OUTDOOR LIGHT-PAINTING PHOTOGRAPHY

THE ESSENTIAL FIELD GUIDE

ERIC PARÉ & KIM HENRY

ilex

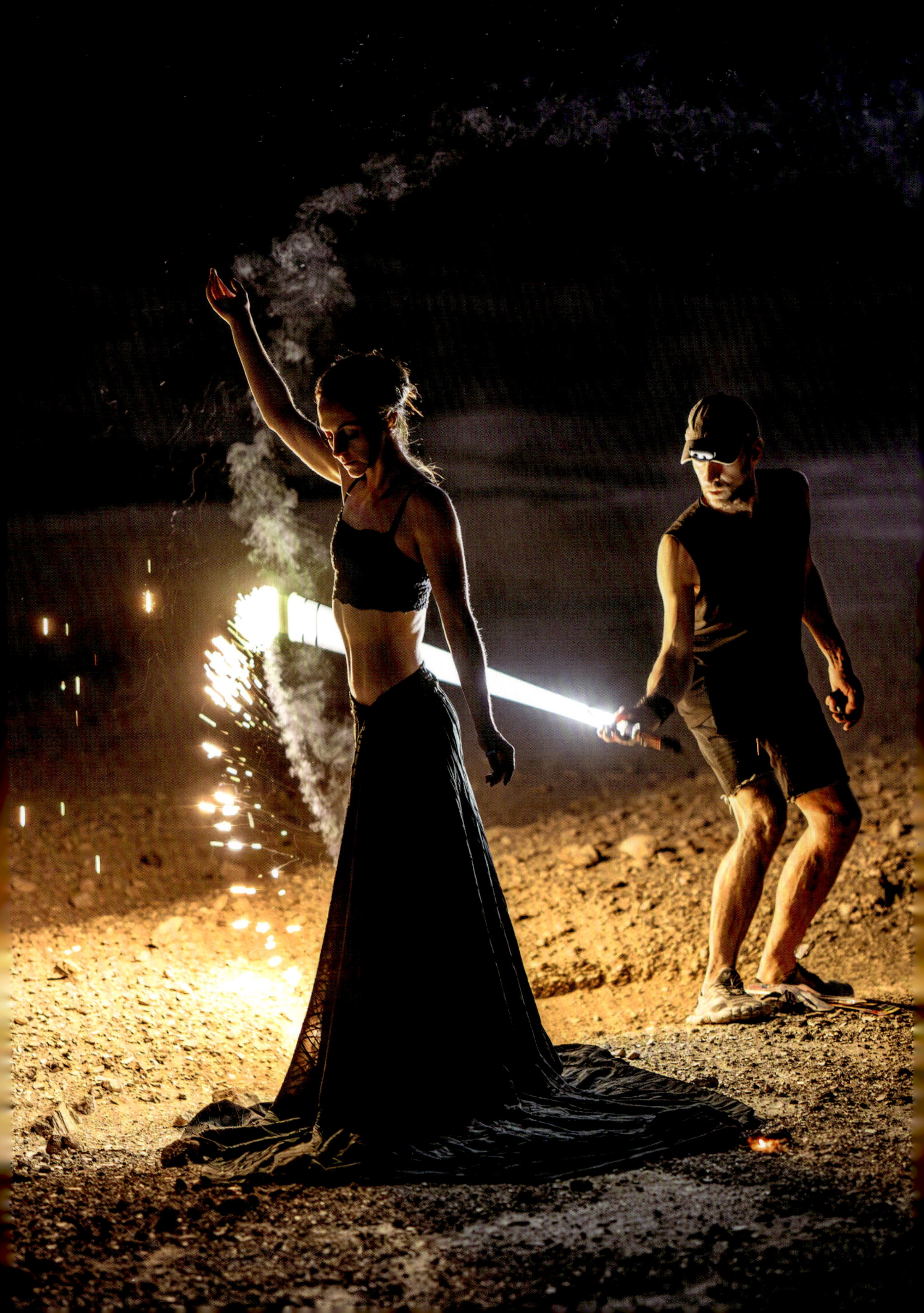

Contents

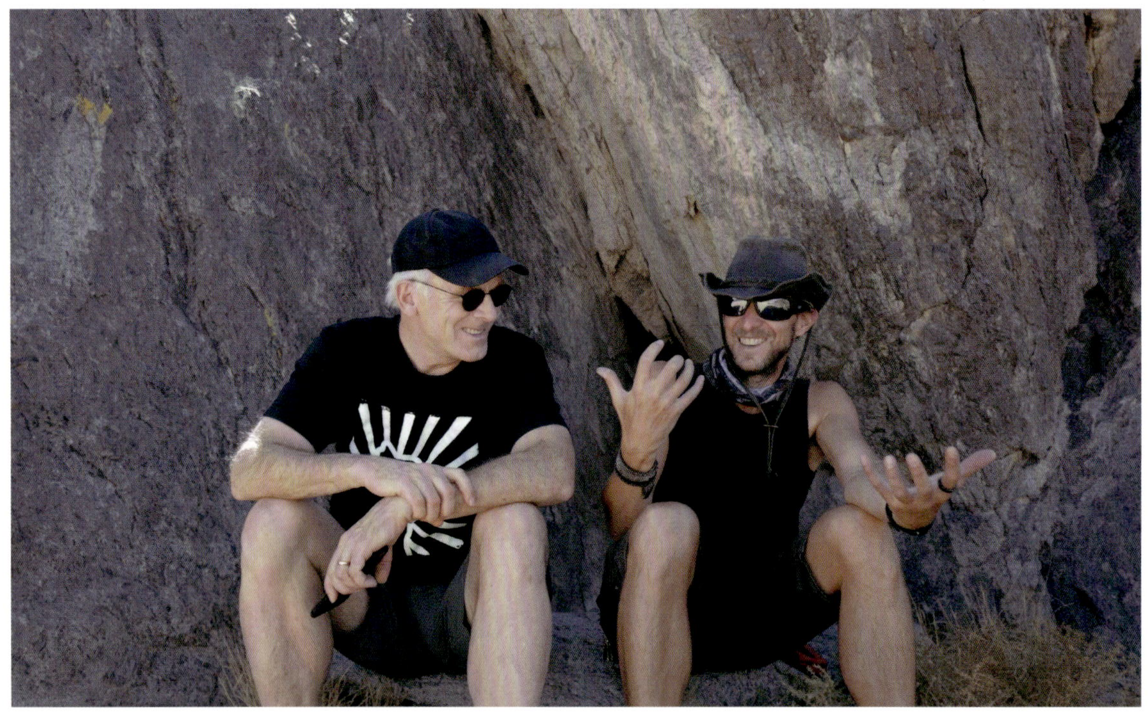

ABOVE **Russell and Eric talking about art and life. 2019, Death Valley.**

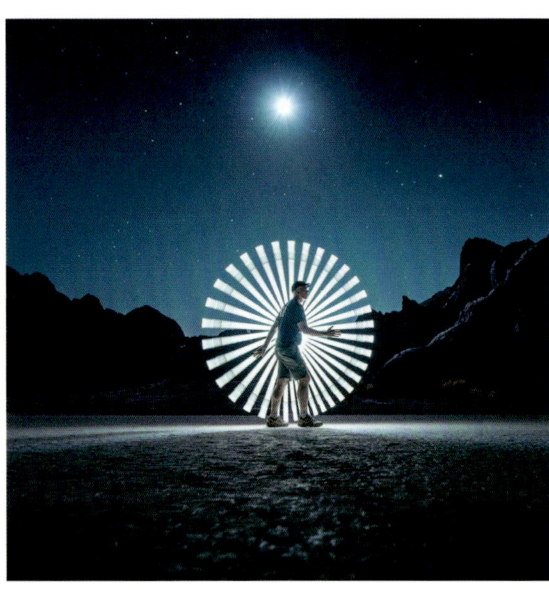

ABOVE **Russell by Eric, 2019, Death Valley.**

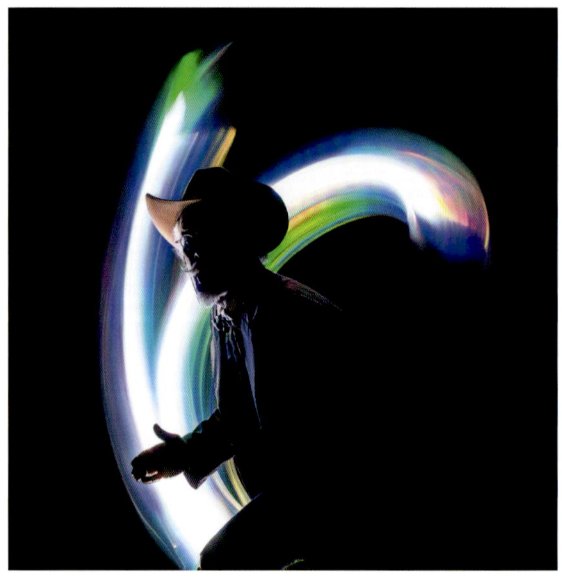

ABOVE **Russell by Eric, 2015, Adobe HQ.**

Foreword

Art, technology, and education have always been at the heart of my career at Adobe, where I've spent the past 40 years helping to shape digital-imaging tools such as Photoshop and Lightroom. But beyond software, I've always been most passionate about the people who use these tools to push creative boundaries. That's why it's been such an honor to witness and support the journey of Eric Paré and Kim Henry, two artists who have not only pioneered a new form of light painting but have also inspired a global movement of creators.

I first met them as an admirer of their work, but after taking one of their workshops, I saw firsthand how their unique blend of photography, dance, and light transformed into something truly magical. This book is more than just a collection of stunning images; it is an invitation to learn, explore, and create. Eric and Kim have always been generous in sharing their knowledge, and now, through these pages, they are passing on their expertise to you. Whether you're a seasoned artist or a curious beginner, I hope this book sparks your imagination and encourages you to experiment with the limitless possibilities of outdoor light painting.

Russell Preston Brown
Senior Principal Designer, Adobe Inc.

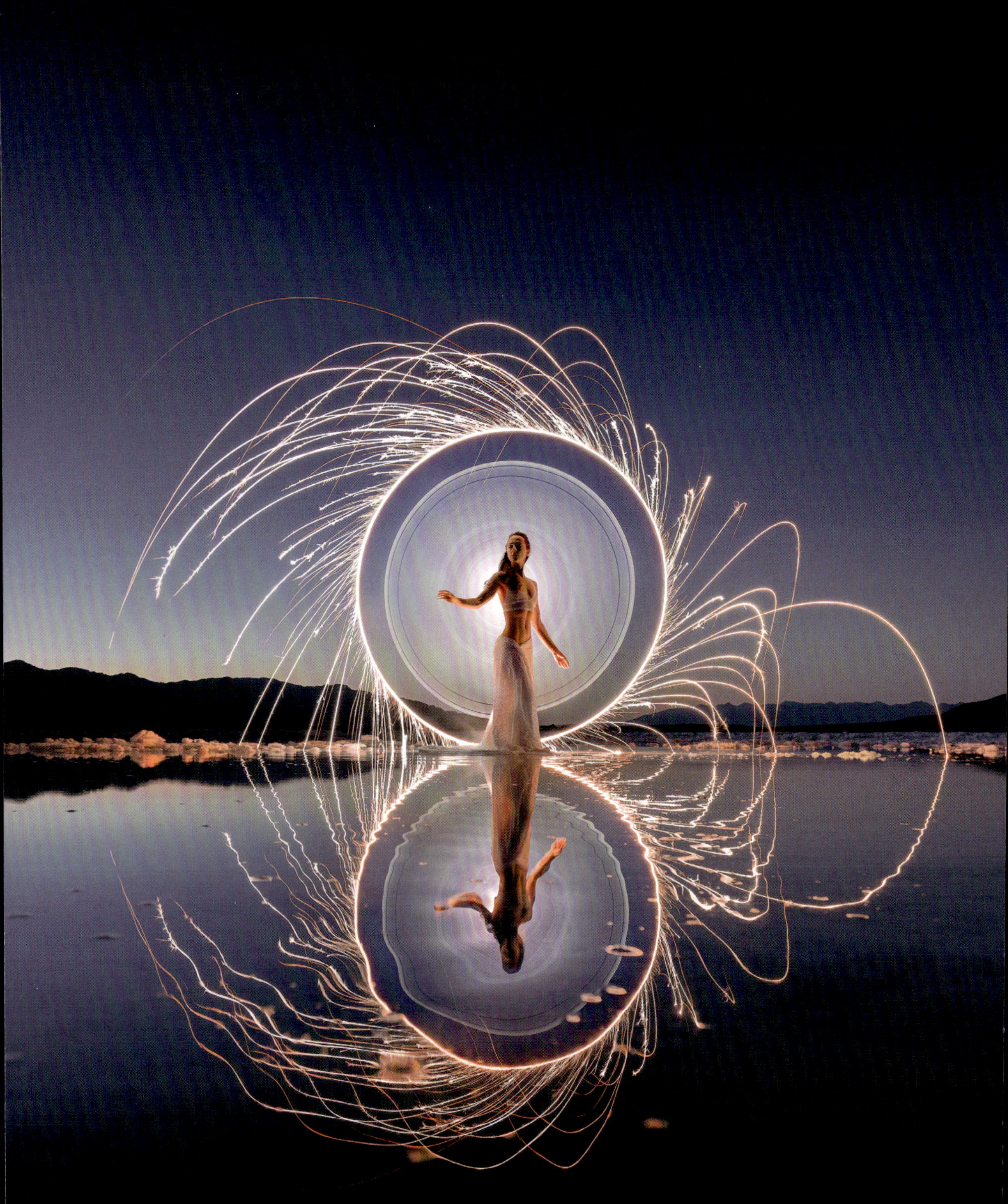

1

Introduction

A creative constraint can spark a decade of exploration. This chapter traces the origins of our light-painting journey and introduces ideas, tools, and intentions that shape this unique form of photographic expression.

Introduction

Let's be honest. When you first heard about light-painting photography, what was the first thing that came to your mind? A naïve looking heart drawn on a black canvas? At least that's what I (Eric) used to think light painting was about. I've got nothing against that, but my interest was elsewhere. My whole perspective (and my world, quite frankly) shifted when painting with light became the answer to a creative constraint I was facing.

To cut a long story short, my previous career as a programmer and my experience as a photographer led me to code software that could control multiple cameras simultaneously. In 2012, I was experimenting in a tiny black studio with a circular 24-camera rig. As I was trying to figure out how to light my subject, it became clear that I needed a very concentrated light source that wouldn't reveal the cameras or the lighting equipment in the frame. The answer was light painting, and I spent hundreds of hours practicing, trying to master (or at least understand) what I was doing. Over the course of a few months, I began to define what would become my signature: the 1-second light-painting portrait.

In early 2013, I dove into the creation of an ambitious personal project: LightSpin. To make this short film come to life, I created half a million pictures of contemporary dancers in the dark combining light painting, stop-motion, and bullet-time techniques. During this process, I met dance artist Kim Henry, who had a profound impact on the project. Sharing complementary skills and interests, we quickly became creative partners, traveling around the world making art.

In 2015, we stumbled across a long plastic tube in a hardware store somewhere in San Francisco. This simple four-foot tube guard was not made to create art, but rather to protect industrial fluorescent lights. We bought one, intending to insert a flashlight inside and use it as a long light-painting tool. We tried our idea that same night on the beach. Little did we know that this tool would once again change the course

of our artistic journey, allowing us to create art that merges light painting and landscape photography. A whole new world of possibilities was opening.

As a light painter, I am not behind the camera; I'm physically in the frame, alongside the model, actively participating in what is being created. The performative aspect to this type of photography is very fulfilling to me. When you're deeply invested in a night session, there's no room to think about anything else. It's a powerful experience to say the least.

This book is based on ten years of experimentation, and is designed to be a tool that you can rely on and be inspired by as you prepare, go out, and create your own light-painting photographs. It is as if a part of us will be with you in the field, although we're not here to impose absolutes or truths; we're here to share our method, derived from over a decade of light-painting photography. Take what you find useful and make it your own.

Like any craft you might aim to master, this technique requires practice, although its essence is simple. Trust us, the process is a beautiful one to dive into. Whether you are new to photography or light painting, or experienced in either or both, we believe you'll find something valuable in these pages. And if it impacts you in a positive way, we hope you'll pass the light on to someone else.

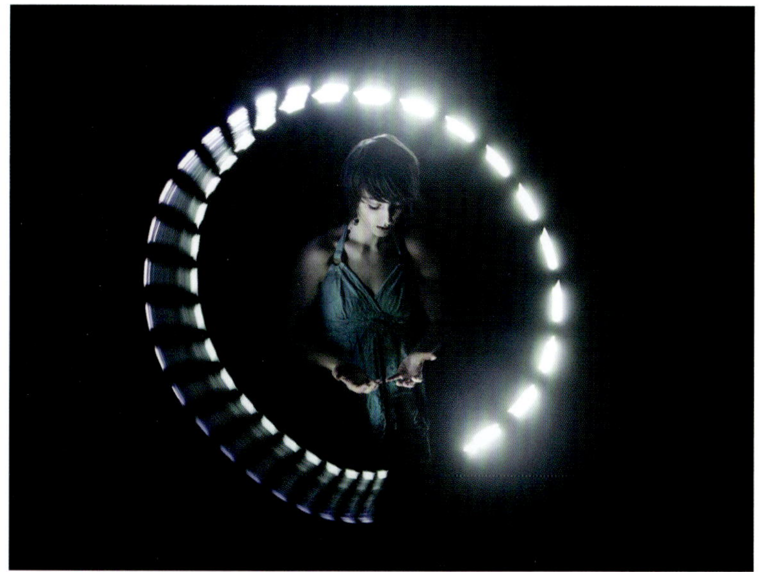

ABOVE **Our light-painting journey started with a small 24-camera rig in Montreal, Canada.**

ABOVE **A single frame of Kim Henry from the project *LightSpin*, 2013.**

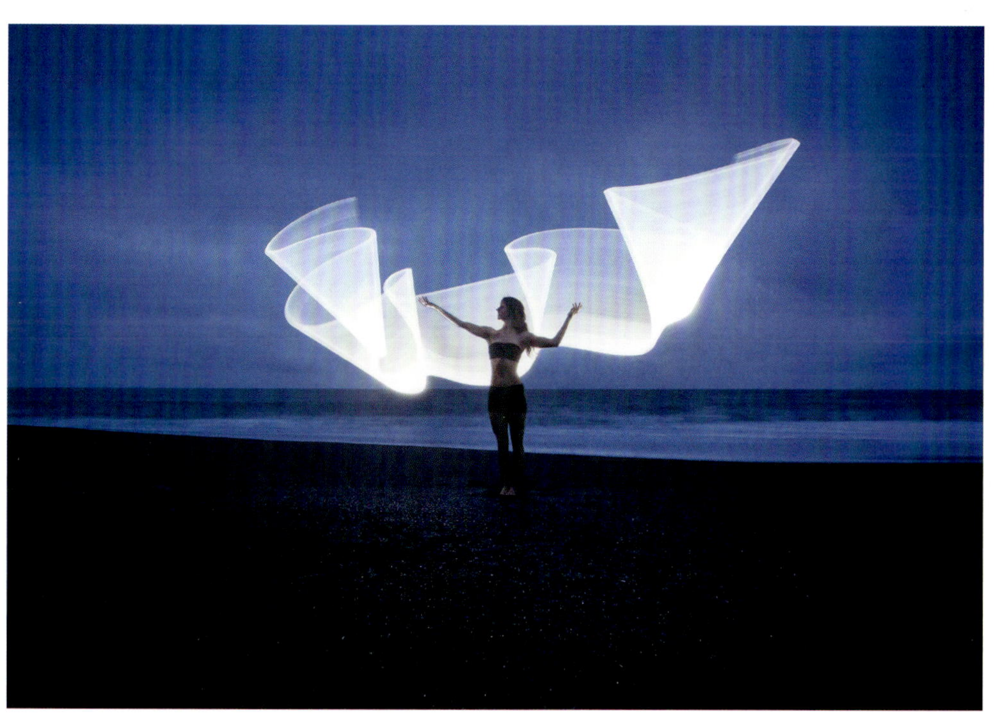

ABOVE **San Francisco, 2015. This image was created on our first night using a plastic tube guard with a flashlight inside as a light-painting tool. This is our first successful outdoor light-painting picture.**

What is light painting?

Is light painting a photographic technique or an artform? We believe it can be both. It is the intention with which we approach and use it that makes the difference. Light painting is usually defined as the technique or art of moving a light source, in a dark environment, while taking a long-exposure photograph. But for us it is more than that. It is a way to be and relate to the world.

There are three main approaches to light painting:

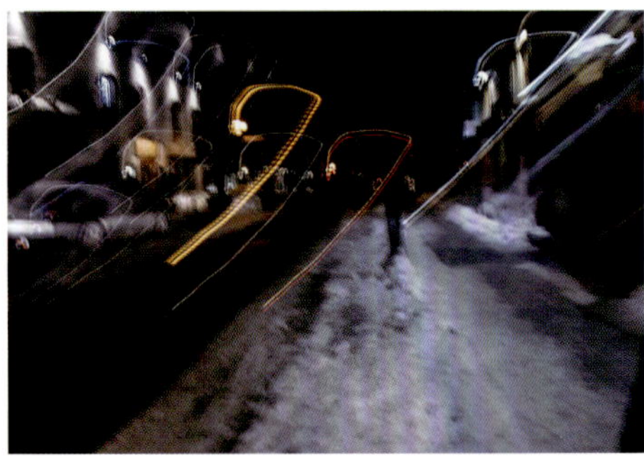

1 **Moving the light source in front of the camera:** The traces of light are visible and integral to the image, acting as a subject.

2 **Moving the light from outside the frame to illuminate a subject:** The impact of the light is visible but not its trails. This is sometimes used as a lighting technique in landscape astrophotography to reveal a subject in the scene.

3 **Moving the camera intentionally to create light traces from stationary lights:** You might already have created something like this (shown above) with your smartphone by accidentally moving it while taking a picture in a low-light environment.

For the purpose of this book, we will be referring solely to the first approach when we talk about light painting; moving the light source in front of the camera.

RIGHT **The trace of light, created by a sparkler in this example, is a central visual element in the composition, alongside the human subject.**

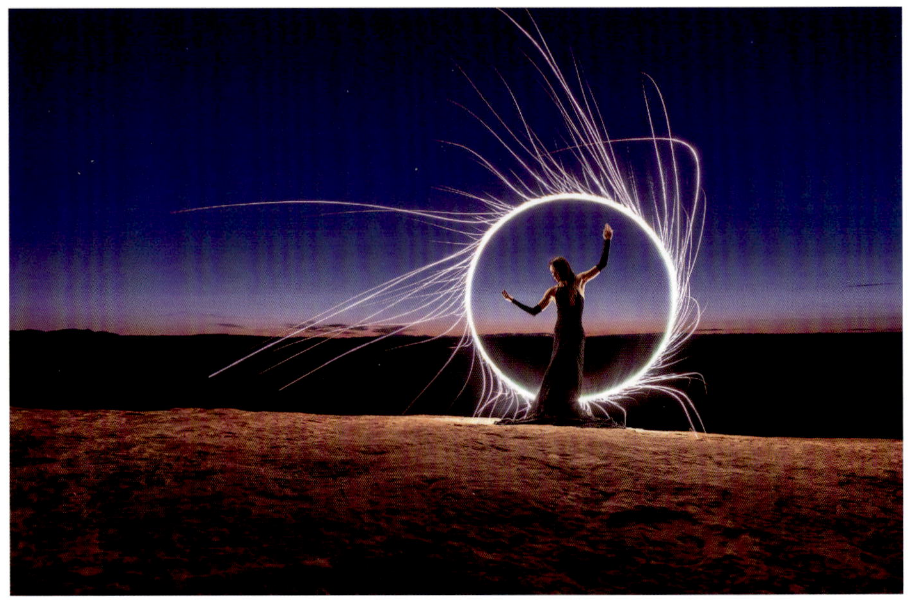

HISTORICAL CONTEXT

As light painting and long-exposures go hand in hand, we could suppose that the former would be as old as photography itself. In the early days of photography, exposure times were necessarily long due to technical limitations, making any moving light source visible as a trail.

The first known light-painting image was created around 1889 by Étienne-Jules Marey and Georges Demenÿ, who attached incandescent bulbs to the joints of an assistant with the purpose of studying human motion.

Although early experiments such as these were mostly serving scientific purposes, light painting eventually started to appear in the explorations of artists using photography as a medium. During the 1970s and 1980s, few artists experimented with light painting outdoors using film, as the process was challenging and the results unpredictable. However, digital cameras made outdoor light painting and night photography far more accessible. Photographers could get instant feedback through image previews, allowing for faster experimentation and learning. This, combined with increasing low-light sensitivity and the overall quality of the cameras' sensors, allowed the artform to reach a new level in the 21st century.

VARIETY AND VARIATIONS AS A NORM

Whether the artist moves the light to "draw" in the space or uses their entire body to paint in a dance-like manner, light painting often involves a physical expression from which a performative element emerges. This unique relationship with the medium fosters a creative process that distances the artist from conventional photographic practices.

Light painting can explore non-representational visual language using motion, time, and visual abstraction. The result often inspires a sense of wonder and awe. As light painters, we don't aim to capture reality but rather participate in the creation of our own. And this process is highly personal.

The degree of abstraction, as well as the aesthetic of the artwork, will vary greatly from one artist to the other, influenced by their interests, skills, and personal background, as well as the tools they choose to use to create their pieces. Some have carved an artistic style for themselves by narrowing the focus of their practice, developing an expertise that makes their art instantly recognizable.

Making outdoor light-painting photographs can be a playful and joyful creative experience. It can also be an almost sacred one, a moment of connection to oneself, others, nature, and the sublime all at once. In any case, most say it's addictive, in a good way!

Before we dive into the technique we use, we want to share the work of two skilled artists we love, who are masters at their craft and generous with their knowledge. They both create outdoor light-painting art with a very different aesthetic to ours, which speaks to the importance of the personal creative voice of the light painter in the making of their art.

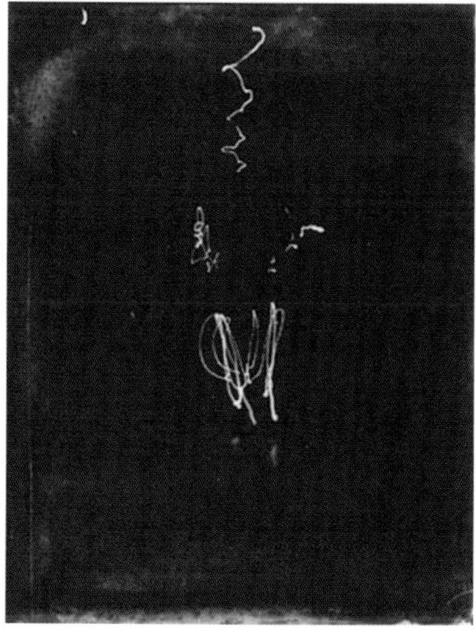

ABOVE *Pathological Walk from the Front,* circa 1889.

Profile **Denis Smith**

Denis Smith is an Australian-based artist and educator who uses light painting as a medium to push himself physically, creatively, and technically. Known for his mesmerizing "Balls of Light," Denis has been creating light-painting art and sharing his passion with others for more than 15 years. You can find Denis's work at: *denissmith.com.au*

How would you describe your approach to outdoor light painting?

Over the years I have learned to have different expectations. Coming home with great images has become secondary. Fun, adventure, and excitement lead me down the path, and enjoying the experience of creation is paramount. Setting realistic expectations means I can sometimes come home with "nothing," so great images are a bonus. My very first images were on beaches and in the mountains; it was where I found solace, where I healed. These days I am looking through these eyes again, and my practice has come full circle.

What do you enjoy the most about creating outdoors?

Making images outdoors is hard, but I love that. New locations and the experience of planning for weather, moon phases, and access is always exciting. There is something magical about being separated from humanity, being alone, which is incredibly easy in Australia. When the journey has been challenging, the result is always sweeter. The nature of being outdoors means that the environment is always changing, so day to day, season to season you can explore new ideas in the same landscape.

What do you find most challenging about it?

After 15 years of exploring all types of light painting, finding new ideas to bring to the landscape is incredibly challenging. I started traveling and making images in distant locations, which added a whole new level of complexity

around planning and execution. You learn to accept "failure," but with a focus on the journey it is rare that I leave a place disappointed.

What is your average exposure time?

When I am outdoors my average exposure time would be 120 sec., regularly pushed out to 240 sec. For years I only made images under moonlight, for a "daylight" look, and this pushed my exposure times to the extreme. The most beautiful part of this was

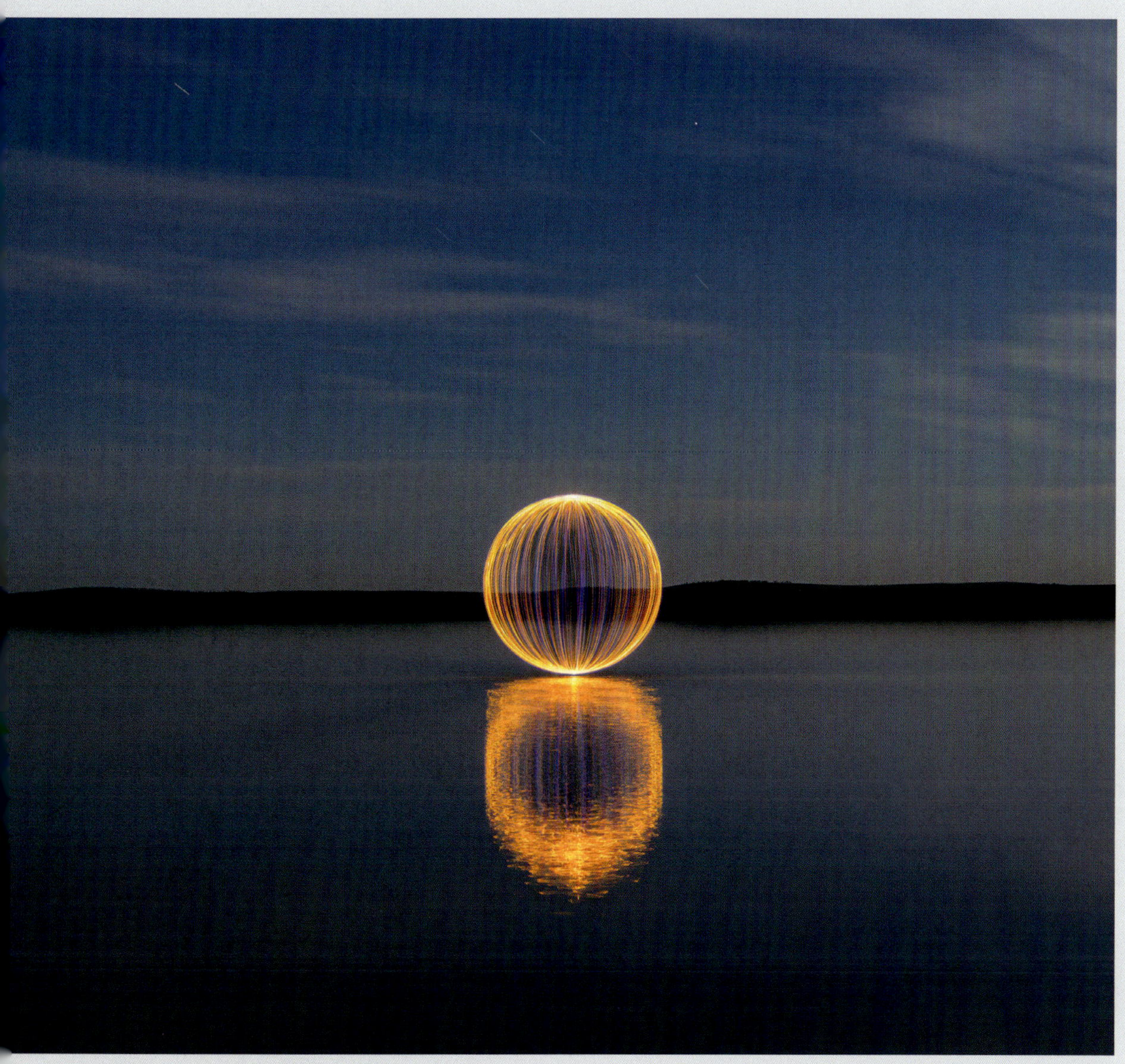

learning to use the exposure time for meditation, silence, and to breathe in the location.

Is there anything lately that sparks a sense of curiosity or excitement in your creative journey?
As light painting continues to explode in popularity, I work hard to push myself. My practice has changed a lot, and is more internal, more personal. More than ever, I care less about what others think of my work, which is allowing me to explore ideas in a fresh way. I rarely look at other light painters' work for inspiration. For the last couple of years I have been looking to other genres of art, music, writing, and cinema for inspiration. There is a deep sense of freedom when your only critic is yourself. Freedom, exploring, and finding inner peace is where my practice started, and I have come full circle, wrapped in light.

Profile **Darren Pearson**

Darren Pearson, alias DARIUSTWIN, is a light-painting artist known for his glowing skeleton figures. For more than a decade, Darren has been crafting intricate forms and playful scenes that blend with the surroundings, using a freehand drawing technique. He also brings his characters to life by meticulously capturing hundreds of sequential long-exposure images to produce masterful stop-motion pieces. You can find Darren's work at *dariustwin.com*

How would you describe your approach to outdoor light painting?

My approach to light painting outdoors is a delicate balancing act between the idea, the environment, and the weather. I try to do my homework before going out: if I'm shooting at the beach, I check the tide chart for high/low tide; if it's in the desert, I check the wind forecast so that I don't end up with a mouthful of sand. These bits of information can be the difference between a dream and nightmare shoot.

What do you enjoy the most about creating outdoors?

The thing I love most about creating outdoors is the sense of solitude I get when hiking. I feel a smallness of being and I get to appreciate the nocturnal sights, sounds, and smells of a world that is equal and opposite to the daytime.

What do you find most challenging about it?

The part I find most challenging about outdoor light painting is giving up control to the environment itself. Sometimes my initial plans don't work and I have to act in a nimble and dynamic fashion to create something that will work with the landscape. I try to be receptive and loose, going with the flow rather than fighting it.

What is your average exposure time?

My exposure time varies based on the complexity of my freehand drawings. They often take a few minutes, sometimes five minutes or more. It's rare for my exposures to be under a minute unless they are single-line designs.

Is there anything lately that sparks a sense of curiosity or excitement in your creative journey?

I like the idea that "necessity is the mother of invention." Personal and collaborative innovations can open doors to new possibilities, and I try to work on projects that will lead to creative breakthroughs in the near and long-term. I am constantly looking and finding inspiration in travel, art, music, and cinema (old and new).

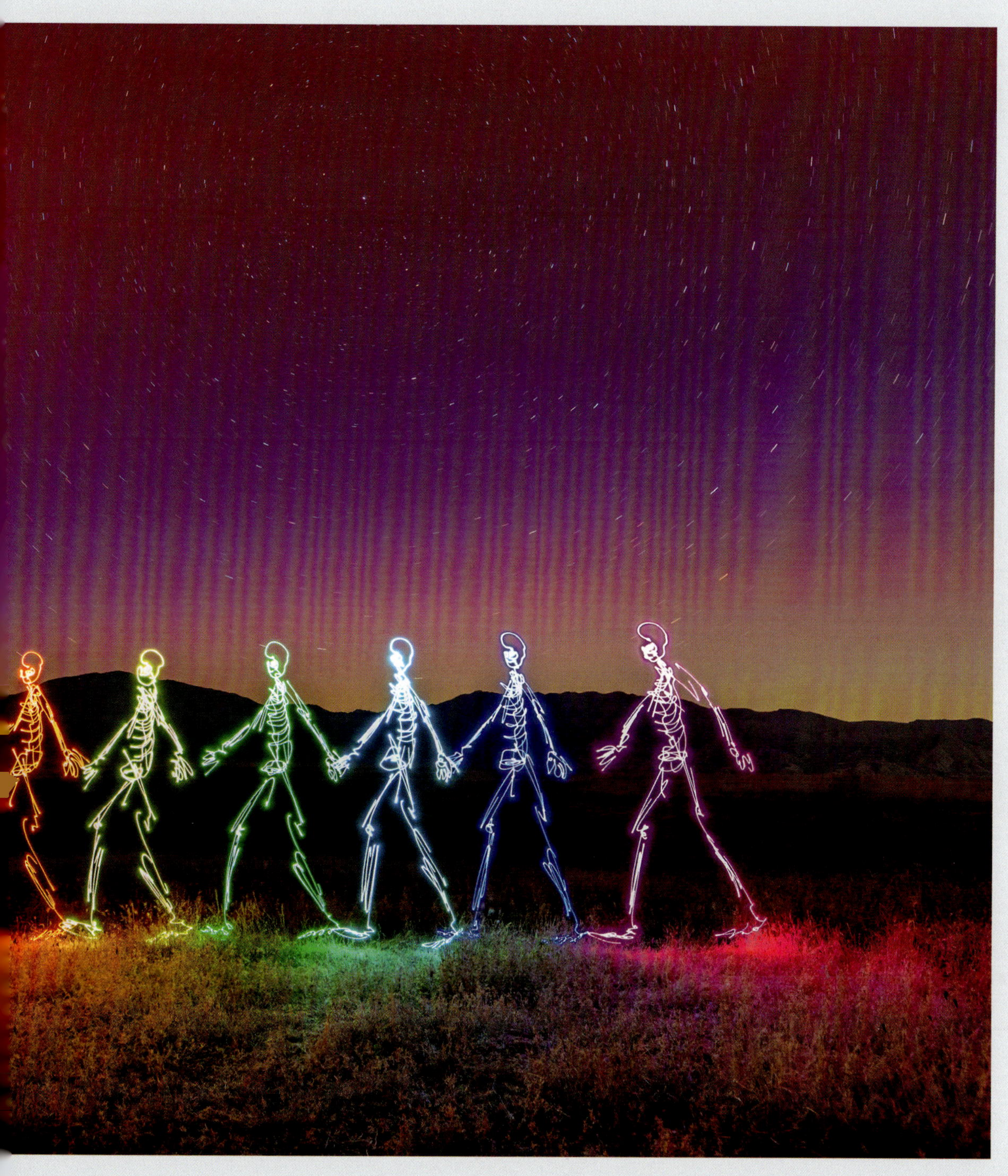

Technique overview

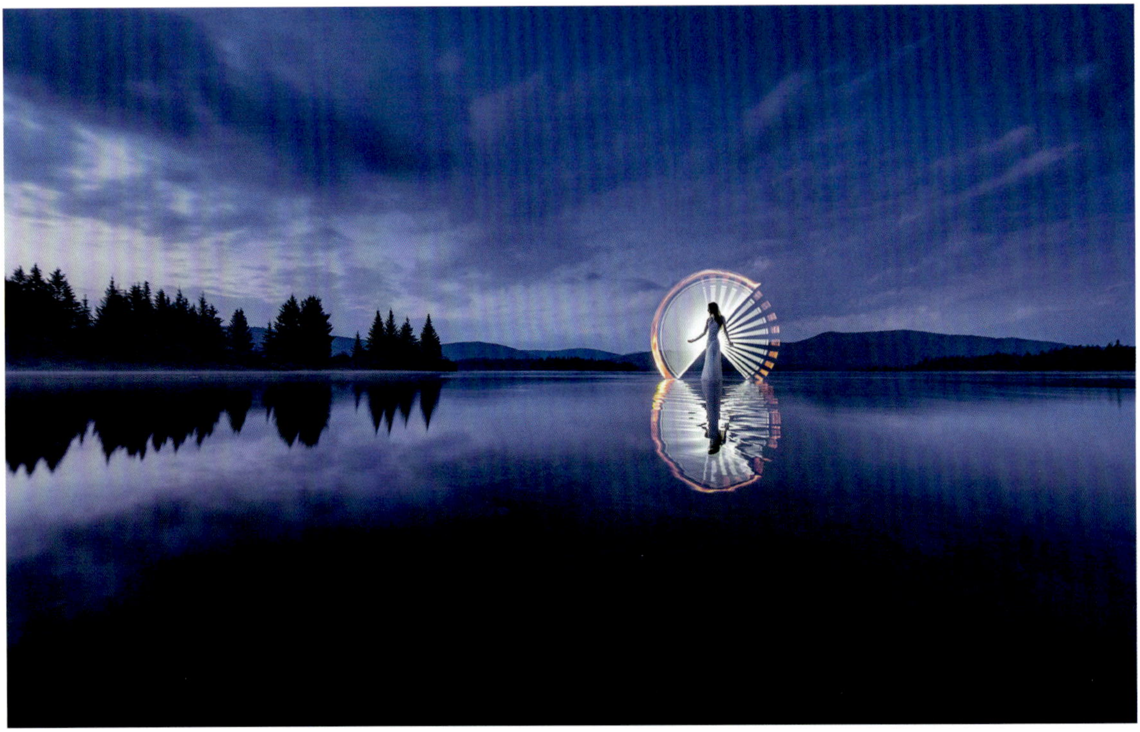

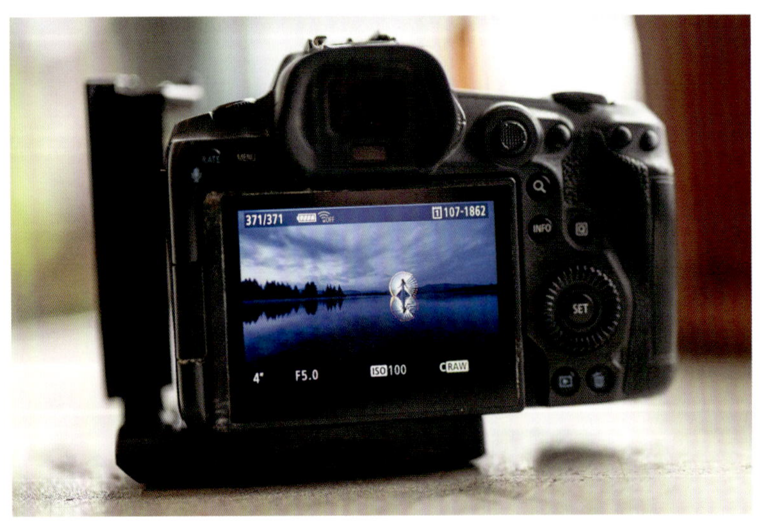

Is it real?

Yes. It is.

Over the years we have often been asked if our images are "real" or not. Every time, we're happy to share that not only are these photographs achieved in camera, but the technique that creates them is quite simple!

Most of the images presented in this book are single exposures, meaning that the landscape and the motion of light with the human subject are captured within a single shot. Our complementary skills have led us to develop a distinctive aesthetic that combines landscape photography, human performance, and light painting. Yet while most of the images we create feature a human subject with the light painting, the core technique can be adapted to match your own creative vision.

We'll go into much greater depth in the following chapters, but let's start with the basics:

→ **Tube light painting:** This is the name we use for our technique, which refers to the tool we use to create the traces of light.

→ **The tool:** We primarily use a plastic tube with a flashlight inserted inside (see below) to generate the light. It's a simple tool that creates beautiful light effects.

→ **Long exposure:** Every image is captured using a long exposure, typically between one and eight seconds (more on that in chapter 3).

→ **The process:** The light painter triggers the camera and then creates light trails during the exposure, typically staying behind the model and turning the light on and off to paint the desired shapes.

→ **Light source:** There is no additional light source besides the tube and the ambient light of the landscape. There are no artificial lights outside of the frame and no flashes are used.

→ **Subject stillness:** The subject remains motionless during the exposure to avoid creating a ghost effect, where they would appear blurred. We will cover this in more detail in Getting a sharp subject (see page 64).

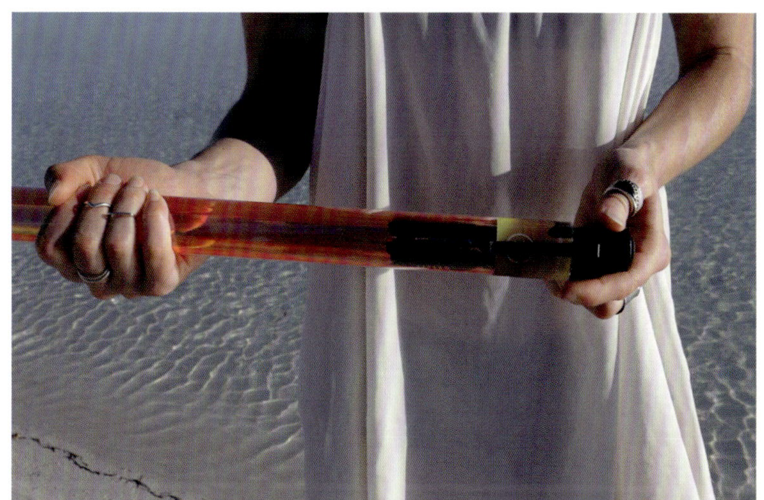

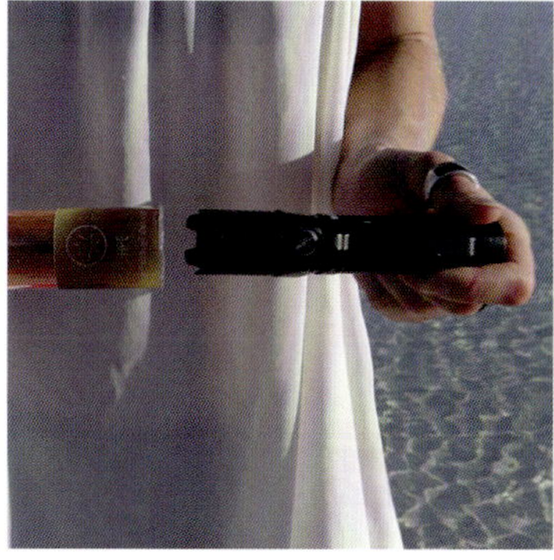

LEFT & ABOVE **A plastic tube with a powerful flashlight inserted inside is the perfect tool.**

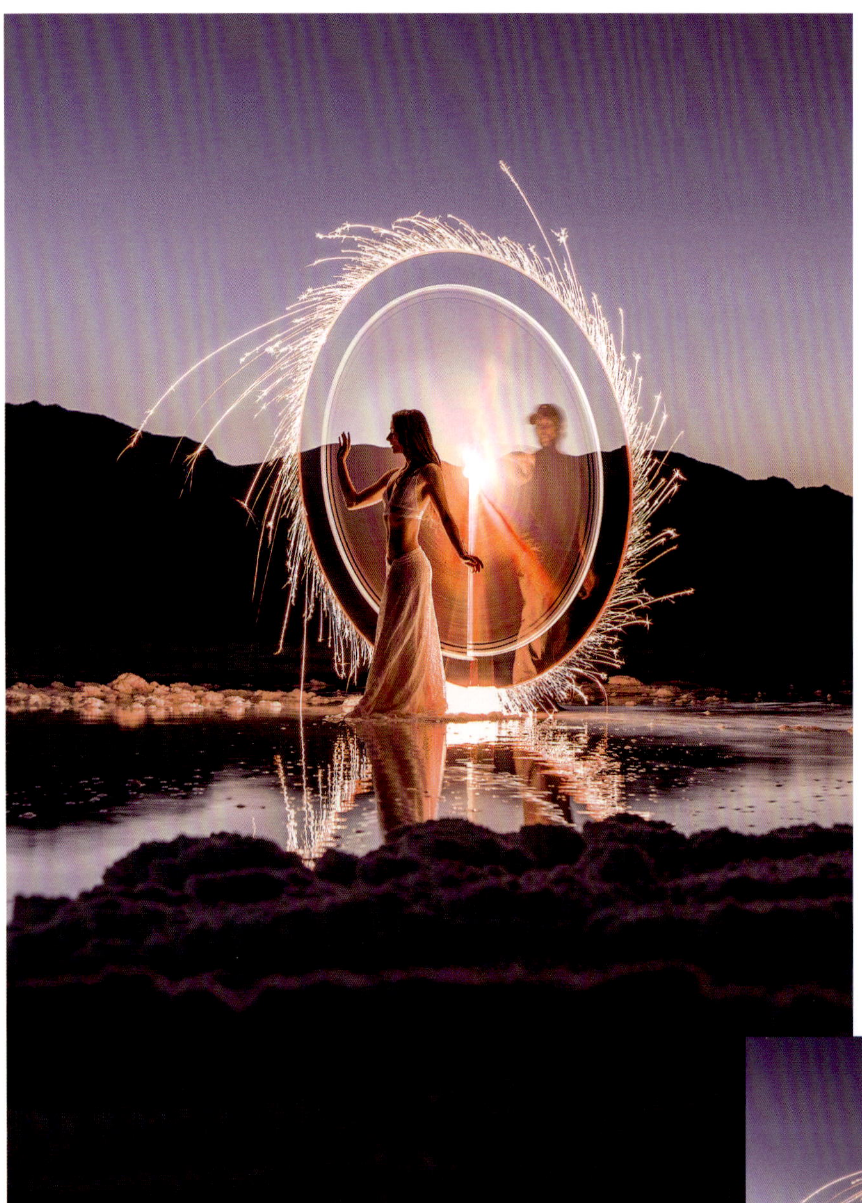

ABOVE & RIGHT **Two views of the same shot, the first one revealing Eric with the light. While we typically work as a duo, this creative process can also be enjoyed in a small group, with friends or family!**

Terminology

We use the terms outpaint and inpaint to define how the light painting is executed relative to the exposure time. Both techniques can be performed with the tube light-painting tool and as you progress through this book you will learn how they can be useful in different environments to serve your creative vision.

OUTPAINT

→ The light source remains on throughout the exposure.
→ A beginner-friendly technique that requires minimal equipment manipulation.
→ The ideal entry point for those new to light painting.
→ Light-trail duration matches the camera's exposure time.
→ Creates continuous, unbroken light traces.

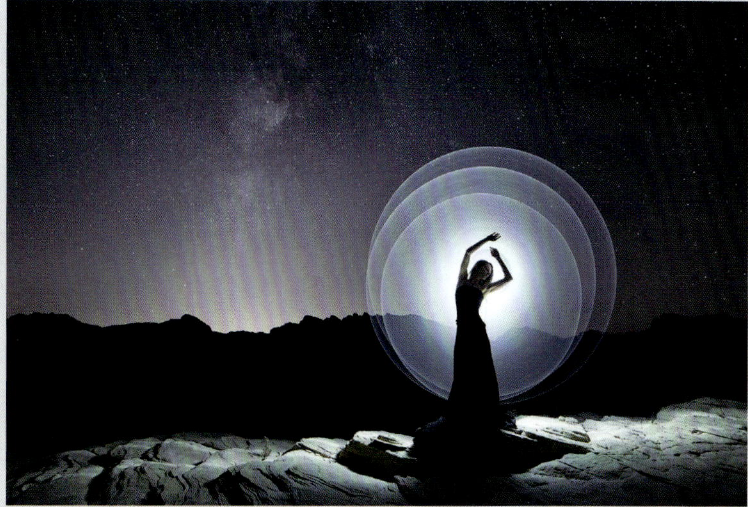

ABOVE **For this outpaint image, the light was turned on continuously for the 8.2 sec. exposure time.**

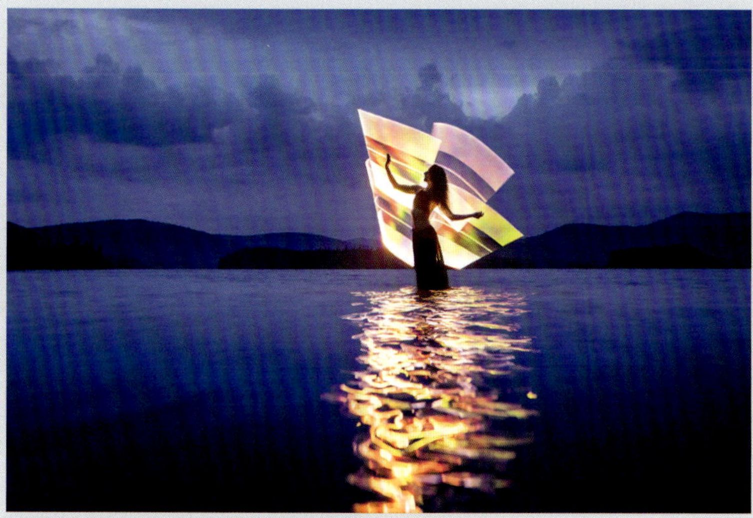

ABOVE **For this inpaint image, the shape was created by turning the light on and off multiple times during the exposure.**

INPAINT

→ The light source is selectively activated and deactivated during the exposure.
→ Creates multiple distinct light trails within a single exposure.
→ The light-painting duration is shorter than the camera's exposure time.
→ Requires a flashlight with responsive on/off capability (preferably pressure switches).
→ Allows you to create more complex, layered light shapes within the frame.
→ Offers greater precision and creative control over light placement.

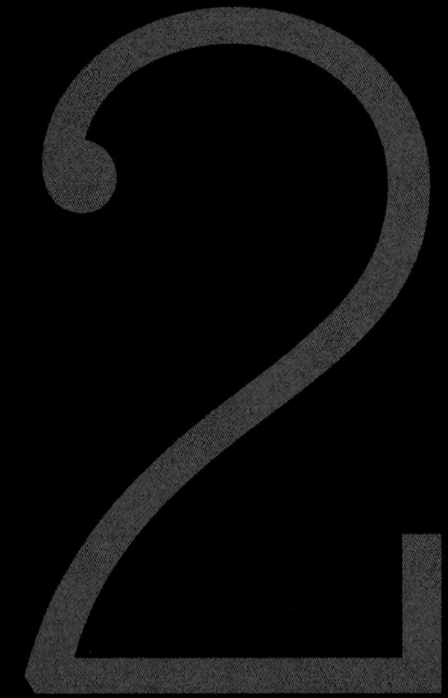

2

What's in my bag

From handmade tools to trusted gear, this chapter shows what we carry in the field. Balancing accessibility and efficiency, each item plays a role in creating, adapting, and staying ready for the unexpected.

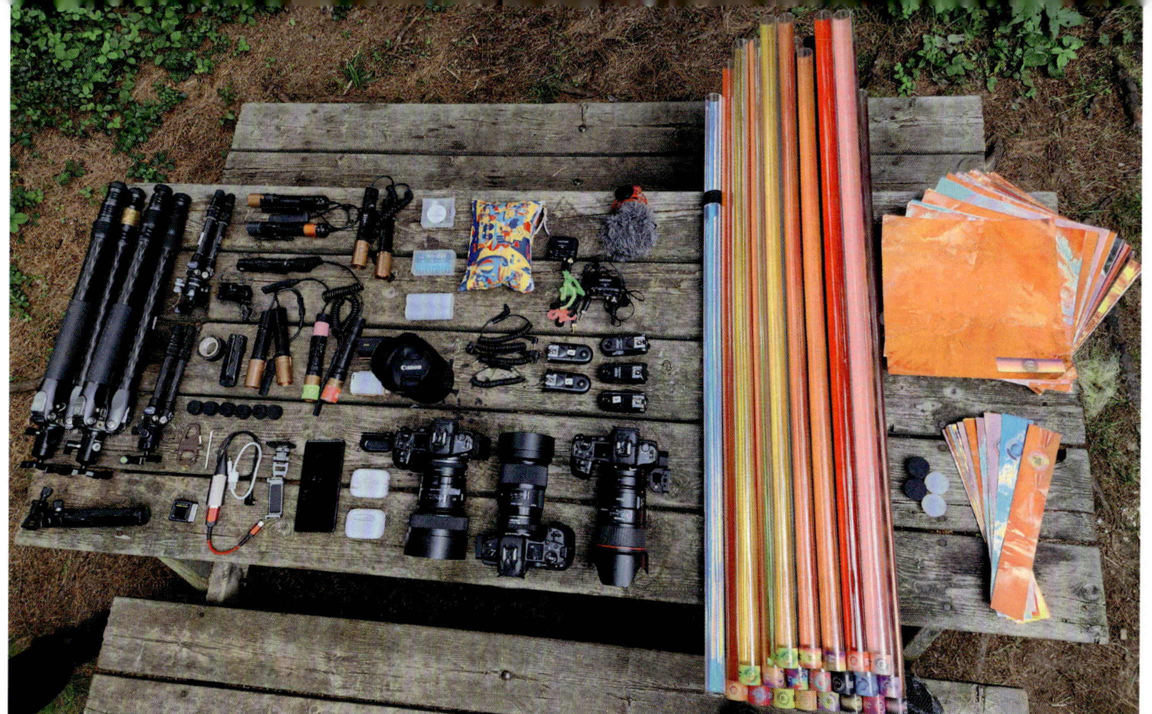

When we are teaching high school teenagers, we show them it's possible to start doing light-painting photography using only a smartphone, a water bottle as a tripod, a cheap flashlight, and a sheet of paper as a light-painting tool. Accessibility to equipment shouldn't prevent anyone from experimenting with this creative outlet.

That said, I'd be lying if I said that equipment doesn't matter to me. Optimizing your gear leads to better-quality images and a simpler, more enjoyable process. This chapter takes a look at what's currently in my bag.

CAMERA BAG

Before we dive into what's inside, a quick note on the bag itself. I use a hiking backpack with front access to the main compartment. Inside, I organize my gear with various colorful pouches and bags. I've been using this type of bag for over a decade. It offers good size, comfort, versatility, and security (as it doesn't signal that I'm carrying expensive photography gear). However, there are so many camera bag options on the market these days that you can easily find something suitable for your needs and preferences. Whatever you choose, make sure it's ergonomic. You want to keep your back healthy for years to come!

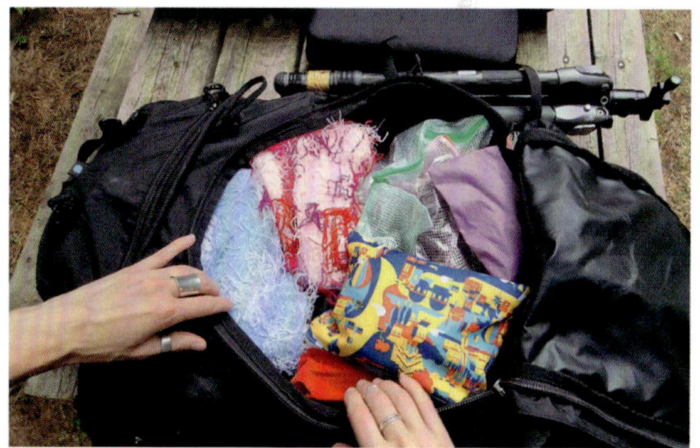

Photography equipment

CAMERA BODY

You only need one camera, and the brand you choose doesn't make a difference in terms of image quality. DSLRs (Digital Single-Lens Reflex) and mirrorless cameras are all pretty good at this point in time. I currently shoot simultaneously with three Canon R5 mirrorless cameras for specific reasons:

→ To document the process, either by filming or capturing behind-the-scenes pictures from different perspectives.

→ To shoot different compositions for every sequence of images (vertical and horizontal, for example). Things sometimes happen quickly, and shooting with more than one camera allows me to maximize the creation time we have.

→ To have the option of using two focal lengths to create a single image (more on that in chapter 7).

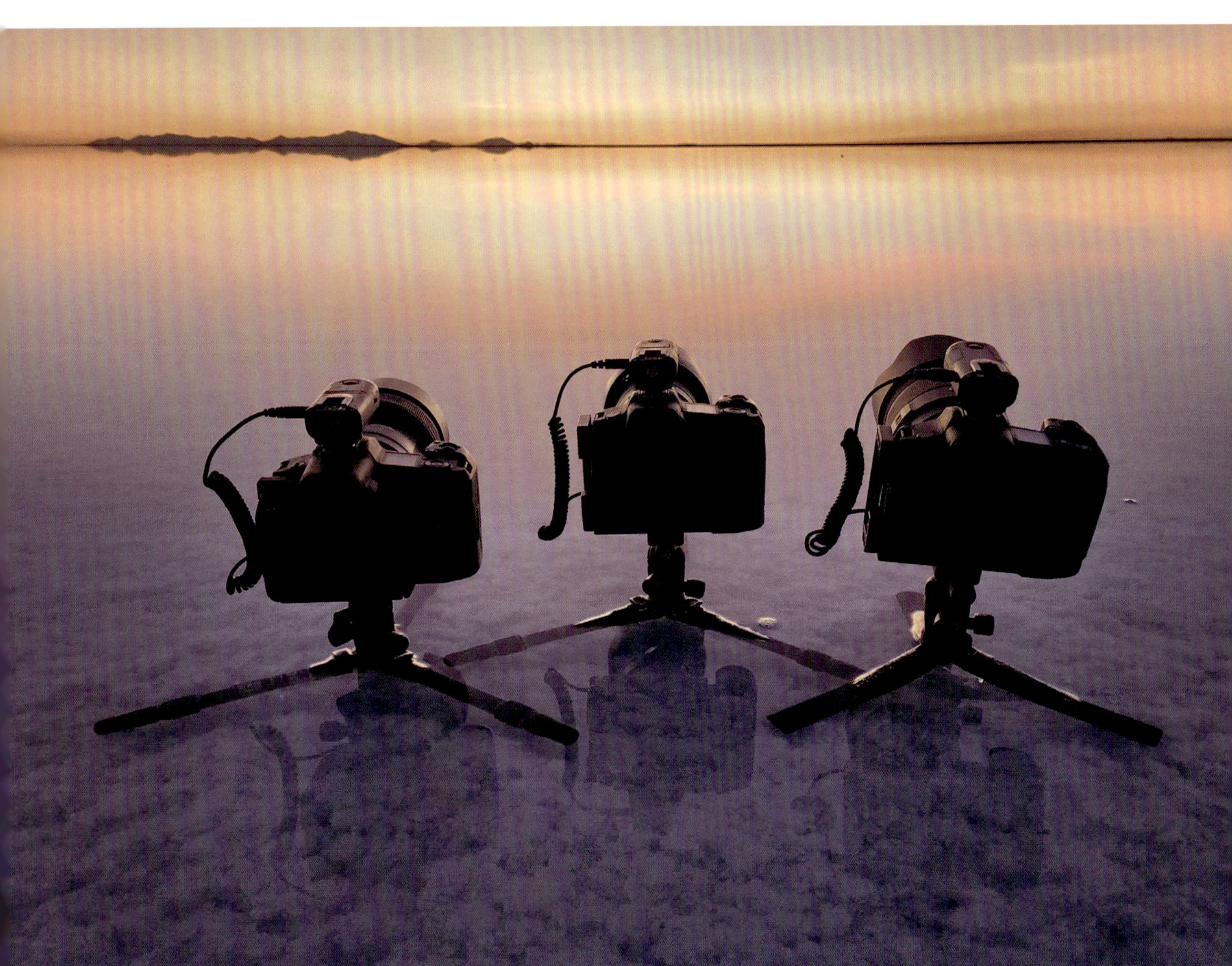

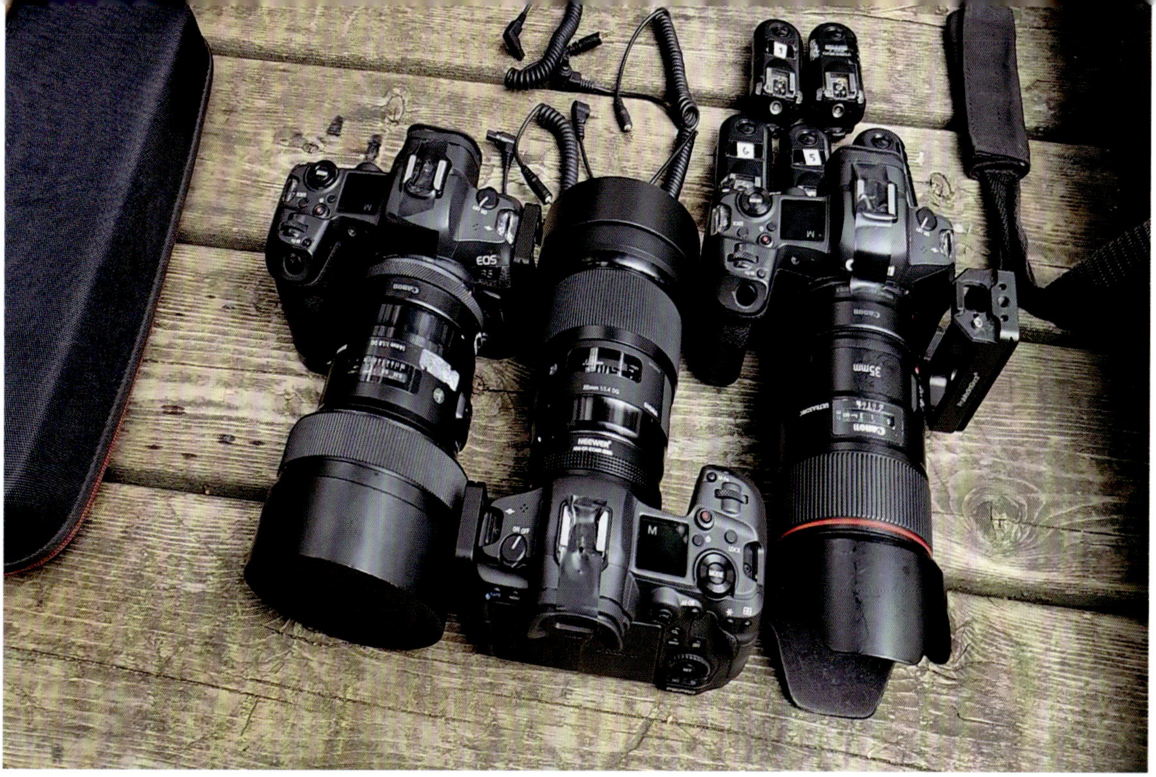

LENSES

I typically carry at least five prime lenses, ranging from 14mm to 50mm. However, if I had to recommend only one lens to start with, I would suggest a 24mm f/2.8 prime lens. Since we mostly shoot in low-light environments, having a wide-aperture lens that allows more light to reach the sensor is essential. Most of my favorite lenses open as wide as f/1.4.

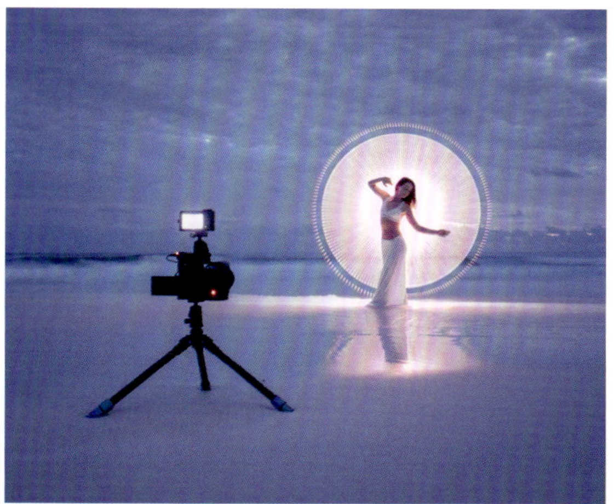

TRIPOD

There's no way around it, you need a tripod to hold your camera steady for light-painting photography. Depending on the location and conditions, I will either use large, sturdy tripods or small, lightweight ones. When I work with big tripods I do so without a center column, as I usually want the camera to be close to the ground. A larger tripod is especially useful in windy conditions or when shooting near moving water. However, I love using small tripods whenever I can, as they can give a very low perspective and are easy to carry.

L-BRACKET

Not essential, but very handy for quickly switching between horizontal and vertical compositions during a shoot. I prefer using an L-bracket rather than adjusting the tripod head, because a bracket offers better weight distribution, which improves camera stability.

MEMORY CARDS

You don't need expensive or high-performance memory cards to capture light-painting photographs, but it's crucial you have enough storage and backup cards in case one (or more) fails during a shoot.

CLEANING KIT

On top of a basic camera-cleaning kit, I usually carry disposable lens wipes when shooting near water or in very humid environments; sometimes I have to clean my lenses every few shots, and a regular lens cloth isn't sufficient.

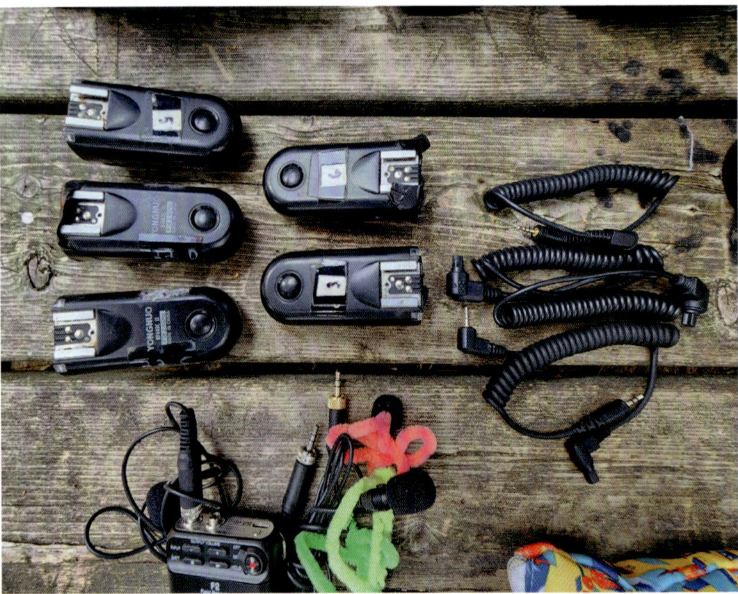

REMOTE TRIGGERS

As the photographer is in front of the camera painting with light, this technique either requires a third person to trigger the camera, or a remote triggering system. Remote triggers are advertised as flash triggers, but they make a perfect wireless trigger system for light painting. They come in pairs: one unit attaches to the camera's hot shoe while the other stays in hand to trigger the shot.

RIGHT **I personally love the Yongnuo RF-603 II, as it is affordable, reliable, and easy to use (an advantage in low light). Mine have traveled through a lot of rough conditions and still work. You can pair multiple units together if you are shooting with more than one camera but make sure you get the correct cable for your camera model when you purchase the triggers.**

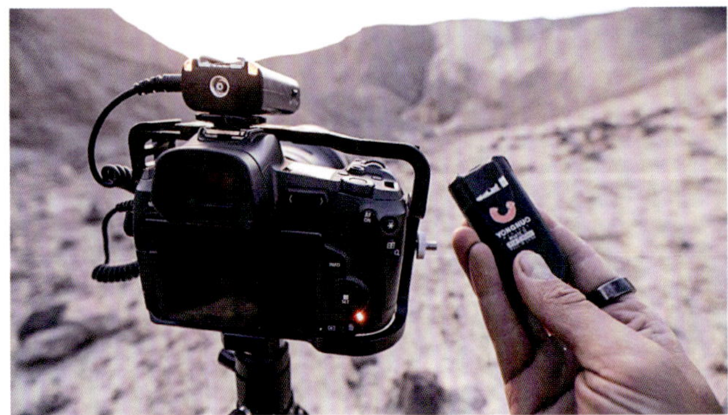

An example of our setup in the field

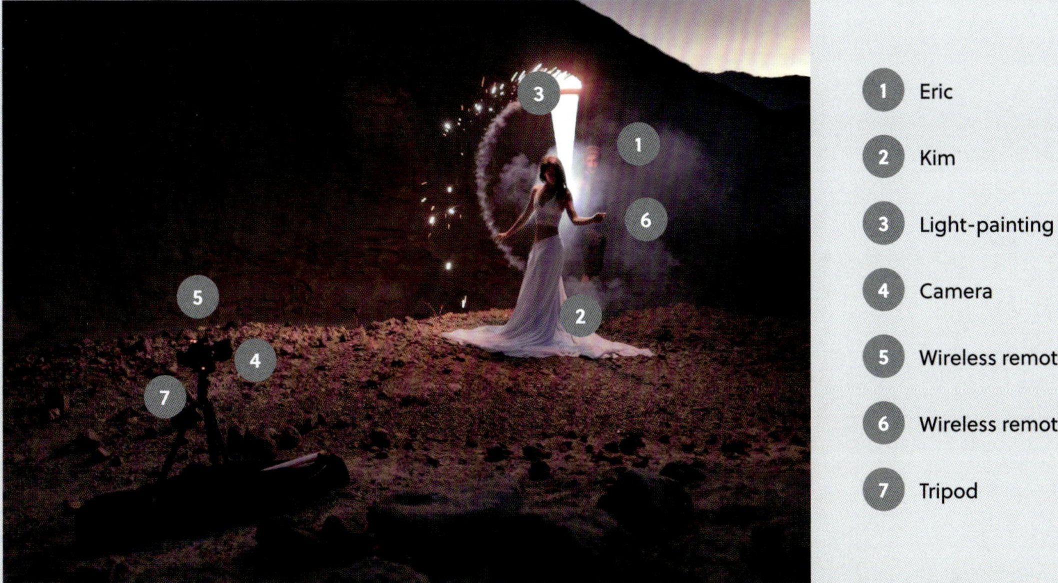

ABOVE **Setting the stage for a light-painting shoot with a camera, tripod, wireless remotes, and a light-painting tube to hand. The end result is shown below.**

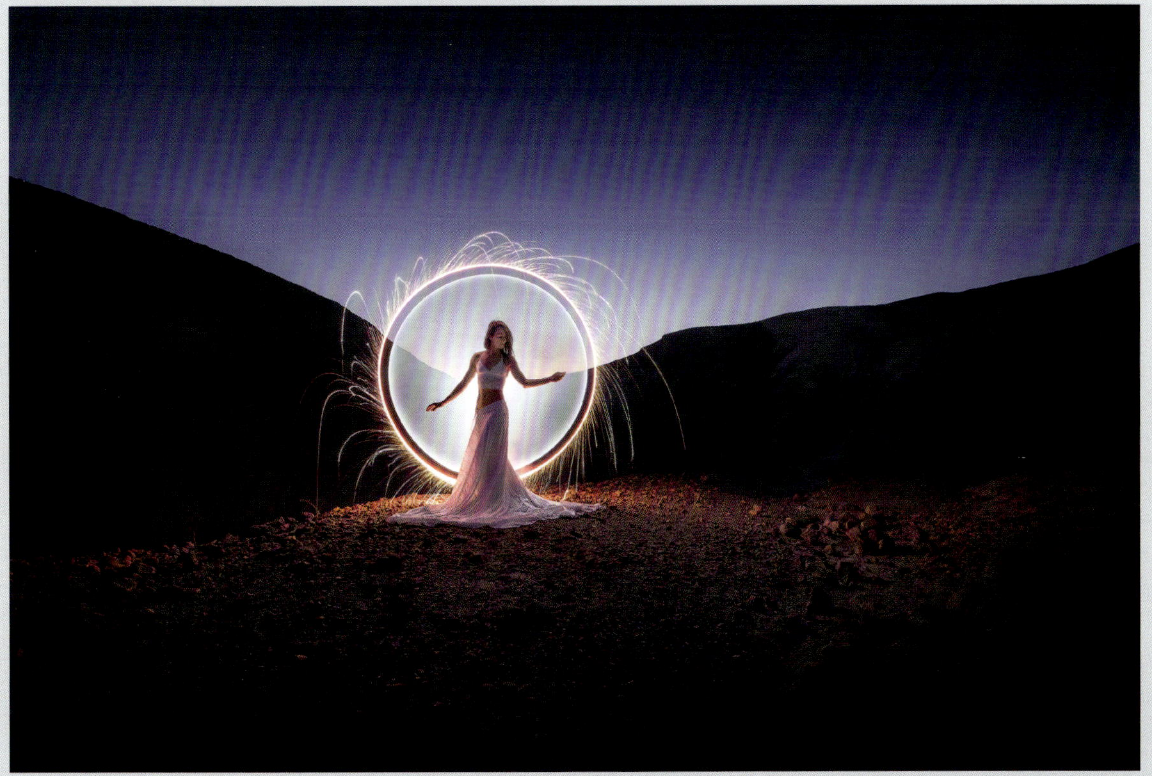

Light-painting equipment

The equipment you use doesn't need to be complex, expensive or highly sophisticated to start creating. In fact, many artists enjoy making their own tools, and we're no exception. Below are the essential light-painting tools I rely on to create most of my outdoor light-painting images... And you'll see that most of the things mentioned were not designed for light painting.

FLASHLIGHTS

Over the years I have tried many flashlights, and unfortunately, none of them are perfect. However, most flashlights with a 1-inch (25mm) diameter head will work. Why such a small head? Simply so it fits easily inside a T8 size tube, which is our main light-painting tool. Tactical flashlights are the most suitable for outdoor light painting, thanks to a few key features:

→ Optimal size
→ Powerful (up to 2000 lumens)
→ Stroboscopic mode (see panel)
→ Optional pressure switch to control the light
   efficiently.

The brighter the ambient light, the more power you will need from your flashlight. At the start of the blue hour I will use a 2000-lumen flashlight at full power, but as the ambient light dims I will reduce the flashlight's intensity using a physical dimmer to block the light. For darker environments, such as a night sky with stars, as little as 50 lumens of power are required most of the time, which means even a $2 flashlight can work.

We dream of designing our own flashlight that would answer all our needs, but until that happens, here are my current suggestions of tactical flashlights to start with for tube light painting:

→ **Folomov Hero 18650s** Around 800 lumens
This is the smallest (and most affordable) tactical flashlight currently available that offers a constant strobe mode and multiple brightness options. Although the manufacturer advertises it at 2300 lumens, stated output is often not entirely reliable. . In our experience, this flashlight is less powerful than the others in this list when tested in the field. Its main drawback is that it can't be easily paired with a pressure switch.

→ **Klarus XT2CR PRO** 2100 lumens
This is the brightest flashlight I currently use. It can be used with a pressure switch and has a constant strobe pattern. It's especially good for blue hour, black canvas, and winter forest shoots, although not the best choice for night-time photography as it has no dimmer or low light level option.

→ **Nitecore P10 v2** 1100 lumens
This is a versatile flashlight with a constant strobe mode, multiple brightness level options, and pressure switch compatibility. However, it's not as powerful as the Klarus, meaning it can't be used early during the blue hour. I also find that its pressure switch is not as sturdy as other models and the buttons are slightly stiff.

This list will most likely change over time, as flashlight manufacturers often change their products and models are discontinued.

Visit *lightpainting.art/book* to see the updated version.

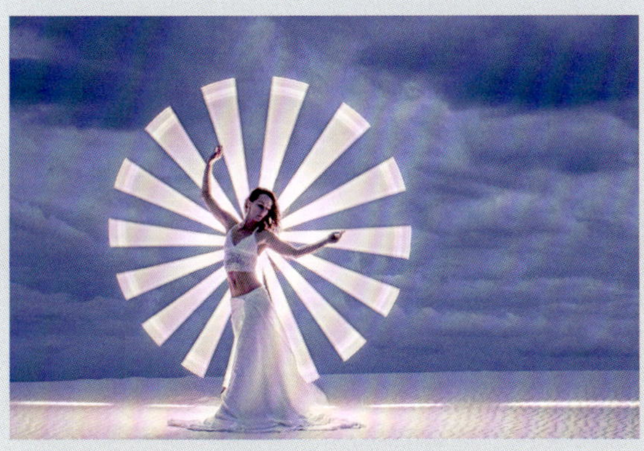

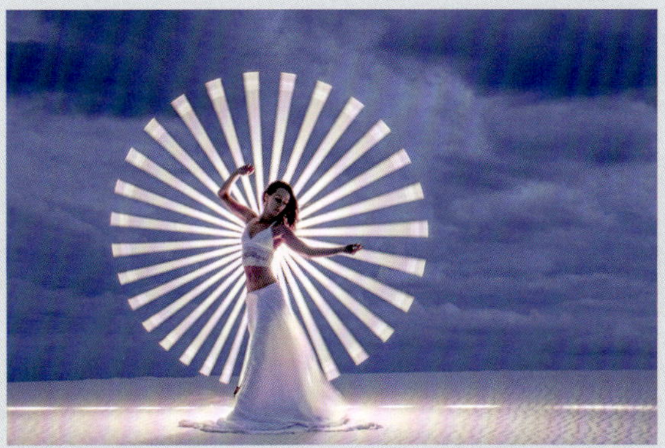

Stroboscopic mode

This mode produces rapid flashes of light at short intervals, which will appear as stripes of light during a long exposure. The interval speed typically varies from one flashlight brand to another, which allows you to change the effect of the light trace. Over the years it has become harder to find flashlight brands that offer a constant strobe mode. Many of them now offer a randomly changing strobe, which changes the frequency of blinking… randomly. This gives us less control on the visual result. At the time of writing, constant strobe is still available on all Olight, Astrolux, Thrunite, Folomov, and Convoy flashlights.

ABOVE **These two shots were created using two different flashlights with different strobe rates.**

REMOTE PRESSURE SWITCH

A remote pressure switch makes it possible to use the inpaint technique by easily turning your flashlight on and off at the press of a button. It also allows you to mix continuous lighting and strobe modes within a single exposure.

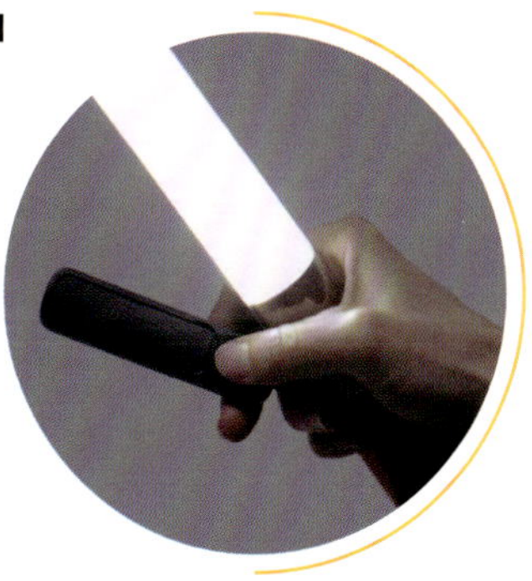

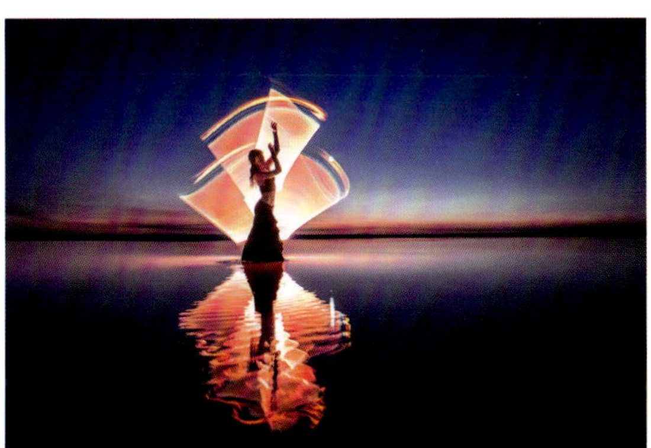

Safety notes

→ **NEVER** aim a tactical flashlight at anyone's eyes. These are very powerful lights.

→ Tactical flashlights can get quite hot when left turned on, so it's a good idea to remove the batteries when you're carrying them in your bag.

→ Speak to the people you create with before using stroboscopic mode. It can be uncomfortable to some, and cause seizures in those with photosensitive epilepsy.

TUBES

This is the main tool we use when creating our outdoor light paintings. In its original form, this is a 4-foot (1.2m) tube guard designed to protect T8 size industrial fluorescent lights. We insert colored gels and other materials inside the tube to change its color and diffuse the light from the flashlight. The tubes are lightweight, easy to carry or manipulate, and create a beautiful light quality.

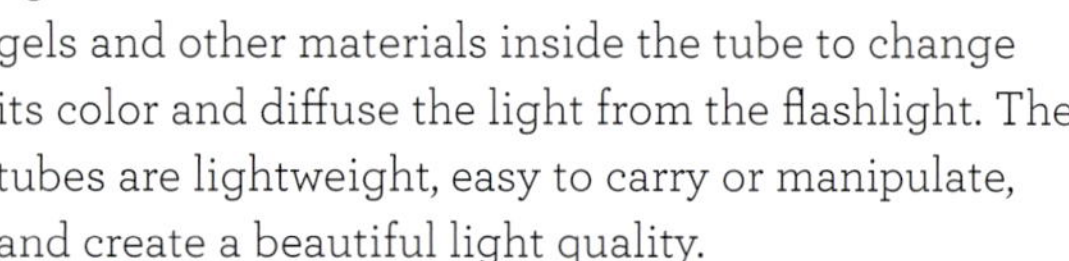

Depending on where we're going and for how many days, we will carry between four and twenty tubes with us. Creating these tubes started as a DIY project, but after a few years we made them accessible for others to buy. We currently have more than 25 colors available, some providing a diffused light quality and others a directional one.

If you are interested in making your own tubes, the easiest way is to buy a clear T8-sized tube guard from a hardware store, or to roll a piece of clear polyester/acetate that you solidify with hair elastics (as having access to plastic tube is hard in some countries). You can insert white parchment paper inside to diffuse the light, or add color, texture, or other modifications to change the quality of the light.

LIGHT-PAINTING SQUARES

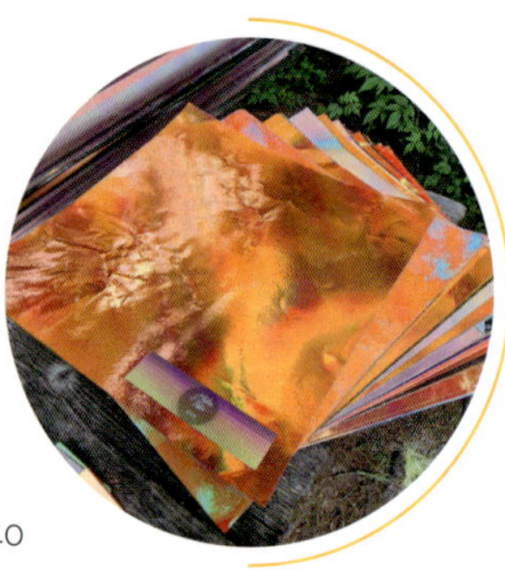

Light-painting squares are the second tool we use most during outdoor shoots. They are very easy to carry, but harder to master than tubes; see page 140 for more details.

TUBE BAG

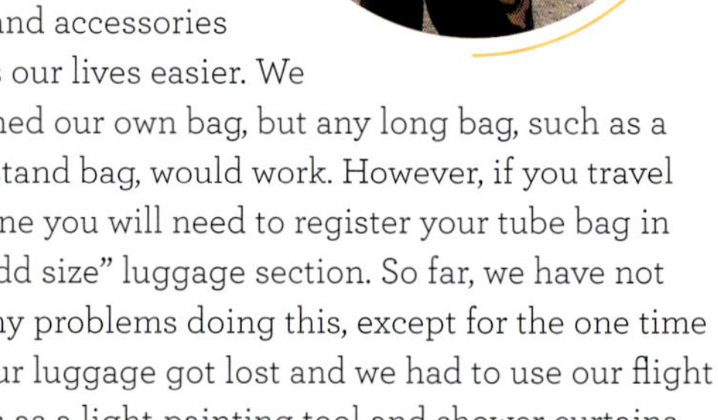

Although we used to travel with three tubes strapped together as carry-on baggage in the early days, having a dedicated bag for all our light-painting tools and accessories makes our lives easier. We designed our own bag, but any long bag, such as a light-stand bag, would work. However, if you travel by plane you will need to register your tube bag in the "odd size" luggage section. So far, we have not had any problems doing this, except for the one time that our luggage got lost and we had to use our flight tickets as a light-painting tool and shower curtains as a dress!

RIGHT **Get creative and make your own bespoke light tube designs at home.**

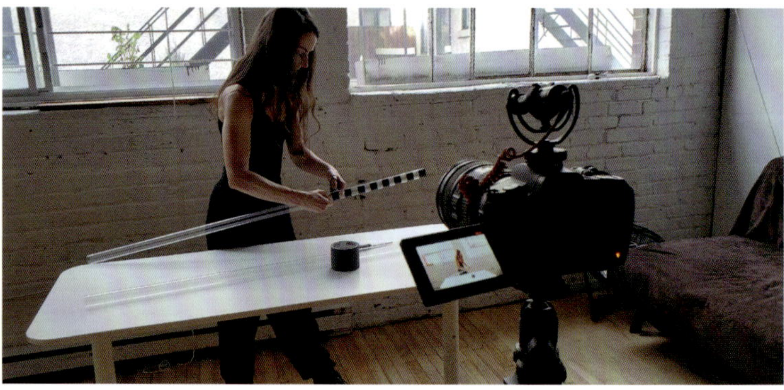

ACCESSORIES

We always carry a
few accessories that
we can use to add
some extra effects
to the light:

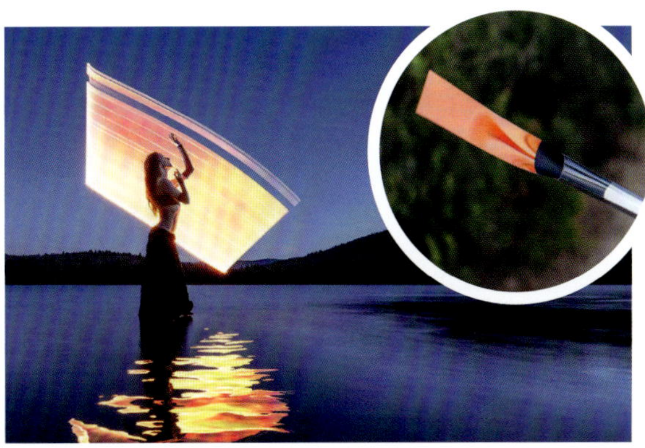

→ **Feathers:** We used
   real feathers for a
   while but switched to
   holographic rectangles to
   optimize both the process and the results. We still call
   them "feathers," though.
→ **Birthday sparklers:** To add dynamic texture to the
   light painting (and a touch of magic!).
→ **Tube caps:** To control the light by blocking or
   bouncing it at the outer edge of the tube.
→ **Hair elastics (or rubber bands):** To hold accessories
   or create dark lines in the tube.

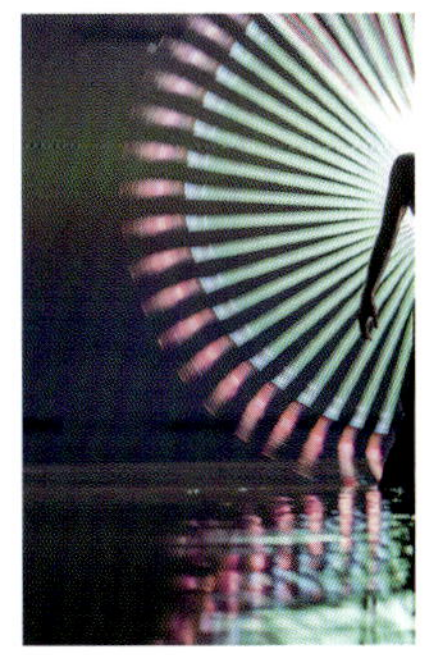

ABOVE **"Feathers" are simply
narrow rectangles that fit inside
the end of the tube. When light
hits the feather, it creates an
outer line in the image.**

LEFT **Feathers are a simple way
of adding a different color at
the end of the light tube.**

Extra gear

Headlamp
Although we work with powerful
flashlights, I like to use a headlamp
during the shoot to avoid draining
my flashlights' batteries.

An extra of... everything!
Batteries for the cameras, the
flashlights, and the triggers; extra
memory cards; extra remote trigger
units. The last thing you want is a
dead battery preventing you from
getting the magical shot you were
hoping for, so make sure you've got
plenty of spares of everything!

Warm clothing
Being prepared for the weather is a
must. If your body is cold, you won't
enjoy the night and everything
from the technical to the creative
aspects will become arduous. Carry
extra layers, as well as spare socks
in case your feet get wet.

Waterproof footwear
If we are shooting in water, we
will both make sure we've got
waterproof footwear and use what
we need once on site. If the water
is on the cooler side we will put
neoprene water socks in our rain
boots, so even if we get water in
our boots we will stay warm a little
longer. If the water's warmer we
might use water shoes instead.

Water
We personally don't snack during
or after a shoot, but if you think
you might need some extra fuel
during the night, have what you
need in your bag. And make sure
you stay hydrated.

Electric tape
Useful for covering the LEDs on
remote triggers and other sources
that might otherwise appear in
the shot.

First aid kit
Even when we are not isolated or
far from the car, we will always have
a first aid kit in our bag.

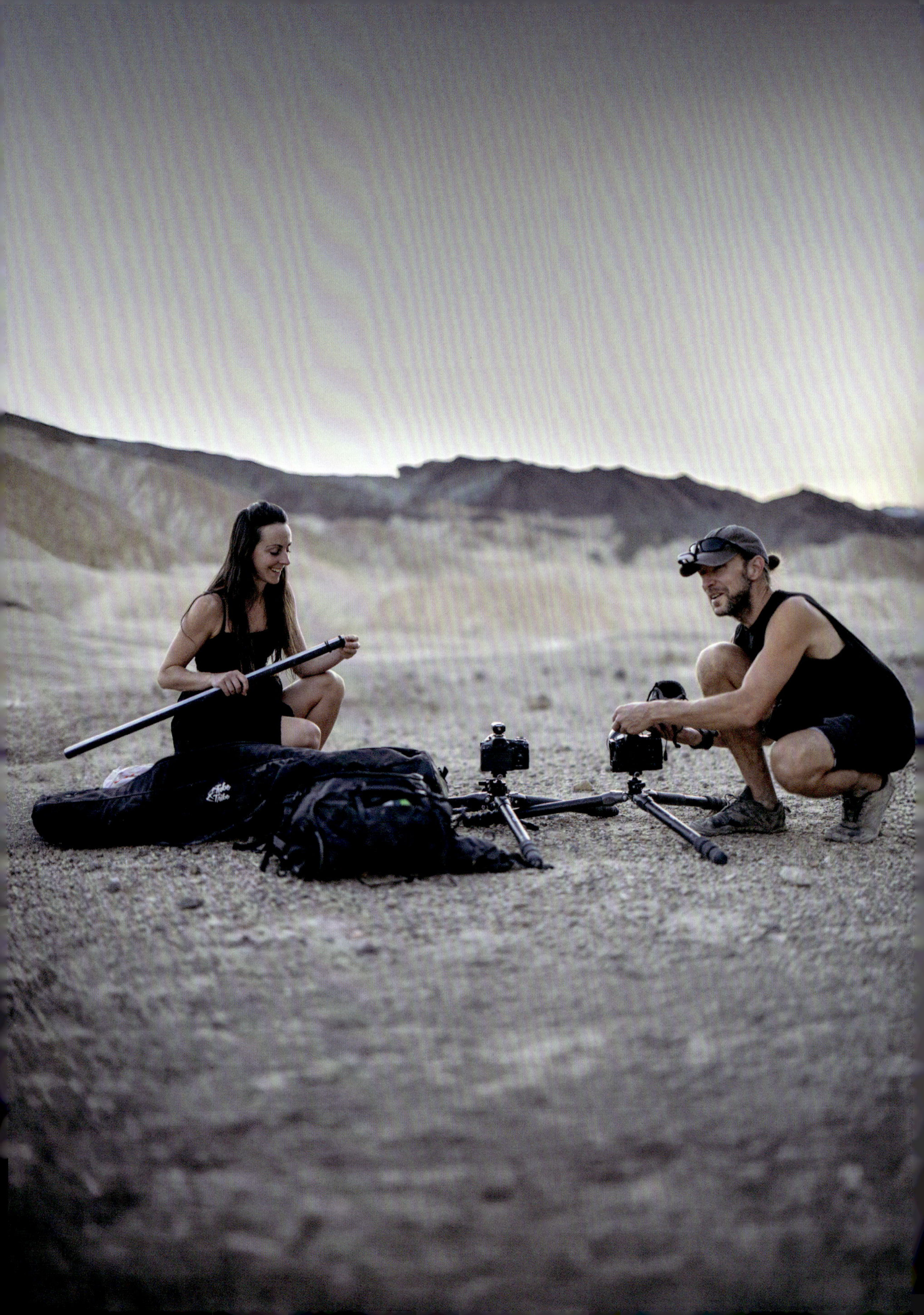

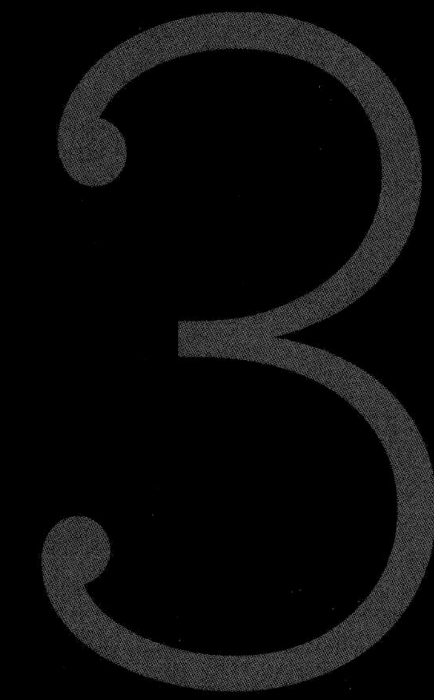

Preparing for the night

The better prepared you are before heading into the field, the more efficient, flexible, and creative you can be. In our experience, things rarely go according to plan, and that's okay. After all, magic doesn't lie in rigidity or predictability. That said, we still want to control what we can.

Initial camera configuration

Camera technology is constantly evolving, and what's relevant for today's cameras may change in just a few months. However, the fundamental principle remains: you need to know your camera well enough to operate it with your eyes closed. Familiarize yourself with accessing the essential settings: ISO, aperture (f-stop), shutter speed, focus, and white balance. These are the key settings I configure on my camera to optimize it for light-painting photography:

→ **Shooting mode: Manual**
In most cases, the camera can't be relied on to measure the optimal settings when you shoot in the dark. You want to be able to control your settings, especially the shutter speed.

→ **Noise reduction: Off**
When this feature is enabled, most cameras will automatically take another "blank" picture after each long exposure, which it uses to detect and remove noise. This second exposure will be the same duration as the first, which breaks the workflow and makes you lose precious time. Even if your camera doesn't create a second exposure, you still don't need to activate noise reduction; current denoiser options in image-processing software often give a better result.

→ **Continuous focus: Off**
Disable continuous focus if the camera is set to autofocus (AF). Otherwise, it will continuously search for a point of focus in the dark, causing your images to be out of focus.

→ **Focus lamp: Off (or taped over)**
It's better to eliminate any extra light coming out of your camera.

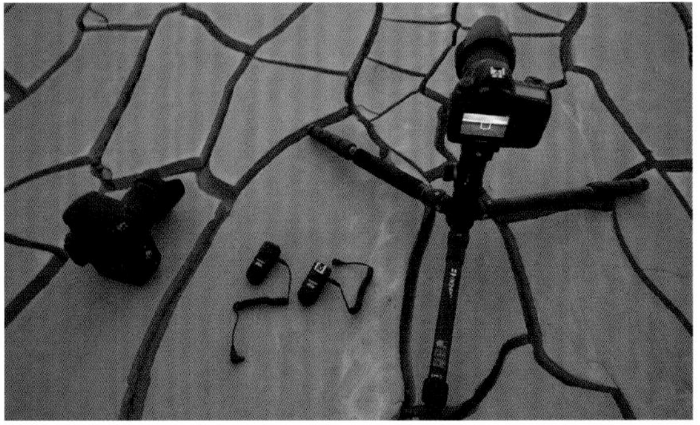

→ **Image stabilization: Off (both camera and lens)**
This might sound counterintuitive, but when you are using a tripod, this feature can introduce blurriness into your images.

→ **Countdown/exposure delay: Off**
As you will be in the frame with your model, you want to control precisely when the exposure starts, which is why it's a good idea to use a remote trigger.

→ **Picture profile: Neutral**
Outdoor light-painting photographs are typically high contrast, with a wide range between the highlights and the shadows. A neutral picture profile will provide a better starting point for editing.

→ **Shooting format: Raw**
This doesn't affect the capture process, but it does make a significant difference during the post-processing phase. The Raw file format records the uncompressed data from your camera sensor, giving you more information to work with. This allows you to make your own choices over the look of the image, instead of letting the camera decide for you.

→ **Back button focus: On**
This is optional, but I recommend setting up back button focus on your camera to separate focusing from the shutter release. I find it increases efficiency during shooting. The setup process varies, but you can easily find instructions online for your specific camera model.

Useful apps & websites

There are lots of useful tools that can ease the planning process, some of which will make complex calculations so you can invest more time and focus on the artistic aspect of the craft. Here are a few apps and websites that we use to prepare for shoots and photography trips:

→ **PhotoPills**
This is by far the app we use the most, not only to plan single shoots, but entire trips. It's a very robust and elaborate tool for photography planning, and we use a fraction of its available features. In a nutshell, we primarily use it to plan blue hour timing, Milky Way positioning, moon phases/position, and star trails. There are countless tutorials within the app or on the PhotoPills website (**photopills.com**).

→ **Weather**
In addition to standard weather apps, we recommend looking at **Windy.com** or **Ventusky.com**. They display animated graphics over a map, giving you real-time updates and forecast data for temperature, cloud cover, precipitation, windspeed, and more. We prefer the desktop versions, but they are both offered as apps as well.

→ **Light pollution**
Darksitefinder.com provides light pollution maps, a simple yet useful tool if you are looking to capture the night sky.

→ **Tide times**
If you are planning to shoot near the coast, you'll need a tidal forecast. We refer to the **Tide-forecast.com** website as we plan our shoots, but you can also use tide forecast apps, such as **Tide Charts**.

→ **GPS tracking**
Apps such as **Geo Tracker** help record your path and make it easier to get back to your car at the end of the night. We also use it during location scouting to mark promising spots with GPS coordinates, so we can return easily, either later that evening or in future sessions.

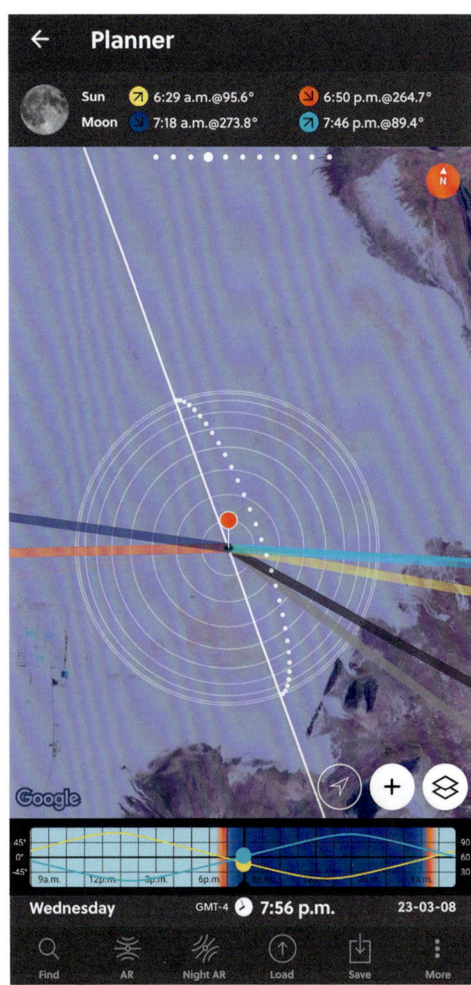

Location scouting

Your choice of location and the weather conditions can inform the creation of your images in multiple ways. The constraints imposed on you, as well as what you notice at a particular place at a certain time, can impact your lens choices, composition, light-painting shapes, and much more.

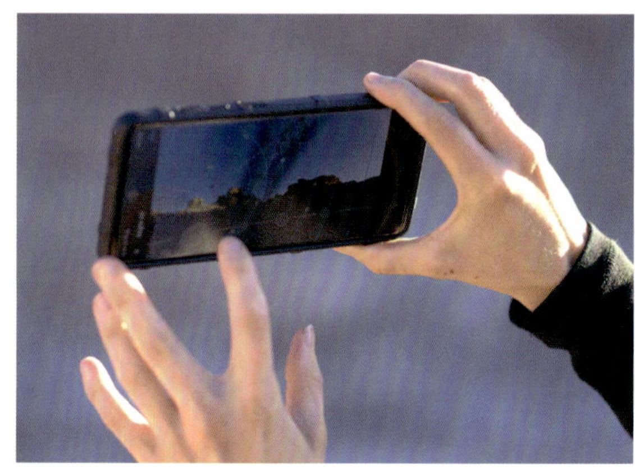

PAY ATTENTION

While you are exploring the potential of a location and looking for appealing visual features, keep an eye on the following key elements:

→ **The sunset glow direction**
When the Sun drops below the horizon, it creates a glow in the sky as well as a gradient at each side of it. This will be your primary ambient light source. Use PhotoPills Augmented Reality to track where the Sun will be positioned below the horizon.

→ **The Milky Way and the Moon**
If you're planning a night shoot, determine where the Milky Way and/or the Moon will appear later that night. PhotoPills Night AR helps visualize these positions on location.

→ **Light pollution sources**
Watch for any artificial light that might affect your shots. Although it can be hard to spot distant city glows when you are scouting a location, nearby lights from streets, buildings, or facilities are usually easier to identify and avoid.

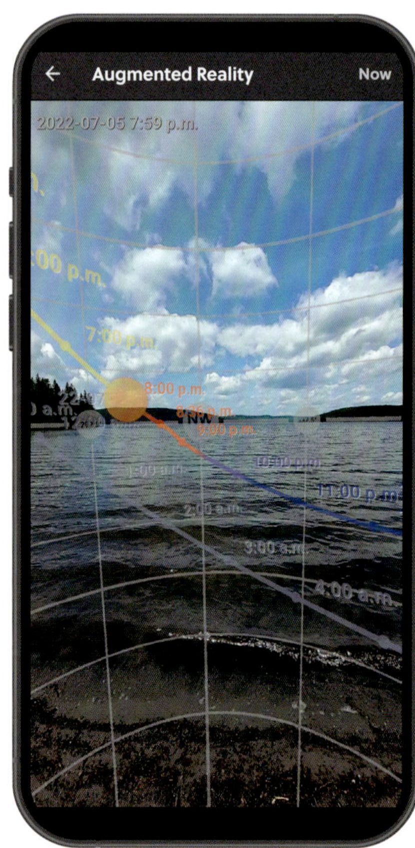

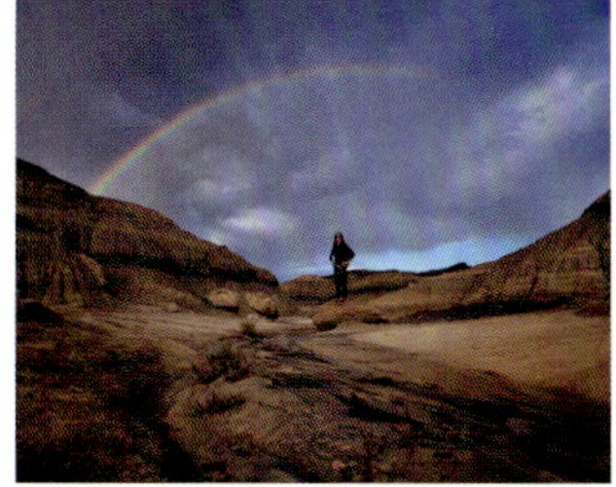
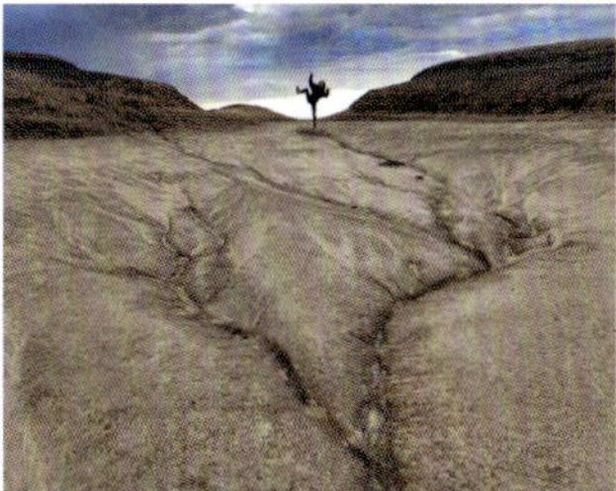
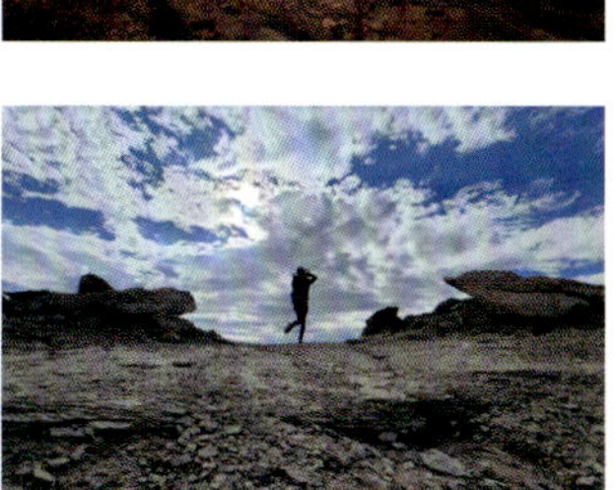
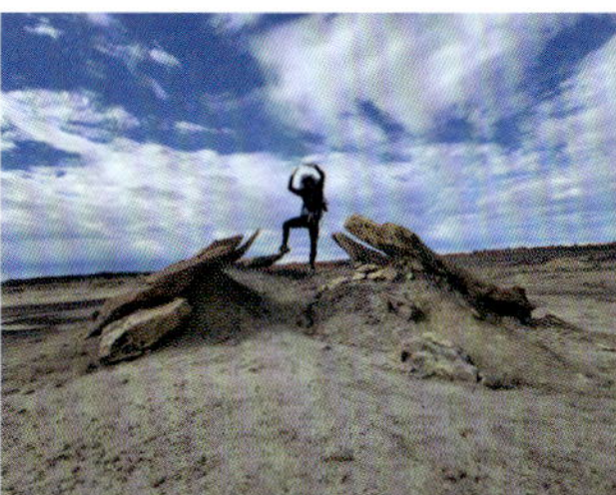
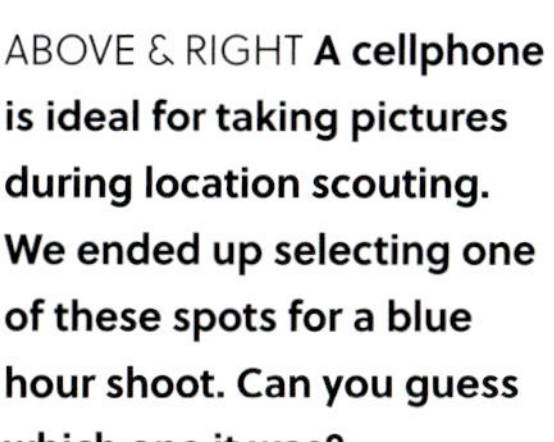
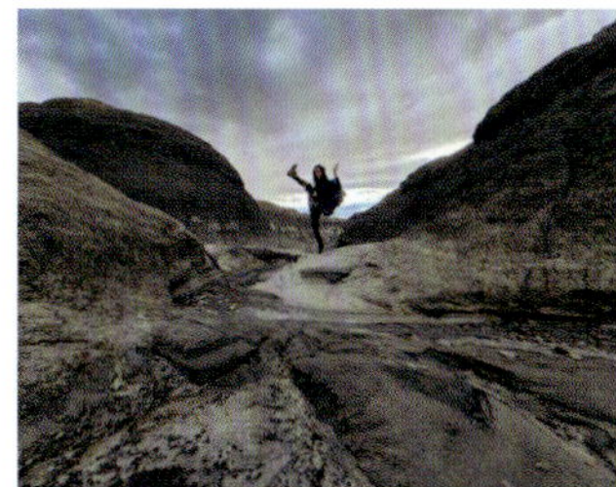

ABOVE & RIGHT **A cellphone is ideal for taking pictures during location scouting. We ended up selecting one of these spots for a blue hour shoot. Can you guess which one it was?**

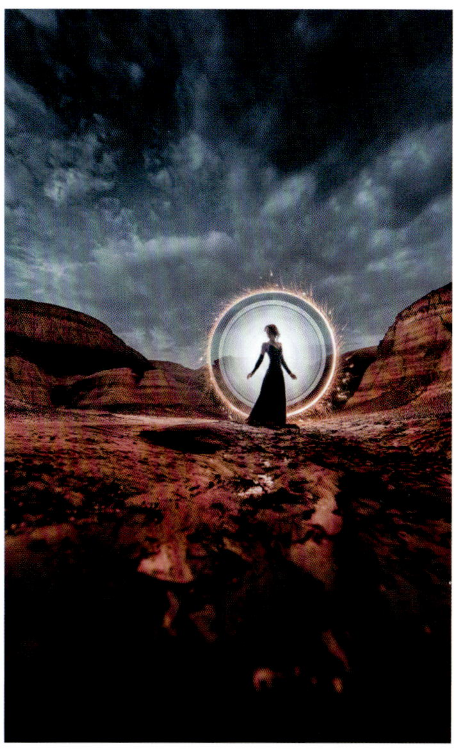

ABOVE **The image we created later that evening.**

SAFETY CONSIDERATIONS

How we experience a location can change a lot once the night has fallen. Areas that seem easy to navigate in daylight can become challenging at night, and you'll need to constantly move back and forth between your camera and the model during the session. As you scout, look for shooting spots where:

→ You can safely move between the subject and the camera.
→ You have space to move behind the subject (no cliff edges or drop-offs!).
→ Your footing is ideally stable and consistent.

We recommend testing various compositions with a handheld camera or smartphone before taking your tripod out of your bag, as this will give you greater freedom to efficiently test safe angle possibilities.

Composition

There's probably a mathematical or methodological way to analyze and choose a good composition, but in practice, we often need to rely on quick and intuitive choices. These are informed by previous experiences, so the more you observe images and reflect on how they make you feel and what you appreciate about them, the better you'll recognize those patterns in the field. Like any skill, this develops through repetition.

You've likely heard of the rule of thirds or the concept of leading lines. These and other composition guidelines can be helpful, but they're not universal. Many techniques exist to guide the viewer's eye, and plenty of books have covered the topic. We won't dive into theory here, but we do want to share a few ideas specific to our process.

Your location scouting should already have narrowed down your composition options. From there, consider the following:

→ Is there an interesting foreground element or texture?
→ Is there water that could reflect the light painting?
→ What is the shape or structure of the horizon separating sky and landscape?

The light painting and human subject naturally become strong focal points in your picture, but what's in front of and behind them also matters. These secondary features add layers and depth in an image. You can think of secondary points of interest in three major zones: the foreground, which might include textures, reflections, or rocks; the middle ground, with elements like trees, dunes, or mountains; and the background, where the sky plays a role featuring sun glow, clouds, stars, or even the Milky Way. The more elements you add, the harder it becomes to maintain visual balance.

A key part of this technique is positioning the human figure in relation to the rest of the composition. The subject's size and placement not only provide a sense of scale, but also help create balance and emotional resonance in the image.

The areas surrounding the subject, as well as the ones between them and the secondary points of interest, are important to consider. Strategic use of negative space emphasizes simplicity and minimalism, bringing the focus to the interaction between the light, the human form, and the natural landscape. Uncluttered compositions and the absence of distracting elements in the frame enhance this artistic approach.

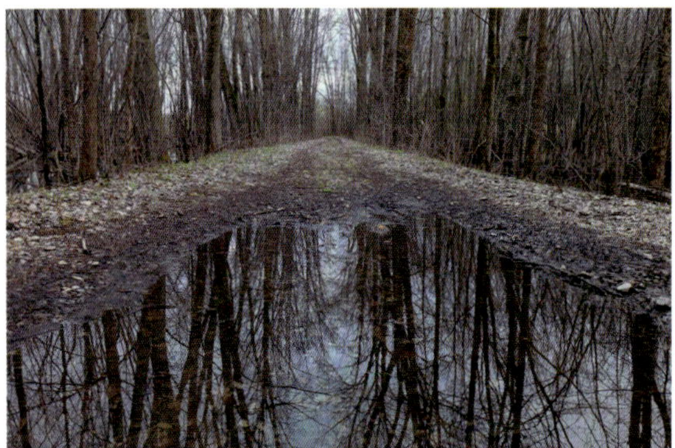

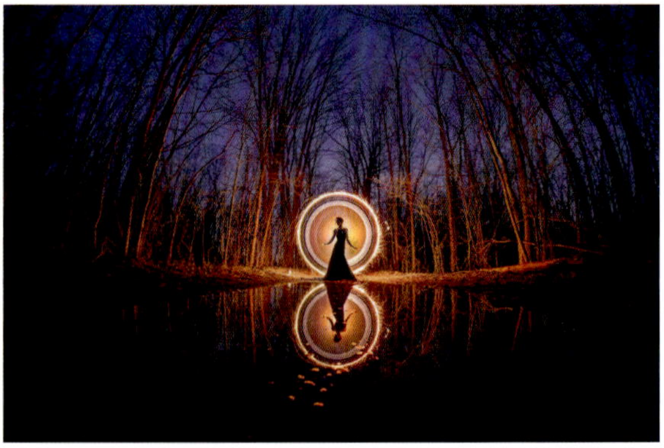

ABOVE **A water source doesn't have to be large. Even a simple puddle can create wonderful reflections when shot with a wide-angle lens from a low perspective.**

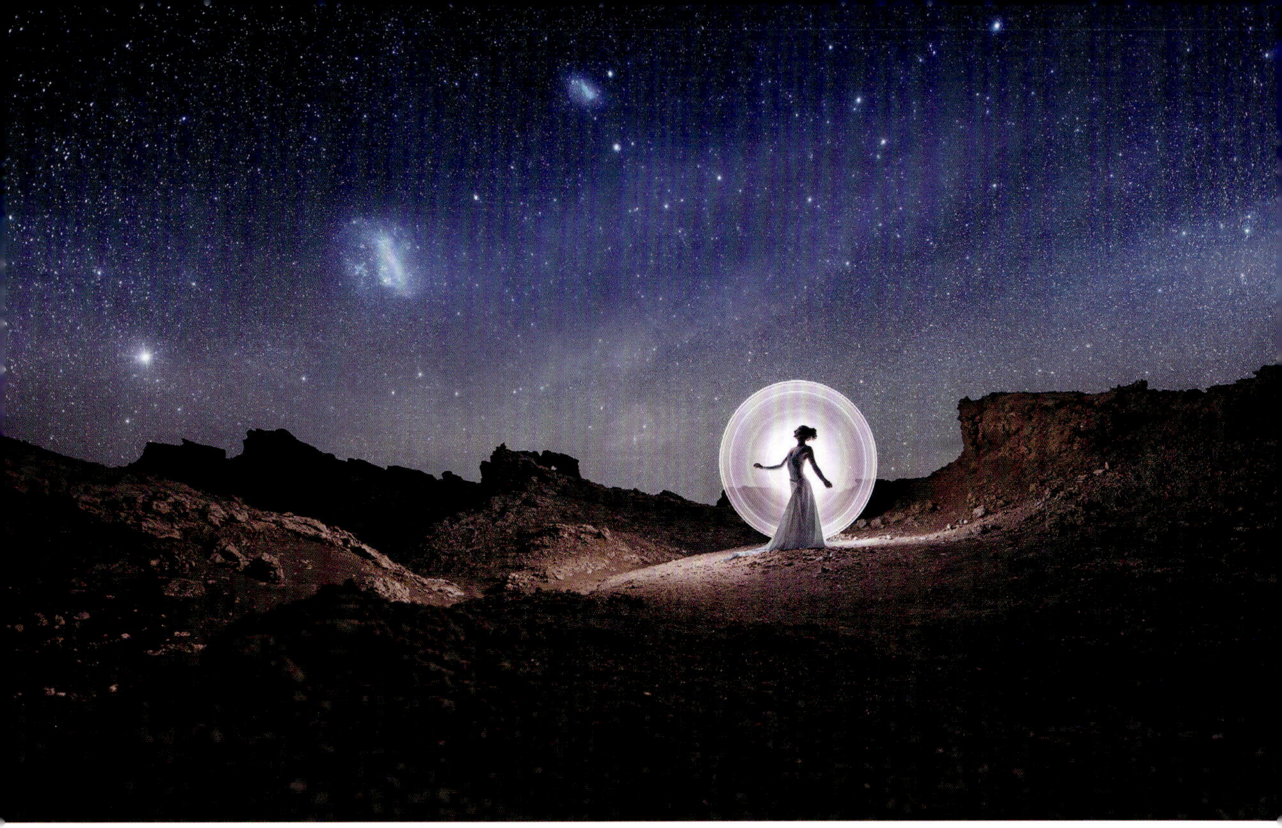

ABOVE **When possible, we place the subject where their scale allows us to perceive the vastness of the landscape, emphasizing its magnitude. Here, Kim's body and gaze direct the viewer toward the negative space, drawing their focus to the Magellanic Clouds.**

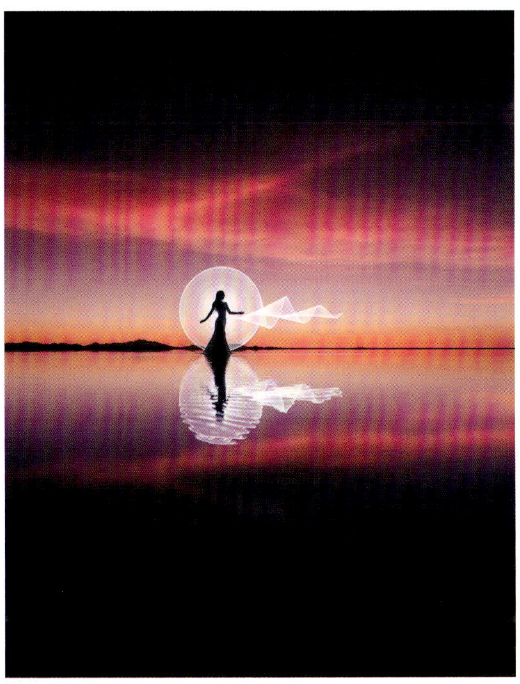

LEFT **The light-painting shape can be used to fill the negative space and create a balance with the other compositional elements.**

Get ready to shoot

CAMERA AND SUBJECT POSITIONING

Once you are confident with your chosen spot and approximate composition, ask the model to enter the frame and move to the position you have in mind. If possible, give them a light tube they can turn on, as this will make it easier for you to visualize their placement.

RIGHT **Use the live view on the rear camera screen to check the composition and fine-tune the camera position, the model's position, or both, to achieve the desired balance.**

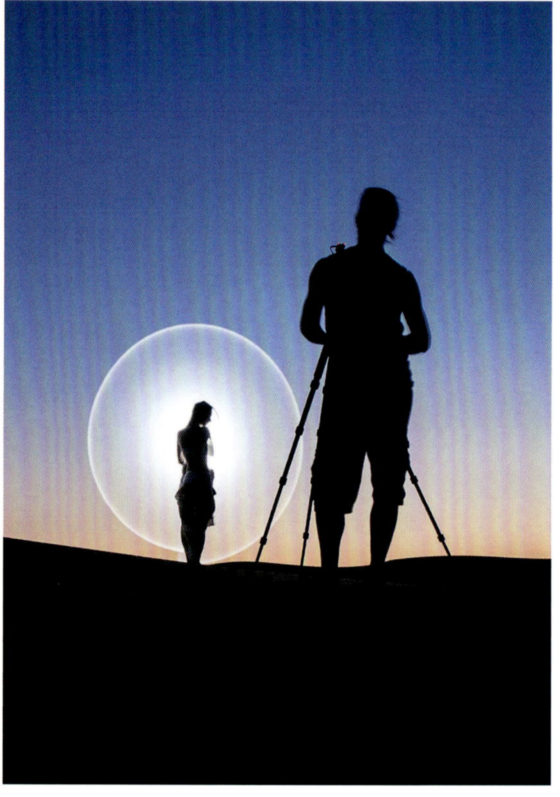

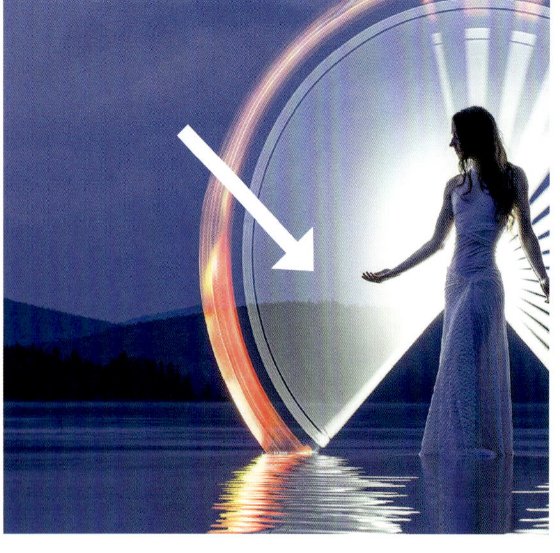

LEFT **Whenever possible, I like to try to position the model's upper body above the horizon line. The partial transparency through the light tube will then reveal background elements that add depth to the image.**

FOCUSING

When you have finalized your composition, the next step is focusing. The most efficient way to do this is by using your camera's live view LCD screen. If there is not enough ambient light for your camera to focus automatically, shine a light on your model or ask them to illuminate their face or body using the light tube. Then, move the focus point to your subject and press the back focus button.

An alternative to using back button focus is to switch to manual focus. In both cases, this will prevent your camera from trying to hunt for focus with each shutter press, which will not only cause delays, but can easily lead to out-of-focus shots. When the focus is set, you shouldn't need to adjust it unless either the camera or the subject moves, although I still check the focus now and then during a session, just to be sure.

EXPOSURE

If you remember only one thing from this section, it should be this: always expose for the background. Every time we teach, we sound like a broken record as we repeatedly remind people to "expose for the background first," but it's the foundation of it all.

There are no perfect settings for outdoor tube light painting. The ideal settings will depend on location, time of night, weather conditions, and ambient light conditions. However, the key principle is to seek a balance between the exposure settings for the landscape and the brightness of the light-painting shape.

Here's how we do it:

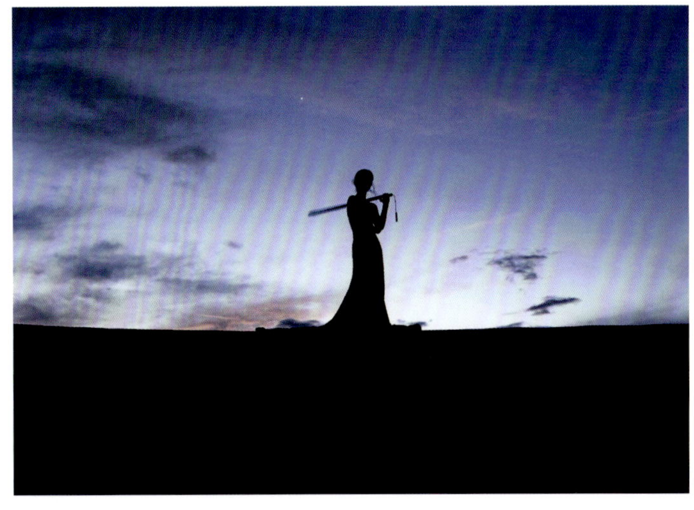

1 Expose for the background
Before doing any light painting, take a long-exposure photograph to determine the settings required for a properly exposed background. These settings will vary, depending on your shooting conditions.

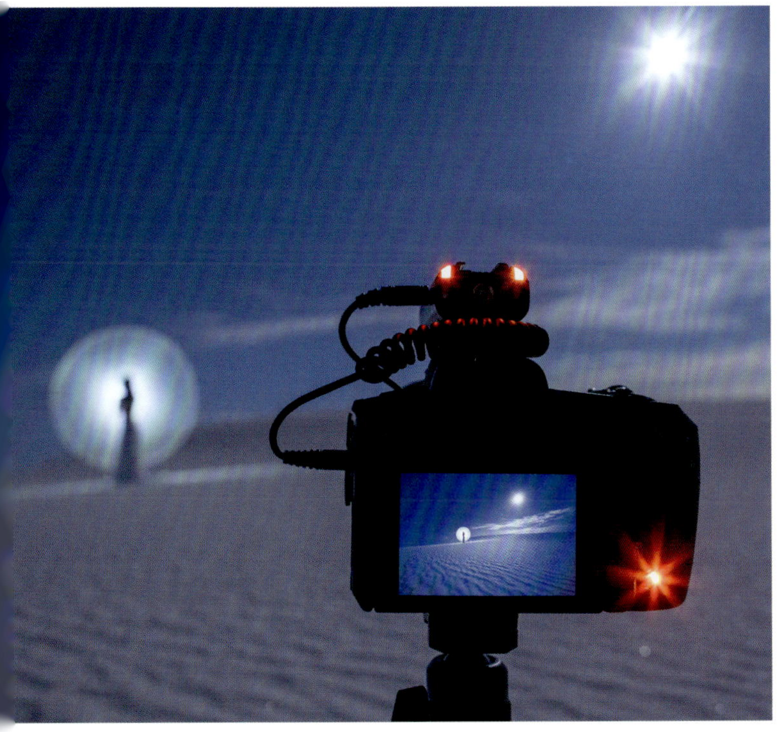

2 Adjust the brightness of your light painting
Using the settings from the previous step, make another test and add a simple light shape. Evaluate the result and adjust your flashlight's brightness as needed. Repeat the process until you reach the point where your light painting is balanced with the background exposure. A common mistake is to make the light painting either too bright or too dim relative to the background. We personally aim for a light trace with some transparency, as revealing the background through the light adds depth to an image. The darker the sky, the less bright your light painting will need to be.

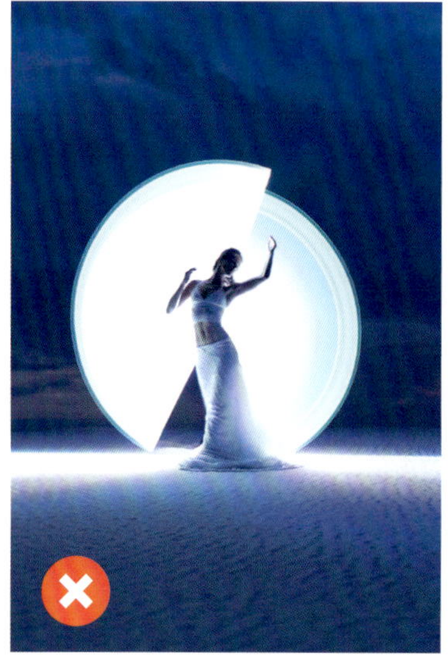 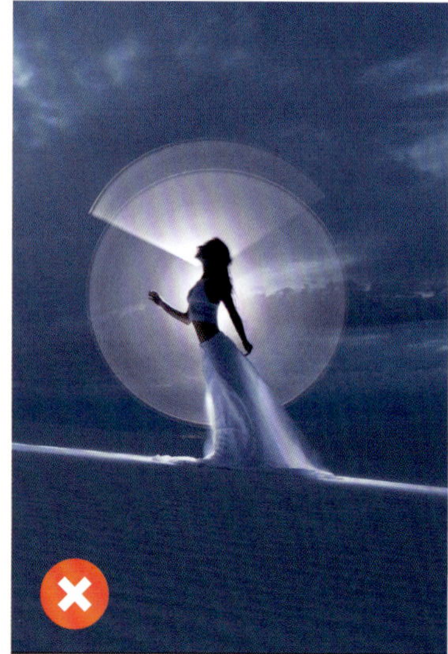 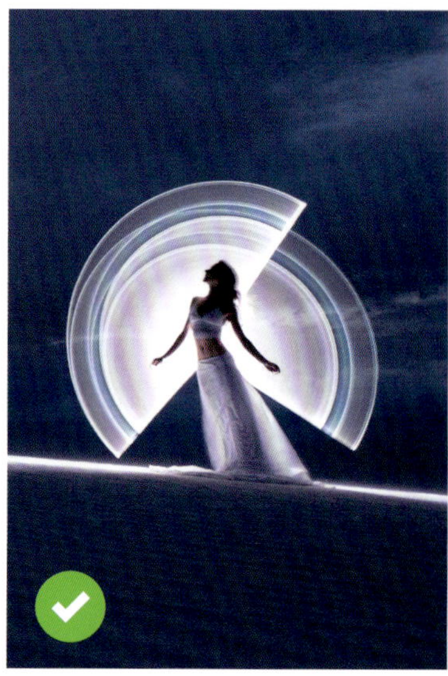

ABOVE **From left to right: too bright, too dim, and balanced light-painting traces.**

Two factors affect light-painting brightness: the power of the flashlight and the speed the light is moved at. The more powerful the flashlight, the brighter the trace of light will be. Most flashlights lack built-in dimmers that work when using their respective pressure switch, so DIY solutions are often necessary. For flashlights under 500 lumens, electrical tape over the head works well, but with high-power flashlights (2000 lumens) the tip can get so hot that the tape melts. We use homemade silicone dimmers that we insert on the flashlight tip, which is the most reliable and effective method we have found for controlling the brightness. This even works with strobe mode, which is programmed at maximum power on all flashlights.

You can also control the brightness of the light by changing the speed you move it at; the quicker you move the light, the fainter the light painting will appear. Swift movements also tend to produce smoother light trails.

Keep in mind that if the ambient light is changing during a session (during the blue hour or moonset, for instance) you will need to check and adjust your exposure settings and light intensity to maintain their balance.

FIXED SHUTTER SPEED VS. BULB MODE

Many light-painting artists use their camera's Bulb (B) mode to manually control the duration of their exposure, and with exposure times that are longer than 30 seconds this is usually the simplest option.

However, while I used to work with B mode, I switched to fixed exposure times several years ago. In most cases, I use the inpaint technique, where I selectively activate the light during an exposure, as this gives me more freedom with my light-painting shapes. Working with fixed exposure times simplifies this process, as I only need to press the remote trigger once to start the exposure and can then focus entirely on light painting.

A fixed exposure time also makes it easier to obtain a consistently well-exposed background; B mode relies on you manually starting and ending the exposures, so is always slightly less precise.

Wireless trigger reliability is another factor that impacted my choice. Over the years, we probably missed thousands of shots while using Bulb mode due to glitchy signals and premature trigger releases.

It's particularly frustrating to lose images because of equipment failures during the precious minutes of the blue hour window. Using fixed exposure times eliminates this issue entirely, as the camera handles the timing automatically without relying on continuous wireless communication.

WHITE BALANCE

Assuming you're shooting Raw (which you should be), it is easy to adjust the white balance in post-processing. However, I have realized over time that if I set my white balance to the correct value when I shoot, I get an instant confirmation that the shot is good and the color of the tube suits the surroundings. To set the white balance I always use a manual Kelvin temperature setting, starting the night at around 5200–6200K and gradually adjusting down to 2800K as the conditions change.

The white balance setting will affect how tube colors appear in your final image, so if you want a white light to actually look white, you will need to compensate with your tube color selection. The warmer the white balance setting, the cooler the tube color should be (and vice versa).

These two images were taken on the same night, the first one at the start of the blue hour and the second toward the end of it. To maintain the deep blue in the sky of the second picture, the white balance was set to 3800K, which meant using a warmer-tinted tube to ensure it appeared as a white light. If we hadn't changed the tube, the light would have appeared blue.

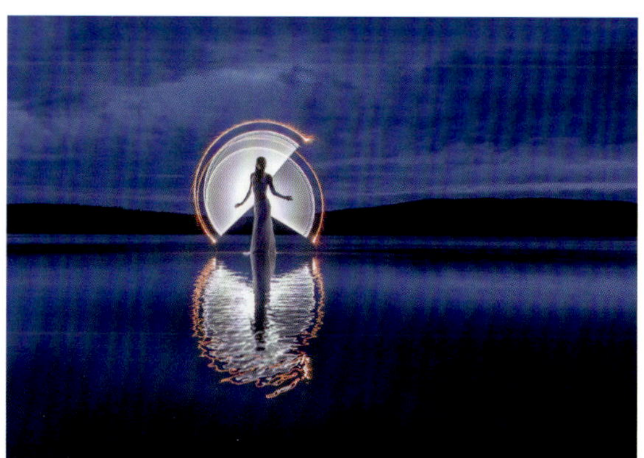

Exposure: 2 sec. (with ~2 sec. light painting), f/9, ISO 400
→ White balance: 5800K
→ Flashlight: 2000 lumens (bright)
→ Tube: Solid White

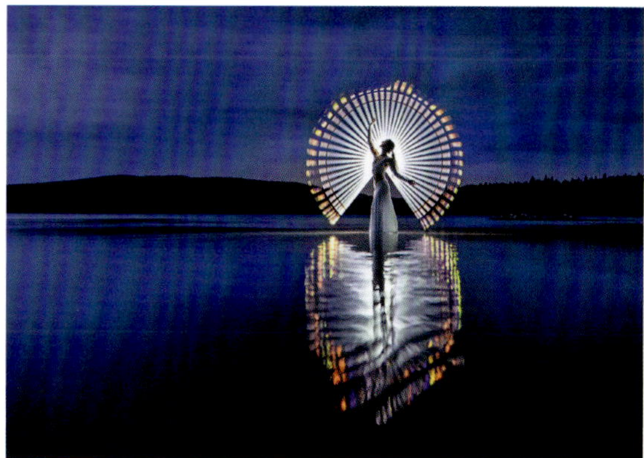

Exposure: 6 sec. (with ~2 sec. light painting), f/1.4, ISO 1250
→ White balance: 3800K
→ Flashlight: 100 lumens (dim)
→ Tube: Warm tint (Warmish)

Workflow

If you have followed the previous steps, you are pretty much ready to start creating. After many years of refinement, this is what our typical workflow looks like. Of course, you can adjust this according to your own preferences, but we find that these steps offer the simplest, most efficient, and enjoyable experience in the field:

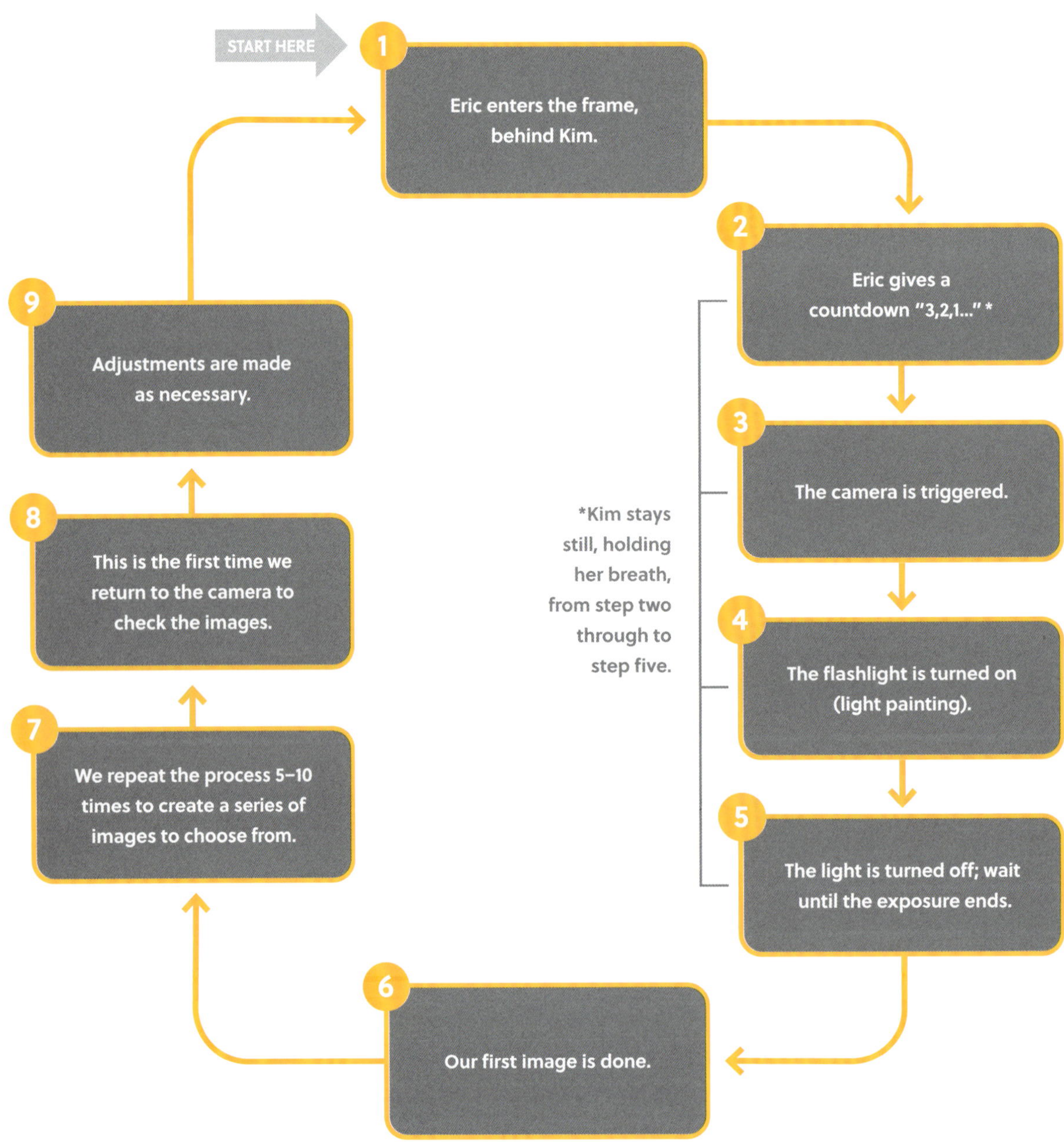

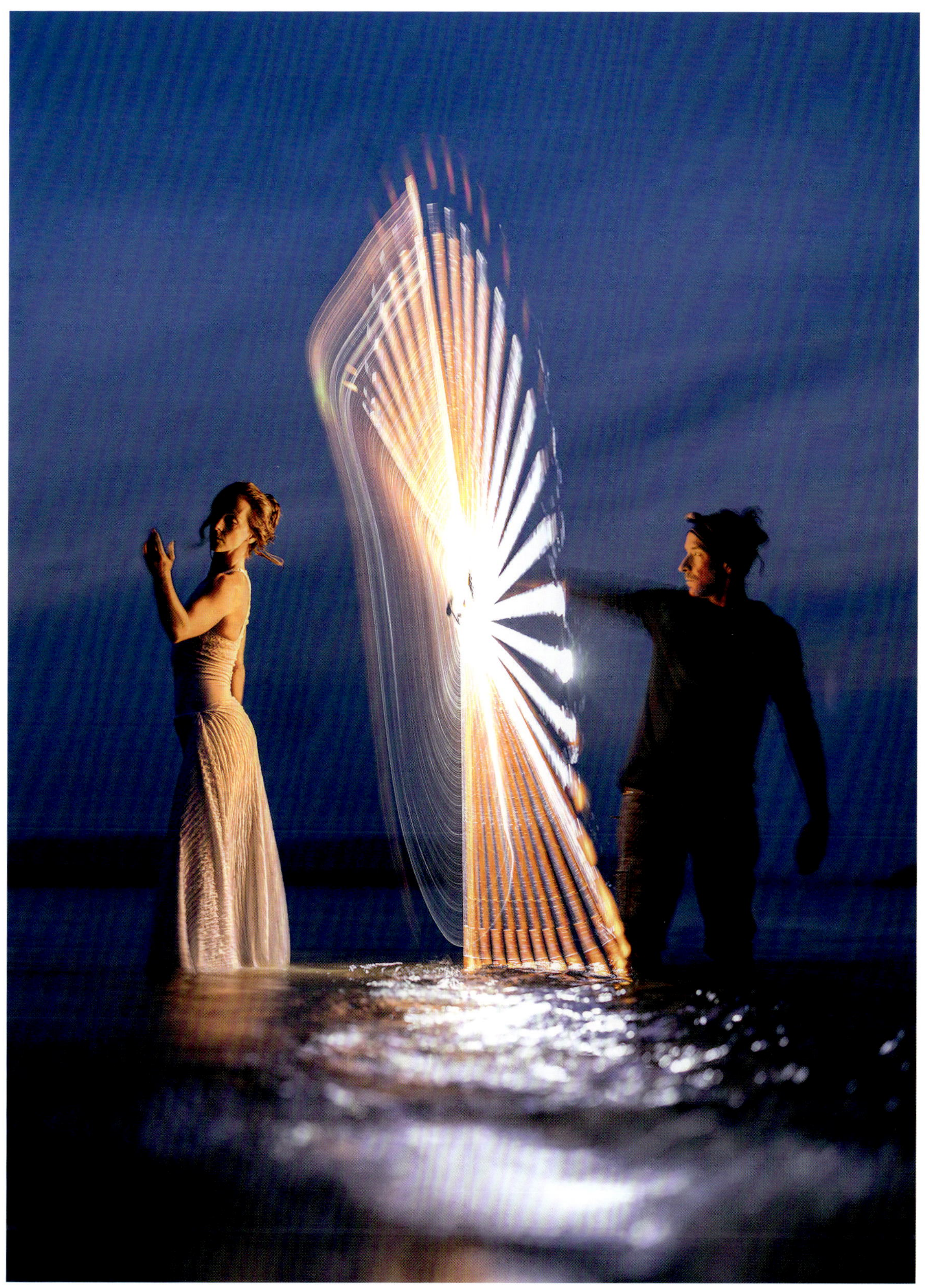

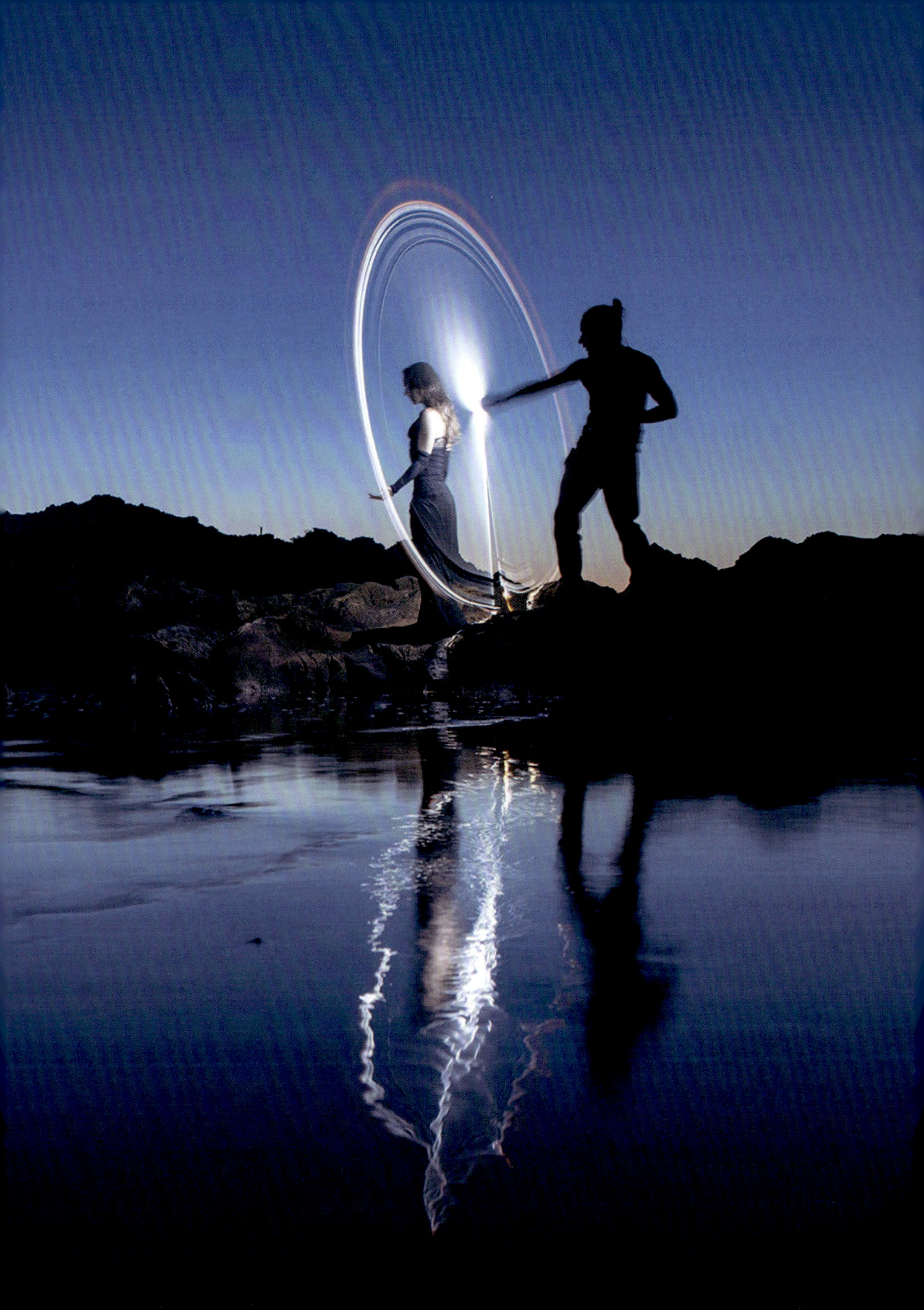

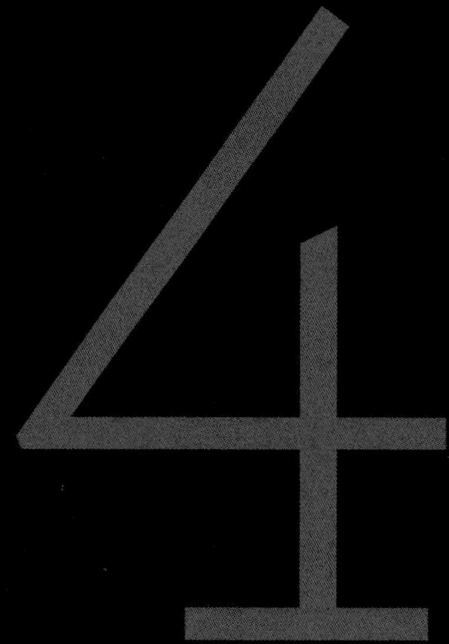

4

Starting with light

Photography inherently involves capturing light, so understanding how light impacts a landscape and/or a subject is very important. But there is an extra layer of complexity when we add hand-crafted light into the mix. Because the movement of the body directly influences the movement of the light, it's sometimes helpful to consider the light as an extension of the body.

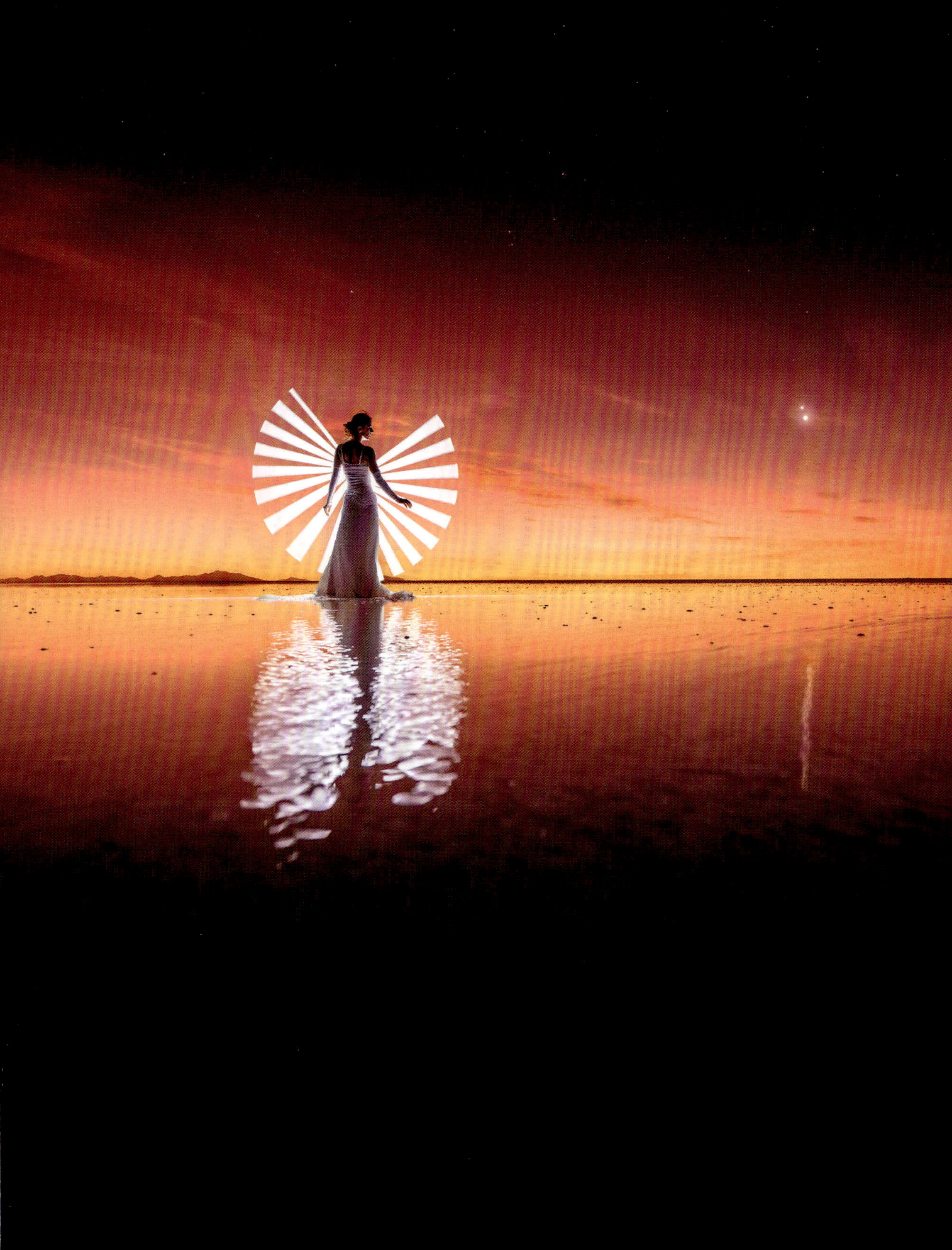

The environment

In outdoor light painting, the goal is generally
to create images that harmoniously integrate
two types of light: the ambient light from the
landscape and the artificial light used for
painting. An understanding of both light sources
is needed to ensure the light painting blends
organically into the natural environment,
particularly when a human subject is involved.
This process is far more nuanced than painting
with light in a controlled dark environment, and is
not approached in the same way.

When creating outdoors, the primary sources of
natural light are the Sun during the early blue hour
and the Moon at night. The direction and quality
of the ambient light has a significant influence on
your composition, as the appearance of a subject
is shaped by how light strikes it. The ambient light
naturally creates highlights and shadows in the
landscape, and can be used to add depth and texture
in an image.

Therefore, the first step is to spend time
observing how natural light transforms a scene
as you move around and change your angle in a
location. Front light, back light, side light, top light
(and everything in-between) will each create unique
combinations of shadows and highlights that will
affect your final image.

Generally speaking, light coming from behind
the camera (which would be called "front light" as
it lights the front of your subject) will reveal details
in both the landscape and the model, but the lack
of shadows results in almost no contrast or texture.
In this context, the light painting will have little to
no impact on the landscape or the subject, often
resulting in a flat-looking image. A light coming
from behind the camera may also reveal your
tripod's shadow in the shot, so while there are some
exceptions, this type of lighting rarely produces the
most pleasing results.

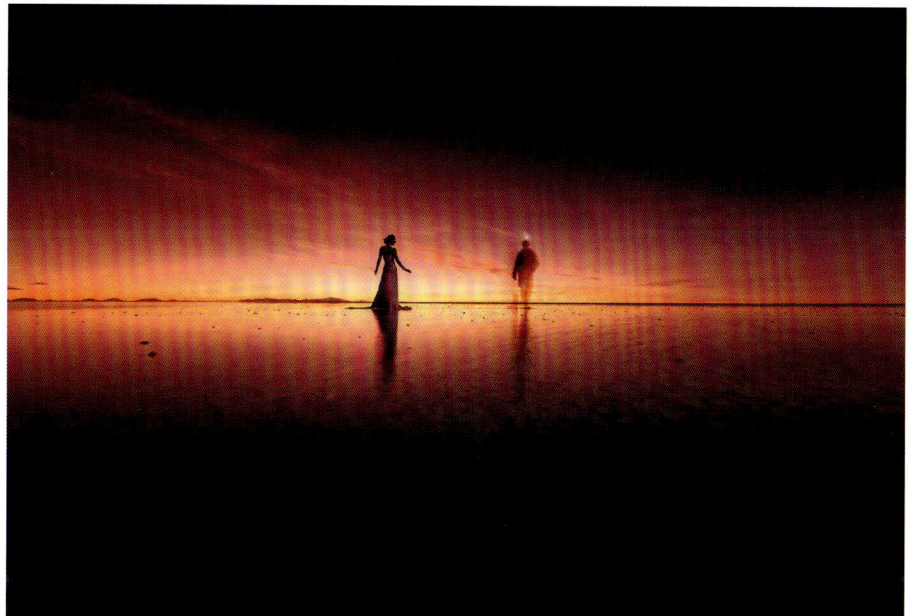

LEFT **Photographed
under a low moon,
this image reveals
the impact of the
ambient light on
the landscape and
the model.**

FAR LEFT **The light-
painting image
created in this
context.**

A single light source

"The only source of light is the one in my hand."

This has been my motto since the start of my light-painting journey. It might not be entirely true if we consider the natural sources of light present when we shoot outdoors, but the essence stands: there are no other artificial lights involved. There are no flashes and no additional light on the subject coming from outside of the frame. If I illuminate the subject, it's with the same light-painting trace that is visible in the picture.

But why? Wouldn't it be simpler to use a flash to ensure the subject is sharp and visible in every shot, rather than trying to do it by hand? My short answer is "No." Simply put, flashes often kill the mood, making images less organic and the creative process less enjoyable.

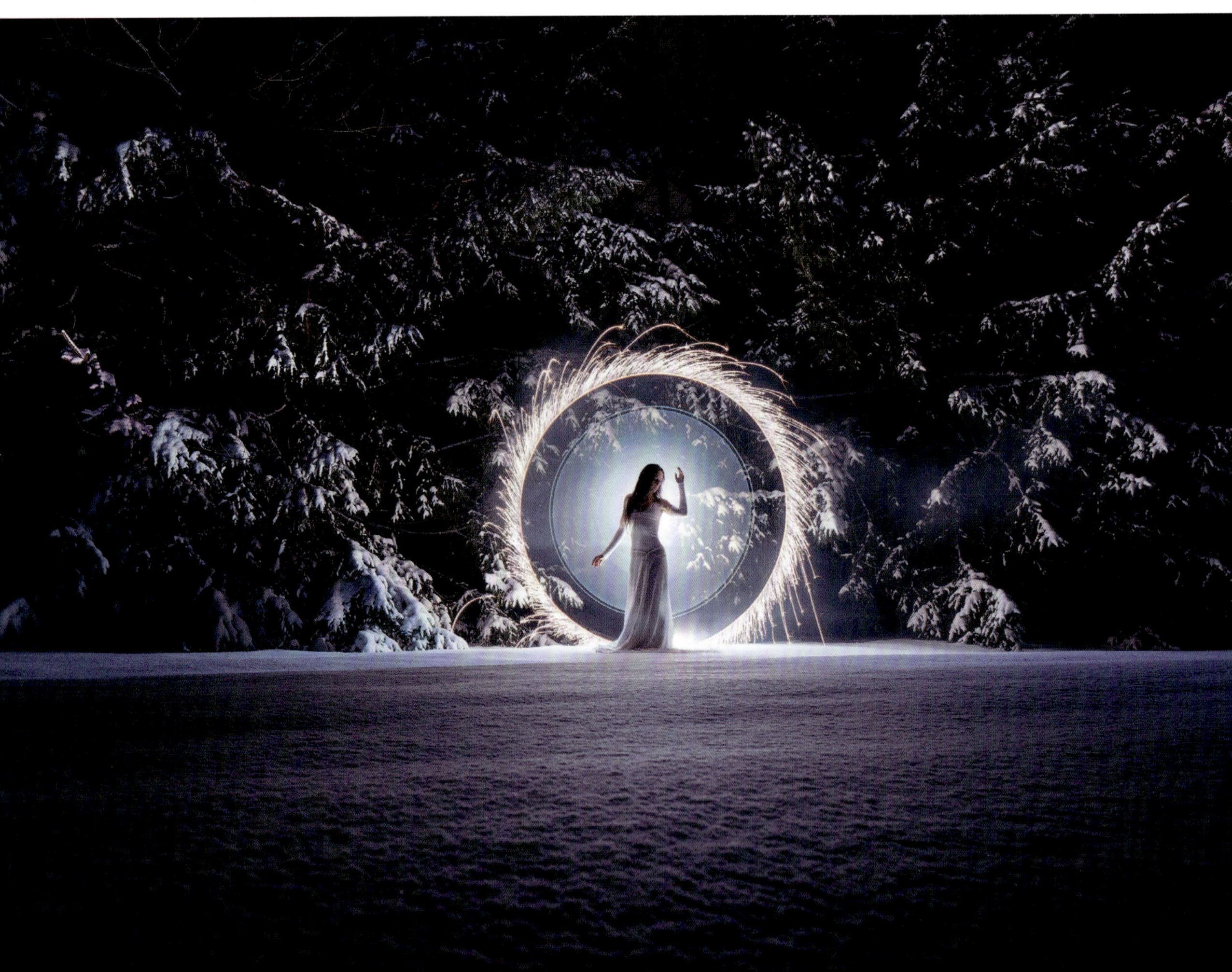

Here are a few reasons why we avoid additional light sources:

→ **Color consistency:** To match the colors between the light on the model and the light painting, I would need to use matching gels on any flash, changing them every time I switch tube colors. This extra step significantly slows the process.

→ **Equipment efficiency:** Extra gear means extra weight, limiting your location options. Carrying more equipment sometimes makes it impractical to reach remote or interesting spots.

→ **Directionality of light:** Unless intentionally creating unease and visual tension when the viewer looks at an image, I want a consistent light direction in an image. For the same reason we want to avoid a front light directed at the subject from the ambient light, a flash behind the camera creates flat, unappealing light, while side-positioned flashes can appear in frame and require post-processing removal. Even then, the light on the subject rarely feels like "it belongs" in the scene, because in most cases it would be disconnected from the light-painting shape or the ambient light.

→ **Subject movement:** Using a flash increases the risk of the model moving between the flash exposure and the light-painting trace, resulting in an unwanted black outline.

Simply put, while it's not impossible to create aesthetically pleasing images using additional artificial light, this is not what we teach or recommend partly because we prefer simplicity. This is an artistic choice and a philosophy. By mastering your tool and learning to work with a single light source the process becomes more intuitive and fulfilling, at least in our experience.

For similar reasons, we try to avoid any light pollution or artificial light sources that affect the location, such as streetlights. Keeping the scene clean ensures we have more control over how we craft the light on the model and the image as a whole.

THE TOOL

We usually aim to achieve several things with our light-painting tool:

→ Create visible traces of light that blend well with the landscape.
→ Separate the subject from the background.
→ Add visual impact to the subject.
→ Have a visual impact on the surrounding landscape.

The direction and quality of the painted light is determined by the tool we choose and how we paint within the scene relative to the camera. We'll be diving deeper into this in the following chapters, but for now consider these four elements as you look at any outdoor light-painting image:

→ How does the ambient light impact the landscape?
→ How does the ambient light impact the human subject?
→ What effect does the light painting have on the human subject?
→ What effect does the light painting have on the landscape?

Light-painting shapes

When it comes to the shapes you can create in your light paintings, the possibilities are endless. We strongly encourage you to explore how you can use the light in your own way, but to help you get started we will give you a few foundation shapes to try. These will allow you to familiarize yourself with the tool and deepen your understanding of how your body movement affects the light painting you create.

A common feature of all these shapes is that they are primarily executed behind the subject relative to the camera, helping to separate the subject from the background using the light. Apart from the shape called "Steps", each of these can be executed using both the outpaint and inpaint techniques so most of them are good options if you don't have a flashlight that can be turned on and off easily. As you master these shapes and understand how your movement with the light affects the way it illuminates the subject and scene, the possibilities will grow.

STARTING WITH A CIRCLE

One of the most frequently asked questions every time we share this technique is "How do you create a perfect circle?" By "perfect", most people mean a circle that looks smooth and symmetrical, with no visible start or end points.

Although this may seem difficult, the circle is a great place to start. When drawing a circle, the whole body remains stable (motionless) while only the arm rotates. By comparison, other shapes require moving your entire body to control the light, which is more complex for most people.

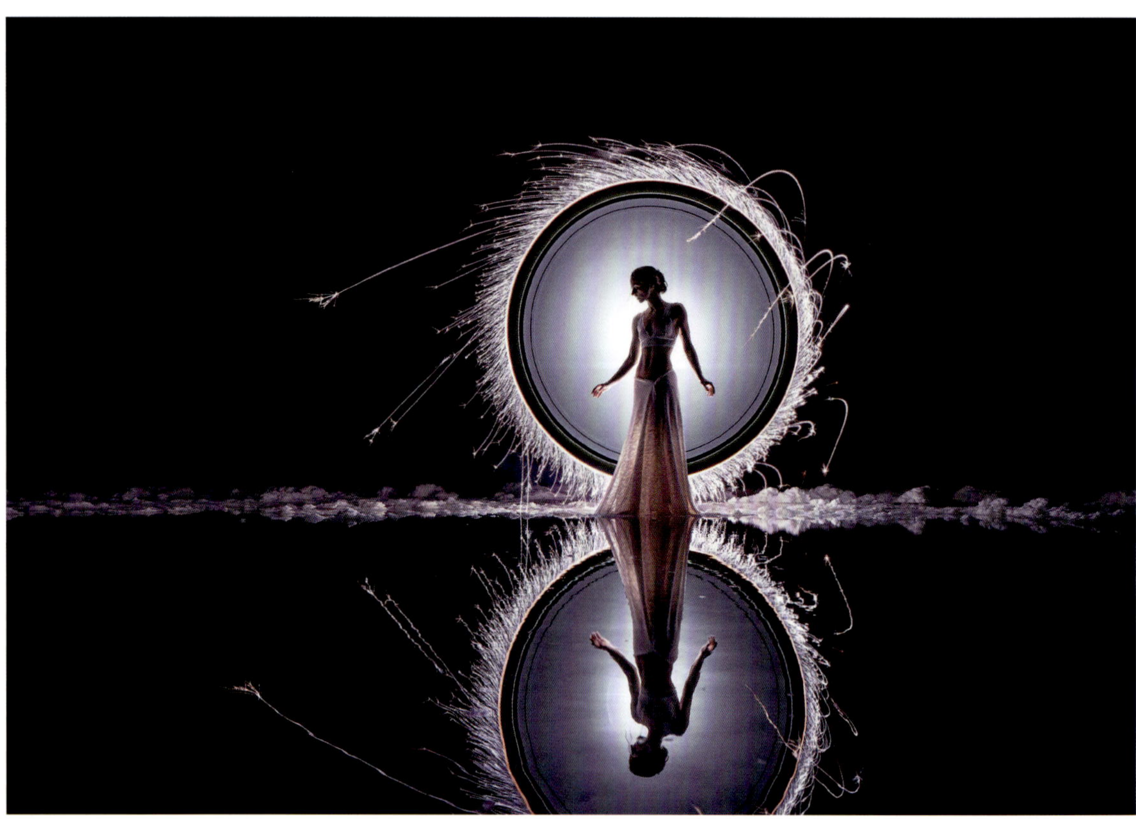

The key steps for a perfect circle are:

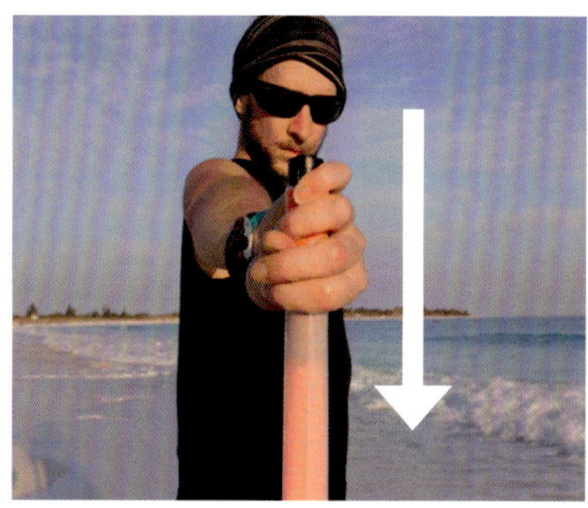

(1) Stand sideways
Stand with your feet perpendicular to the camera plane. This will help you maintain consistency and control during the movement.

(2) Start with the tube pointing down
Start with the light tube behind one leg of the model, pointing downward. This hides the overlap where the circle begins and ends, making the shape appear seamless.

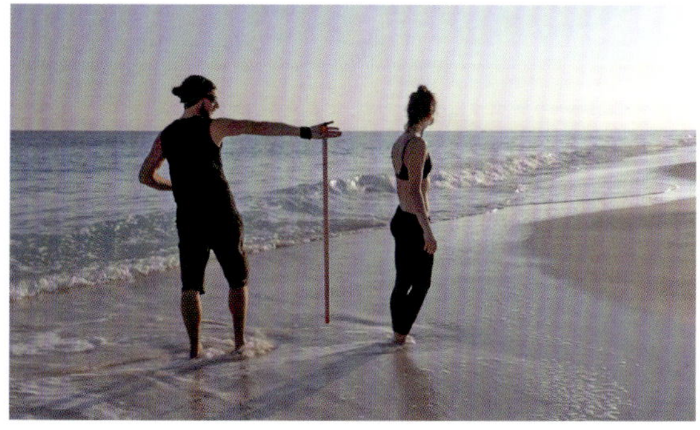

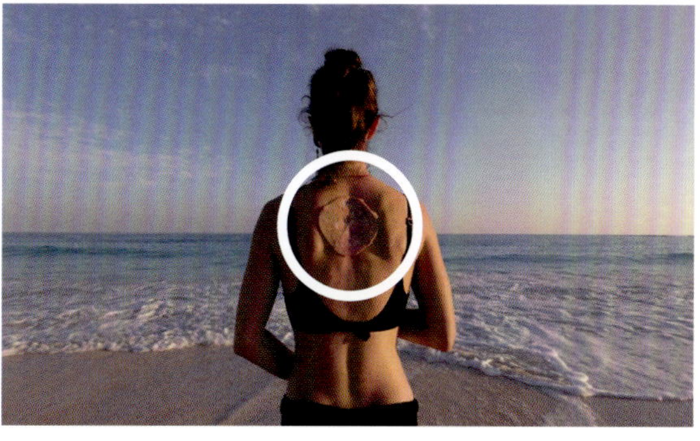

(3) Extend your arm
Create a straight line from your shoulder to your wrist and the tube. A bent elbow makes it much harder to achieve a precise and steady rotation.

(4) Anchor your rotation with a reference point
To maintain a consistent axis of rotation, pick a spot on the model's body to use as a target, such as the middle of their upper back (we've got a video where we use a salami as a visual target on the subject's back: an unforgettable trick to keep your axis steady!). Like clock hands moving around a fixed center, your hand holding the tube should stay anchored in one position.

(5) Make your circle…
Start rotating your wrist: clockwise if you're using your right hand, counterclockwise if you're using your left. Let your shoulder follow as your arm stays extended in a steady, even motion. That's it, you've made your first circle!

(6) Maximize your range of motion
We all have different shoulder and wrist mobility. Try opening your hand at the end of the movement, as this small adjustment can make a big difference.

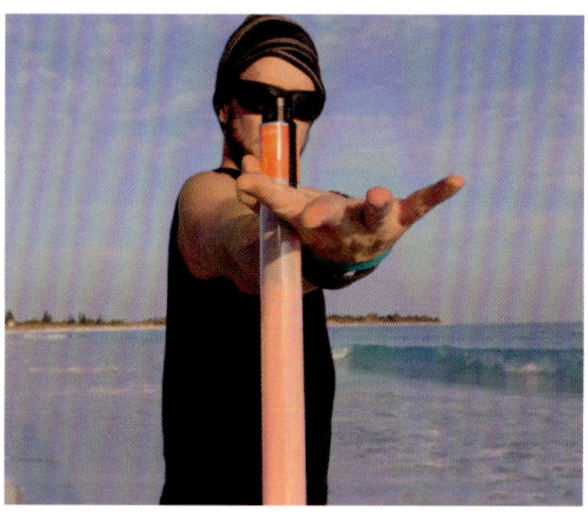

ADDING A TWIRL

Once you've learned to create a perfect circle, you can experiment with variations to add dynamism to your shapes. A simple way to approach it is by adding a light trace to the circle itself, starting with what we call the twirl. This shape works with both the inpaint technique (turning the light off between the circle and the twirl) and the outpaint technique (keeping the light on throughout). Turning the light off helps hide the overlap for a cleaner look.

1 Make a circle

Begin by drawing a full light-painted circle using the technique described earlier. Keep your arm extended, your rotation smooth, and your hand anchored on your reference point.

2 Retrace part of the circle

After completing the circle, hold your position and retrace, moving backward, about ¼ or ½ of the circle. This prepares the structure for the twirl while keeping the motion continuous.

3 Draw the twirl outward

Once you've retraced part of the circle, extend the tube outward, gently rotating your wrist as you go. This motion creates the twisting effect that gives the twirl its name.

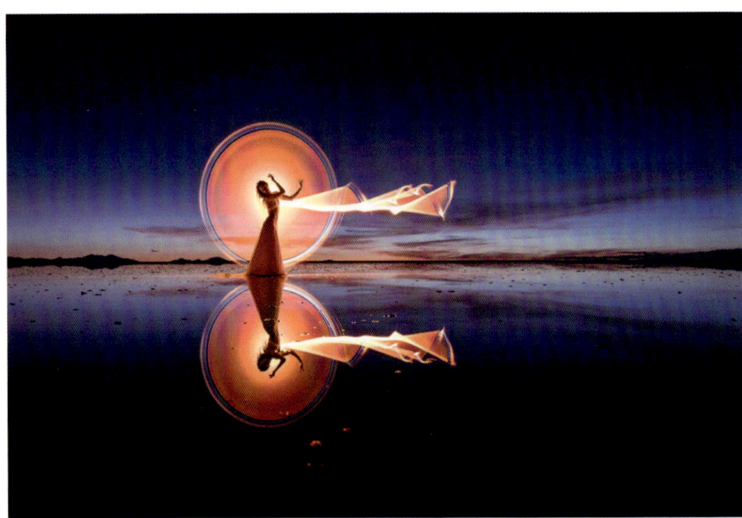

ABOVE **This twirl was made using the outpaint technique.**

RIGHT **A twirl added using the inpaint technique.**

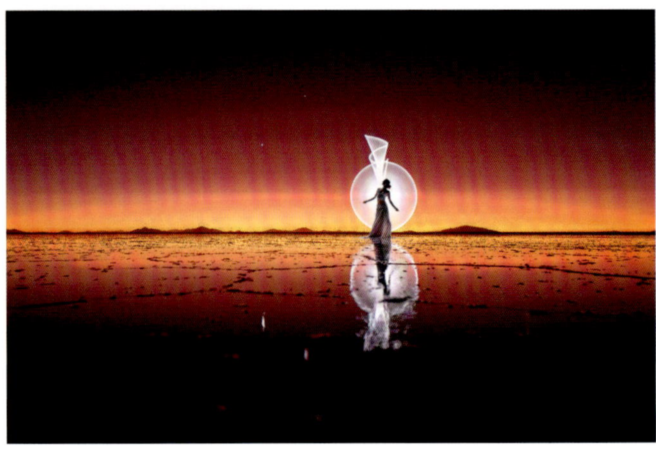

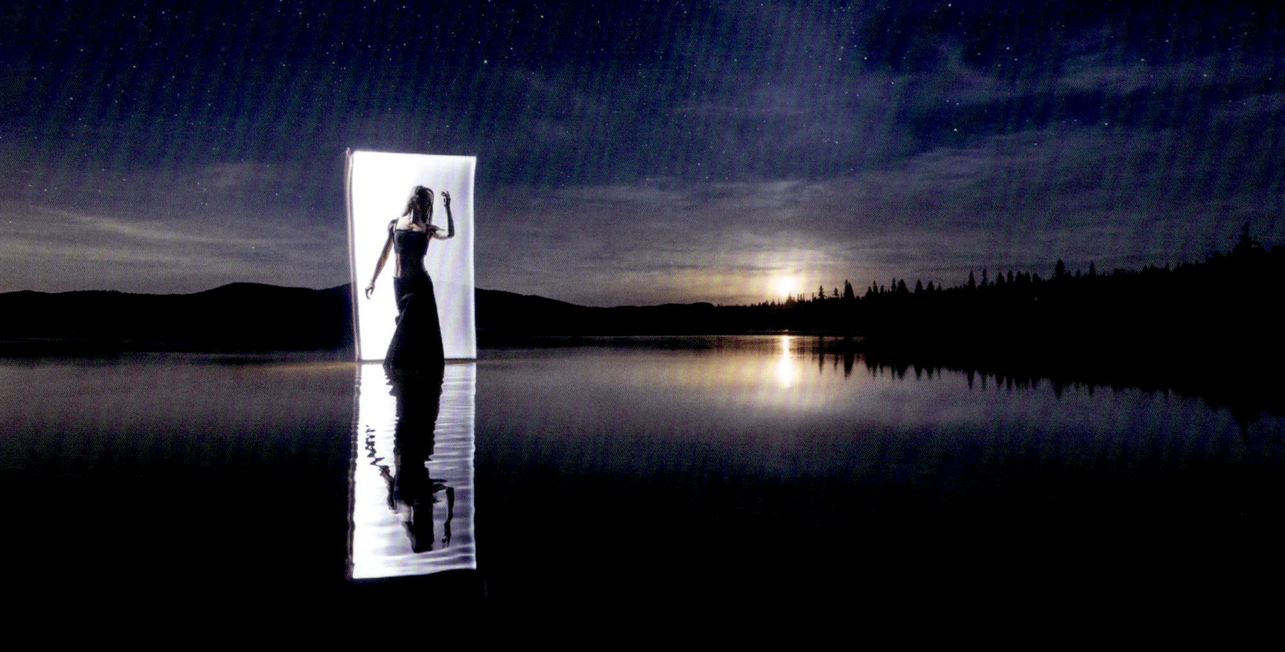

After mastering the circle, the next step is to explore a variety of shapes that add richness and diversity to your light painting. These are some of the forms we've developed and practiced over the years, each with its own character and visual impact. Think of them as starting points rather than rules; there are countless ways to paint with light, and these examples are here to spark your own creativity.

DOOR

1. Hold the light tube above the subject's head, parallel to the ground or at a slight diagonal.

2. Make sure the light is evenly distributed on both sides of their body. The side of the tube you are holding will cast some light on the subject.

3. Move the light in a straight vertical line all the way to the ground.

CANDLE

1 Hold the light perpendicular to the ground, starting with your hand at head level on one side of the subject.

2 Trace a line moving down in a slight diagonal, crossing the subject's body.

3 When you reach the ground, add a curved line, passing behind the model again.

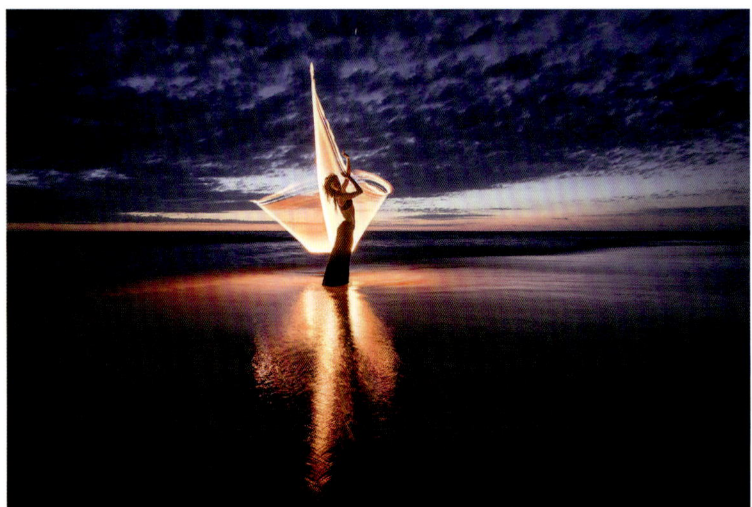

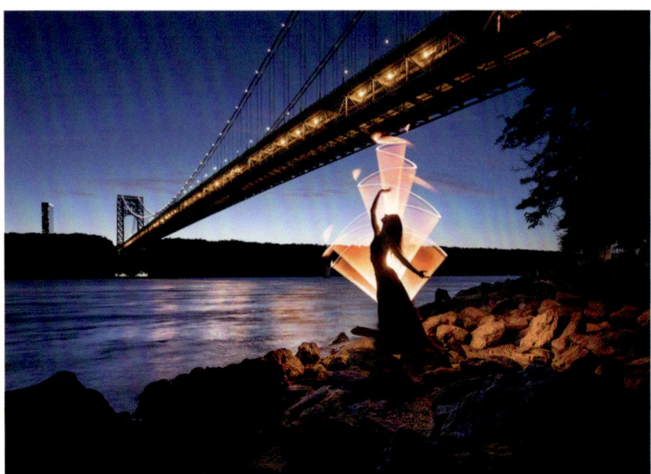

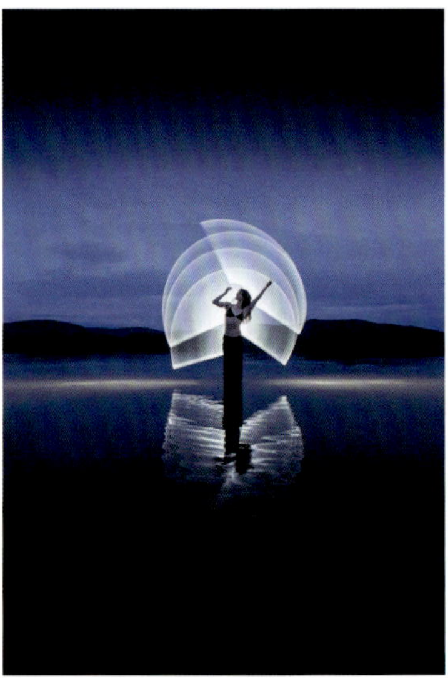

FLOWER

1 Hold the tube at a slight diagonal, with the base at your subject's shoulder height.

2 Move your arm down along an imaginary center line, while rotating your wrist to create a side-to-side wiper-like motion in the upper part of the tube.

3 Gradually increase the rotation width as you move the tube downward.

DEEP FLOWER

1 Start with the tube base behind the model's head, at a slight angle.

2 Move downward, keeping the tube's base aligned with an imaginary center line.

3 As you move down, draw larger arcs of light than the regular flower shape.

STEPS

This shape is one of many possibilities you can explore by turning your flashlight on and off during the exposure (using the inpaint technique).

1. Hold the tube diagonally, pointing upward, with the base above the model's head.

2. Trace a short line and turn off the light.

3. Move the tube down, turn the light on, and trace a slightly larger line below.

4. Repeat the process one or two more times. For your final pass, the tube base should be held at around your model's knee height.

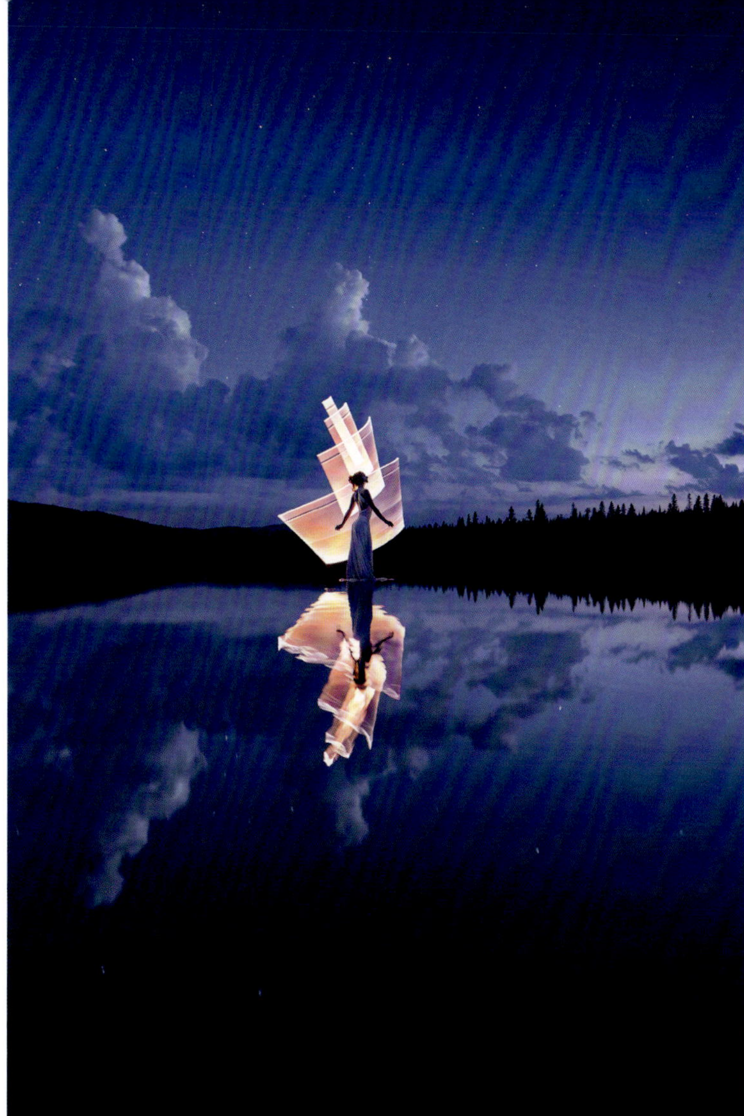

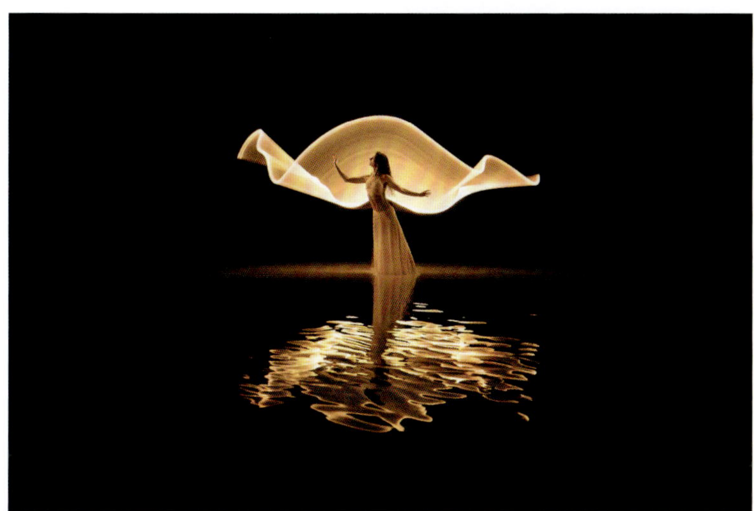

LATERAL SHAPE

1. Starting at one side of the model, trace a line across from one side to the other.

2. Keep the tube base at the model's waist height when passing behind them. If it's too high, you won't see their body; if it's too low, you won't see their head!

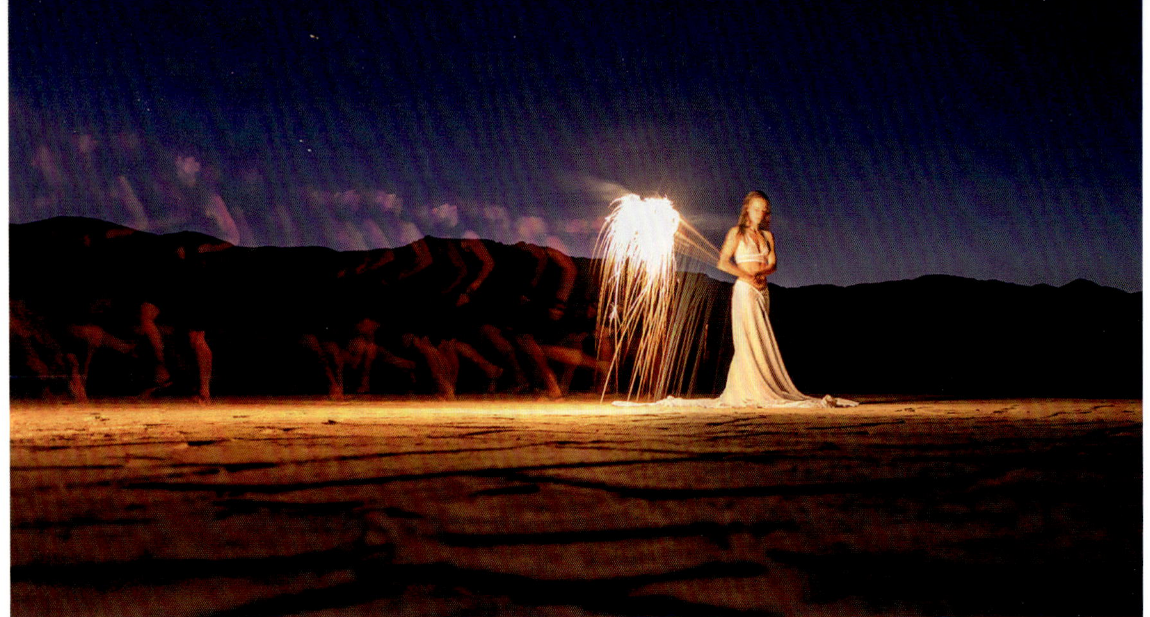

Make yourself invisible

Can you spot Eric on the shot to the right?

Not appearing in the image during the exposure is generally the goal when creating outdoor light-painting images. Part of this art form's magic is the illusion it creates. These images would not be as impactful if my face or my butt appeared behind Kim! There are two main ways you might unintentionally become visible during a shoot, which we will look at here.

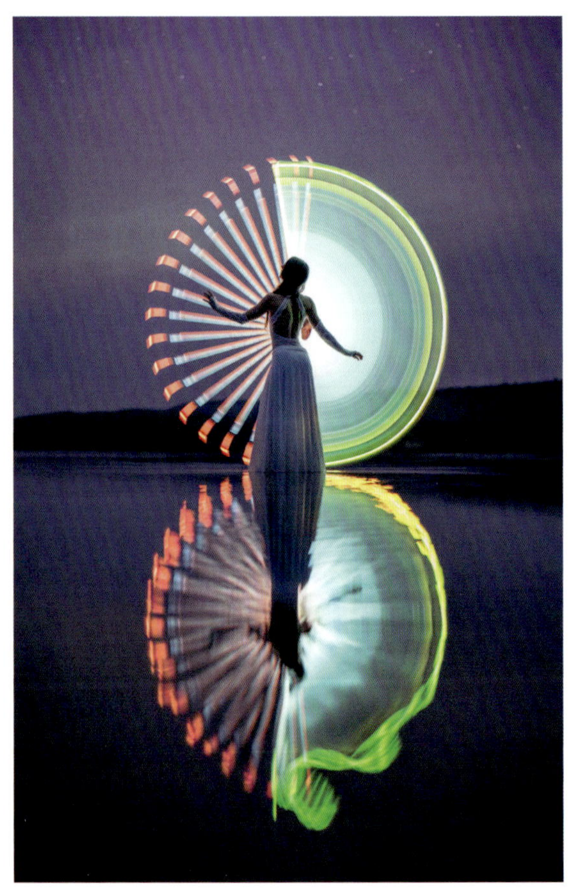

CASTING A SHADOW ON THE BACKGROUND

What appears to be your shadow is actually your body blocking the light from behind you from reaching the camera (typically the sky in the background). This phenomenon is most noticeable during the blue hour. To avoid casting a shadow, consider the following:

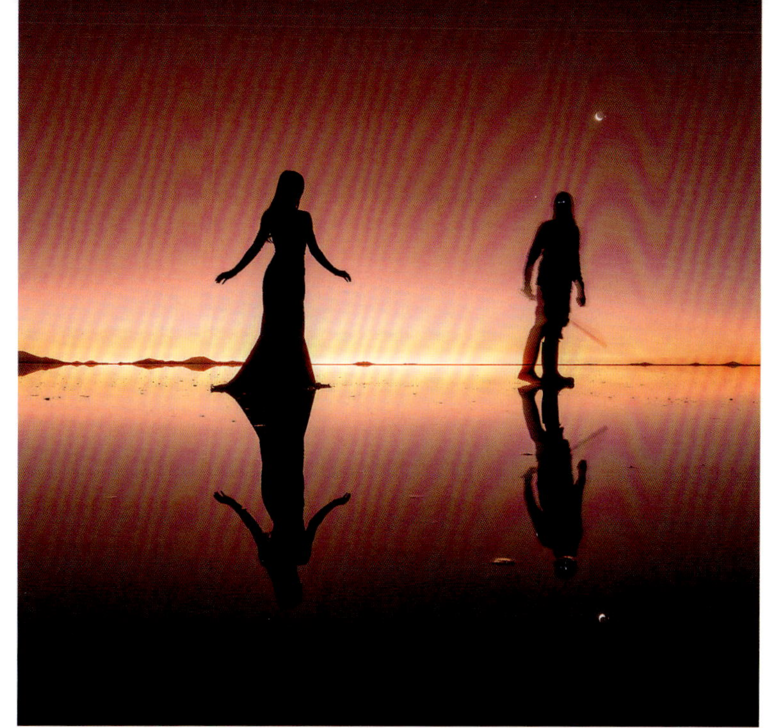

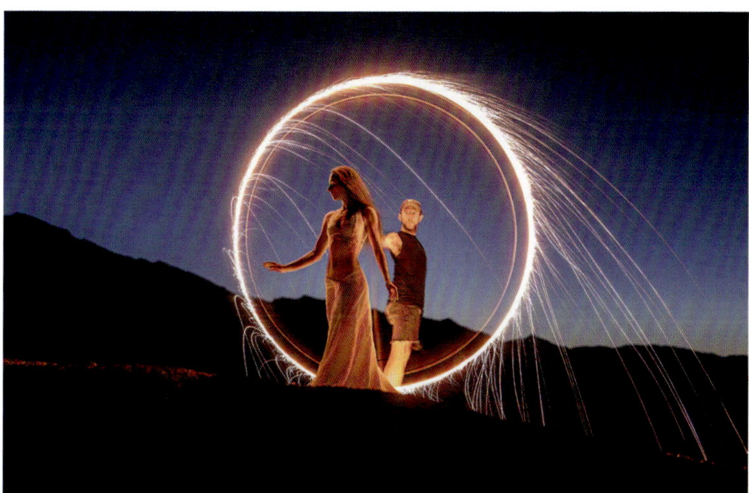

→ **Stay well aligned behind your subject**
This is the most important consideration, as it prevents other issues. Position yourself directly behind your subject from the camera's perspective. Sometimes, turning sideways with both feet in a straight line relative to the camera's position helps you take up less space. If your alignment is off, not only will you become visible, but the shapes you create will appear distorted or asymmetric.

→ **Move quickly when creating lateral shapes**
If you can't stay hidden behind your model while creating a lateral shape, move at a fast, constant pace throughout the exposure. By keeping your whole body in motion (walking) at a fast pace, you reduce the amount of time your body blocks light, minimizing its effect on the background.

→ **Exit the frame during longer exposures**
For captures of 8 seconds or more, complete your light painting within the first 1–2 seconds, then quickly (and safely) move out of the frame. This allows the remaining exposure time to capture only the background light.

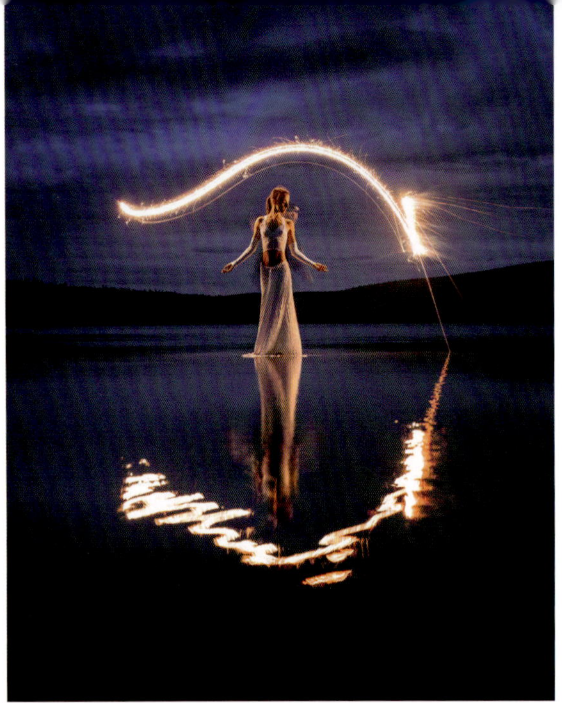

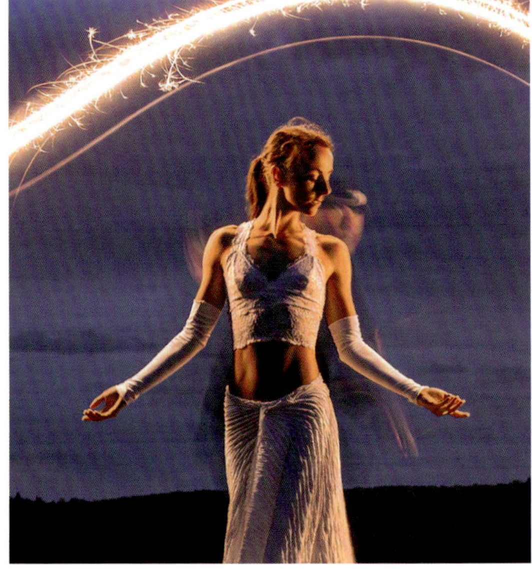

ACCIDENTALLY ILLUMINATING YOURSELF

If you accidentally illuminate yourself with the light-painting tool, you will also become visible, creating a ghostly effect in the image. To minimize this risk:

→ **Wear dark, non-reflective clothing**
  This will reduce the amount of light you reflect.

→ **Direct the light away from yourself**
  Regardless of the tool that you are using, be mindful of how you move it during light painting. Ensure the light is aimed only at the subject and away from your body to prevent unintentionally lighting yourself.

→ **Control the light directionality**
  Some light-painting tools, such as Solid tubes, are designed to emit light in a specific direction. You can further control this by physically modifying the tool, for example, by blocking or blacking out one side, to reduce the amount of light directed toward you.

→ **Move quickly**
  Faster movements limit the time you might accidentally illuminate yourself.

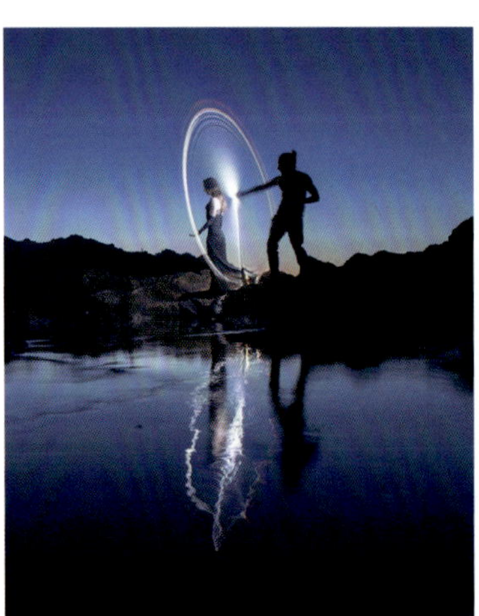

RIGHT **A side view comparing directional (Solid) and diffused (Milky) light tubes. The directional tube blocks light on Eric's side, which reduces the risk of self-illumination.**

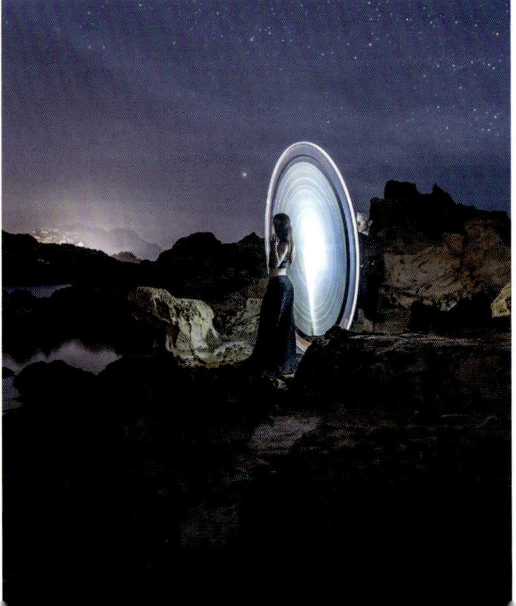

ADDITIONAL TECHNIQUES TO STAY INVISIBLE

→ **Use the model's clothing**
Ask the model to wear loose-fitting clothes – wide-legged pants and long skirts can help hide your feet and legs while you paint.

→ **Hide behind the light painting**
You can easily disappear behind the light painting shape you create. For instance, bringing the light trace all the way to the ground behind the subject can effectively mask your feet and legs, as shown here.

→ **Position the subject higher than yourself**
Position the model on a rock, ledge, or elevated element in the scene. Use the object they're on to hide yourself from the camera as you paint.

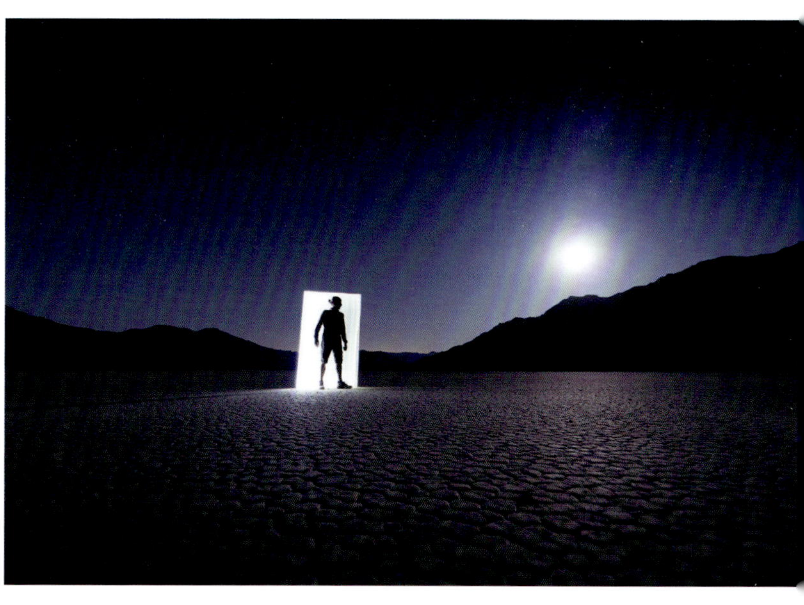

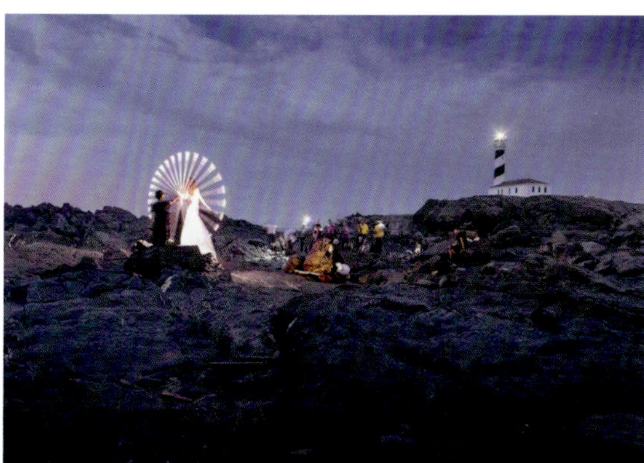

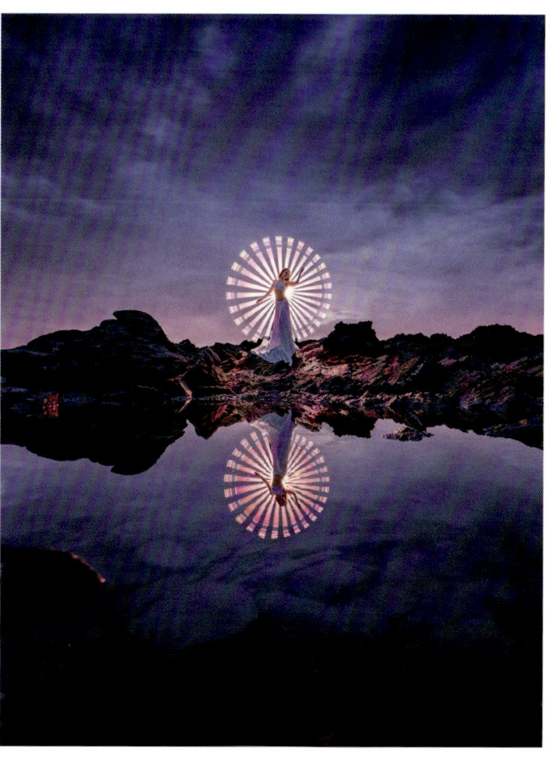

ABOVE & RIGHT **At this location, I was on a lower surface than Kim, hiding behind rocks, which made it easier to conceal part of my body. We doubled ourselves in the behind-the-scenes image. Can you spot us?"**

Silhouettes

Creating silhouettes is a great way to add a sense of mystery to your images that leaves space for the viewer's imagination. A silhouette forms when the subject is backlit, either by ambient light combined with the light painting, or by the light painting alone if there's no ambient light.

In order to create a powerful image that doesn't confuse the viewer, the body expression of the subject must be easy to read. In other words, the silhouette must provide enough information for us to understand what we are looking at. Creating negative spaces between parts of the body will increase its readability. A simple way to define the silhouette is to create space between your model's arms and torso. Also, having the model look sideways (either by turning their head only or their whole body) will help reveal their face contour.

BELOW "What does she have on her head?" There's nothing wrong with creating confusion if that's intentional, but if it's not your goal, make sure the person you work with knows when they are backlit and help them adjust their body position if needed.

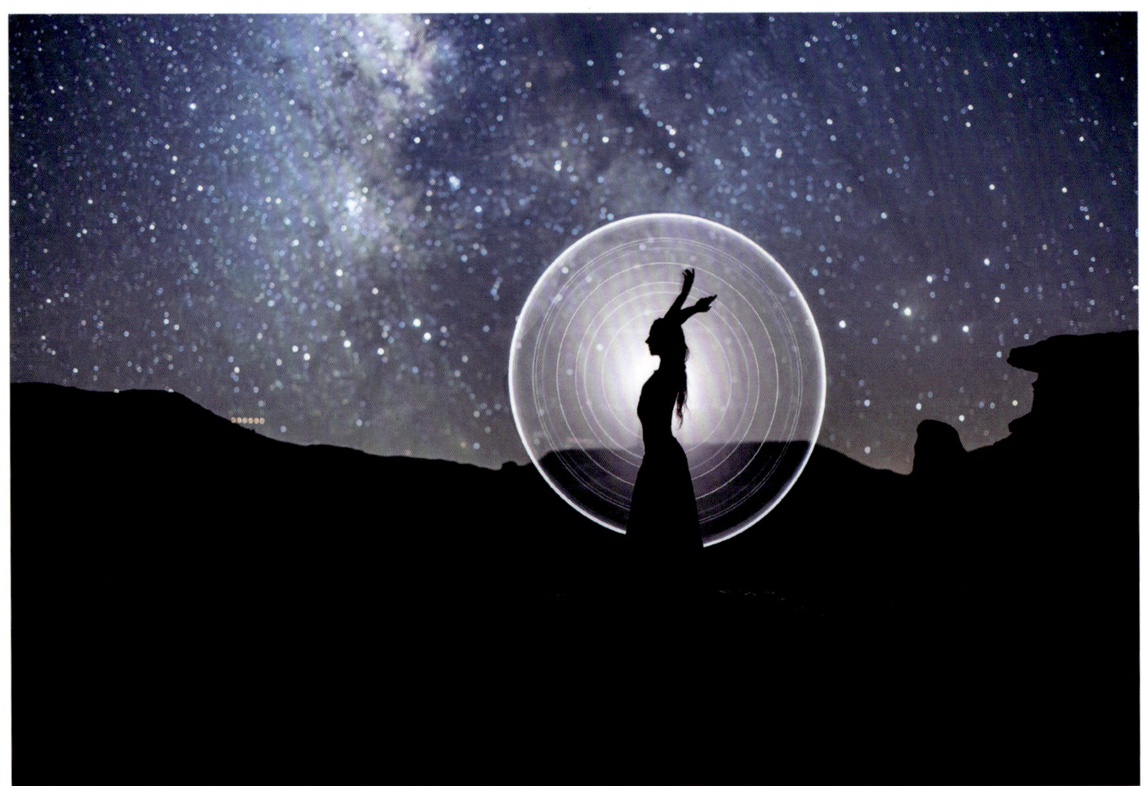

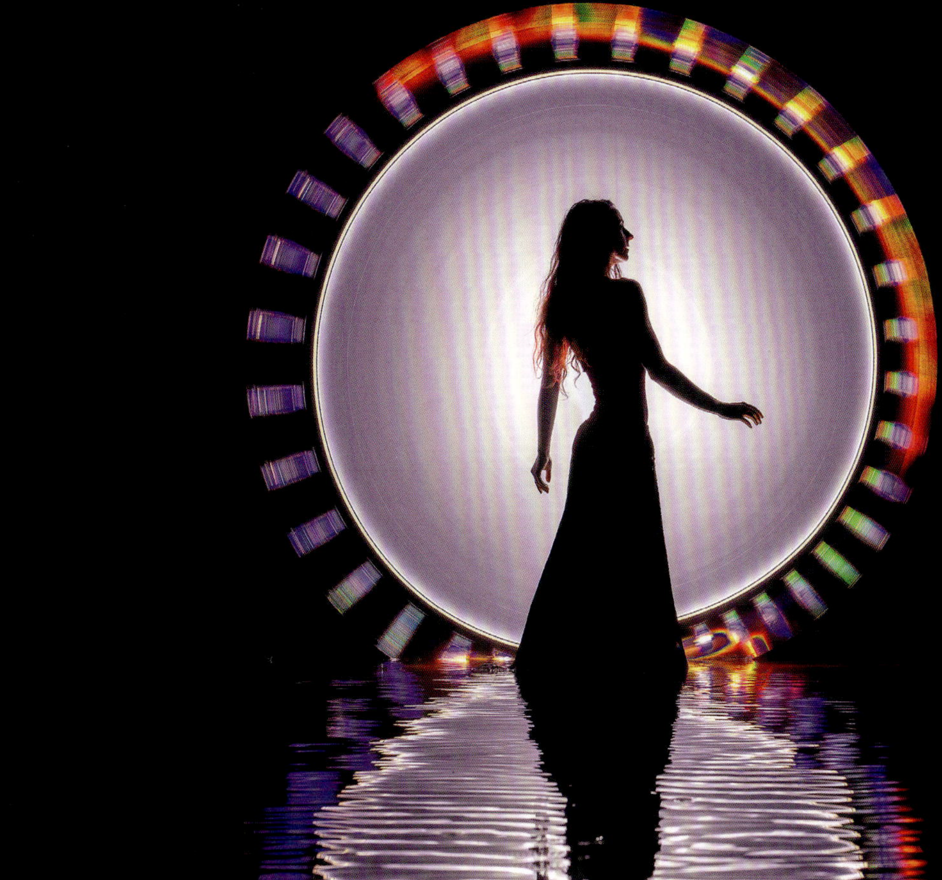

ADDING DEPTH AND MOVEMENT

To incorporate a sense of movement and three-dimensionality, create curves and spirals that complement the body's natural lines and angles. The first thing to play with is the relationship between hips, shoulders, and head. Avoiding alignment of these three points introduces slight twists and rotations that create spirals and curves in the body.

To increase the dynamism of the body shapes, create uneven and asymmetrical negative spaces by modifying the pose (bending only one arm, for example) or having the model maintain the pose while rotating slightly so the camera sees a different perspective.

ABOVE **Some images feature partial silhouettes, where light subtly reveals certain body parts. In this image, you need to look closely to see Kim's face.**

Lighting your subject

If you don't want to create silhouettes you can still make your subject visible without introducing additional artificial lighting.

Overcast sky during the blue hour: As the light is diffused by clouds, it softly illuminates the subject. Choose a shooting direction where the sunset glow is positioned behind the camera.

Moonlight: The Moon can light both the subject and the landscape. A low moon can provide side lighting, while a very high moon can provide slightly offset top lighting. Although this lighting may not be flattering for every landscape, it tends to work beautifully above water or with light-colored foregrounds.

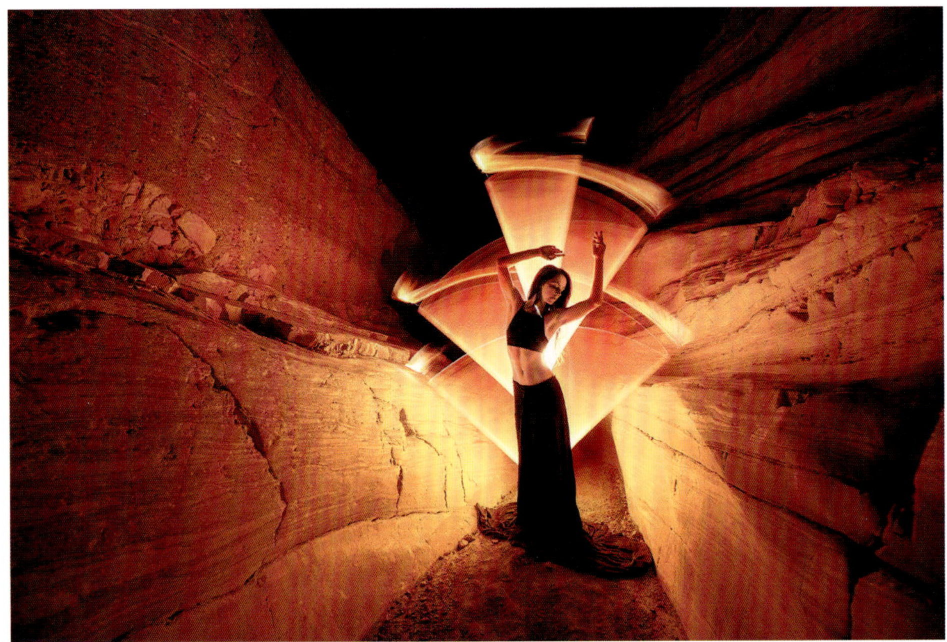

Use available surfaces to bounce the light: Surfaces in the environment can act as natural reflectors. Light reflecting off the ground, especially water or light-colored terrain, bounces on to the subject. Other elements of the landscape can also be used to reflect light, such as large rocks or natural walls.

RIGHT **Be careful when you are aiming a light at nearby surfaces. If it is too intense it may create harsh lighting. For this image we blocked the tube end with a black cap to cast a softer, diffused light on the scene.**

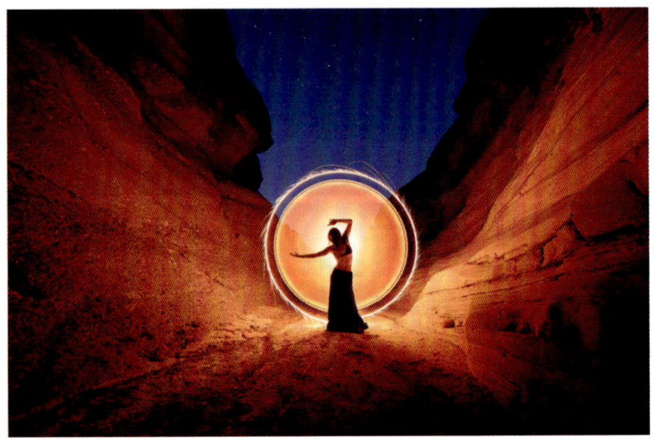

Use your light painting to illuminate the model: You can use your light-painting tool to illuminate the subject by bringing the tube slightly in front of them from one side while you create your shape. Before you shoot it is a good idea to test your light-painting shape so you understand how it affects your subject.

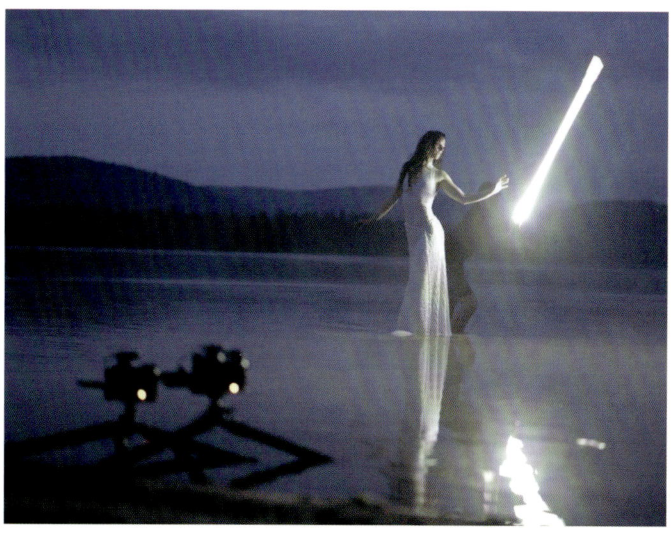

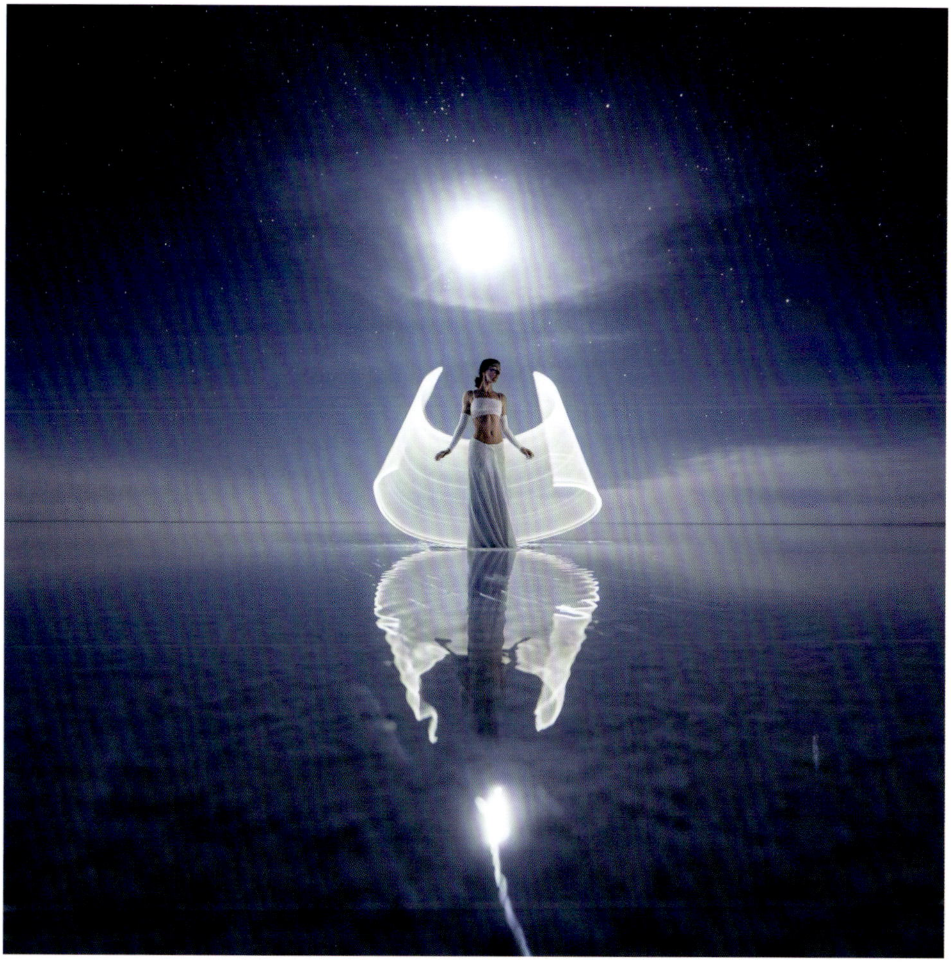

Getting a sharp subject

Working as a team makes this process easier, although this can be slightly overwhelming at first, especially if you're working with someone for the first time. The model plays a vital role in creating the final picture: from an artistic perspective they serve as a strong visual point of interest in the image, and from a technical standpoint their stillness is essential to prevent blurriness in the photograph.

However, most people aren't used to posing for long-exposure photographs, so clear communication about the process is essential. It is crucial that your model remains motionless, not just during the light painting, but throughout the entire exposure.

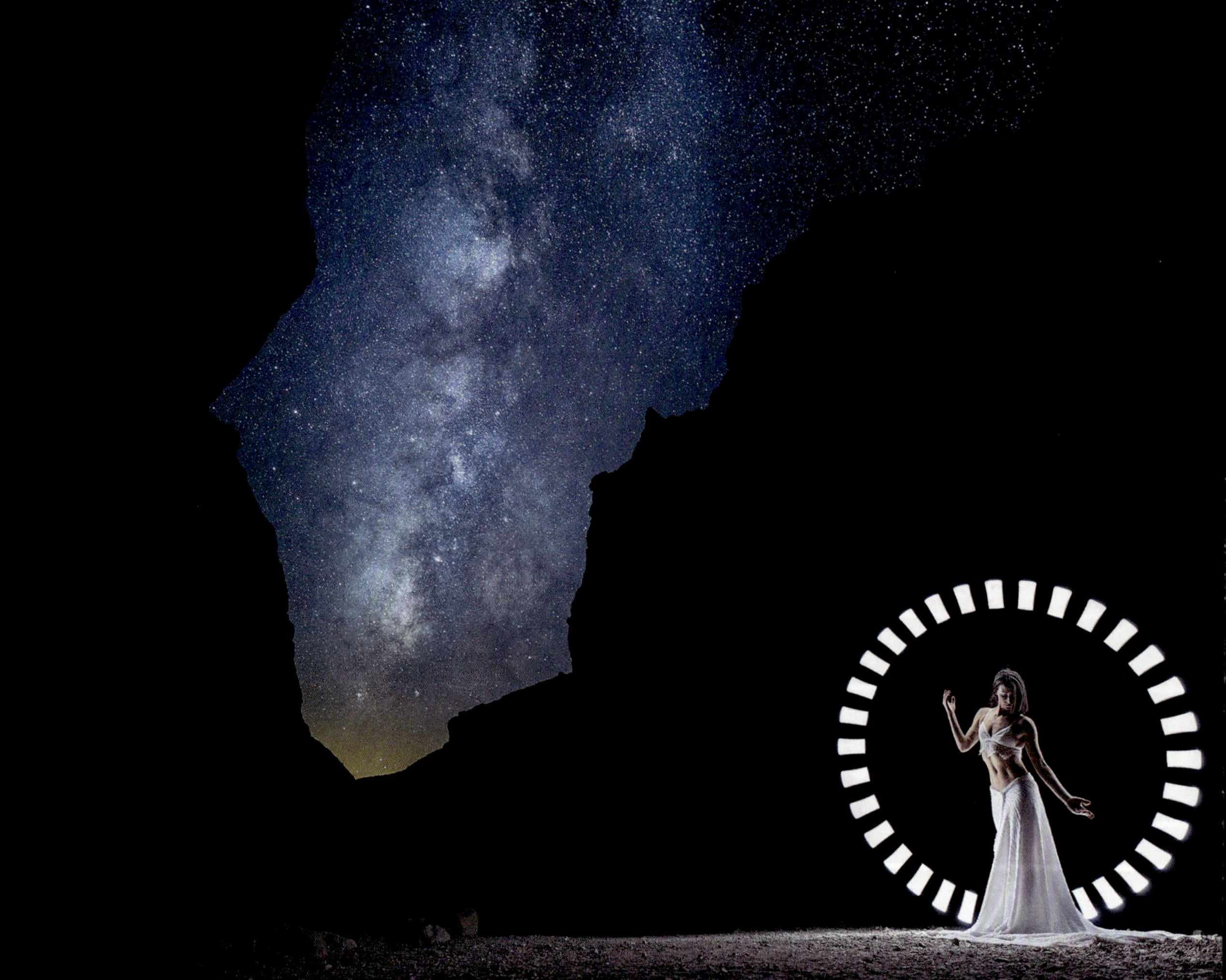

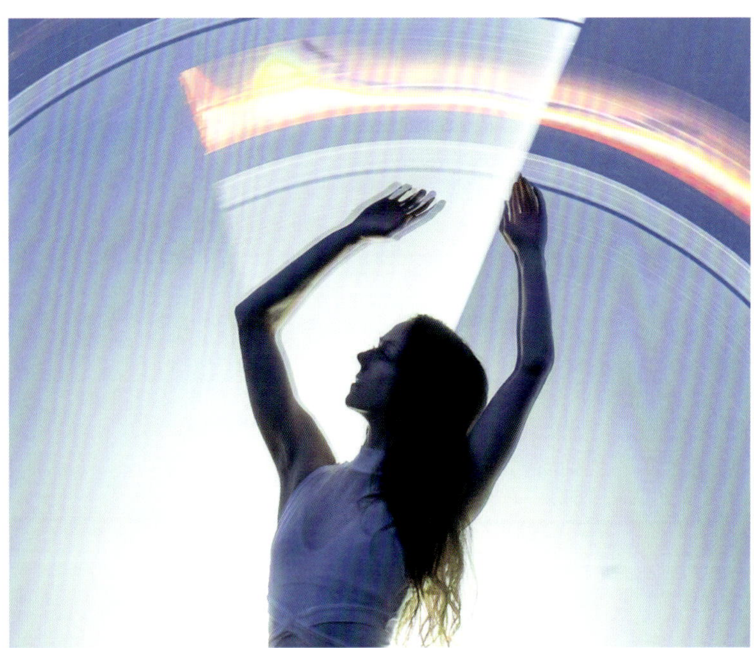

ABOVE **If there is ambient light in the background directly behind the model (from the sky, for example), movement can create a black line along the body's contour, where the background light is not blocked consistently.**

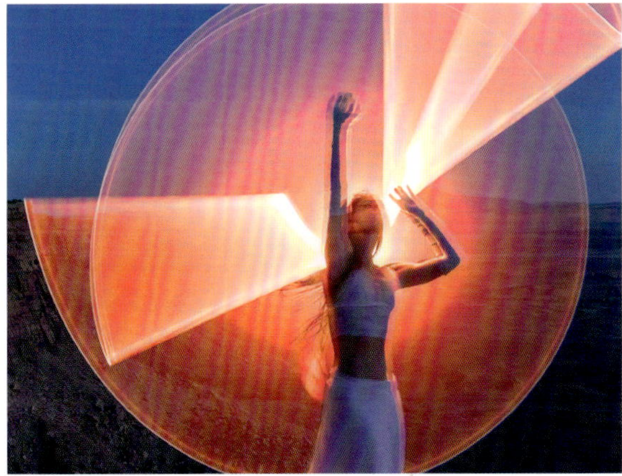

LEFT **If the model moves while they are lit by ambient light from any angle, their face and body may appear blurry or distorted.**

LEFT **Positioning the model in front of a landscape feature (like the rock wall in this image) creates a dark background that blocks ambient light, making it easier to get a sharp subject. We also typically keep our exposure times at 8 sec. or less to minimize the risk of blur; the longer the exposure, the more chance there is of having a blurry subject in the picture.**

THE LIGHT PAINTER'S ROLE

When it comes to achieving sharp images, it is a team effort between the light painter and the model. When you are starting out, our best advice for achieving good results is to keep it simple and have fun. As you practice and gain experience, you'll be able to make your experiments more complex and play with various concepts. Here are our top tips for the light painter:

→ **Give clear instructions:** Use a countdown to prepare the model. We use a simple "3,2,1…" (triggering the shutter on "0"), but you can adapt it to something that works better for you and your collaborator. Whatever you choose, be clear and consistent.

→ **Avoid the scanner effect:** Don't move the light over the same body area multiple times during the exposure. If you do, it increases the risk of not having a sharp subject because your model might have moved slightly between the two passes.

→ **Create simple shapes:** Use single, swift movements with the light to minimize the time the subject is illuminated for. Creating silhouettes (backlighting only) is another effective way to limit the impact of the subject's movement in the shot.

→ **Move quickly:** Whenever possible, paint with the light as quickly as possible while maintaining control. The faster you move, the less time the model is exposed to the light. As you move faster, you might need to increase the brightness of your light source to keep the exposure balanced between your light painting and the background. Adjustments depend on your flashlight power and the ambient light conditions at your location.

→ **Position your subject strategically:** Placing the subject further away from the camera makes small movements less visible. Conversely, placing your subject closer to the camera will make any motion (and blur) more noticeable.

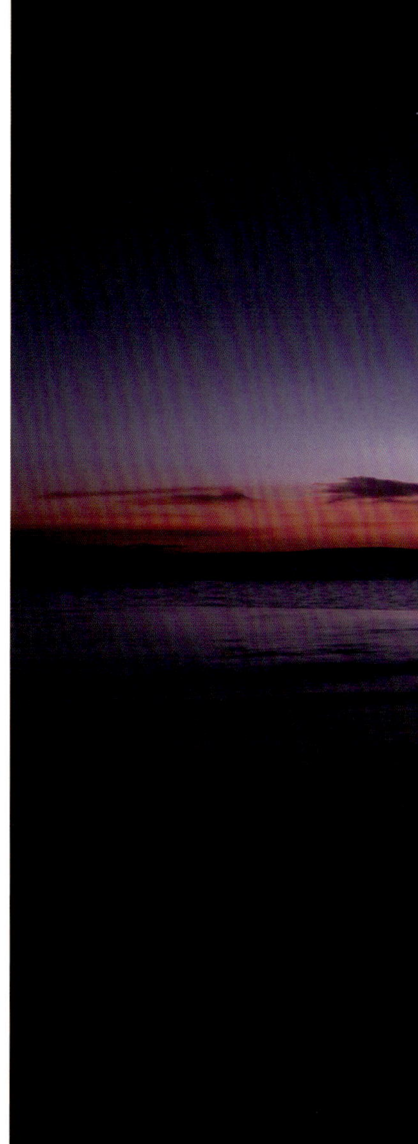

THE MODEL'S ROLE

While the light painter plays a significant part in creating a sharp image, there are several things the model can do to improve their stability and minimize movement during the light-painting process:

→ **Hold their breath during the exposure:** Even the movement of their rising thoracic cage from breathing is enough to introduce blur. Asking your model to hold their breath from the end of the countdown until the exposure is complete is a good way to maximize stillness.

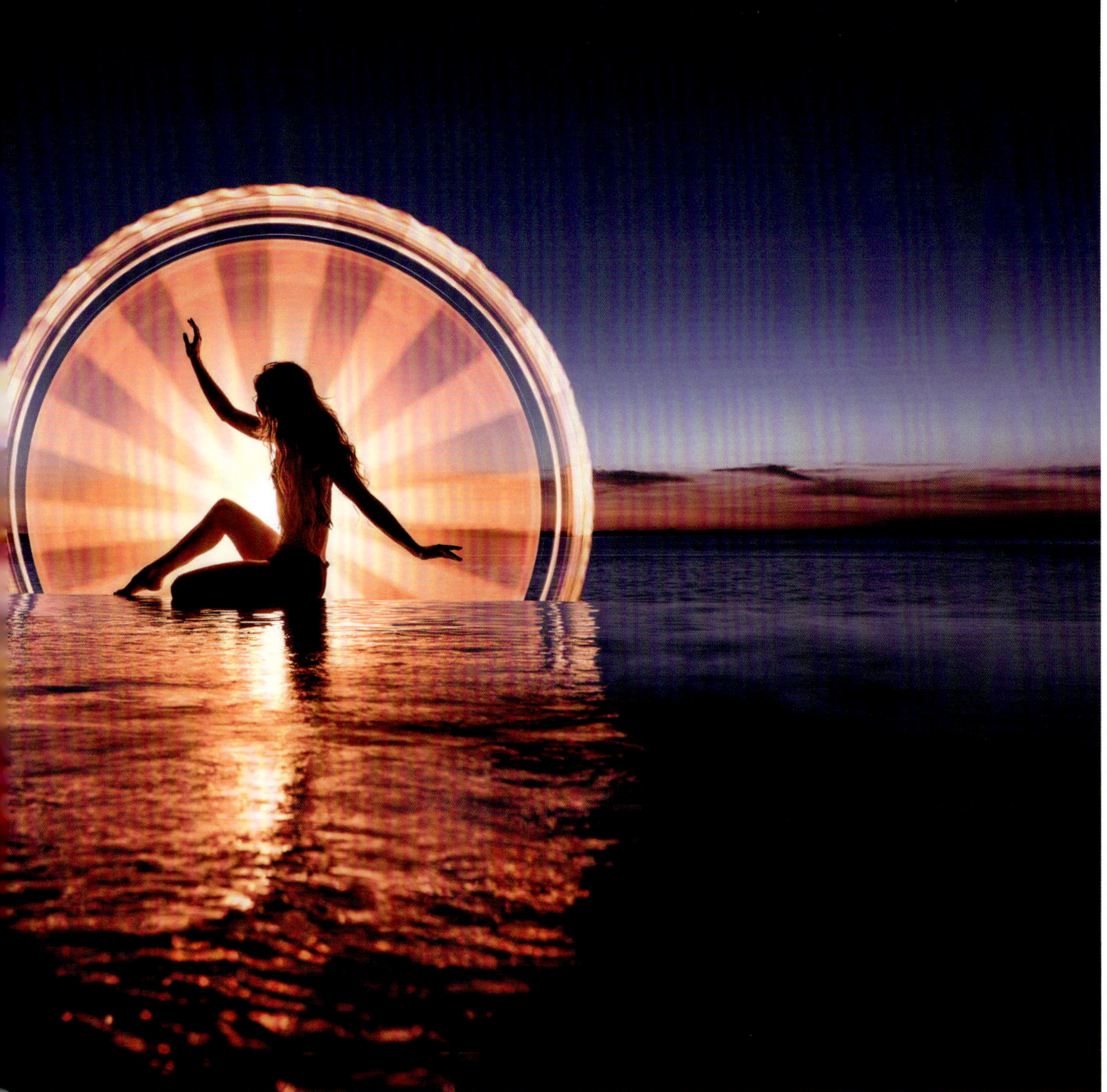

→ **Choosing stable body positions:** The more stable your model is, the easier it will be for them to stay motionless. Standing on a solid surface with their feet shoulder-width apart is usually a good place to start; seated poses offer even greater stability. Once again, start with simple poses and build complexity over time.

→ **Using vision as an anchor:** Have you ever tried to stand on one leg while looking at something in front of you, and then closed your eyes? If you haven't, you should try it. It's a lot of fun! It also illustrates the significant role that vision plays in balance. A lack of visual information affects our proprioception and postural control, even if we are standing on both feet. Having your model focus on a fixed point during the exposure will help minimize body oscillations.

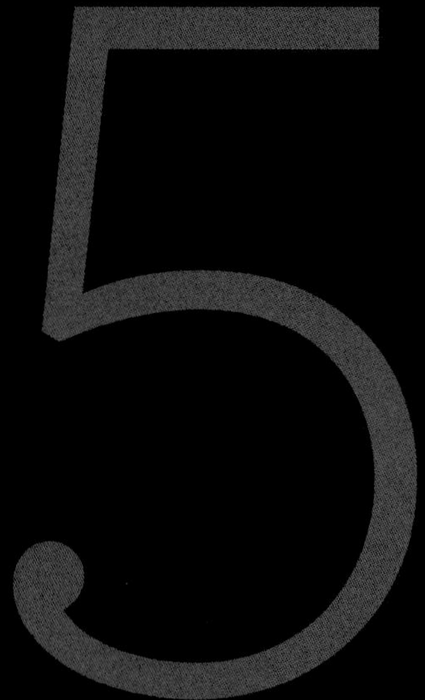

Shooting scenarios

In this section you will find guidelines and tips for most of the situations you could encounter while creating outdoors. These all relate to landscape photography or landscape astrophotography but are often specifically adapted to the light-painting technique we share in this book.

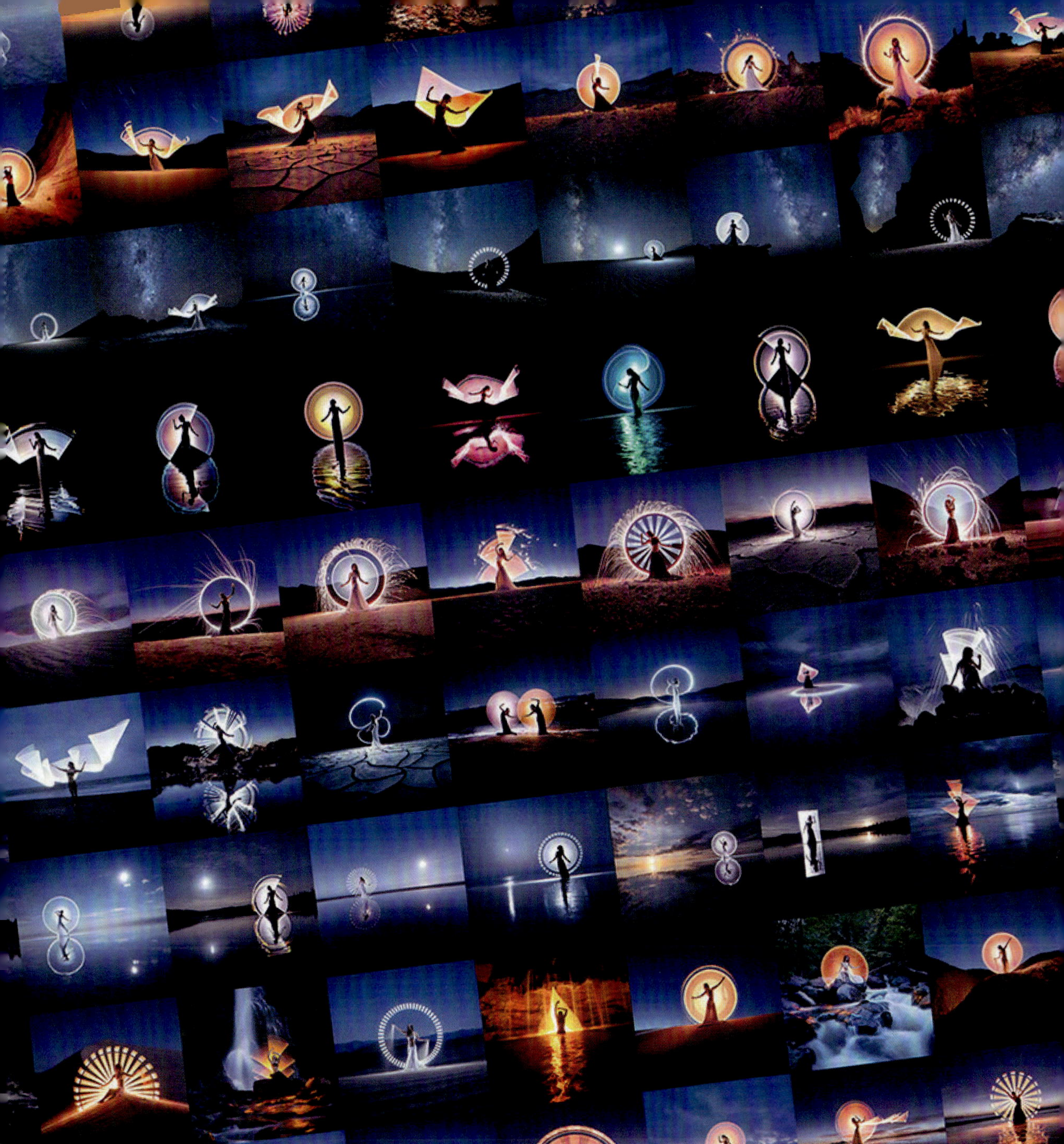

Despite all the preparation you make in advance, there are many reasons why things won't go according to plan once you're in the field. Having an idea of what you want to achieve is a good place to start, but curiosity and flexibility are essential to the creative experience.

There is almost always the option to shoot outdoor light-painting images, and the more scenarios you are familiar with, the more adaptable you will become in the field.

Black canvas

The "black canvas" is the simplest and purest expression of the outdoor light-painting art presented in this book, and a great entry point to experiment with the technique. By eliminating most of the landscape elements, it brings the focus on the light painting itself, enabling you to practice making light shapes and deepen your understanding of how the light impacts the subject (see page 62 – Lighting your subject).

Unless there's a major change in the ambient light (moonrise, for example) the settings will remain the same for the whole session. This makes it the closest thing to practicing in a studio, although the outdoor environment still impacts the scene in subtle ways. This is especially true when using water to reflect the light painting. From a small puddle to an ocean shore, a shallow lake, a creek, or anything in between, almost any body of water can be used to create reflections for the black canvas. Start by exploring locations you already have access to near your home. You might be surprised by how effective simple or overlooked spots can be!

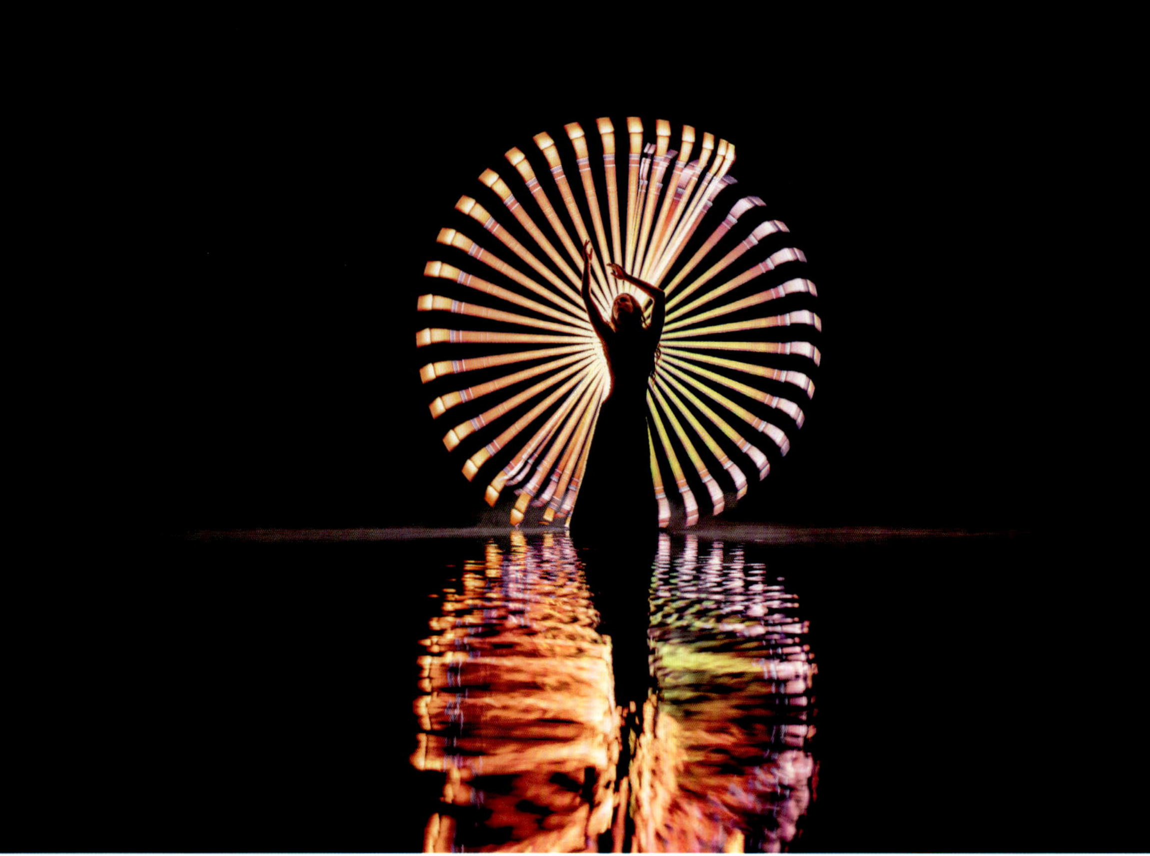

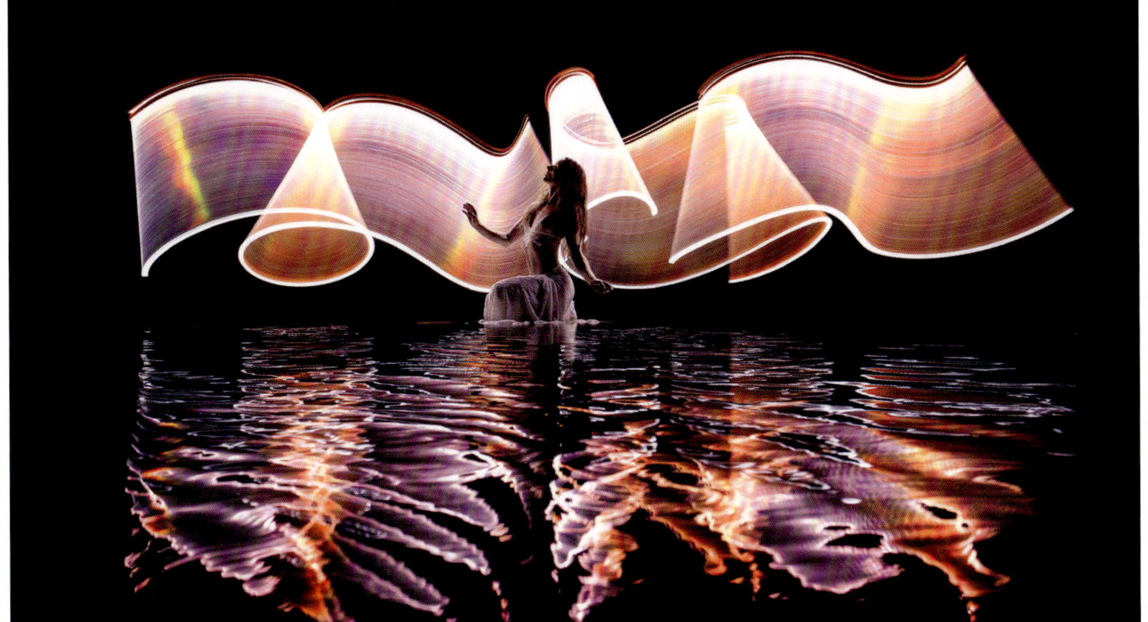

PLANNING

There are many reasons why we would want to let go of the background and use the environment as a black canvas, ranging from the technical to the artistic. It may be that the background simply doesn't look interesting as we get close to nighttime, or perhaps the clouds are "messy," making it hard to create a balanced or appealing composition, or the cloud coverage is very high, resulting in a featureless dark sky at the end of the blue hour. Distant light pollution can also become more visible at night, and it may be that it can't be incorporated into the composition. Lastly, ambient light can affect the subject and/or foreground when using an exposure time of 6 seconds or more for instance, making it impossible to capture the night sky without the rest of the scene being affected.

Not using the background can also come from a desire to create a minimalist image that puts the emphasis on the light painting and the subject, rather than its integration in the environment.

In each of these cases you can adjust the settings and composition to exclude most of the background and middle ground elements. There is at least one exception, though: if the Moon is bright enough to illuminate the scene, it makes it impossible to get a really black background.

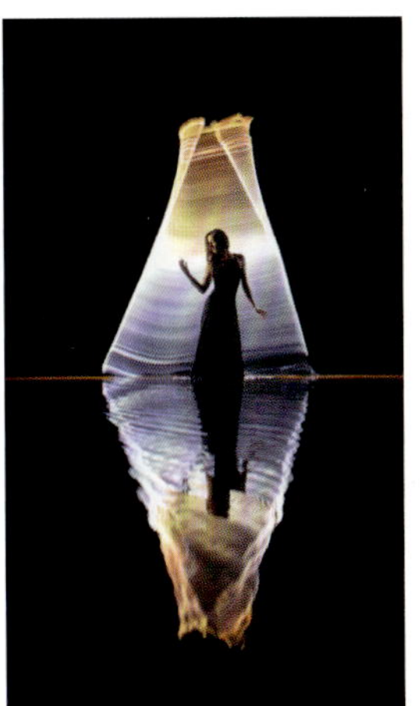
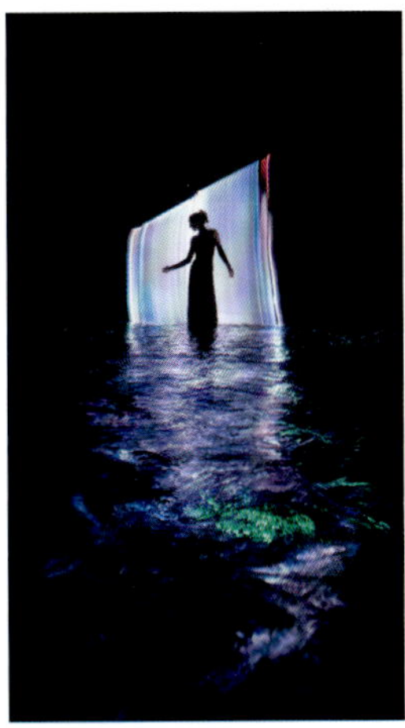

ABOVE From a recognizable reflection to total abstraction, the degree of distortion created by the environment in the body of water adds an extra layer to an image.

CAMERA SETTINGS

The following settings will provide a good starting
point for your black canvas images:

→ Exposure: 4 sec. (light painting ~4 sec.), f/6.3, ISO 200
→ White balance: see the datasheet on page 168
→ Flashlight power: 2000 lumens

If you still see the background with these settings,
reduce your shutter speed; if your light trace is too
dark, increase the ISO or use a wider aperture. The
white balance will vary depending on the tube color
you're using.

TOOLS

As there isn't a landscape to harmonize with,
the light-painting possibilities open up in terms
of colors, textures, and shapes. With a black
background, there's no need to consider how
your light interacts with the environment, so you
can push things further and make bolder color
combinations. I especially enjoy using holographic
tubes and feathers in these setups; their iridescent
nature catch the light in unpredictable ways,
creating rich, saturated colors that stand out
beautifully against the dark. Without the need to
"match" a scene, the creative choices become more
about contrast and motion.

COMPOSITION

Black canvas images are usually well suited for a
central composition, as there is nothing else besides
the light painting, the model, and their reflection.
 We aim to include the entire reflection in the
frame. If the water is moving because of wind or
waves, framing the shot vertically allows more space
for the abstract reflection.

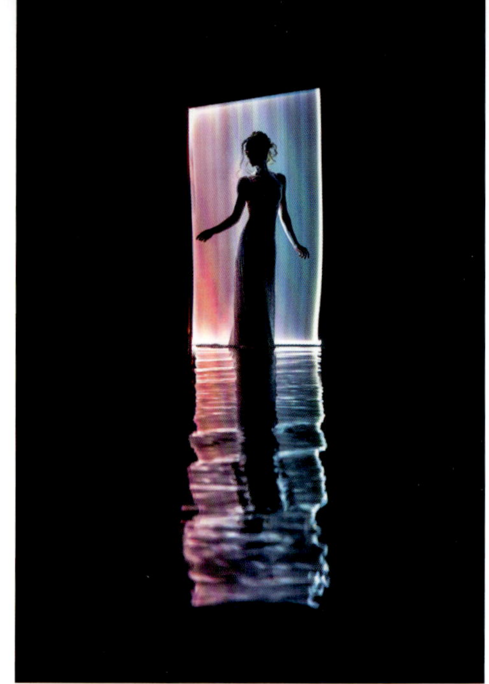

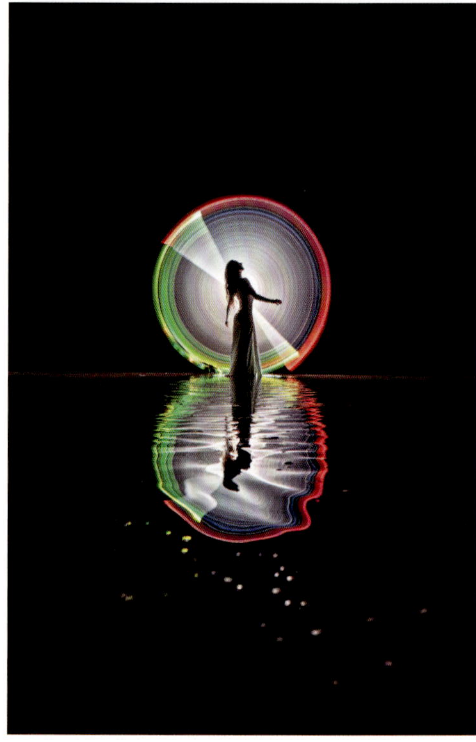

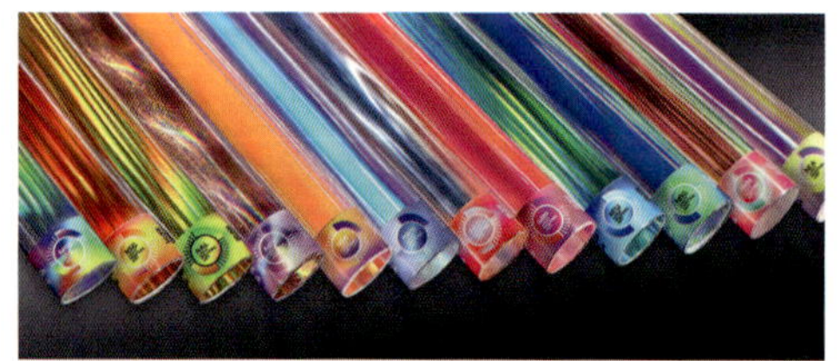

LEFT & ABOVE **Black canvas sessions are where the holographic
tubes truly come to life, allowing their vibrant colors
and dynamic effects to really stand out against the dark
background. We have 12 different varieties of holographic
tubes (and feathers) that we don't hesitate to combine during
these sessions.**

Case Study **Black canvas**

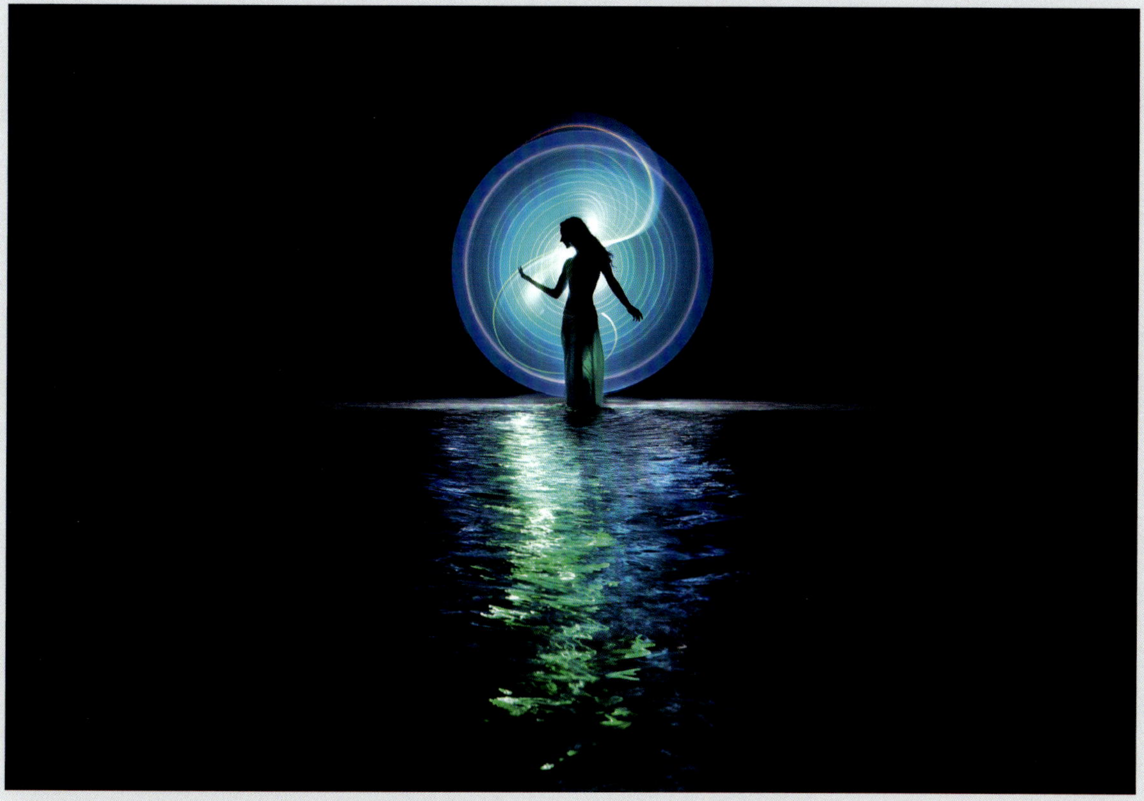

Environment: Beach | **Focal length:** 24mm | **Exposure:** 4 sec. (light painting ~2 sec.), f/8, ISO 400

We were on a week-long creative trip at the beach and had hiked for about an hour with our camera gear to get to a remote location where we could shoot away from artificial lights. We went for a swim and slowly prepared as the Sun was setting, but unluckily for us, the clouds were messy and it was windy, making the sea very agitated.

We found a pool of water where we could keep some reflections, but this only worked if we got rid of the background. So, we spent the whole session getting back to the essence of what we do: focusing on the shapes and colors of light painting without letting the environment impact the image. The only problem with that is we lose track of time and create for hours, as the conditions don't change much!

DID YOU NOTICE?

If you look closely at the light-painting shape, you can see brighter lines creating smaller circles in the main shape. Over time, we have noticed that the older our tubes get, the more texture we see in the light. This is due to sand or other particles inside the tube reflecting the light, or scratches on the tube that make some parts look slightly brighter. You can add texture intentionally to your tubes by inserting a piece of plastic that you scratch with sandpaper. One of the easiest materials to use for this DIY project is a piece of acetate cake collar (a thin, flexible plastic usually sold in rolls and used to wrap around the sides of a cake for support or decoration).

The Moon

If you're starting your tube light-painting journey, working with the Moon is a good place to begin. This is mainly because the moonlight simplifies the creation process; you can see what you are doing with more ease, and things are moving much slower than they are during the blue hour.

As the Moon acts as an additional ambient light source that impacts the whole scene, our favorite approach is to include it in the image whenever possible. This type of back lighting naturally accentuates the texture and details of the foreground in a unique way.

PLANNING

To determine the phase of the Moon, as well as its approximate trajectory during the night, we use the Planner feature in PhotoPills for every creative session we plan. In most night photographs we want to make sure the Moon doesn't interfere with our capture of the night sky, so we look for a new moon phase or a period during which it is under the horizon. However, in this context, we want the Moon to shine.

In our experience, working with the Moon as a subject is optimal when it is at an elevation of 1–30 degrees above the horizon. When the Moon is higher than 30 degrees it is much harder to incorporate it

and create a balanced composition. Of course, this depends on the features of the landscape you're in, as well as how wide you shoot; the wider your lens, the more time you have with the Moon in the frame.

How much time you will have exactly will depend on your location, the time of the year, and the moon phase. Sometimes it takes less than 2½ hours for a full moon to rise to 30 degrees, but on the same night at a different latitude, the elevation will stay below 30 degrees for the whole night, allowing many more hours of potential creation. If you don't need a precise timeframe, a good rule of thumb is to allow around two hours after moonrise or before moonset for your shoot.

RIGHT **PhotoPills provides a visualization of the moon phase and its rising and setting times for a given date and location. The direction of the moonrise and moonset is indicated by the thick blue lines on the map.**

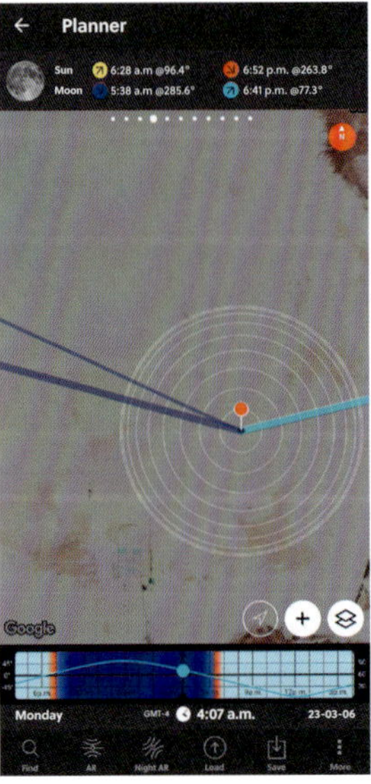

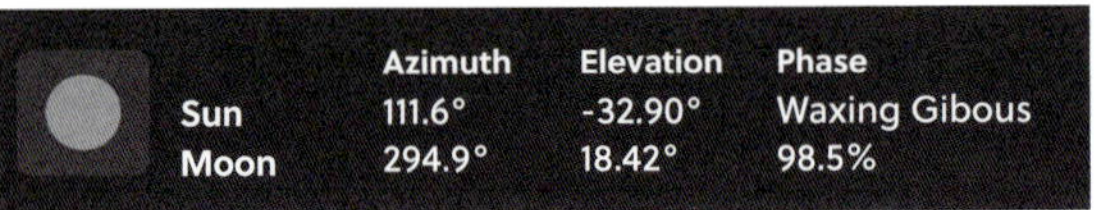

	Azimuth	Elevation	Phase
Sun	111.6°	-32.90°	Waxing Gibous
Moon	294.9°	18.42°	98.5%

ABOVE **Here we see the elevation, phase, and percentage of illumination of the Moon at a precise moment for the same date and location. Its direction corresponds to the thin, dark blue line on the map.**

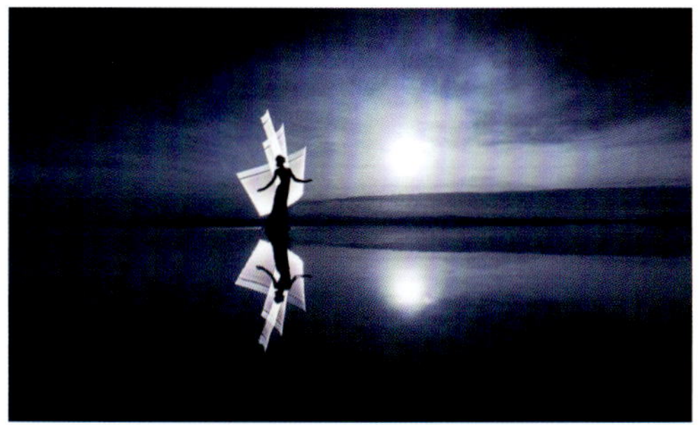

ABOVE **This is the finished image that we created in the conditions shown.**

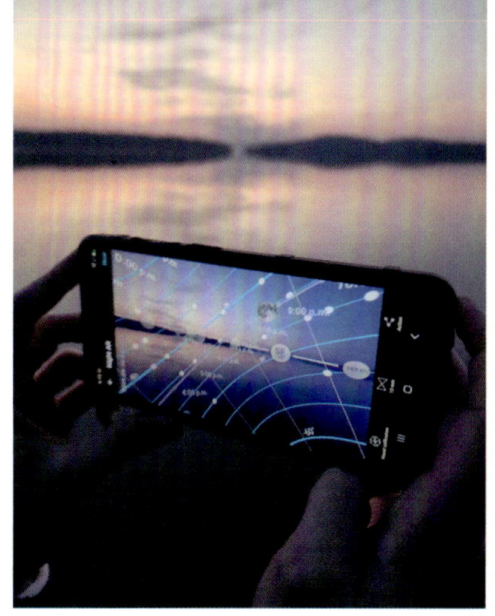

LEFT **You can use the PhotoPills Night AR tool to visualize the trajectory of the Moon and plan a composition that includes the other elements of the landscape.**

What is moon elevation?

Moon elevation is the angle, in degrees, between the Moon and the horizon as seen from an observer on Earth. It varies daily and is influenced by both latitude and altitude:

→ At mid-latitudes there are greater seasonal height variations, with a higher maximum elevation during the winter months and a lower elevation during summer.

→ Close to the equator the Moon appears higher in the sky. At the equator it also appears to rise and set almost vertically.

→ At high latitudes there are small seasonal height variations and a lower maximum elevation. If you were to shoot at the North or South Pole during the winter months, the Moon could remain above the horizon for up to two weeks.

→ The higher the altitude (at any given latitude), the higher the Moon will appear to be above the horizon.

When you are shooting in a relatively flat landscape that offers a view of the horizon, capturing a moonset or moonrise creates unique colors in the sky.

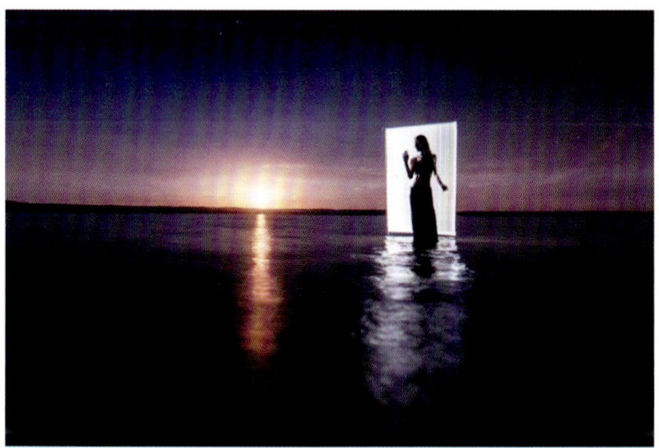

ABOVE **2.29 degrees elevation, 77.7 percent illumination**

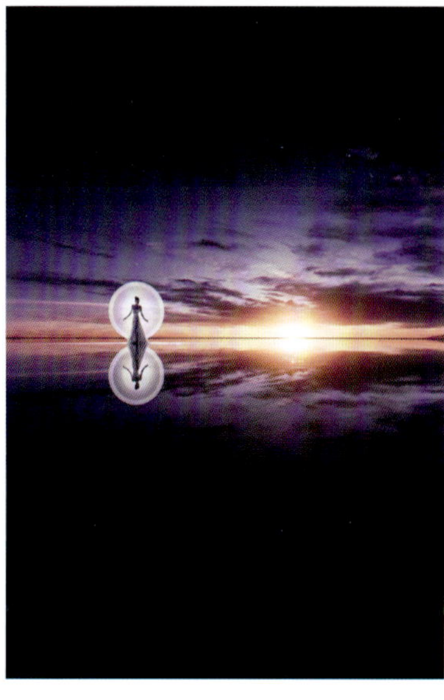

LEFT **1.34 degrees elevation, 90.7 percent illumination**

There are endless moon elevation and illumination percentage combinations, as these examples show:

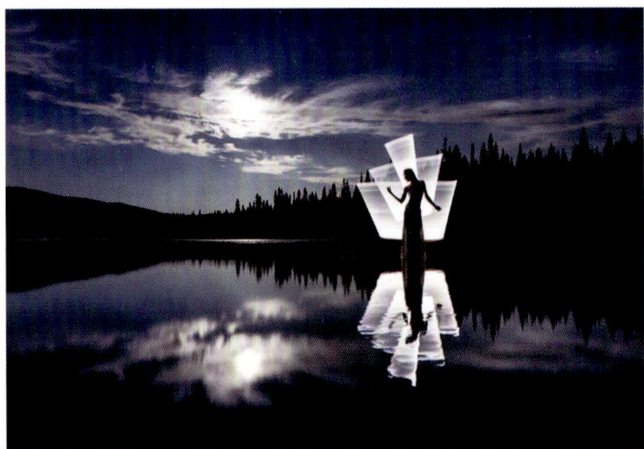

ABOVE **10.9 degrees elevation, 49 percent illumination**

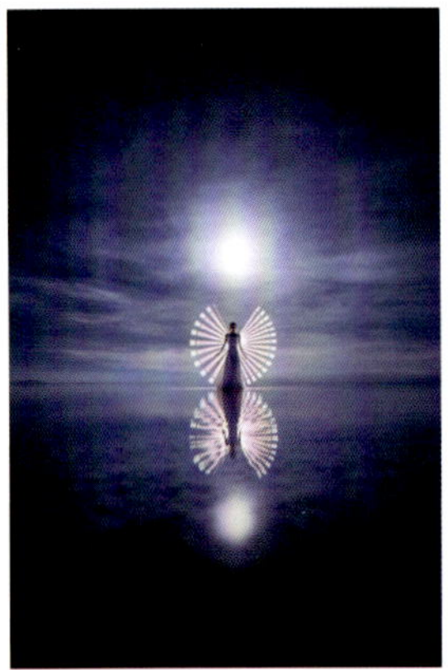

ABOVE **24.2 degrees elevation, 99.2 percent illumination**

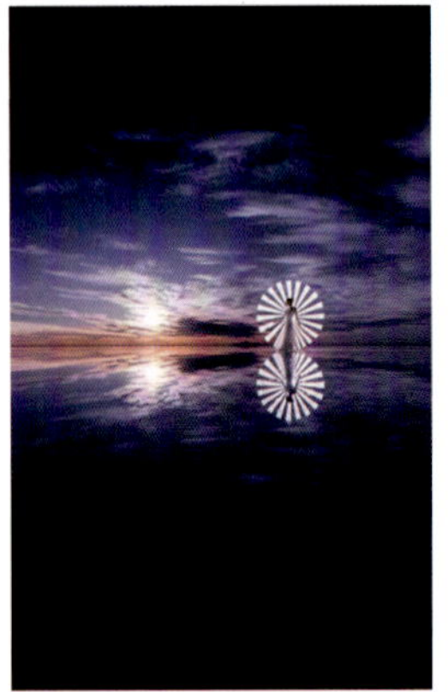

ABOVE **4.6 degrees elevation, 90.6 percent illumination**

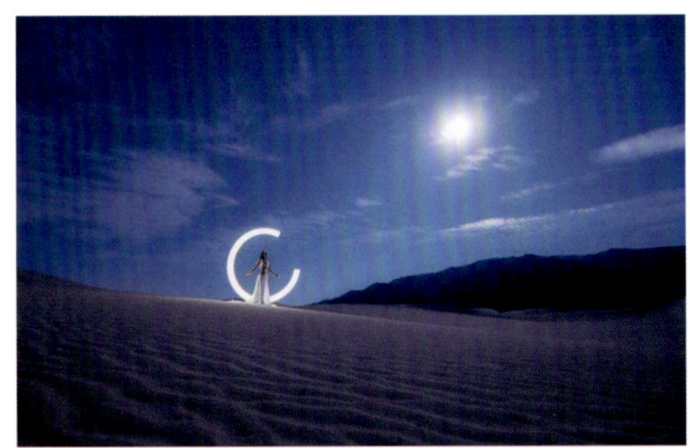

ABOVE **32.35 degrees elevation, 99.3 percent illumination**

CAMERA SETTINGS

Depending on the phase and elevation of the Moon (and therefore its perceived brightness), your exposure settings can vary considerably, although once you find the settings you need to get a well-exposed background they will remain constant for a little while. The biggest variations will be experienced when the Moon gets closer to the horizon, or if it gets covered by clouds, as the ambient light will become much dimmer. On a clear night, use these settings as a starting point:

Nearly full moon at ~10–30 degrees elevation
→ **Exposure:** 4 sec. (light painting ~2 sec.), f/2.8, ISO 400
→ **White balance:** ~4000K
→ **Flashlight power:** 200–400 lumens

Nearly full moon, close to the horizon
→ **Exposure:** 4 sec. (light painting ~2 sec.), f/1.8, ISO 1600
→ **White balance:** 3200K
→ **Flashlight power:** 50–100 lumens

TOOLS

I typically use a cool white balance setting at night, including when we work with the Moon, as it enhances the blue tint of the sky. I never feel the need to add a lot of color to these scenarios, so I tend to use a tool that will mostly appear white. This means choosing a tube with warmer tones to compensate for the cool white balance setting; if I were to use a regular white tube, not only would the light painting have a blue tint, but so would the model's skin. My favorite tubes for this type of image are:

→ **Warmish tube:** to create a white light.
→ **Pinkish tube:** to create a white light with a pink tint.

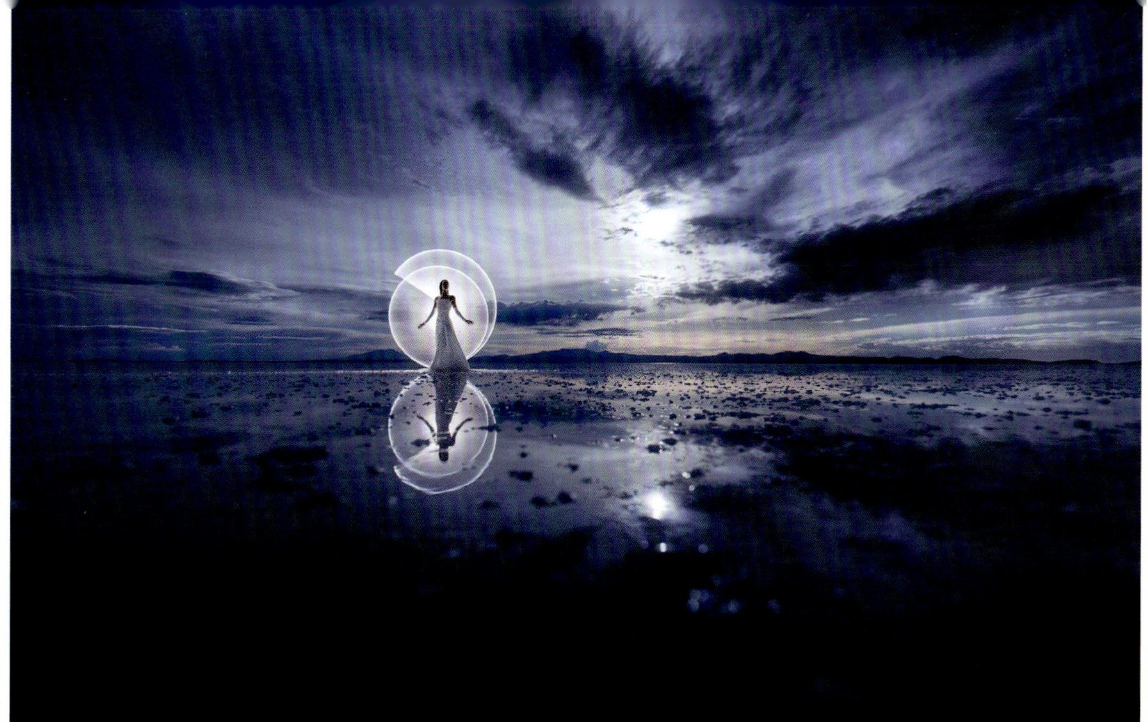

COMPOSITION

When choosing your composition consider the clouds, the shape of the horizon, and the elevation of the Moon. The Moon can add incredible atmosphere to your image, especially as it casts shadows within cloud formations, giving them depth and dimension. Because it's such a bright visual element, it naturally draws the eye – so think of it as a counterbalance to your light painting. Aim to create a sense of relationship or interaction between your subject and the Moon by positioning it thoughtfully, ideally in a way that echoes or complements your subject's form or direction. If the Moon is too high in the frame or too far from your main subject, the image can feel disconnected.

That said, elements like clouds, the shape of the horizon, or features such as mountains and rock formations can influence how that balance is achieved. For example, when the terrain rises sharply, you may need to place the Moon slightly higher in the frame to maintain visual balance. Also consider how dense or dynamic the clouds are, as they can redistribute visual weight across the composition.

ABOVE **The Moon adds a natural bright area in the frame that can create a beautiful counterpoint to the light painting. How you use this counterpoint depends on the other elements you need to balance, as well as your own preferences.**

BELOW **If the Moon is high enough to be directly above the subject, it can suit a portrait orientation and/or a central composition.**

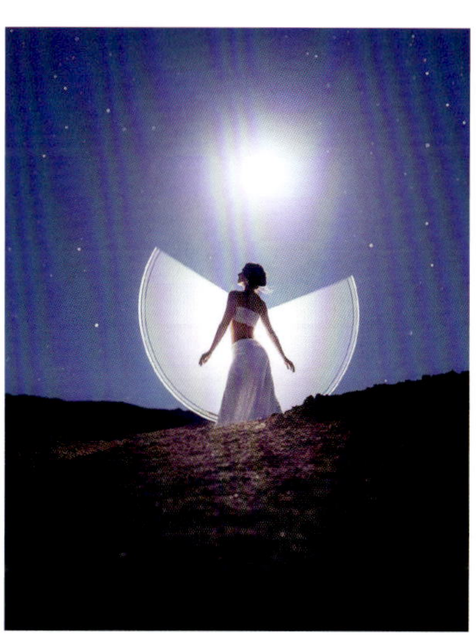

NO MOON IN THE FRAME?

Sometimes it can be impossible to include the Moon in a composition, even if it is low in the sky. It may simply be outside the frame. If that's the case, but you still want to experiment, use the Moon to illuminate the scene from the side. This tends to work best if the Moon is lower in the sky, fairly small, or partially hidden by clouds or other landscape features such as mountains or trees.

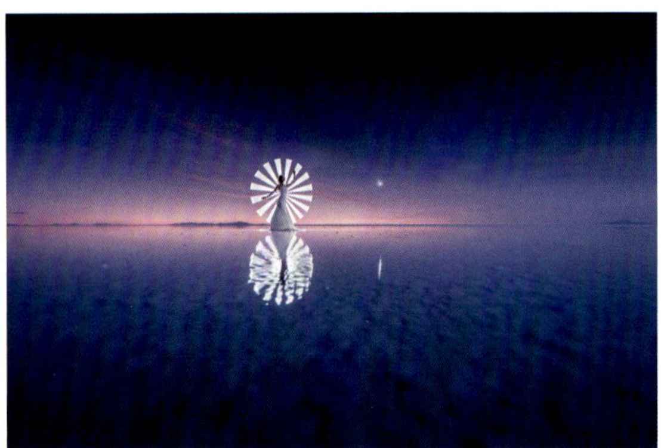

ABOVE **This image was created at the end of the blue hour, with pastel colors in the sky. Notice how the moonlight impacts both the subject and the landscape.**

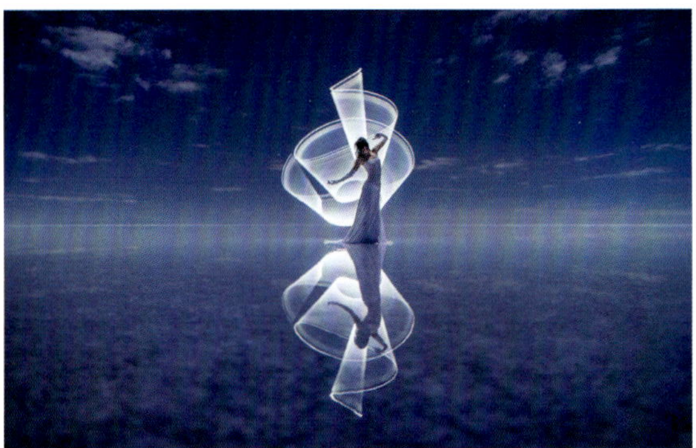

ABOVE **In this image, the Moon was above our heads, acting as a top light on the scene (elevation 81.6 degrees, with 71 percent of its surface illuminated). The result might not have been as interesting without the foreground reflection, but the only way to know for sure is to try it.**

Case Study **The Moon**

We had embarked on a creative road trip around the USA to spend time outdoors and revisit some of our favorite locations from previous adventures. White Sands was one of our first destinations and we wanted to shoot during the full moon. This proved to be a challenge, as it was not easy to find a good composition that aligned the Moon with a pristine sand dune. With little wind in the previous days, there were countless footprints from past visitors covering the landscape, so we had to venture further from the main hiking trail to find a clean sand dune.

After a few hours of shooting we were quite satisfied with our first night's creations. The Moon was now high in the sky, but before we made the long hike back to our car we decided to try one last shot.

We looked for a high dune that would allow us to shoot from a lower angle, with the camera pointing upward, bringing the Moon back into the frame.

We found what we needed and as we began testing our composition, we noticed a moon halo had appeared. We were rewarded with a glimpse of magic for staying out just a little bit longer. When everything aligns like this, it feels like a gift from the elements. However, the only way to make this magic happen is to increase the odds of being there and ready when it occurs. The more you go out, the more likely you are to witness these unpredictable moments.

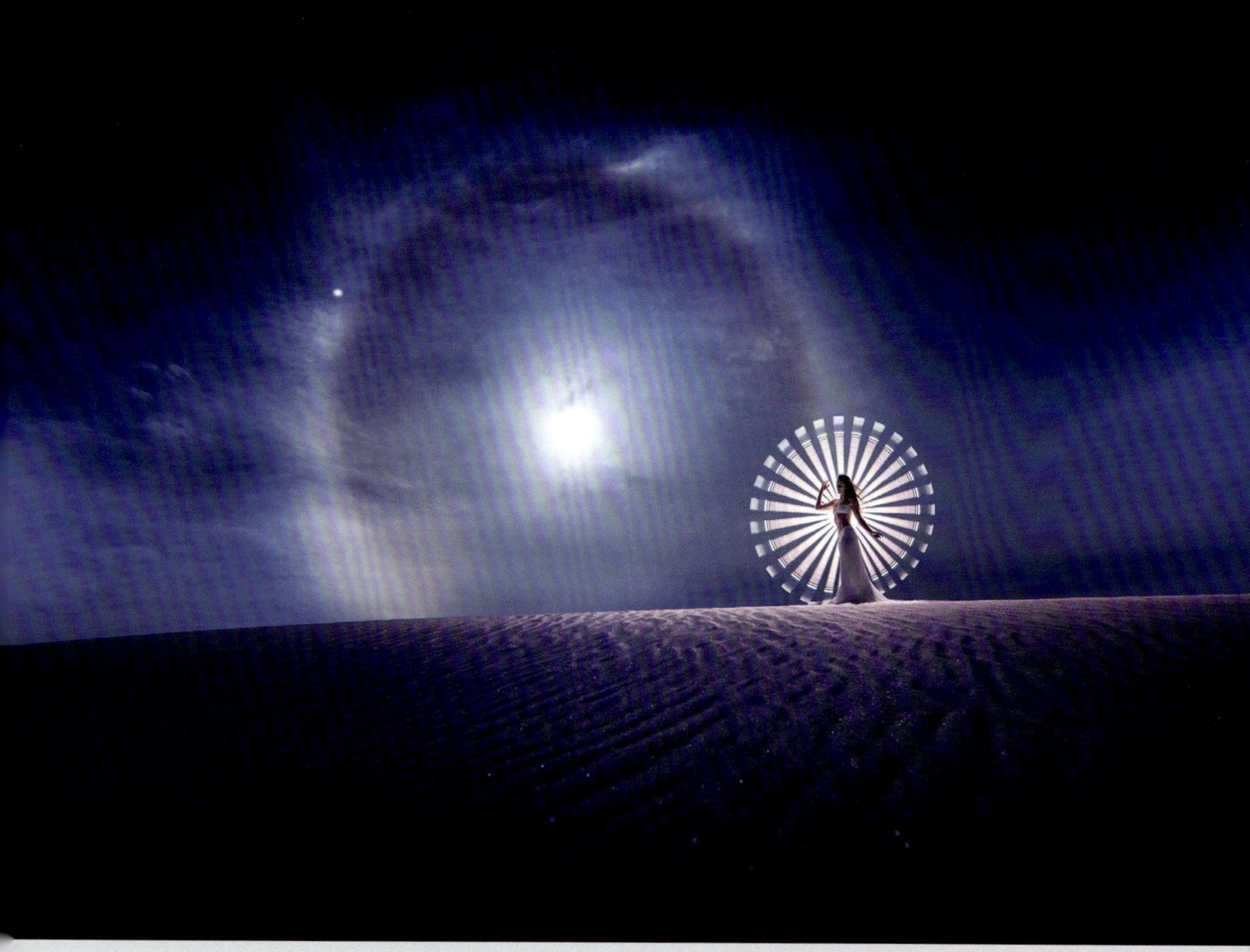

Environment: Sand dunes | **Focal length:** 14mm | **Exposure:** 4 sec. (light painting ~2 sec.), f/2.8, ISO 400

ABOUT THE LOCATION

White Sands National Park is located in New Mexico, USA. What makes it so unique is that the sand dunes are composed of gypsum crystals, making the sand appear white. This area is the world's largest gypsum dunefield in the world, with about 7,650 square feet (710m2) of white dunes in the desert. Although the park closes right after sunset, you can request a permit to stay beyond the opening hours, but this should be done at least one month in advance to ensure you get it on time.

DID YOU NOTICE?

If you look closely, you won't see any footprints in the sand between the camera and Kim. This is not because I removed them in Photoshop, but because I walked around to her from the camera position, rather than walking in a straight line. By walking far out of the frame I ensured no footprints are visible in the sand. It's more time-consuming and physically challenging, though, as I have to run back and forth multiple times during a session!

Blue hour

Unless you are in a high-latitude region at the right time of the year, the blue hour is fairly brief. As the ambient light changes rapidly, maintaining a good balance between the background exposure and the light painting requires constant adjustments, which means fine-tuning your camera settings and modifying the flashlight's power every few minutes. This can feel a little bit overwhelming, but the process can also be exhilarating. For us, capturing the beauty of the day-to-night transition is definitely worth the challenge!

Twilight is separated into three distinct stages: civil, nautical, and astronomical, each of which is defined by the Sun's position below the horizon. For the purpose of this book, when we use the term "blue hour," we are referring to a period that includes both nautical and astronomical twilight, when the Sun is 6–18 degrees below the horizon. This is the optimal twilight period for tube light painting, which typically starts about 30 minutes after sunset. It's not a standard definition, but a practical timeframe specific to the technique we share throughout this book.

There are two opportunities each day to create during the blue hour: morning and evening. Unless you know a location well, the simpler option is to shoot in the evening, after sunset. Scouting a location in the dark (for the morning blue hour) is not easy, and the colder temperatures and early wake-up times aren't ideal for most people.

However, a morning session might be your best option to capture twilight colors in a particular composition facing east. For example, if you want a blue hour picture on a beach on the east coast of the American continent, with the glow of the Sun in the frame, the morning blue hour is your only option.

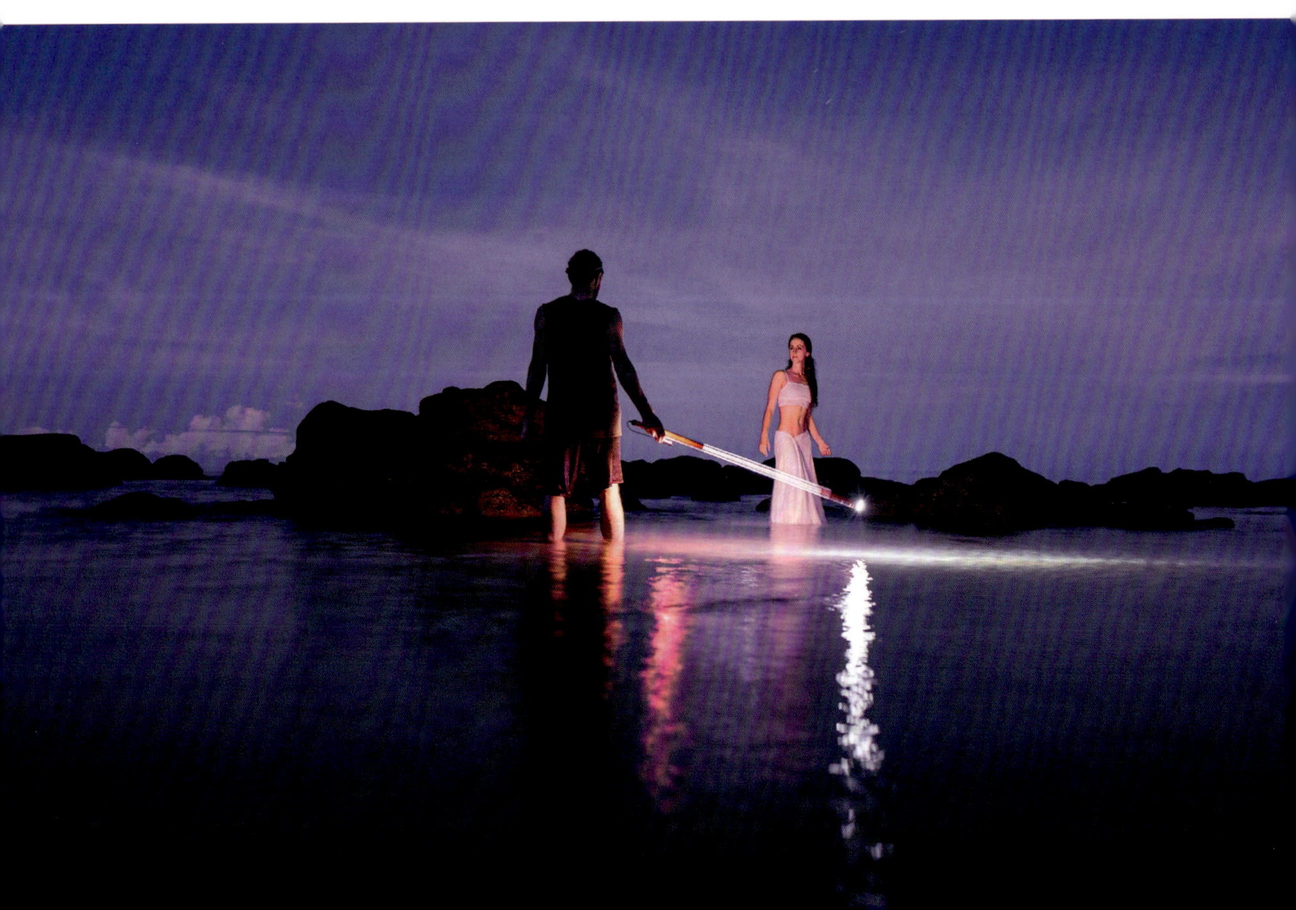

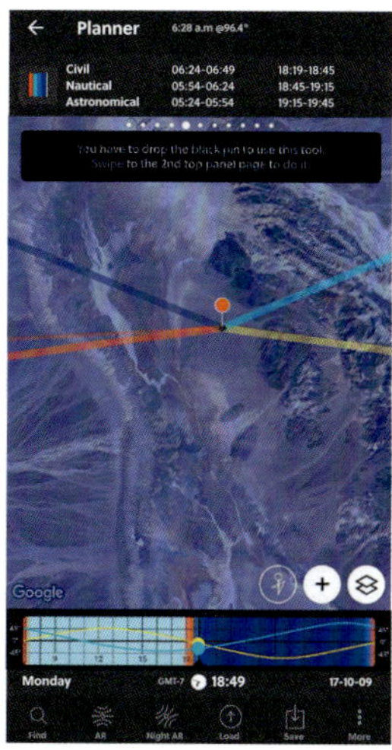

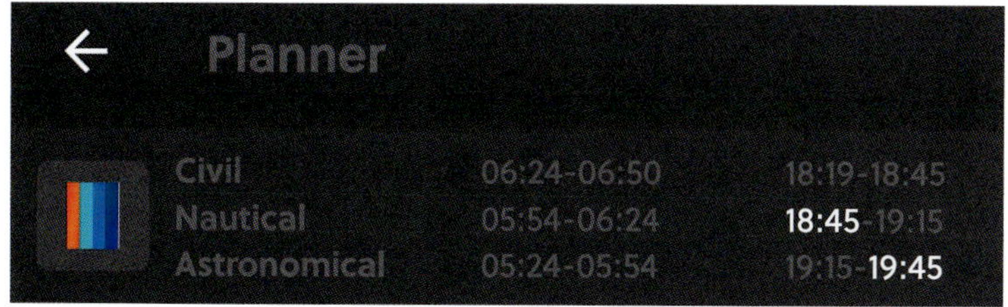

LEFT & ABOVE **The PhotoPills Planner feature can tell you the precise timing of each twilight at any time of year and location. As a rule of thumb, you can create your first well-balanced shot at the start of nautical twilight if you have a powerful flashlight (2000 lumens).**

Civil twilight?

In most cases, the ambient light is too strong to shoot during civil twilight; the light painting will be barely visible and won't have any impact on the environment or the subject. However, with an evening shoot it's a good time to test your composition and practice your shapes.

PLANNING

The cloud coverage will have a profound impact on the choices you make during the blue hour, so it definitely pays to check the forecast before you set out, especially if you are after a specific result or if your location has limitations in terms of orientation or composition.

Clear sky

If the sky is clear, choose a composition that faces west (if shooting in the evening). As the Sun passes below the horizon, the glow of the sunset in the frame will allow you to capture the display of colors above the horizon during the blue hour. If you create in the early morning, shoot toward the east.

Shooting toward the north or south during a cloudless blue hour creates a gradient in the sky, from bright to dark (or vice versa), making it hard to achieve a balanced composition.

If your camera is pointing east at sunset (or west at sunrise), the ambient sunlight will illuminate the landscape and subject from the front, resulting in

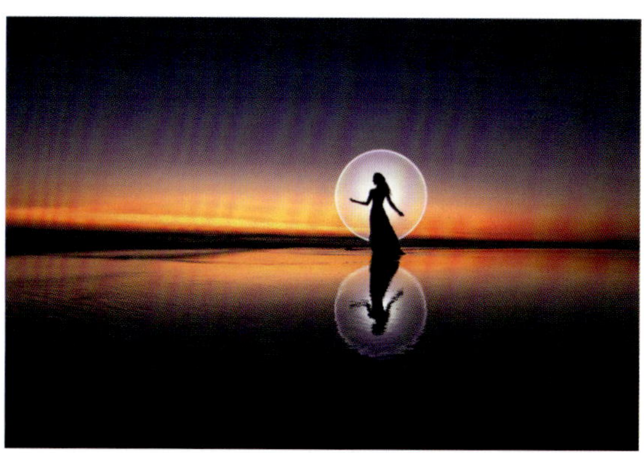

ABOVE **If you want to take advantage of the colors in the sky during the blue hour, put the glow of the Sun slightly off-center in your composition. Position your subject on the other side, in a slightly darker area, to create a balanced image.**

flat lighting that eliminates natural shadows and reduces contrast on the model and foreground.

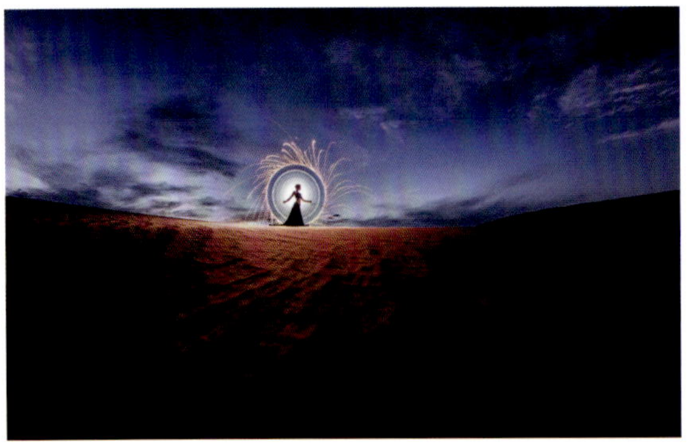

Partly cloudy

This is probably the most challenging condition for blue hour photography. The first thing to do is to identify whether the clouds are covering the area of the sunset glow or not. If they are, the best option is to compose with the clouds in the frame, without worrying too much about the glow's position. Even shooting in a northerly or southerly direction can work in some cases. Pay attention to how the ambient light affects the landscape and model to inform your choice. If the clouds aren't affecting the sunset glow you can treat it as a clear sky, so find a composition facing west (toward sunset) or east (toward sunrise). However, you may need to adjust your composition during the session as the clouds move, so there will be an additional element to consider. The clouds' speed will depend on their altitude as well as the wind speed.

Cloudy

Heavy clouds over the glow of the sunset or sunrise can be quite unpleasant in some cases. However, a cloudy sky offers more composition options. With the Sun's glow covered, the light becomes more diffuse, allowing compositions in most directions; the blue tones of the sky will look best if you are facing east at sunset.

Keep in mind that the ambient light level is lower when it's cloudy, which will affect the timing and length of your session. In the evening you will be able to start shooting earlier than the nautical twilight, but for a much shorter duration, as no stars will be visible during the astronomical twilight and the sky will darken quickly.

CAMERA SETTINGS

As the ambient light changes quite rapidly during the blue hour, so too will your settings. The chart on page 170 demonstrates how the exposure can change at a single location with an almost identical composition, but these settings will give you a broad starting point as the blue hour commences:

→ Exposure: 2 sec. (light painting ~2 sec.), f/9, ISO 100
→ White balance: 5200K
→ Flashlight power: 2000 lumens

The key is to understand how each element changes. The ISO, aperture, and exposure time (shutter speed) increase as the sky gets darker, while the power of the flashlight decreases. The duration of the light painting remains almost the same, regardless of the exposure time. You can execute your light-painting shape within two seconds most of the time.

The main principle is always the same: expose for the background first, then adjust the power of your flashlight to balance with these settings. To achieve balance at the start of the blue hour you will need a powerful flashlight (about 2000 lumens), but as time passes you will need to reduce the power.

TOOLS

My goal is either to harmonize or complement the colors that are present in the landscape. With that in mind, here's a list of my favorite tools for the blue hour:

→ Solid Orange or Milky Orange
→ Sugar
→ Sunset
→ RedPink

I usually start the session with a Solid White tube, but after a few minutes of shooting I'll switch depending on the dominant colors in the scene. The best way to know what works is to test it!

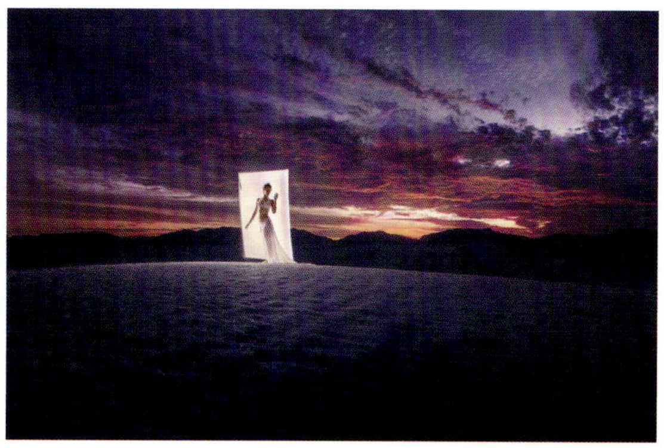

ABOVE **For this shot I used a Solid White tube early in the blue hour. This is currently my brightest tool, which allows me to start a few minutes earlier than any other tool.**

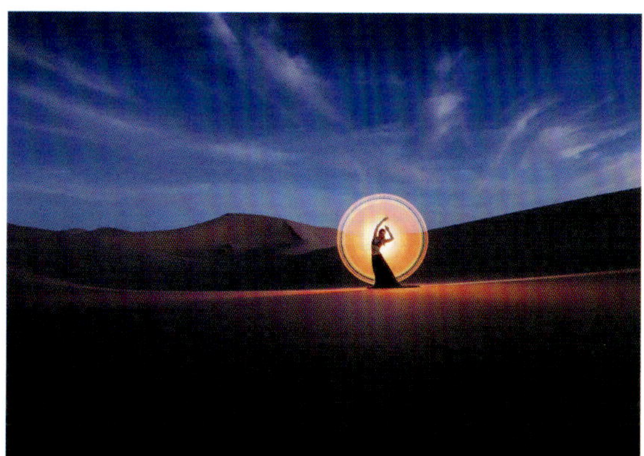

Solid Orange or Milky Orange

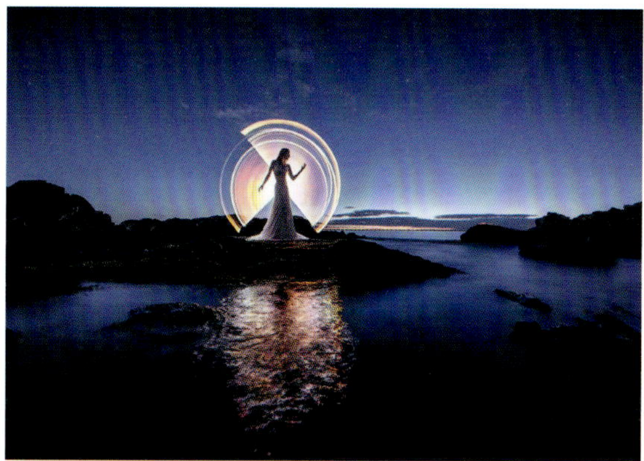

Sugar

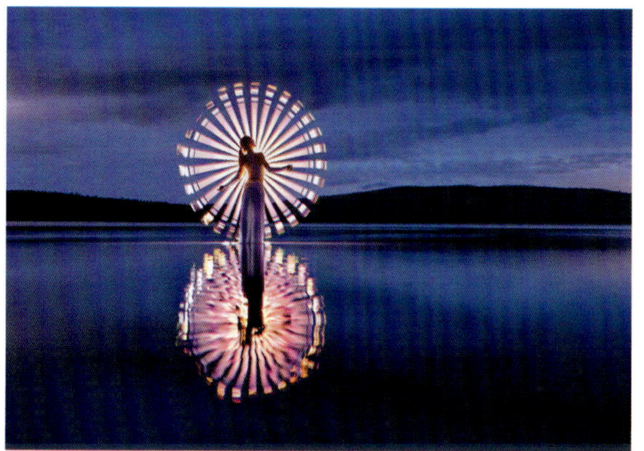

Sunset

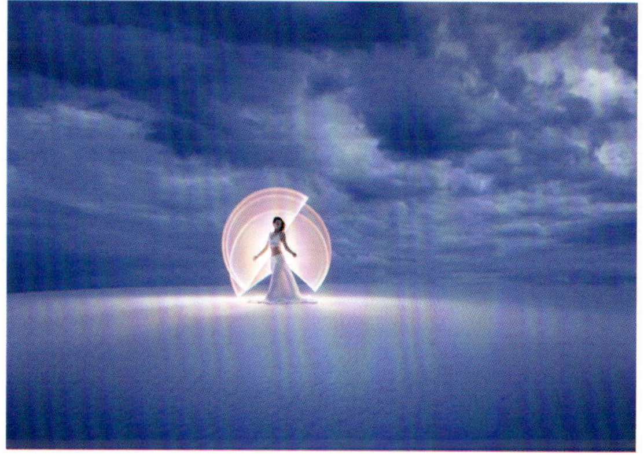

RedPink

Case Study **Blue hour**

Isn't the blue hour supposed to be... blue?

This image was created during a three-week creative trip in one of our favorite places on Earth, Salar de Uyuni in Bolivia. Although it was our fourth time traveling in the area, we prepared months in advance, as we knew it would be challenging in many ways. We were hoping for the best and ready for many things: sleep deprivation, altitude sickness, cold nights, technical and logistical problems, and things simply not going according to plan.

On our first night of shooting we were both puzzled by the colors during the blue hour. The sky was red and pink! It was hard to believe, but there it was in front of our eyes. We later learned that these colors were caused by particles of volcanic ash circling around the southern hemisphere. They were the result of an eruption that had happened about a year earlier near Tonga, in the Pacific Ocean. We were delighted to be able to witness and capture these unusual colors in a place that is very dear to us.

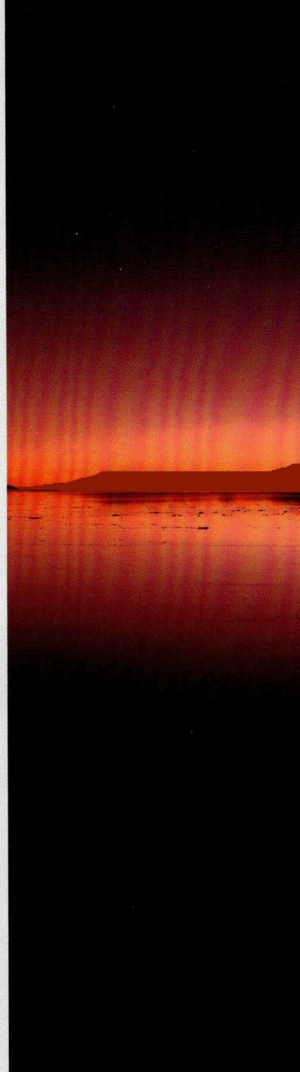

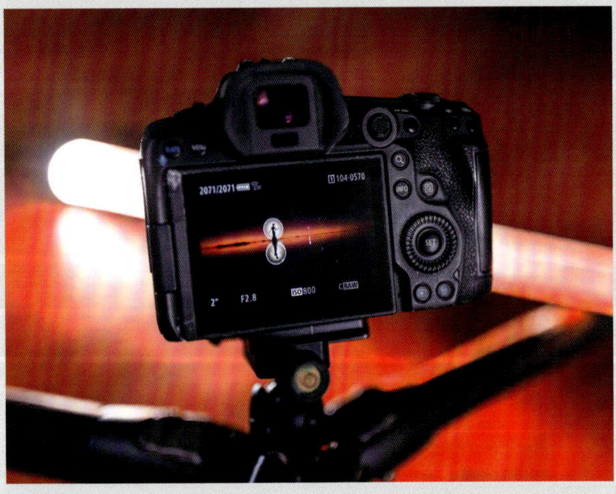
ABOVE **The colors as captured by the camera.**

ABOUT THE LOCATION

Salar de Uyuni, located in southwest Bolivia, is the largest salt flat on the planet. It sits at an elevation of about 12,000 feet (3,700m). During the rainy season, between December and April, a thin layer of water accumulates that transforms the "playa" into a giant mirror. The display of clouds and their reflection creates an ever-changing landscape.

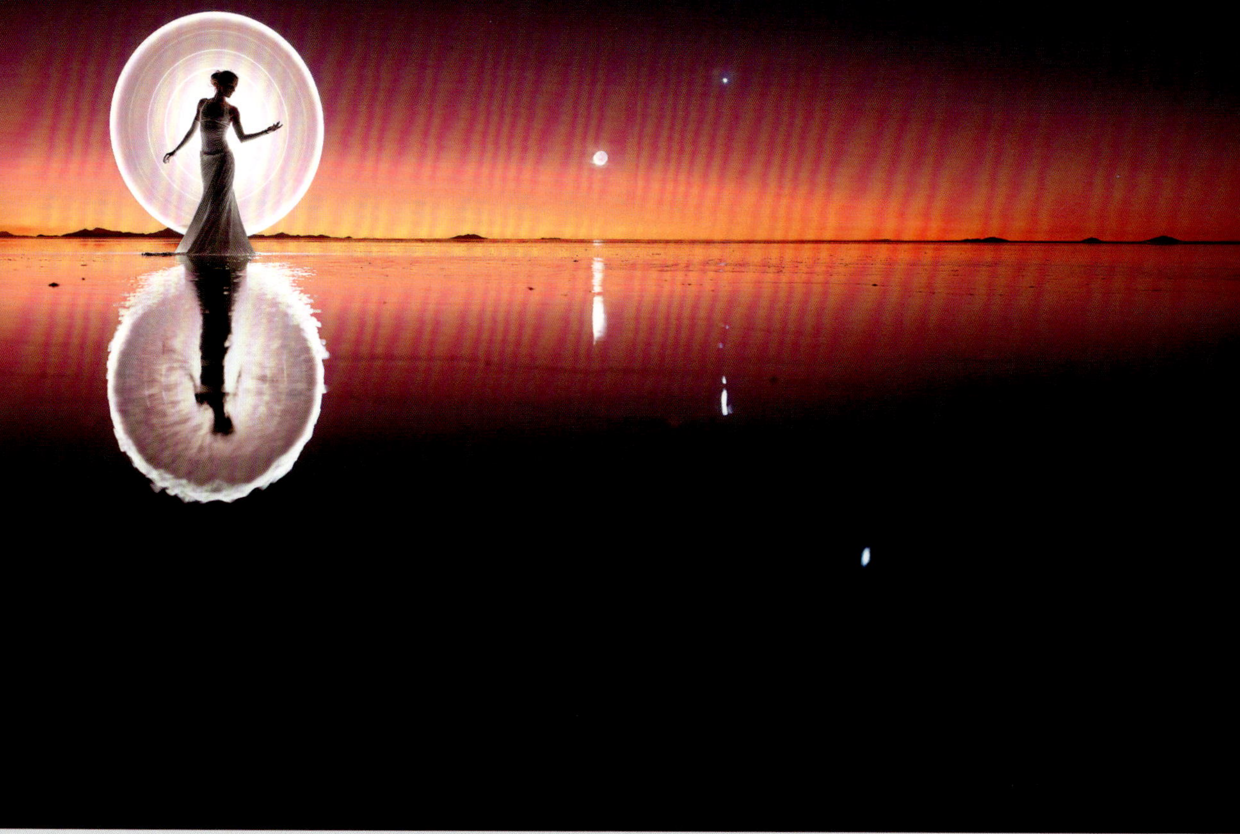

Environment: Salt flats | Focal length: 24mm | Exposure: 2 sec. (light painting ~2 sec.), f/2.8, ISO 800

DID YOU NOTICE?

There are three bright celestial objects in the composition: from left to right we see the Moon, which was in its first day of waxing crescent phase, Venus, and Jupiter. This was the only evening when we could capture that precise alignment, and while you might think that everything was planned, that was not the case. For these kinds of trips there are lots of things we can't control, so we show up and adapt to what is there. We were not expecting to have a clear sky during the rainy season, so it was a beautiful surprise. We were at the right place at the right time.

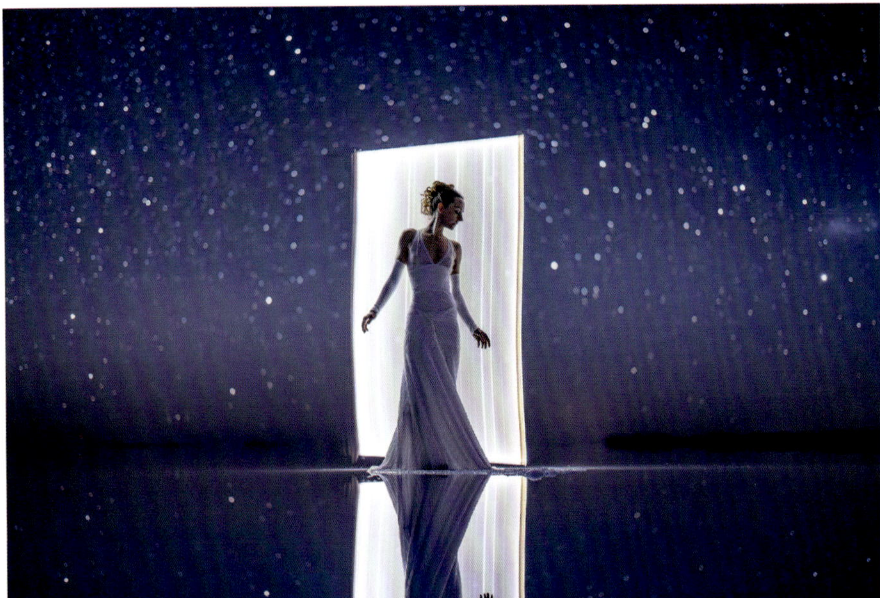

After the end of astronomical twilight, we enter nighttime. If the sky is clear enough to see the stars, especially on a moonless night, this can be a good opportunity to experiment and play with this technique. Unless there is a major change in the ambient light, such as the Moon rising, your camera settings will remain the same, which means the pace of creation is much slower.

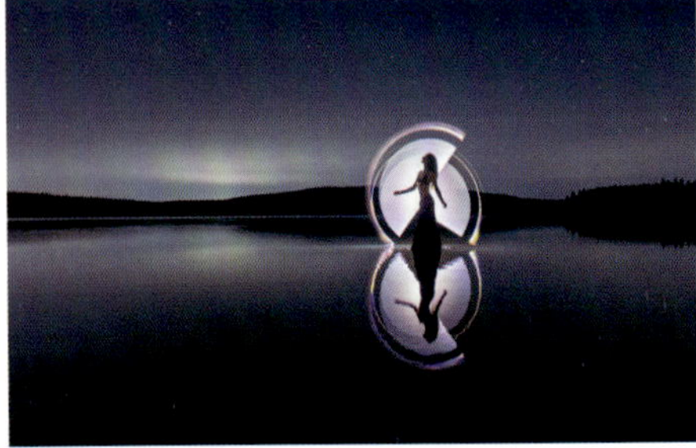

ABOVE **In this image, the bright area at the left side was created by light pollution from a distant city. Using the light pollution as an additional element in the photograph is often the best way to control its impact.**

PLANNING

When choosing a location, be aware of any artificial lights nearby, as well as distant city glows. Streetlights and house lights close by will likely impact the foreground and/or subject, which is the main thing you want to avoid. If you can't access a dark sky, don't worry, because even if you only capture the brightest stars visible, you can still create beautiful images, just as long as you stay away from artificial lights on location. It also helps to shoot when the Moon is either not visible or very small (illuminated 25 percent or less), as this will limit its impact on the landscape and your subject.

CAMERA SETTINGS

To quickly test your composition in the dark, dial in the following settings:

1 sec., f/1.8, ISO 51,200

If your camera can't reach these exposure values, don't hesitate to make adjustments. Use the highest ISO and lowest aperture you can.

Here's another example:

→ 2 sec., f/1.8, ISO 25,600

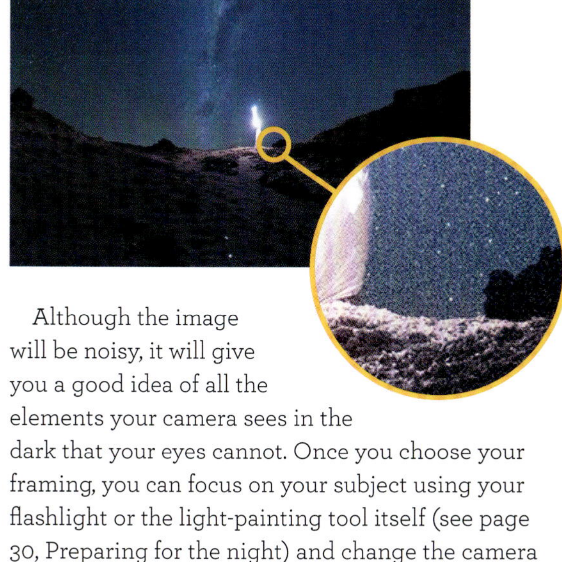

Although the image will be noisy, it will give you a good idea of all the elements your camera sees in the dark that your eyes cannot. Once you choose your framing, you can focus on your subject using your flashlight or the light-painting tool itself (see page 30, Preparing for the night) and change the camera settings to shoot with the stars. The settings we recommend are pretty much always the same when shooting with stars or the Milky Way.

But remember that this is a guideline, not a rule, so always make a test exposure for the background first:

→ Exposure: 8 sec. (light painting ~2 sec.), f/1.8, ISO 3200
→ White balance: 3200K
→ Flashlight power: 50–100 lumens

If your lens doesn't open up to an aperture of f/1.8, increase the shutter speed to 13 sec. or increase the ISO to 6400 instead. We would recommend changing the ISO over the shutter speed because the longer the exposure time, the harder it will be for the model to remain still.

A great thing about shooting dark night skies is that you don't need a powerful flashlight to balance the tube brightness with the background. Any 50–100 lumen flashlight that fits in a tube would work. If you only have a powerful tactical flashlight, physically block the light to dim it down (see page 40, Exposure section from Preparing for the night).

TOOLS

Similar to the Moon and other nighttime scenarios, I usually choose tools with a warmer tint to counterbalance the cool white balance I use to enhance the sky's colors, such as:

→ Warmish tube: to create a white light.
→ Pinkish tube: to create a white light with a pink tint.

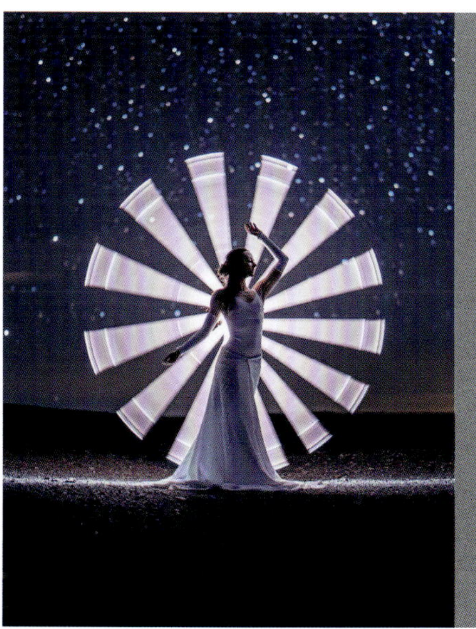

Should we focus on the stars?

This is not something you'll hear often, but we never focus on the stars. As the subject is in focus and we aim for a single exposure, the stars won't be in focus. It's a choice we make not only because of the technical constraints, but also because of aesthetic preference. I personally appreciate how out-of-focus stars look a little bit bigger. If you want your stars to appear sharp, the way to do it is to make multiple exposures: one for the light painting and another for the sky, changing the focus point between the two shots. However, combining the images can be a challenge, because the stars visible through the light-painting trace will appear bigger and won't be in the same position in the sky when you merge the two pictures.

LEFT **Out-of-focus stars are more apparent when captured with a longer focal length. This one was taken with a 50mm lens.**

Case Study **Stars**

We were on a creative road trip in late summer, and had the chance to organize a night shoot with our friend, Russell Preston Brown (who many of us affectionately call Dr. Brown). He has played a significant role in our journey. It was partly because of him that we were in San Francisco in the summer of 2015, where we found our first plastic tube.

On this particular trip we were spending two weeks in Death Valley National Park, and had rented a high-clearance 4x4 to go to the Racetrack Playa. We'd never been there before, but were pretty excited to discover a new area. We probably would not have gone there by ourselves, as it's a remote and fairly inaccessible location, and the temperature drops significantly at night due to its higher altitude. But we happily packed our camping and photography gear for the adventure with Dr. Brown.

When we got there, we played for a few hours under the stars by ourselves. We love to shoot in unrecognizable landscapes, and when the background is filled with stars but we can't see galaxies or specific constellations, it's as if the sky is contributing to making the landscape anonymous. Sometimes it allows us to daydream and wonder if we are even on Earth.

At some point during the session, Dr. Brown suggested we try using a small light to illuminate part of the rock formation in the background. If it had just been the two of us, we would never have gone in that direction, but as we were on a creative adventure with our friend we decided to break our own rule. This is the only time I can recall doing that.

ABOUT THE LOCATION The Racetrack is a large dry lakebed ("playa") located 3,714 feet (1,132 m) above sea level, in Death Valley National Park. It is known for its many mysterious moving rocks. The road to get there is rough and it's not recommended that you attempt the journey in a regular car, as there's a high risk of getting a flat tire and no cellphone service in the area. If you visit after a period of rain you need to make sure that you don't walk on the delicate surface of the playa when it's wet, as your ugly footprints will scar the beautiful landscape for years.

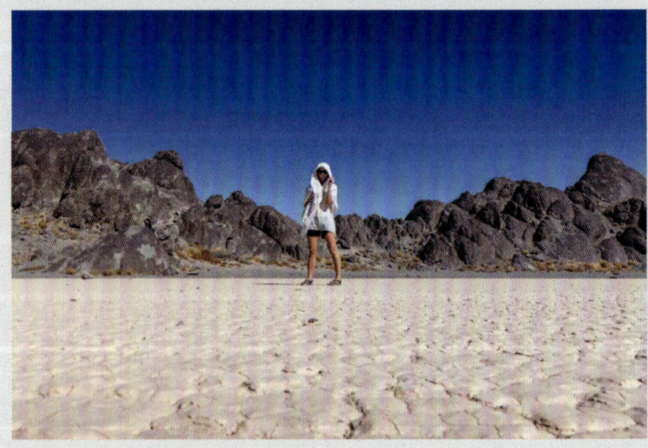

ABOVE **The playa during the day.**

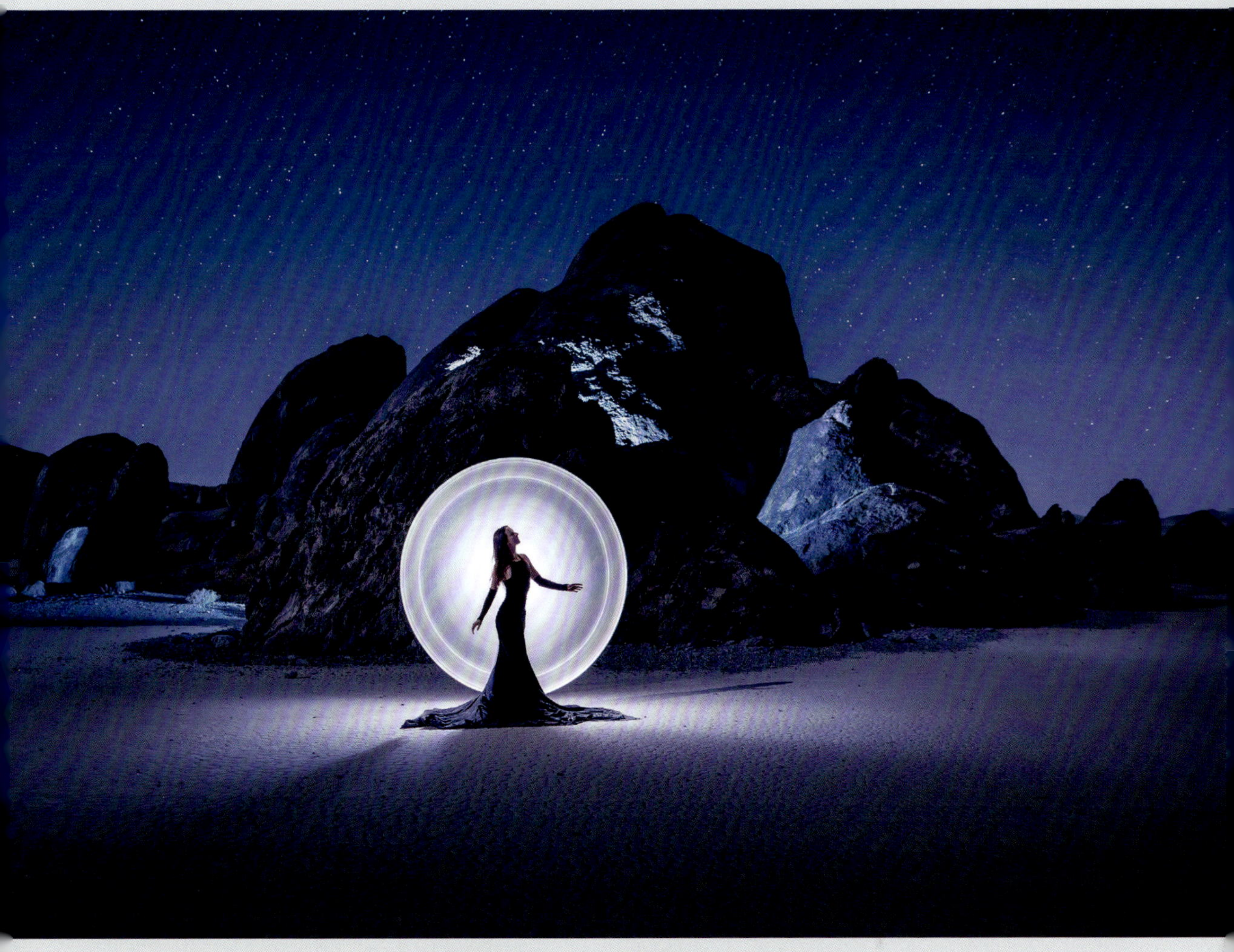

Environment: Desert | **Focal length:** 24mm | **Exposure:** 8 sec. (light painting ~1 sec.), f/2, ISO 80

DID YOU NOTICE?

Looking at this image, there is a lot of detail in the rock formation, the foreground, and the subject. This is caused by the moonlight coming from a near 45-degree angle, behind the camera. You can also see the photographer's and model's shadow if you look closely. Not including the Moon in our composition is not something we do often, as it significantly increases the potential blurriness of the subject.

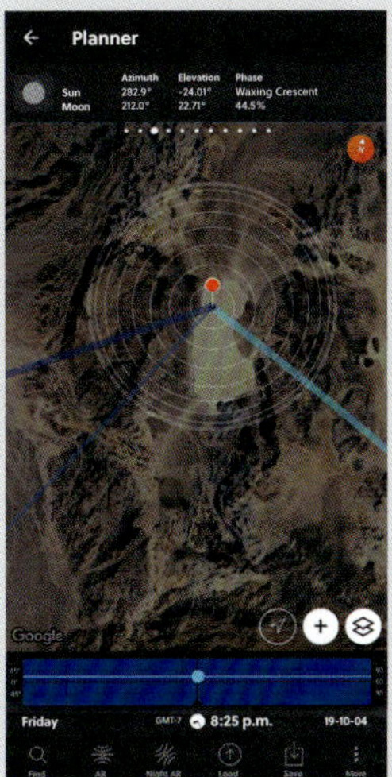

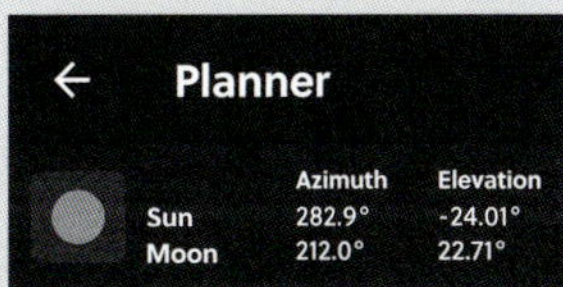

LEFT & ABOVE **The Moon was 44.5 percent illuminated and had an elevation of 22.71 degrees when the main image was made.**

Milky Way

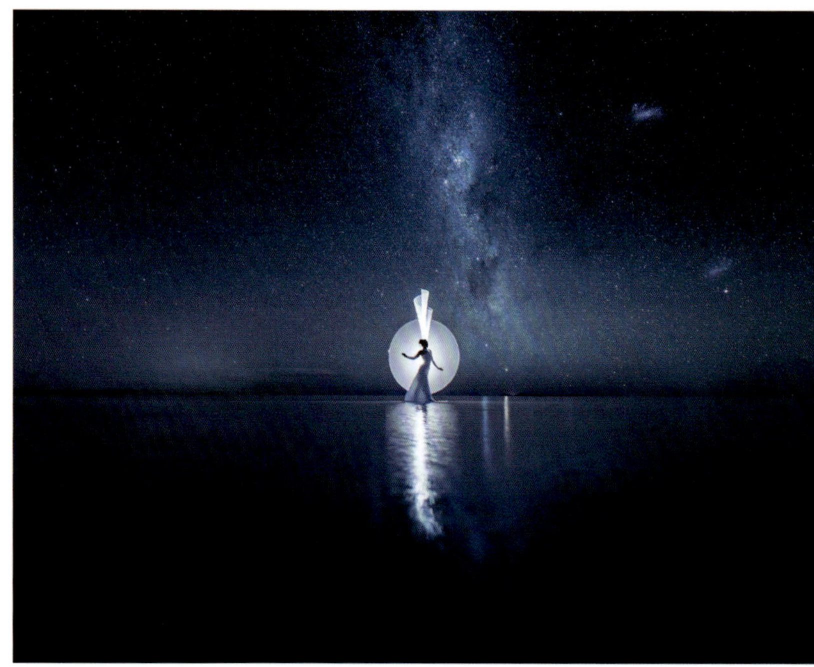

Depicted in many mythologies as a road, a river, or a path, the Milky Way has been a source of wonder and fascination since humans were able to share stories.

The fact that we can get a view of our own galaxy from within is in itself pretty fascinating when you think about it. One thing is certain, the Milky Way is a beautiful element to include in an image if you have the chance to see it in the night sky.

PLANNING

Several elements usually need to come together if you want to capture the Milky Way.

Dark environment: You always want to avoid artificial lights and light pollution, as stray light in the environment will prevent you from seeing the Milky Way, as well as most stars. Sky glow from distant urban areas can wash out the dimmest stars, potentially preventing the Milky Way from being visible, especially when it is close to the horizon. The further you are from urban areas, the better. You can use **Darksitefinder.com** or another light pollution map to look for a location with limited light pollution in the direction of the southern sky. Why south? Because this is where you will see the Milky Way core. Depending on the hemisphere and time of the year, it can be toward the southeast, south, or southwest.

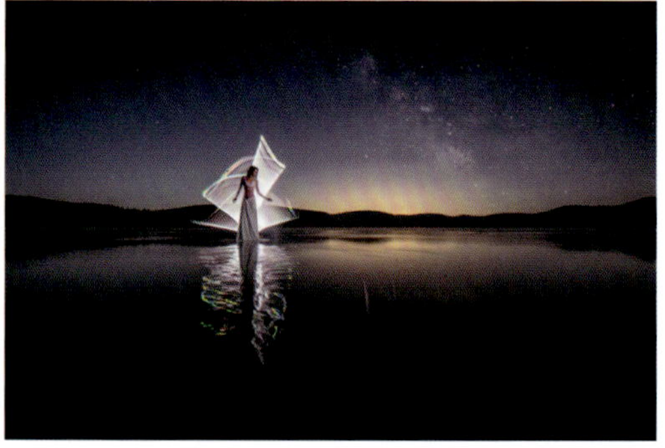

ABOVE **Here, we had to include the city glow in our composition if we wanted to shoot. The Moon was 35 percent illuminated with an elevation of 14.6 degrees, which also affected the visibility of the Milky Way.**

Dark, moonless sky: The Moon also makes it hard (if not impossible) to see the stars, and therefore the Milky Way. There are exceptions; if you are in a very dark environment, the Milky Way can be captured with a setting moon, especially if it's close to being a new moon.

Clear, cloudless sky: A cloudless night not only increases the visibility of the stars, but also your composition options. The Milky Way is an important element, but just a few clouds in the frame can quickly limit your composition. Other elements that can negatively impact the visibility of the Milky Way include dust, haze, smoke, and moisture in the air.

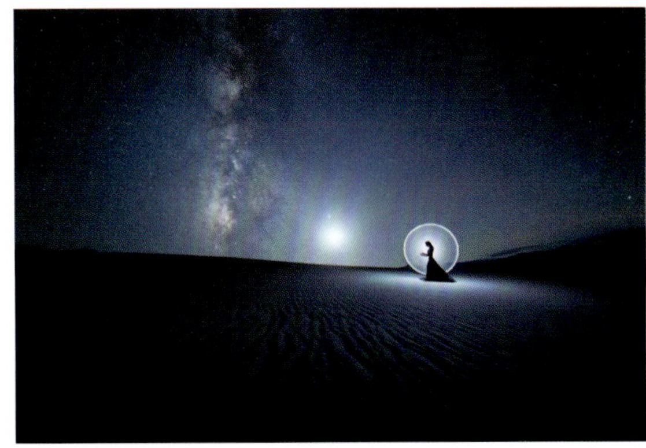

ABOVE **Even if the Milky Way is not easily visible to the naked eye, your camera can see it. Because of the brightness of the crescent moon, the exposure time was shorter for this shot than normal.**

THE RIGHT SEASON

Although the Milky Way is visible throughout the year, its galactic core (generally considered the most photogenic part) rises above the horizon at night for approximately nine months, between early February and late October. In reality, the visibility period is much shorter in most locations around the world, as the galactic core is hard to see or capture when it's close to the horizon.

This period is often referred to as "Milky Way Season" by photographers, although "Milky Way Core Season" would be more accurate. The visibility of the galactic center will vary greatly depending on your latitude: the further south you go, the longer the Milky Way Core Season lasts. In the northern hemisphere, the galactic center stays relatively close to the horizon (and below it at latitudes above 61 degrees north), whereas the southern hemisphere experiences a greater elevation variation; during the winter months it can appear both overhead and very close to the horizon within the same night.

PhotoPills Planner is helpful when it comes to identifying the best time of year (and day) to go to a given location to capture the galactic center, and this is even more useful if you have a precise idea in mind. Once you're in the field, the PhotoPills Night AR tool makes it easy to see the direction and orientation of the Milky Way and plan your composition ahead of time.

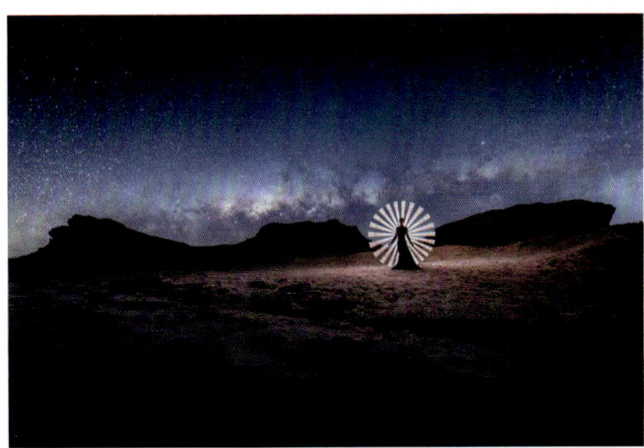

ABOVE **This image was planned using PhotoPills's Night AR tool.**

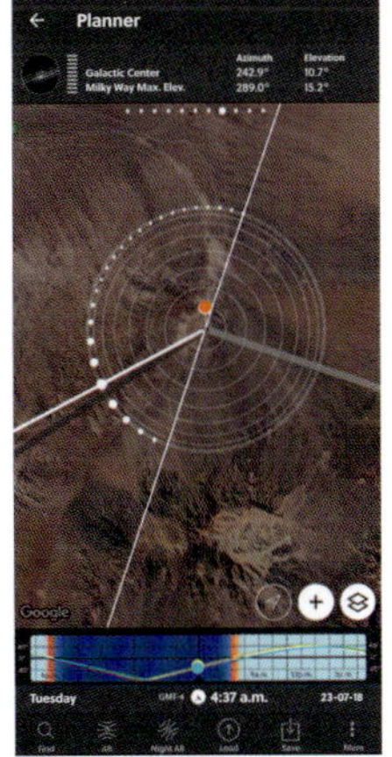

LEFT **PhotoPills Planner can show the visibility and elevation of the Milky Way core for a specific time and location. The direction of the galactic center is indicated by the thick white line.**

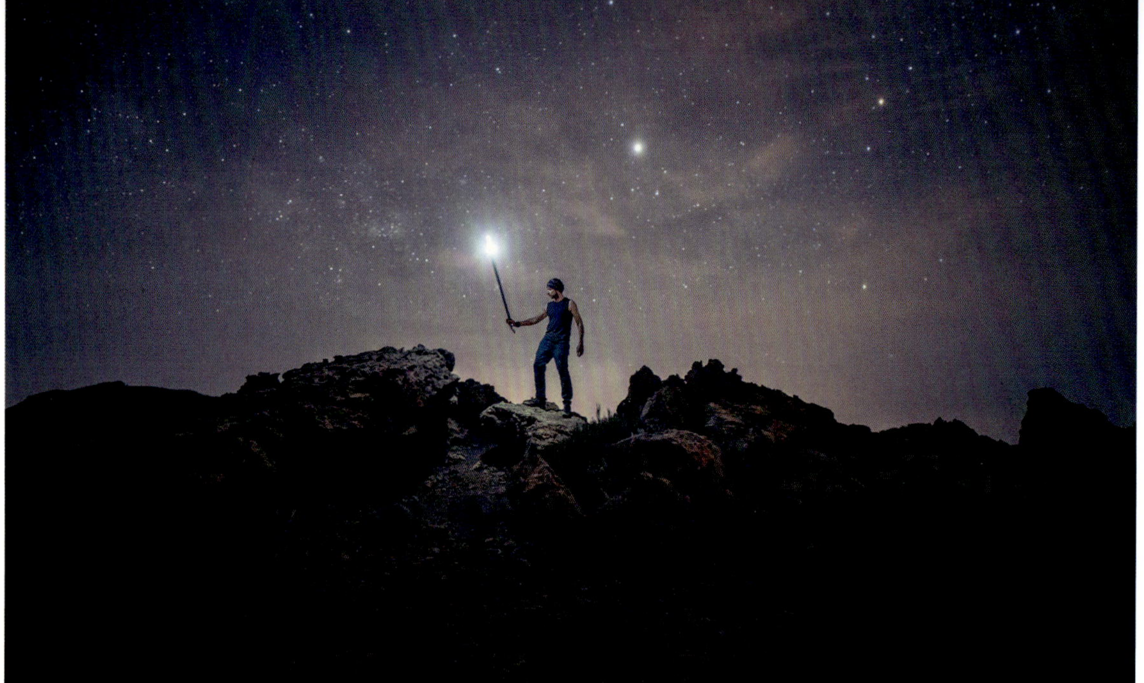

TOOLS

In addition to the neutral colors I use at night (Warmish and Pinkish tubes), a tool I love using with the Milky Way is the Black tube.

The Black tube is an extension that I attach a smaller tube to. It is used in the same way as other tubes (by holding a flashlight at the base of it), but creates perfect outline circles, rather than solid discs of light. When I'm working with this tool, I use a small reflective tube to get directional rather than diffused light, which lets me light up the subject as well as the foreground.

With this tool, keep your flashlight at maximum power (or close to maximum), and don't worry about seeing through the light painting. What you're looking for is a tiny light around your subject. This is a great way to create a beautiful light on your subject late at night.

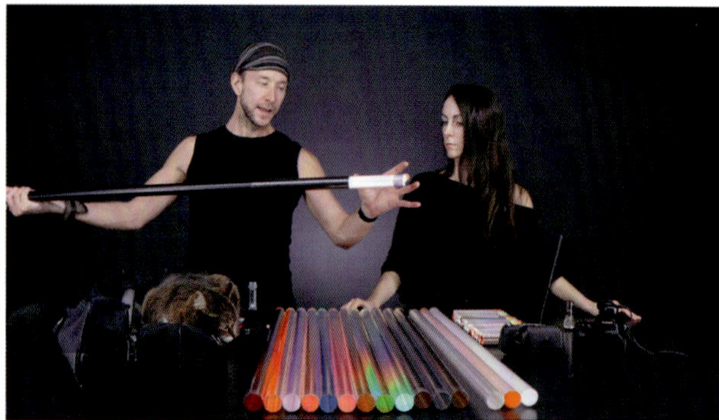

RIGHT **Using a small tube on top of a Black tube naturally illuminates the scene and the subject. As there is no light directly behind the model, you need to be very precise with your alignment when using this tool, otherwise you will be visible from the camera's perspective.**

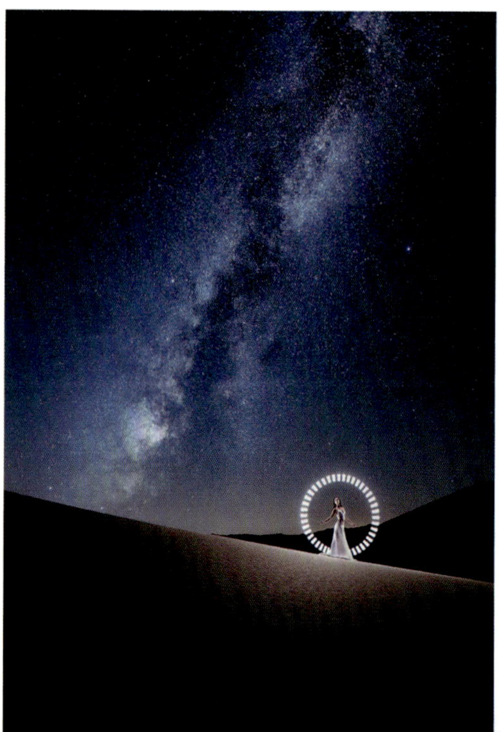

COMPOSITION

The Milky Way is an imposing element in our night sky and perhaps the biggest challenge is finding a balanced composition that includes it, the landscape, and your light painting/human subject. Generally, a portrait orientation is more suited to a vertical or slightly diagonal Milky Way, whereas a landscape orientation tends to enhance a horizontal Milky Way.

This is not always the case, though, as it also depends on the architecture of the horizon line and the other elements you choose to include in the image. All these variables should guide your positioning of your model and your light painting. As a general guideline, have the model look toward the Milky Way.

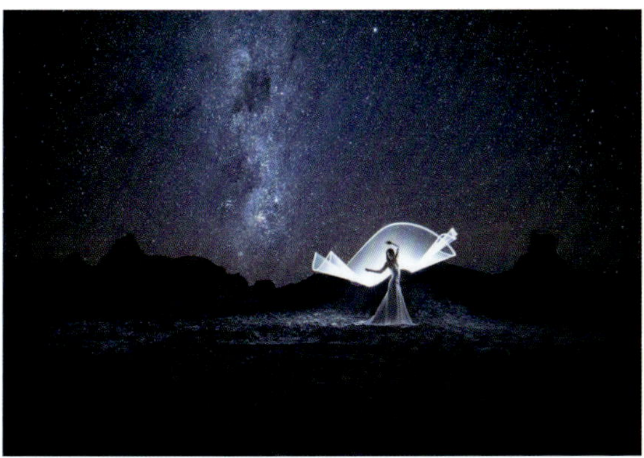

Vertical Milky Way: When the Milky Way is vertically oriented, I tend to place the subject close to it in the frame, making them both share the center of the image in the composition.

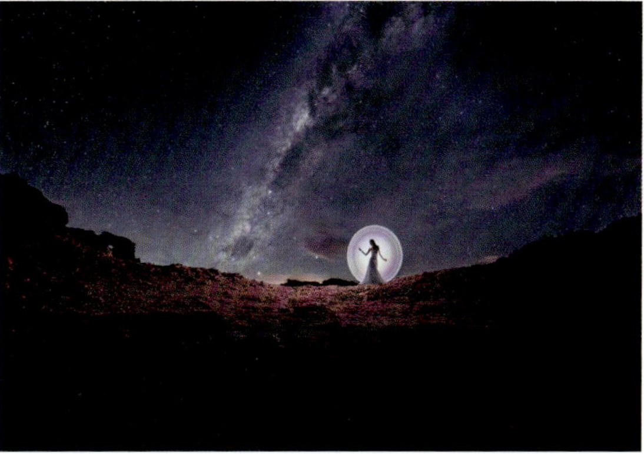

Diagonal Milky Way: It usually looks more balanced if the subject is positioned under the Milky Way.

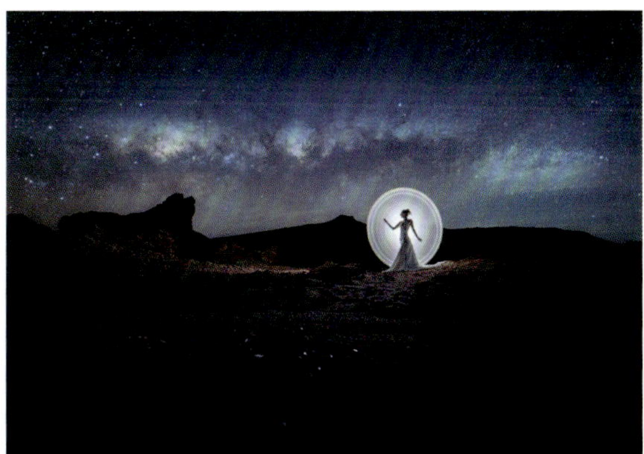

Horizontal Milky Way: In this case, the model and Milky Way were positioned to create balance among multiple compositional elements, including the Milky Way core, the rock formation in the middle ground, the architecture of the horizon line, the foreground texture, and so on.

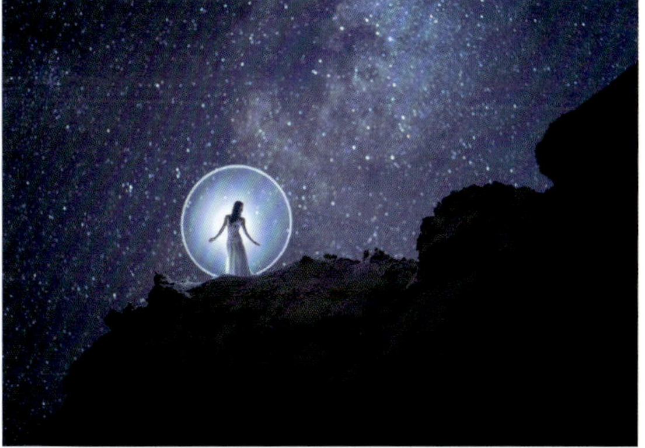

In the Milky Way: Positioning the subject higher on a rock formation and shooting from below with an 85mm lens gave an unusual perspective. As always, don't hesitate to explore and try something different.

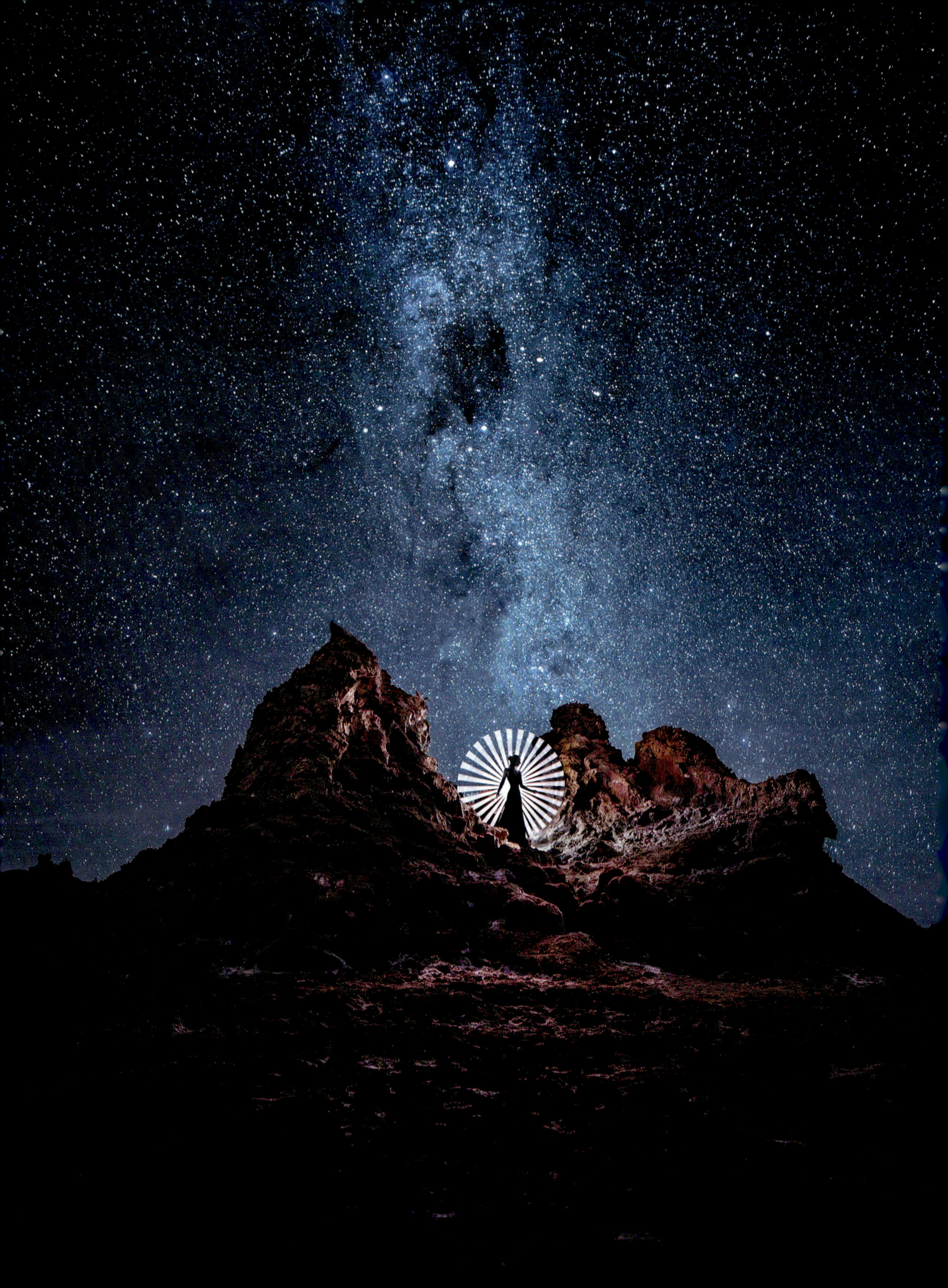

Case Study **Milky Way**

This image was created on the last evening of a short creative trip in the Atacama Desert. We had visited the region a few years earlier, when we were still in the process of figuring out how to optimize our technique to shoot with the night sky. Like our previous visit, we went during winter. Although the temperatures get cold at night (below freezing point), there are very few visitors at this time of year, which is a positive counterpoint.

After nearly a week of shooting long hours in the cold nights, living in a campervan with no access to a hot shower, we were tired and quite satisfied with what we had created so far. On our last night, we questioned whether we needed to go out and shoot again, but decided we had to create until the end. After all, we had no idea if and when we would have another opportunity to capture or see such a majestic night sky.

After a cold blue hour session, Eric went to do some location scouting in the dark, finding a setting in the middle of nowhere, surrounded by rocks and stars. The fact that we kept exploring until the last minute allowed us to create a piece with a unique and unusual composition.

ABOUT THE LOCATION

The Atacama Desert is a high-elevation plateau located in Chile, and one of the driest places on Earth. Because of its high altitude, dry air, extremely low light pollution, and nearly absent cloud cover, this place is a dream-come-true for star lovers.

DID YOU NOTICE?

When we see images of the Milky Way, we usually see its galactic core, which is one of the most impressive displays of beauty we have access to. However, don't hesitate to capture other parts of the Milky Way if the galactic core is covered by clouds, below the horizon, or simply can't be included in your composition for some reason. Here, we were in the southern hemisphere in July, capturing a vertical Milky Way. This meant the galactic core was directly above our heads and impossible to include in the frame. By not limiting yourself to capturing the galactic center, you will expand your creative possibilities and ensure that Milky Way Season never ends.

Environment: Desert | **Focal length:** 24mm | **Exposure:** 10 sec. (light painting ~2 sec.), f/1.4, ISO 3200

Winter

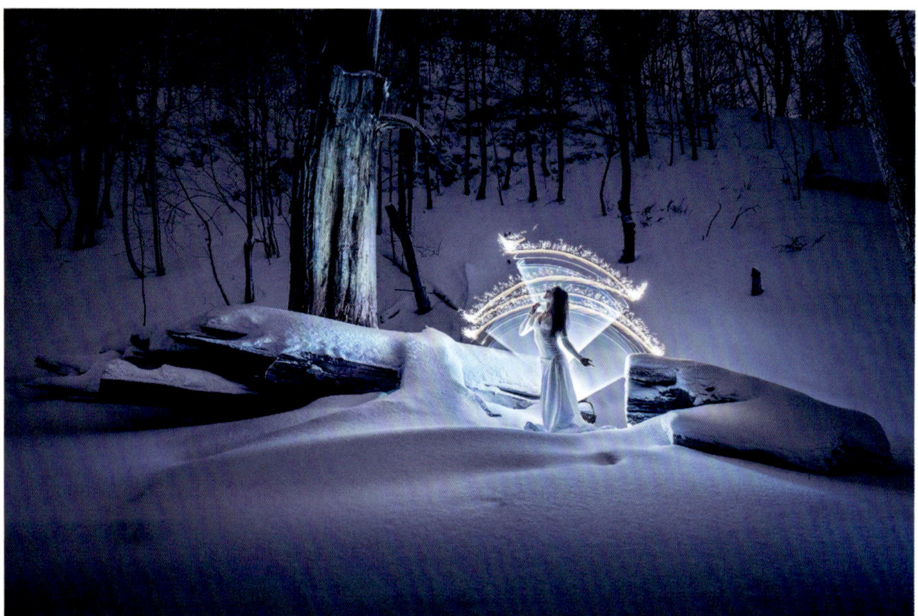

For us, winter is mostly associated with forest landscapes, which will be the focus of this section. Creating tube light-painting images in winter settings can be quite magical, and doing it in a forest at night makes the technical side of things very simple. However, the cold weather adds a layer of complexity that is worth addressing: if you choose to play outside at night during winter, be ready to embrace discomfort.

If you're photographing a person, their safety (as well as your own) should be the priority. Your shooting time will be limited in cold weather, and we will only work for periods of about 15 minutes when the temperature is between -5°C and -15°C, compared to several hours when it's warm outside. When it's colder than that or very windy we stay inside, although you might be tougher than us and brave colder weather. In any case, being well prepared before heading out is key.

PLANNING

To get a beautiful, pristine snowy foreground, the snow needs to be very fresh and not too heavy. That means you either have to go out during the snowfall (if it's safe to do so), or head out right after it stops, assuming that happens during the blue hour or at night.

If you prioritize the fresh snow in the foreground, you are unlikely to be able to capture a clear sky with stars in the background at the same time. As we love to create in the forest, we don't usually see the sky in the background anyway, so we skip twilight and start to shoot when it's close to nighttime.

Unfortunately, pristine snow doesn't last for long. The texture can change within a few hours, and if it's windy the snow on the branches quickly falls to the ground, reducing the immaculate beauty of the foreground. This is obviously not something you have any control over, but if you are well prepared, you can increase your chances of creating something beautiful when the conditions align.

It will help if you familiarize yourself with the area where you want to shoot, so scout it in advance, before the snowstorm. Have a few compositions in mind, as this will make the process more efficient and prevent you from leaving unwanted footsteps in the snow.

Prepare your gear in advance. Having the triggers and cables installed on your cameras and preparing the settings are simple yet helpful steps that can be done before leaving the warmth of your car or home.

Finally, dress for the weather. That means layers, and lots of them. For us that includes heated socks and hand warmers, mittens, a warm hat, winter coat, and good winter boots. Anything you need to stay warm and dry, including your face.

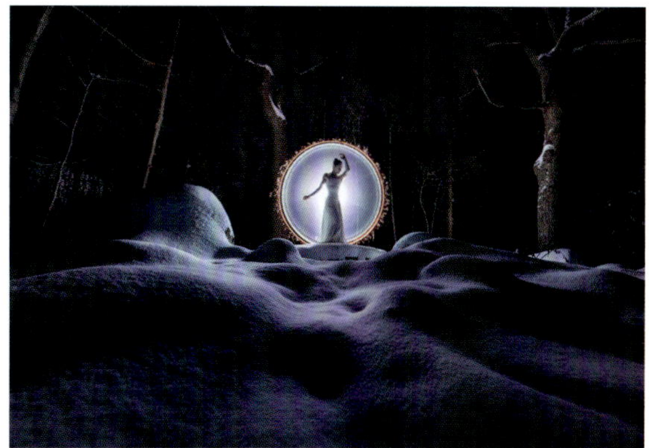

CHALLENGES

Working in snow presents its own difficulties, but the fact that it's usually cold makes it worse. These tips will help you during the process:

→ **Keep the remote trigger inside your mitten:** You want to avoid taking your mittens off to prevent the loss of dexterity. We use mittens with an opening in case we need to manipulate the camera during the session.

→ **Extra battery:** Unlike many landscape photographers, we don't keep extra camera batteries in a coat pocket to keep it warm. Although it's true that batteries drain faster in cold temperatures, in winter we never shoot long enough to justify carrying an extra battery – we get cold before the battery does!

→ **Avoid changing lenses during the shoot:** We don't need wide aperture lenses when we shoot in a forest with snow, as we're not capturing the stars or the sky most of the time. Instead, we usually shoot with a zoom lens, typically a 16–35mm f/4 or a 24–70mm f/2.8 or f/4. This lets us adjust the composition without changing the lens.

→ **Have a cleaning cloth in your pocket:** If it's snowing, you might have to wipe your lenses between each series.

→ **Leave no trace:** To keep the foreground free of footprints, both the model and light painter need to avoid walking between the camera and the subject's position. After you choose your composition, get your model to walk outside the frame (guiding them using live view) and enter from the side once they're far enough away. When they're close to the desired position, have them walk straight toward the camera. The goal is to hide any footprints behind the subject and the light painting. Shooting from a low angle will also help to hide distant footprints. This same technique can also be used when you're shooting in sand dunes or on the beach.

→ **Create shorter series:** Depending on how the model chooses to dress, they may or may not need to take off extra layers when shooting. If they do, make shorter series (take fewer shots) before going to the camera to check your results. This will give your model more time to warm up between series. If you work in a small group, a third person can stay hidden and give the model a warm coat between shots. If you have to walk or hike before reaching a warm location, factor that in when you plan your shoot.

→ **After the session:** Make sure your gear is dry before storing it. Extending the legs of your tripod to let them dry can prevent them from rusting.

CAMERA SETTINGS

This is one of the rare occasions when we don't expose for the background first, because there is no background (sky) to take into consideration. When shooting in a forest, start with these settings:

→ Exposure: 2 sec. (light painting ~2 sec.), f/5.6, ISO 200
→ White balance: 5200K
→ Flashlight power: Maximum (2000 lumens)

If your flashlight power is less than 2000 lumens, increase your ISO. You will also have to adjust the brightness of your flashlight according to the brightness of your sparkler if you use one.

If you want to shoot a winter landscape with the stars, the Milky Way, or auroras, refer to those respective sections for the settings (pages 86, 90, and 114). This also applies to the following notes on tools and composition.

TOOLS

For winter scenes in a forest, I typically use a Winter tube, mainly because this holographic tube casts subtle tints of purple, teal, and pink on the white foreground.

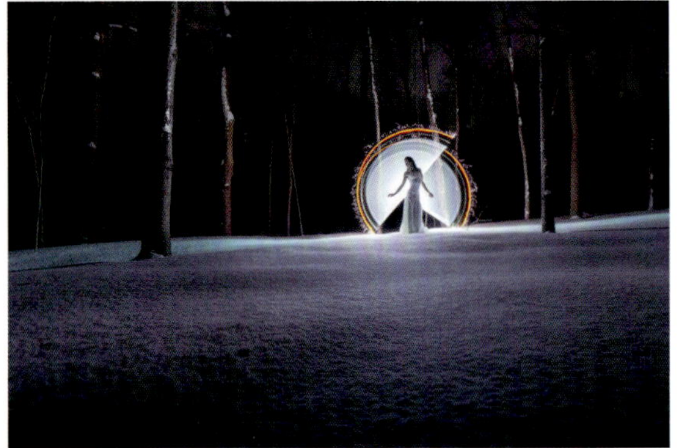

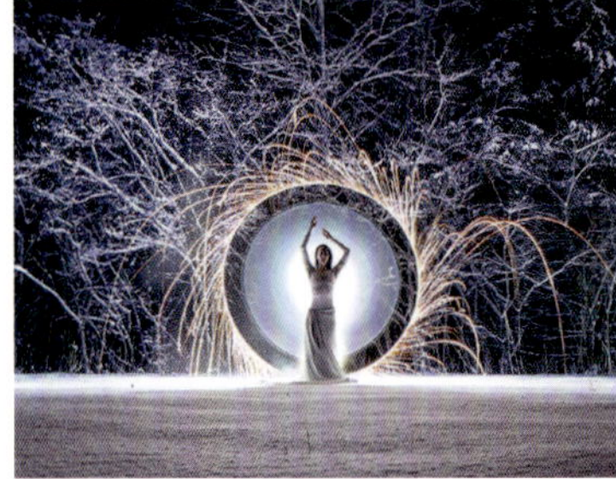

ABOVE & LEFT
I often use birthday sparklers on top of the tube to illuminate a dark forest scene.

COMPOSITION

You can use the landscape elements (the trees) to surround your subject and create a more intimate scene. This might be more specific to shooting in a forest environment than a winter setting, but to us they often go hand in hand.

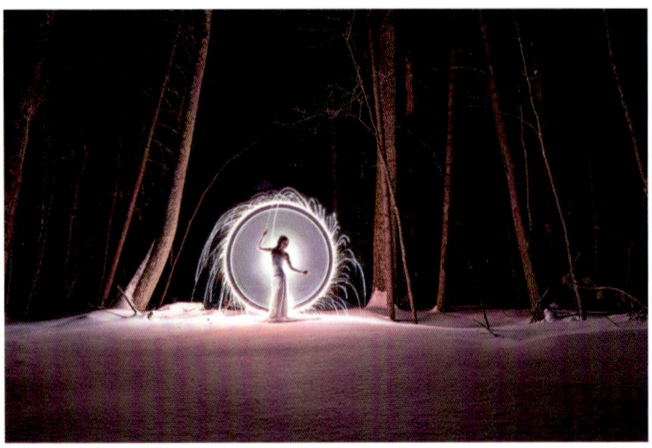

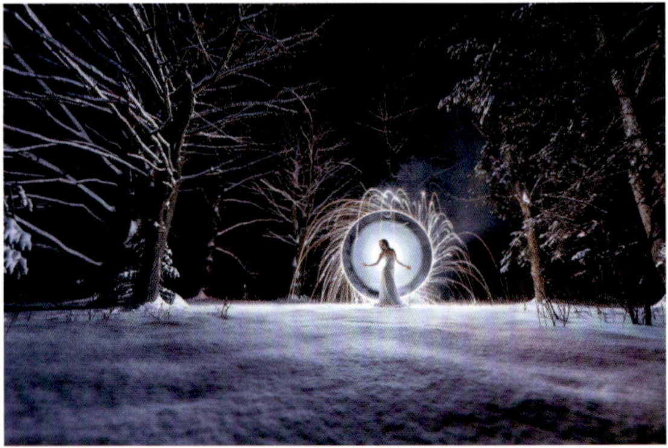

Case Study **Winter**

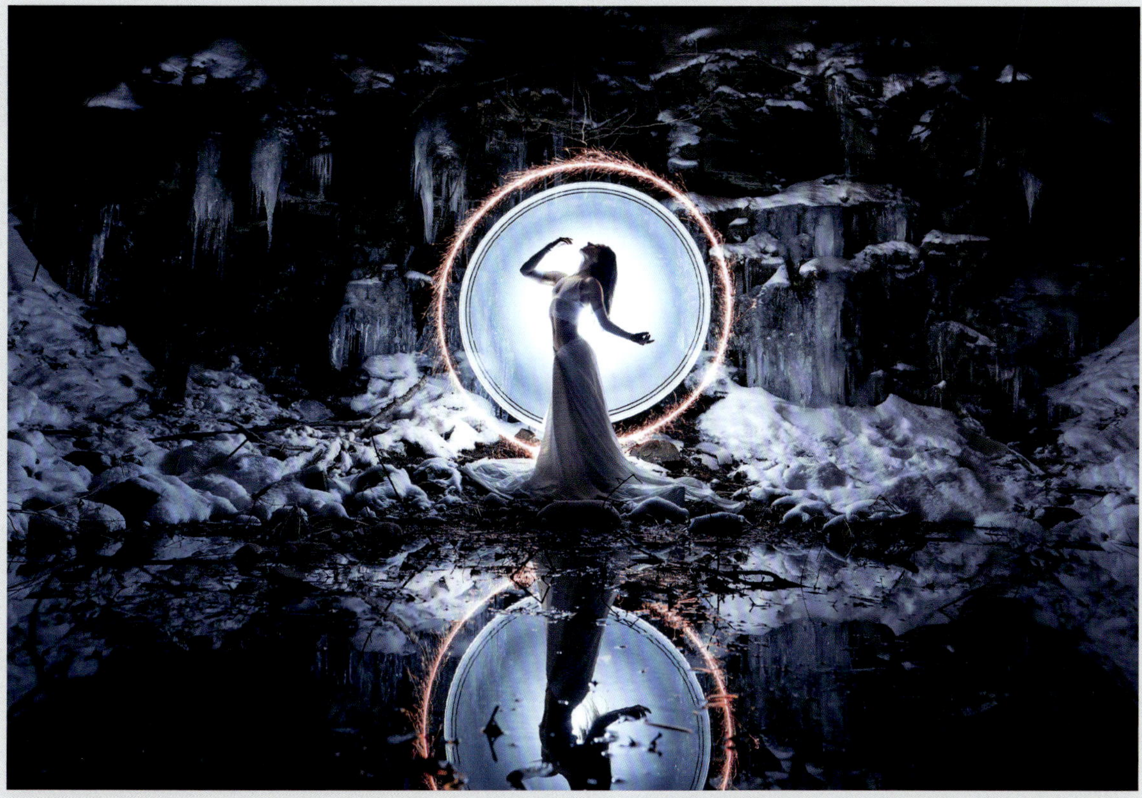

Environment: Park | **Focal length:** 24mm | **Exposure:** 1.8 sec. (exposure and light painting), f/5.6, ISO 400

You don't always have to travel to remote places to see and capture the magic of nature. This image was taken in Mount Royal Park, Montreal, next to a staircase leading to the main belvedere, where people can get an view of the city. As you can imagine, it is usually a busy area.

It was the start of winter and the weather was in its transition period, softly getting colder. We went for a walk in the park, as we often do, and noticed the beautiful configuration of ice on this rock wall, with a pool of water beneath it. It was clear we had to come back later to capture this ephemeral scene, which we knew wouldn't last. We had to cross a small creek to get to our shooting spot, and Eric had to jump across it every time he wanted to go back to the camera. We were surprised he didn't fall in the water.

While it was a relatively warm evening (given the time of year) Eric's fingers were freezing as he manipulated his cameras and the light-painting tools.

A few people walking in the park watched on with curiosity and we heard kids asking their parents what we were doing with our dancing lights and "princess costume." If it had been warmer we would have taken the time to show them the back of the camera and let them have a go themselves, but it was getting cold and we didn't have much time before we needed to pack up and leave. A few hours later, everything was frozen.

Beach

Shooting at the beach can be a beautiful experience, but it brings its own set of challenges. From sheltered lake shores to expansive ocean coastlines, beach environments can vary dramatically. To make the most of this type of location, both the model and the light painter usually have to get in the water so reflections on the wet sand or the body of water can be captured.

As soon as the Sun sets, the beach can become a somewhat chaotic environment to shoot in, especially when there are crashing waves. They can be loud and make it hard to communicate, so much so that we often have to scream at each other, even when we are a short distance apart.

PLANNING

Choose your beach wisely. We usually look for a long, flat beach at low or descending tide or, even better, a shallow lake. Another great option is to find a pool of water left from the previous high tide, especially when it's windy.

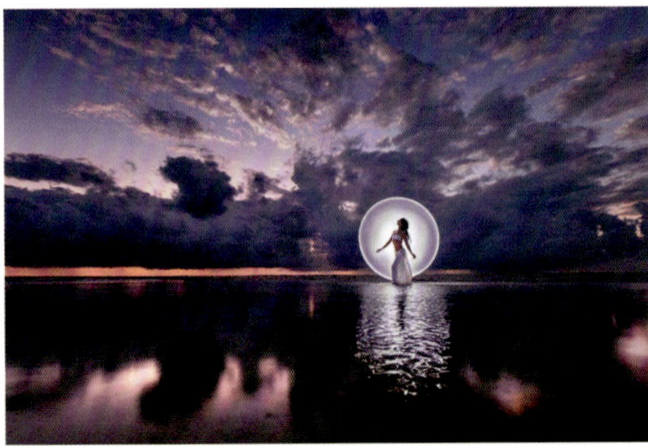

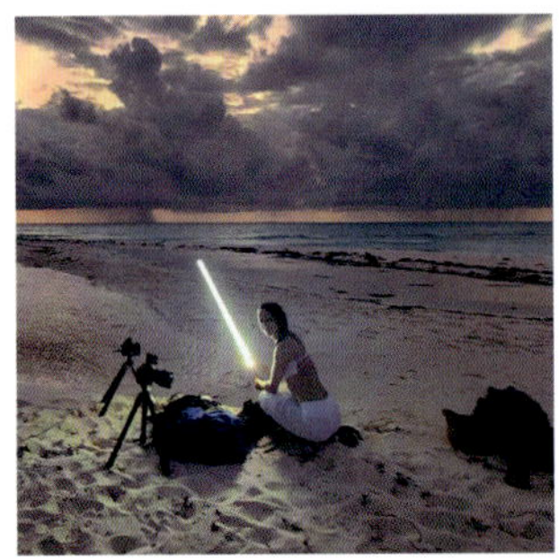

ABOVE & RIGHT
We safely created this image in a pool left on the beach by the receding tide.

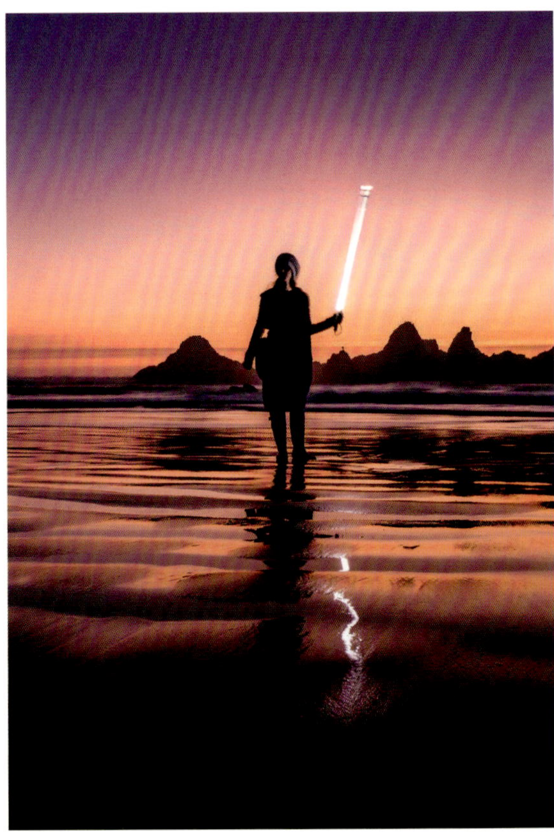

If you're working at a tidal location, one of the most important things to know is the state of the tide – is it coming in or going out? You can use an online resource such as **Tide-forecast.com** or an app like **Tide Charts** to get this information. Also find out if there is a risk of sneaker (or sleeper) waves at your chosen location. You'll have your back to the water a lot of the time, in the dark, so you don't want to risk a large rogue wave sneaking up behind you.

Whether you're shooting by freshwater or the sea, find out what types of creatures (big or small) live in the area. Is there anything you'd rather not encounter while shooting in the dark, such as jellyfish, stingrays, or leeches?

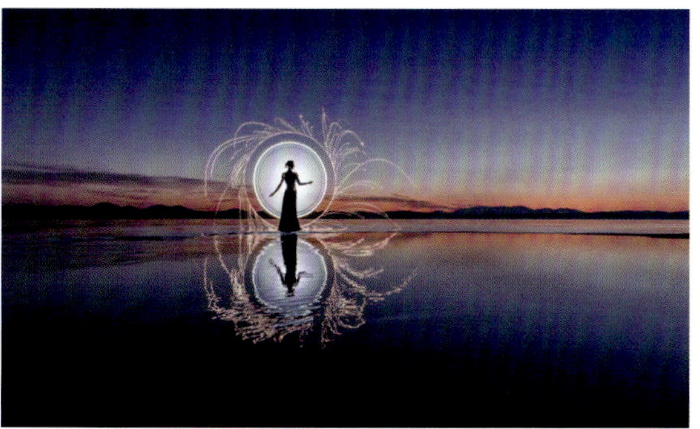 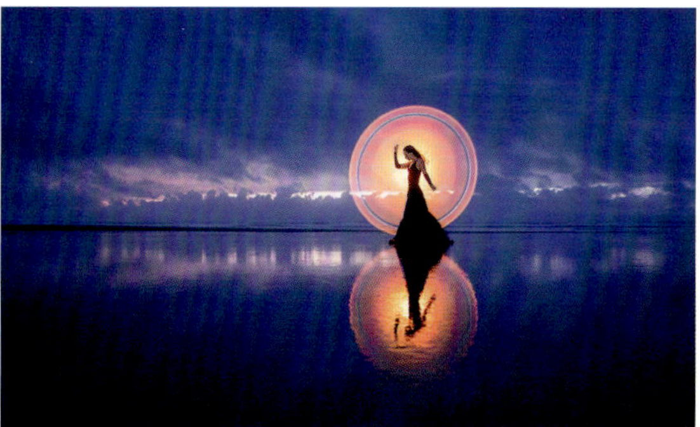

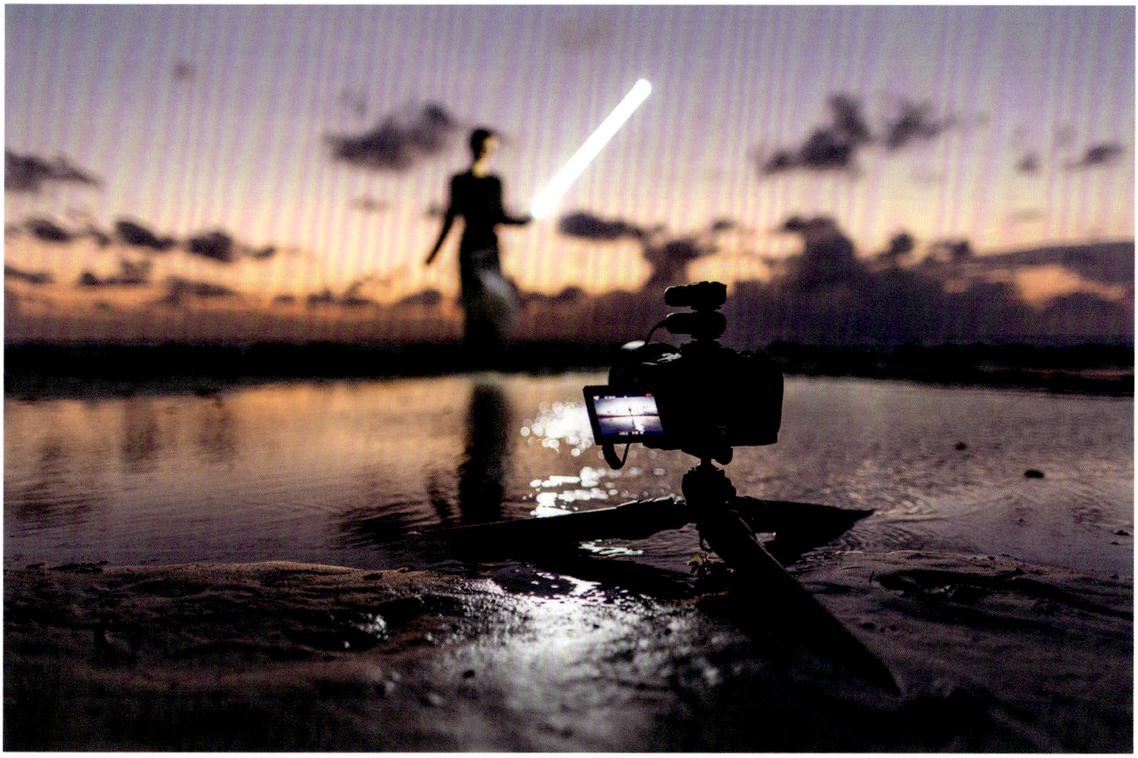

CHALLENGES

Once you have found a beautiful and safe place to shoot, there are some additional technicalities to consider:

→ If you shoot from a low perspective, droplets of water will likely get on your lens. Your regular microfiber cleaning cloth won't last for long, so use delicate task wipes to clean your lens instead.

→ Regardless of the height at which you shoot, if your tripod is in contact with moving water (especially receding waves), it could make it sink in the sand. This can impact your composition and the sharpness of your image if the camera moves during an exposure.

→ Receding waves, even small ones, can make the sand move under your model's feet as they try to stay still. This can result in a blurry subject.

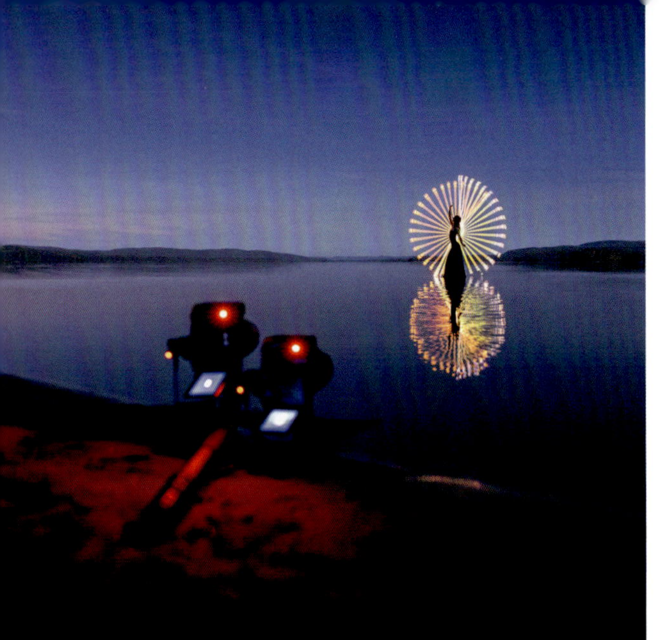

WHAT IF THE LAKE IS NOT SHALLOW?

In most of our images involving bodies of water, it looks like Kim is almost floating above the surface. You can achieve this naturally if the water is very shallow, but rarely are we lucky enough to find that kind of location. Instead, we use heavy duty stackable crates that Kim stands on in deeper water. We have tried various solutions over the years, from an icebox to a short step stool, but the crates are our preferred option, as they are not too heavy to carry and don't float. At some locations we have stacked two crates, so Kim is almost above the surface, while Eric is knee-deep in water.

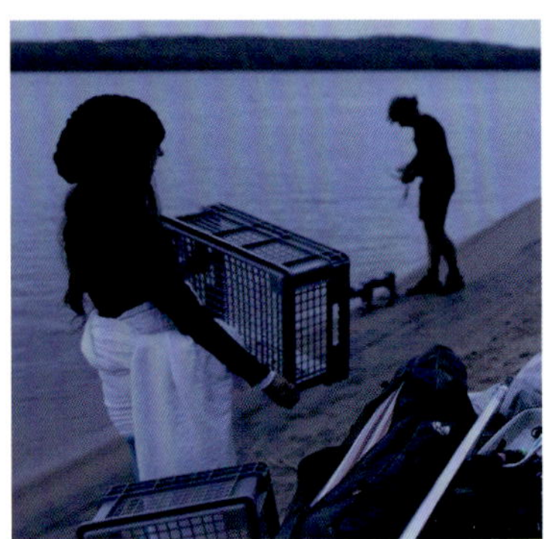

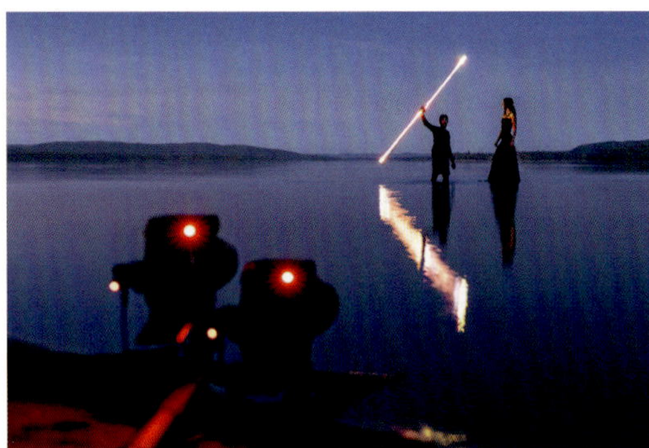

LEFT **You can see Kim holding her plastic crate, and the height difference between us when she stands on two stacked crates in the water (second image).**

CAMERA SETTINGS AND TOOLS

Refer to the section for the type of sky you are shooting (blue hour, stars, and so on) for our suggested initial camera settings and preferred tools.

COMPOSITION

Regardless of the type of beach you shoot at, composition is often a considerable challenge. The orientation of most beaches usually doesn't offer a lot of options to move left or right, limiting the possibilities of aligning your subject with the Sun's glow, the Moon, the Milky Way, or whatever else you want to include.

In addition, when the beach slopes steeply downward it's nearly impossible to get a low enough perspective to make the subject appear above the

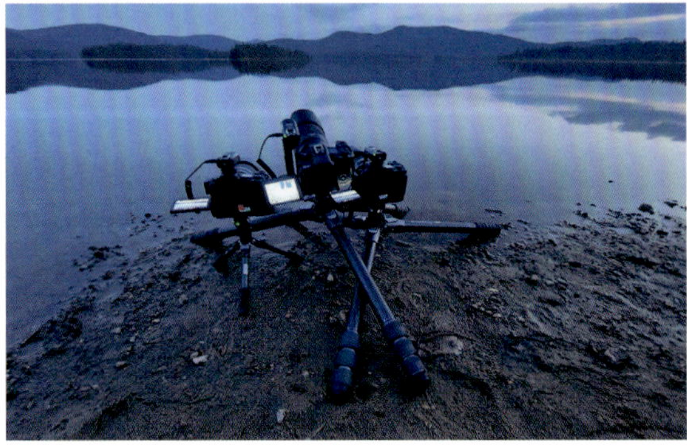

horizon line in your composition. If you're shooting at a lake with a steep beach, your best option is to get your camera quite close to the surface of the water, but be careful not to get it wet!

Case Study **Beach**

Planning a trip when you don't know the area you're visiting can be tricky. Even if you find a location that is well oriented and seems good from images you see on the internet, it's hard to gauge precisely what it will look like once you get there. When we were planning a trip to Vietnam, we did our best to choose a promising, west-facing beach to shoot during the blue hour, with some nice black rock formations in the water. What we could not predict, though, is what the beach would look like at night.

We only had three nights to create in, so we were traveling with the minimum amount of gear we could, but this turned out to be a bad idea. Once we got to the beach, we realized it was much steeper than expected, and our tripods were not sturdy or high enough for the task.

On our first night, we went shooting, despite our jet-lag. As it was getting darker during the blue hour, we saw bright green lights far away in the water. We were puzzled. What could they be? As usual, we allowed the unpredictable to influence our process, quickly adjusting our composition to include the green lights. The following day we learned that these strong green lights were coming from boats in the Gulf of Thailand, and were used to attract plankton as they fished for squid. Often, it's the unexpected elements that make an image more special.

DID YOU NOTICE?
The water got quite deep, quite quickly, but we wanted Kim to stand close to the surface. Luckily, there was a small rock formation that Kim could stand on, which you can see in the image if you look closely. However, to get there, we both had to walk slowly out over loose rocks, hip-deep in water.

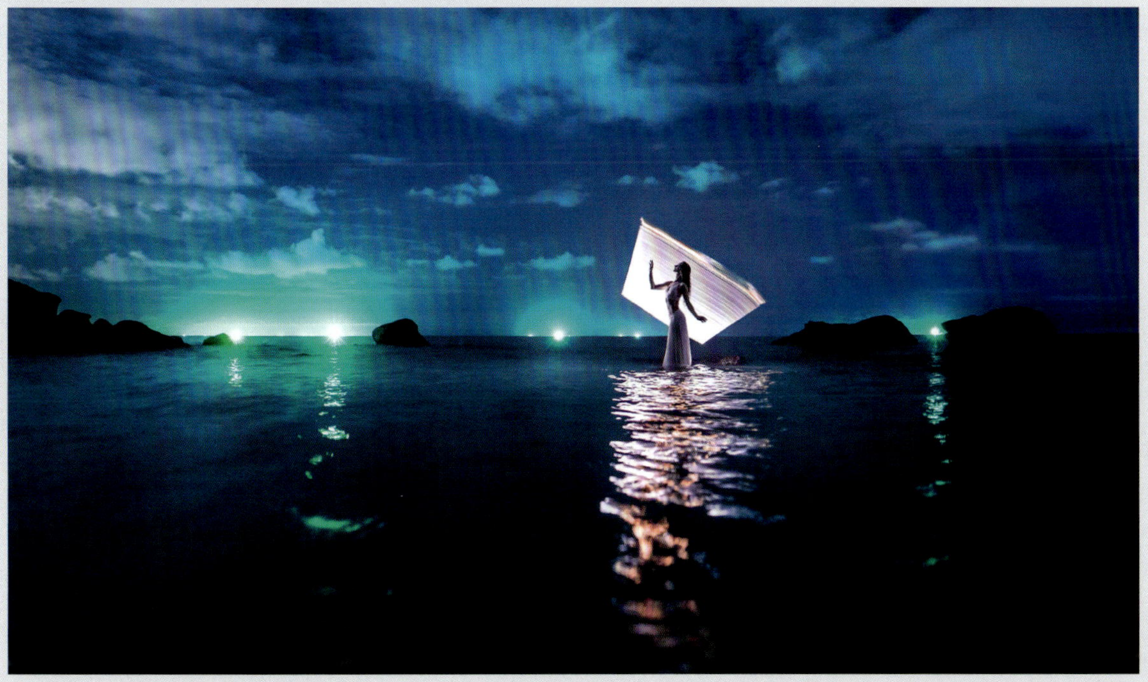

Environment: Beach | **Focal length:** 24mm | **Exposure:** 1.6 sec. (exposure and light painting), f/1.8, ISO 1600

Cityscape

All of the shooting scenarios presented so far have had one thing in common: avoiding light pollution and artificial lights that would affect the subject and foreground. Is that possible to achieve if you're shooting in an urban area? Yes, but it's not an easy task.

We explored creating in urban environments early in our journey, but it's not something we do anymore. The main reason is artistic choice; we prefer natural and vast landscapes where there's no human trace or readily recognizable features. We also prefer the experience of being in nature at night, away from civilization. But if you love cityscapes we can help you on your light-painting journey.

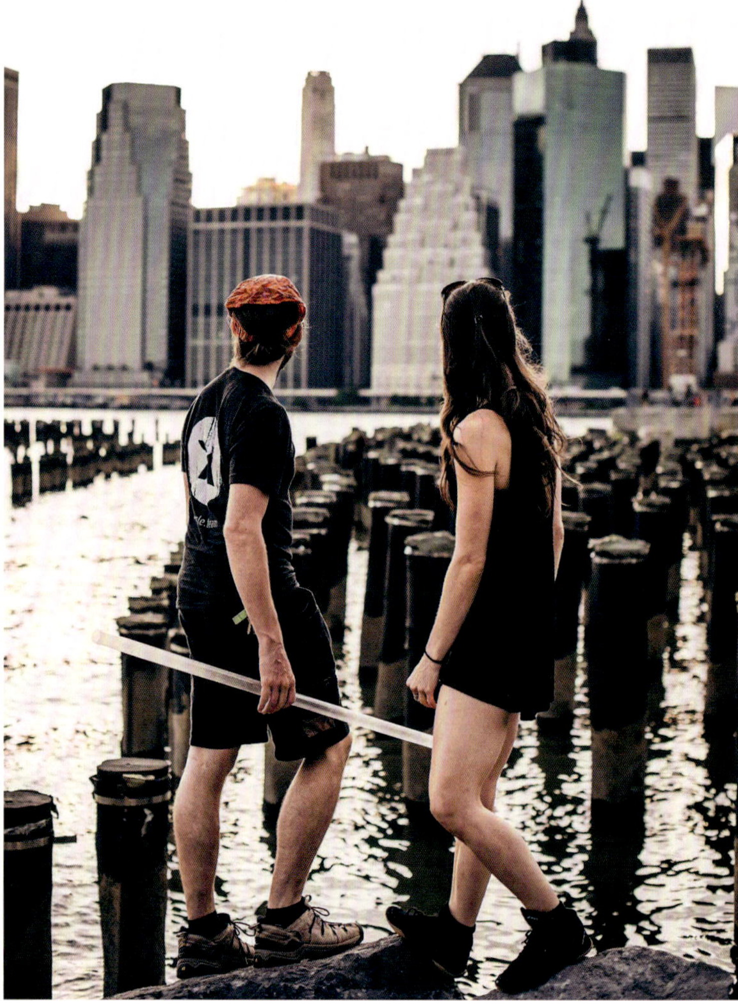

RIGHT **Image taken by our friend Efren Herrera.**

PLANNING

The main challenge is to find a shooting spot where you can minimize the ambient light while positioning your model to create a beautiful composition. The constraint of needing distance between the camera and the model, as well as space behind them for the light painter to move, limits the possibilities in urban settings. For a start, there will likely be more people around you while you shoot, which means more disturbance and potentially greater stress about your gear's safety, which makes the experience less enjoyable. To minimize that last issue, shooting with an extra person who stays close to the camera is a good idea.

When it comes to vantage points, there are multiple options for you to consider:

Street view: The hardest option is shooting at street level in the middle of a city. Flat lighting on your subject and foreground is almost impossible to avoid unless you can position yourself in a dark area, such as a park, where there aren't any streetlights or lights from buildings behind the camera.

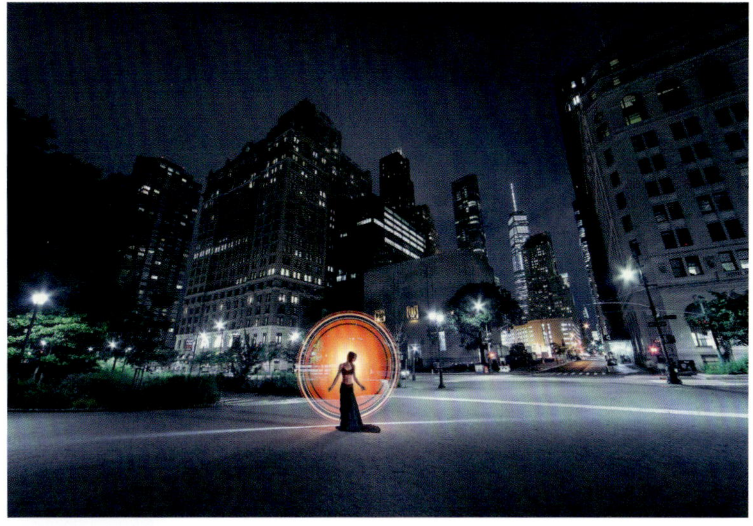

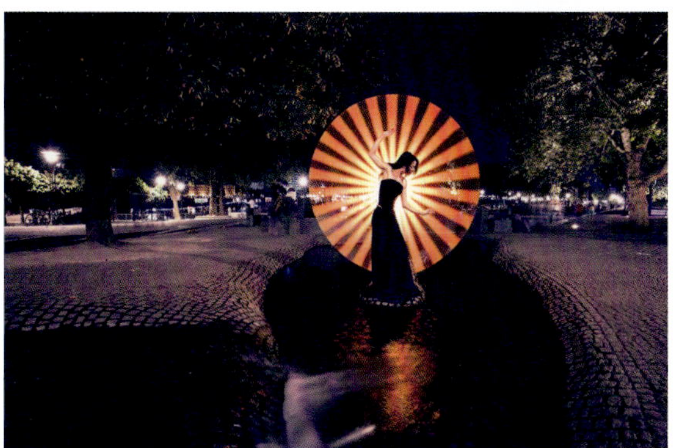

ABOVE **Although this scene is fairly bright, you can see shadows on Kim's body, indicating there's no light coming directly from the front. In this case, we were in a park with very little light behind the camera.**

LEFT **You can guess what is causing the flat, orange light in this shot... This is what happens when you shoot too close to streetlights!**

Higher perspective: An alternative option is to look for a higher perspective, from a balcony or rooftop that offers a city view from above. Make sure there aren't any security lights that can't be turned off, though. We wouldn't encourage anyone to trespass to access a shooting location, so always ask permission from the person in charge of the building.

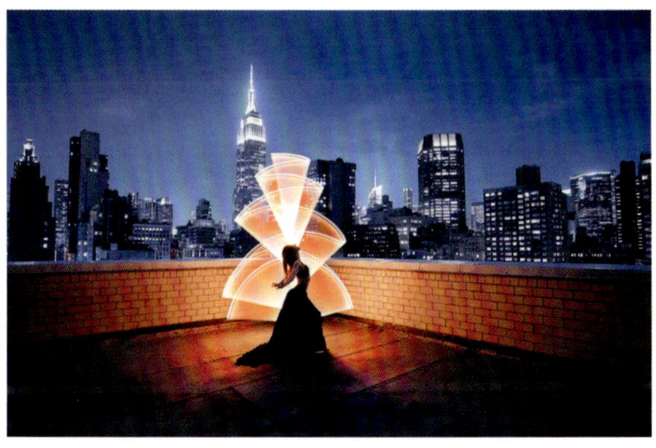

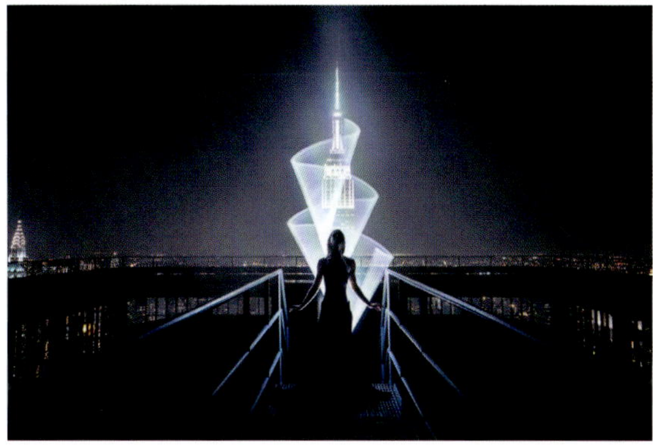

you more freedom, enabling you to use the city lights as a close and slightly more abstract background.

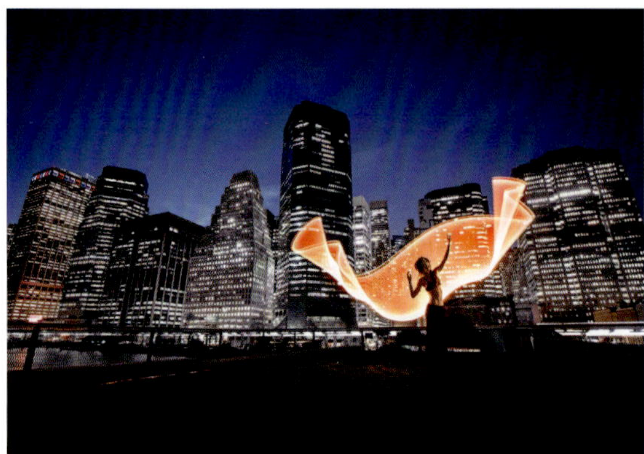

ABOVE **In this image, the light-painting shape creates the lighting on Kim's body. The buildings create a background full of lights, whereas the foreground is barely noticeable.**

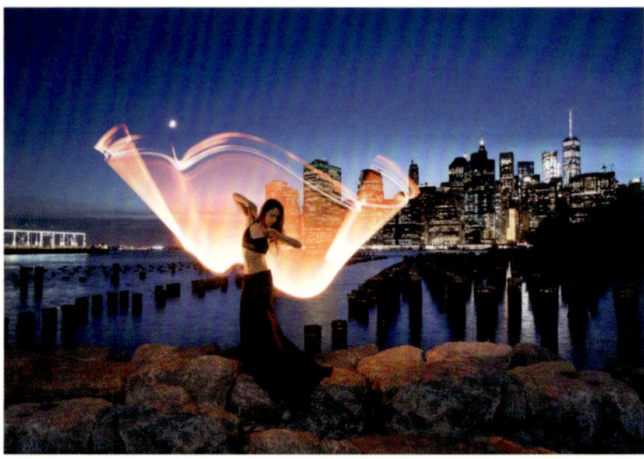

ABOVE **Finding a location slightly further from the city and using the skyline as a background can be a great option.**

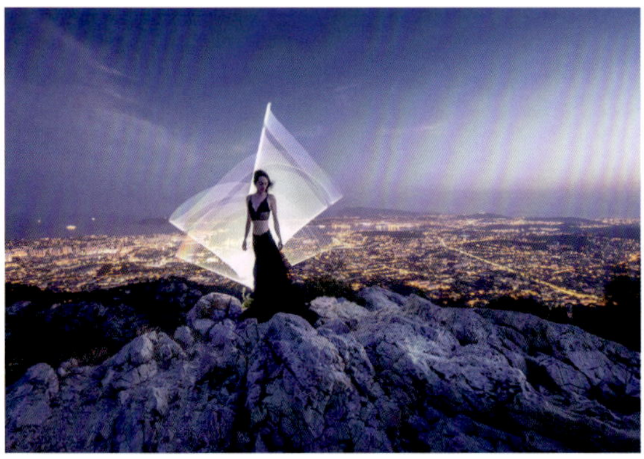

ABOVE **A vantage point that stands above the city (a nearby hill or a park with a viewpoint, for example) allows the city to become a more abstract display of lights in the background.**

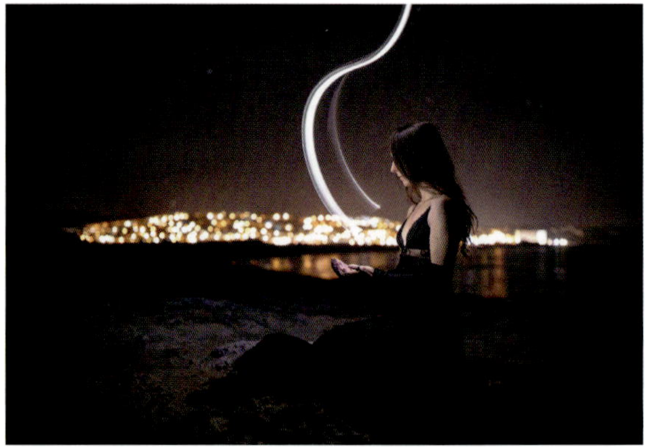

ABOVE **This image was shot with a 35mm lens using a Black tube. As we were both close to the camera, Eric was able to light paint from outside the frame.**

CAMERA SETTINGS

If you are shooting during the blue hour, refer to the settings on page 82, Blue hour. If you're shooting during nighttime, your optimal settings will depend on how much ambient light there is.

TOOLS

The tool you choose should be influenced by the colors of the surroundings, which can vary greatly. Is it blue hour? Nighttime? What is the dominant color of the cityscape? Do you want your light painting to harmonize with it or contrast with it?

Case Study **Cityscape**

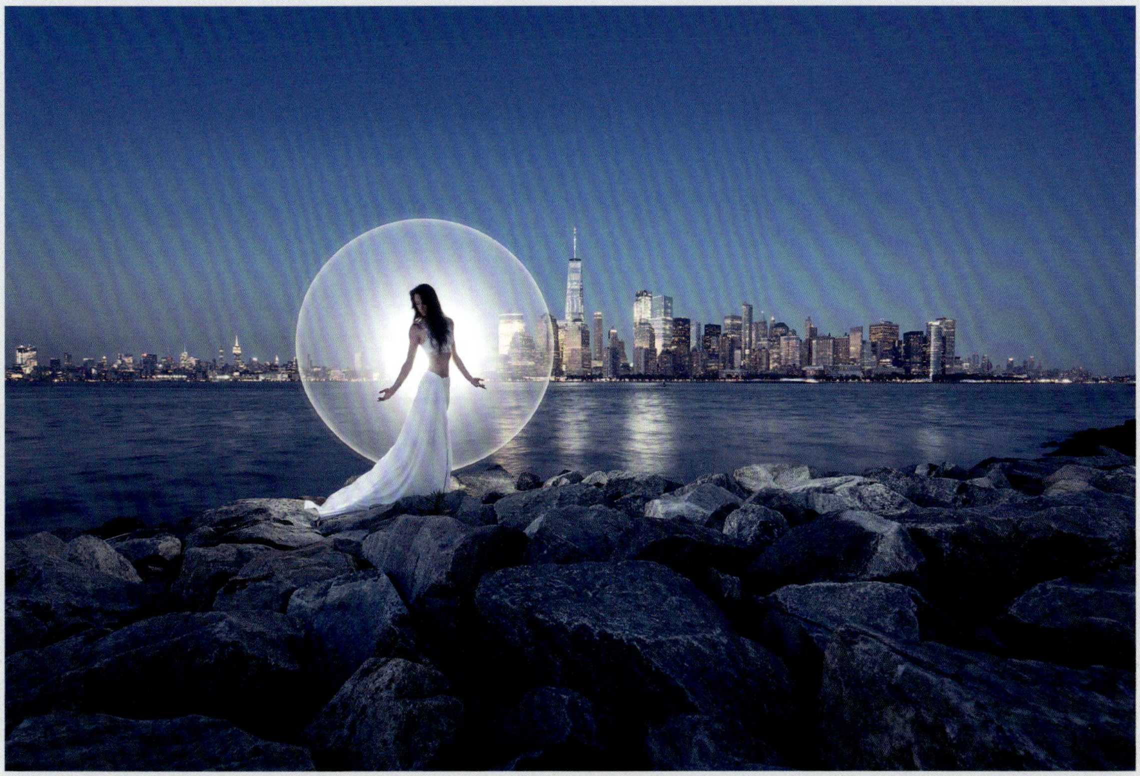

Environment: City | **Focal length:** 16mm | **Exposure:** 2.2 sec. (exposure and light painting), f/10, ISO 400

Whenever we're traveling, we try to meet and create with new people, even if we are only in town for one evening. It's always a good experience to see the city from their perspective while sharing ours. Our expectations about the images are not usually high, as the technique we use is not easy to integrate into a cityscape, but the outcome is not what motivates us during these nights.

On this occasion, it was a warm summer evening, and our new friend Chris had taken us out of the city to show us this beautiful view. The natural elements leading to the skyline in the background really pleased us, which is probably one of the main reasons this image is our favorite of its kind. The session ended up being quite short, as the city lights quickly became too strong and forced us to stop. When we're shooting in a city, we also enjoy how it can make people curious. Some stay and watch, waiting to ask what we're doing. When they see the result on the screen, they light up, which can lead to interesting conversations.

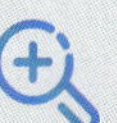 **DID YOU NOTICE?**

It almost looks like this image was captured during the day. This is because it was taken during civil twilight, which is much earlier than our usual shooting time. We generally warm up and do some test series during civil twilight, so we're ready when the ambient light is optimal, and then shoot until the streetlights cast a strong light on Kim, which didn't take long in this instance! However, after the session, we agreed that our favorite shot of the night was one taken during the test series, when it was technically "too early."

Star trails

Incorporating star trails into images offers a unique way to play with time and how we visualize it, allowing us to capture the Earth's rotation. The capture process and post-processing technique are more complex than many other scenarios, which is why we consider it an "advanced" option. We'll address the post-processing later (see page 150), and for now focus on what happens in the field.

PLANNING

To create the best star trails, choose a location that is free from artificial lights, ideally far from urban areas, so that you avoid any light pollution. It is also a good idea to choose a night when the Moon is below the horizon (or not visible), and you want a cloudless sky so your trails aren't obscured.

Be ready to stay on location for a considerable amount of time. Depending on the image you are looking for, it can take anywhere between five minutes and a few hours to capture what you need. Although five-minute star trail images aren't common practice, even very short trails can add a little bit of magic to an image. If for any reason you can't afford to stay more than a few minutes on location to capture extended star trails, we would say do what you can with the time available to you, rather than not trying.

To maximize your trails, consider using a longer focal length, as the focal length will influence the time needed to see star trails in the sky. If you shoot with a 50mm lens, rather than a 14mm, for example, the same five-minute trails become more impactful.

Also, the further a star is from a celestial pole, the longer its trail will appear to be. The north and south celestial poles are two imaginary extensions of the Earth's poles into space, which appear to remain fixed in the sky, as all other celestial objects (stars, planets, deep-sky objects) seem to rotate around them. So, if you were to shoot toward the east or west

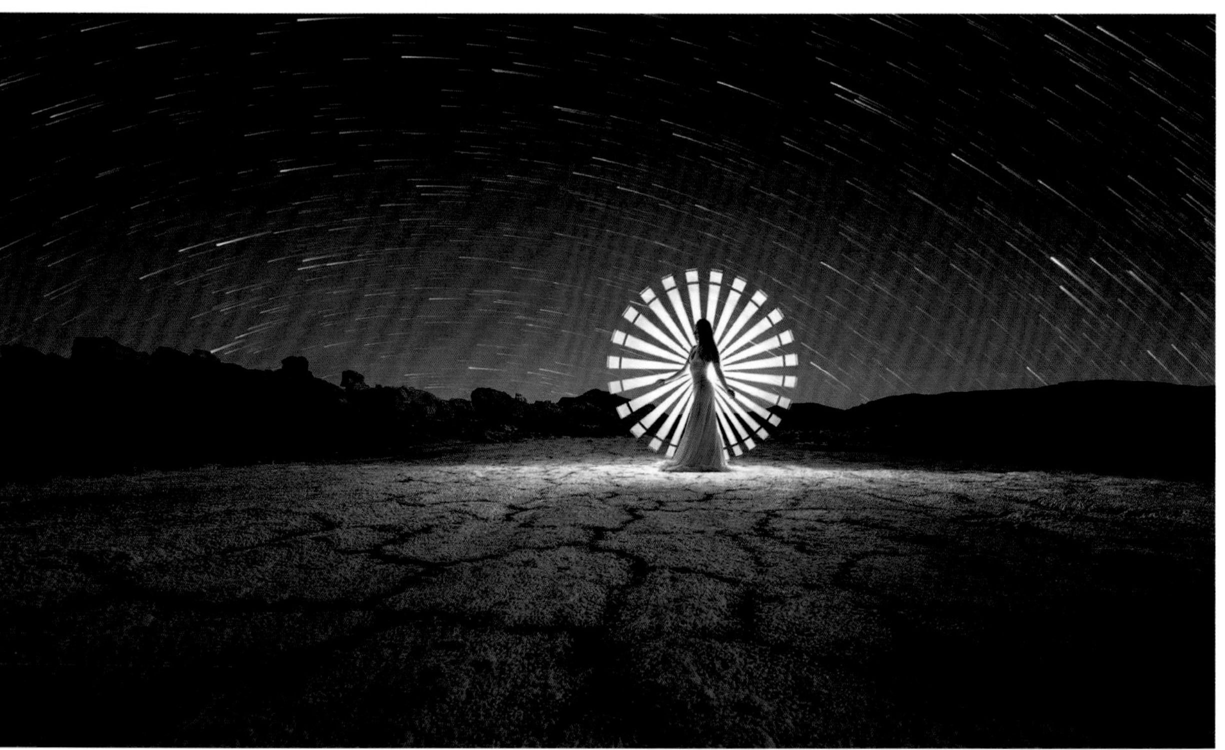

(furthest away from the celestial poles) with a 35mm or 50mm focal length you could obtain star trails that complement your image in just a few minutes.

In the field, we mainly use PhotoPills Night AR to help us plan our composition. It allows us to visualize the star trails patterns based on the direction our camera is pointing in and also makes it easy to identify the celestial pole when needed.

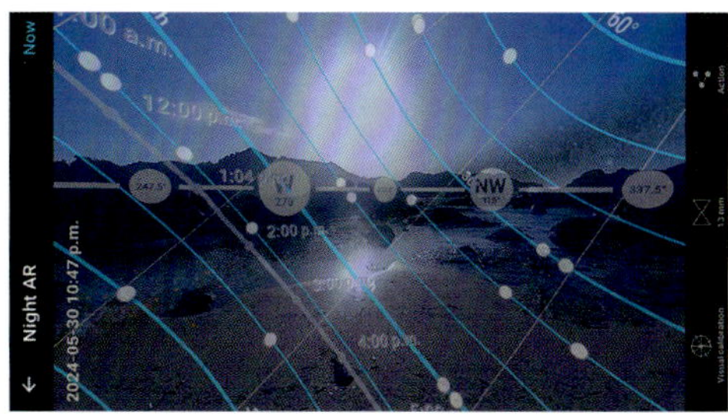

ABOVE **In PhotoPills, the blue lines with moving gray dots show the path of the stars.**

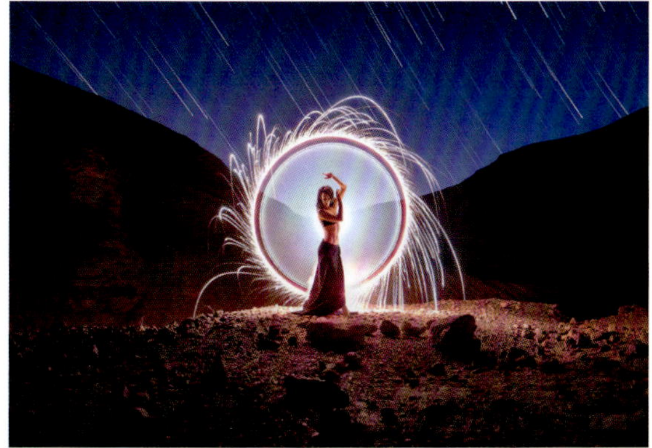

ABOVE **This picture was taken in the northern hemisphere, with the camera pointing west.**

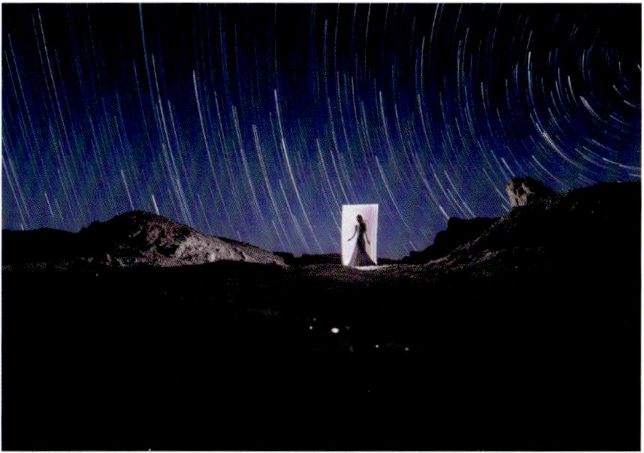

ABOVE **This image was made in the southern hemisphere, shooting southeast with the celestial pole outside the frame at the right.**

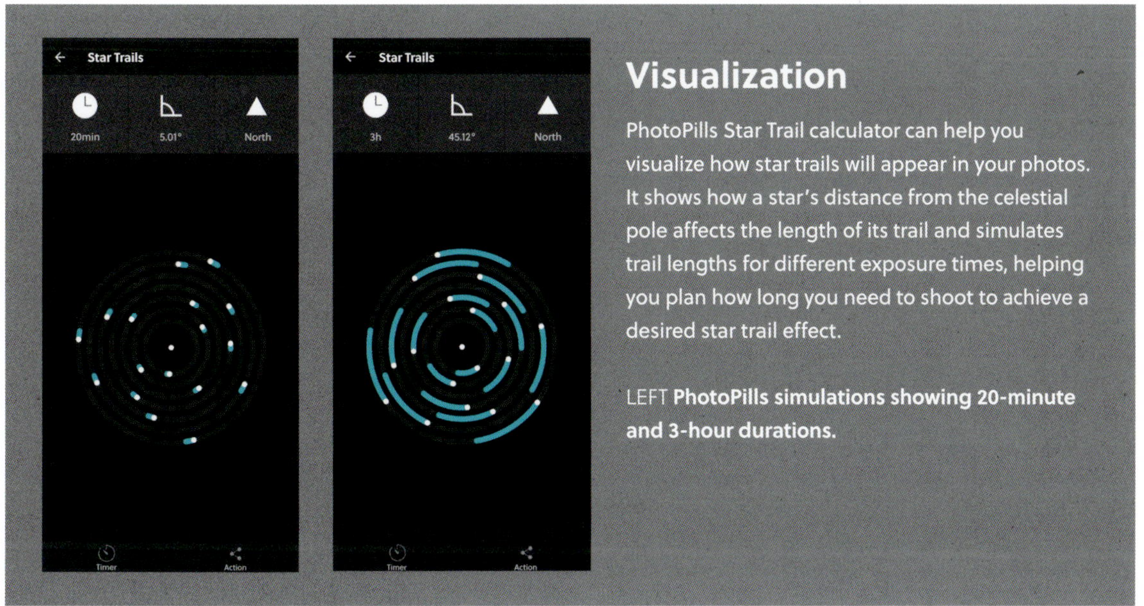

Visualization

PhotoPills Star Trail calculator can help you visualize how star trails will appear in your photos. It shows how a star's distance from the celestial pole affects the length of its trail and simulates trail lengths for different exposure times, helping you plan how long you need to shoot to achieve a desired star trail effect.

LEFT **PhotoPills simulations showing 20-minute and 3-hour durations.**

CAPTURE

The photography process is divided into two parts: one to capture the light painting and another for the star trails. During post-processing, these images are combined to create a final composite. It's not easy, but it's worth the effort.

Part 1: Light painting

Once you have chosen a composition with a pattern of star trails in mind, the light-painting element is pretty similar to shooting with the stars (see page 86) and you can start with the same settings:

→ **Exposure:** 8 sec. (light painting ~2 sec.), f/1.8, ISO 3200
→ **White balance:** 3200K
→ **Flashlight power:** 50–100 lumens

I often make a series of about ten light-painting images. Then I review them and check that the shot (or more than one if we're lucky) looks good and doesn't need anything else. This original frame is the most important thing to me, because there's always a possibility that I might not to use the star trails in the shot. I see adding the star trails to the image as a potential bonus, so the original frame needs to stand on its own.

Even though PhotoPills Night AR gives me an idea of the patterns of the star trails, I still want to confirm that the movement of the brightest stars will look good with the rest of the composition. To do this, I scroll through the pictures I've created in my initial series, looking at the sky and the movement of the brightest stars. If I'm satisfied, I move to the next step; if not, I adjust the composition and create another series.

Part 2: The star trails

When I'm happy with my original frame, I change the settings to capture the star trails:

→ **Exposure:** 30 sec., f/1.8, ISO 200
→ **White balance:** 3200K

Although you could change the focus at the same time as the rest of the settings, and make the stars appear sharp, I prefer it when the star trails look slightly larger, so I leave the focus alone.

I usually let the camera's timelapse mode take images for 30–60 minutes, which gives me 60–120 images, even though I rarely use more than 40 to create star trails. The reason I capture longer trails is because it gives me a wider selection to choose from, so I've got more options for the final composition. Before starting the timelapse sequence, make sure you've got enough space on your memory card and sufficient battery power, as any delay between pictures will result in visible gaps in the star trails.

If your camera doesn't have a timelapse mode and you don't have an intervalometer (an external device for triggering timelapse sequences), you can use the burst mode on your camera instead. You'll need to press the remote trigger from time to time to make sure the camera keeps shooting, so it's a more tedious way of working, but it works if you don't have other options. Alternatively, you can capture star trails in a single long exposure.

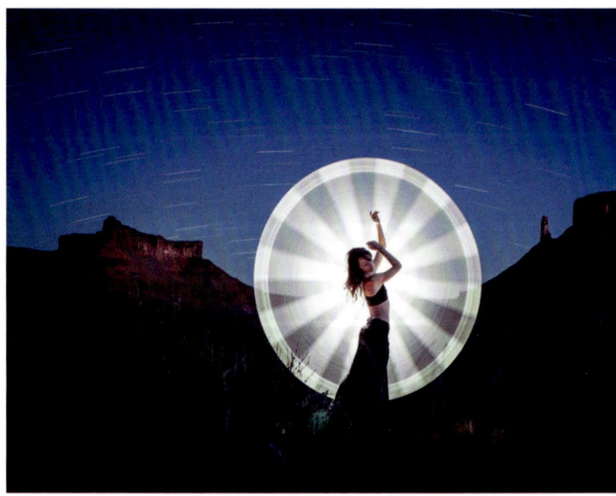

Exposure: 14 mins. (Bulb mode), f/8, ISO 800

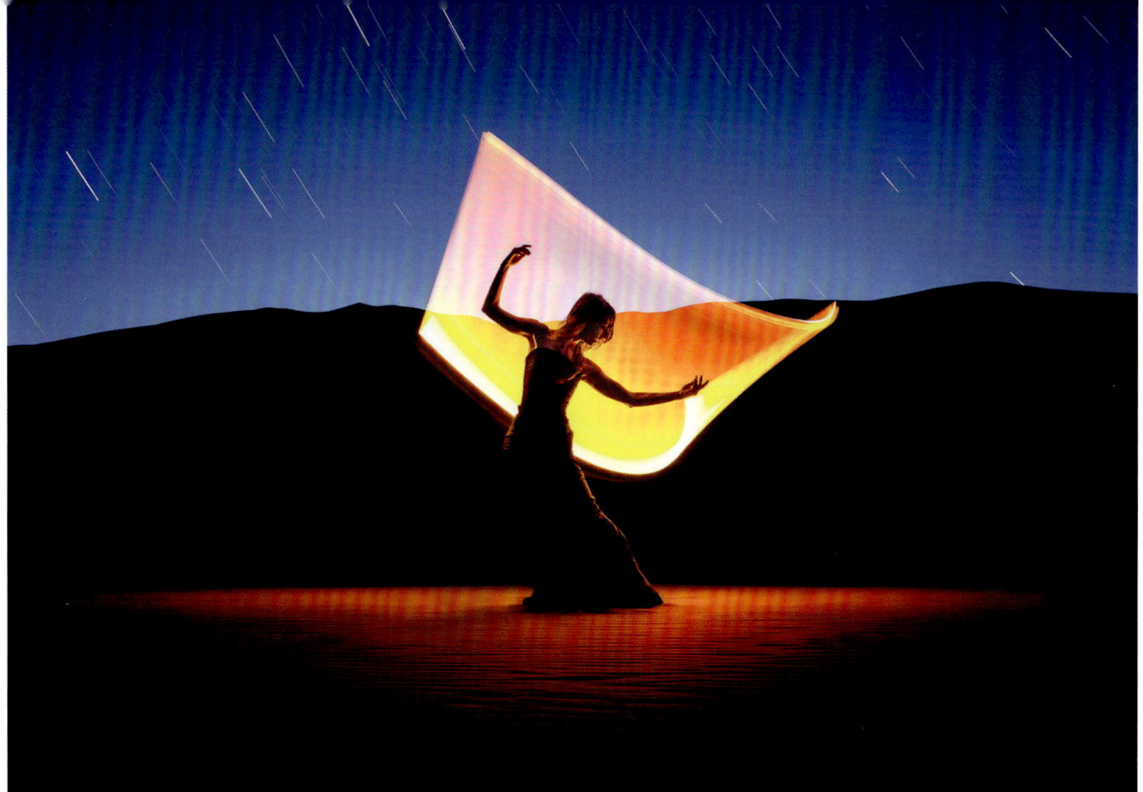

These are two of our early attempts at capturing star trails and light painting. They are composites of two exposures: one for the light painting made during the blue hour, then a second single exposure for the sky taken at the end of nautical twilight. We had to make sure we didn't touch the camera between the two shots.

In theory, it's also possible to capture the light painting and star trails in a single exposure, although this is not something we have attempted or would recommend (it would be too restrictive and the quality of the final image would suffer).

Stacked images vs. long exposure

Although it's possible to record star trails in a single exposure, we prefer to stack our images for several reasons:

→ The risk of something going wrong during a single 30-minute exposure is too high. There are lots of things that can ruin a shot, including airplanes, satellites, the headlights from a passing car, and so on. If you shoot multiple images, these elements can be dealt with more easily in post-production.

→ There's more control over the final result, as you can select a specific part of a trail that works best with the overall composition.

→ I often use "Comet Mode" in StarStaX to give the star trails a fading, comet-like effect when I combine my individual files, which would be impossible to achieve with a single exposure.

Case Study **Star trails**

We have shot at this location at least ten times over the years, but this was the first time the conditions were ideal for shooting after the blue hour. By ideal, I mean not cloudy, not extremely windy, and not cold. These rock formations are close to Favàritx lighthouse, in Menorca, and as you might imagine, a lighthouse has a very strong artificial light that we want to avoid!

That evening, we were teaching a group during a PhotoPills camp, and at night, a lot of the photographers wanted to capture the lighthouse with the Milky Way. We split off from the group and found a spot in the rocky formation where we could hide from the beams of light and keep shooting without photobombing anyone else.

After a few light-painting series, we started the timelapse to capture the star trails. Most of the time when we shoot star trails we either leave the camera running and move away to keep creating, or go back to the car so we can warm up. However, on this occasion we had to wait about 45 minutes in the dark; we had to keep our lights off to capture the foreground in the timelapse and couldn't risk trying to walk anywhere in the darkness. So, we simply gazed at the stars, contemplating the universe.

DID YOU NOTICE?

You can see reflections of the brightest star trails at the bottom of the image, which is not an easy thing to capture. The receding tide had created ephemeral pools of water that transformed the landscape, but the water needed to be very still for a long period of time to create the clear reflections.

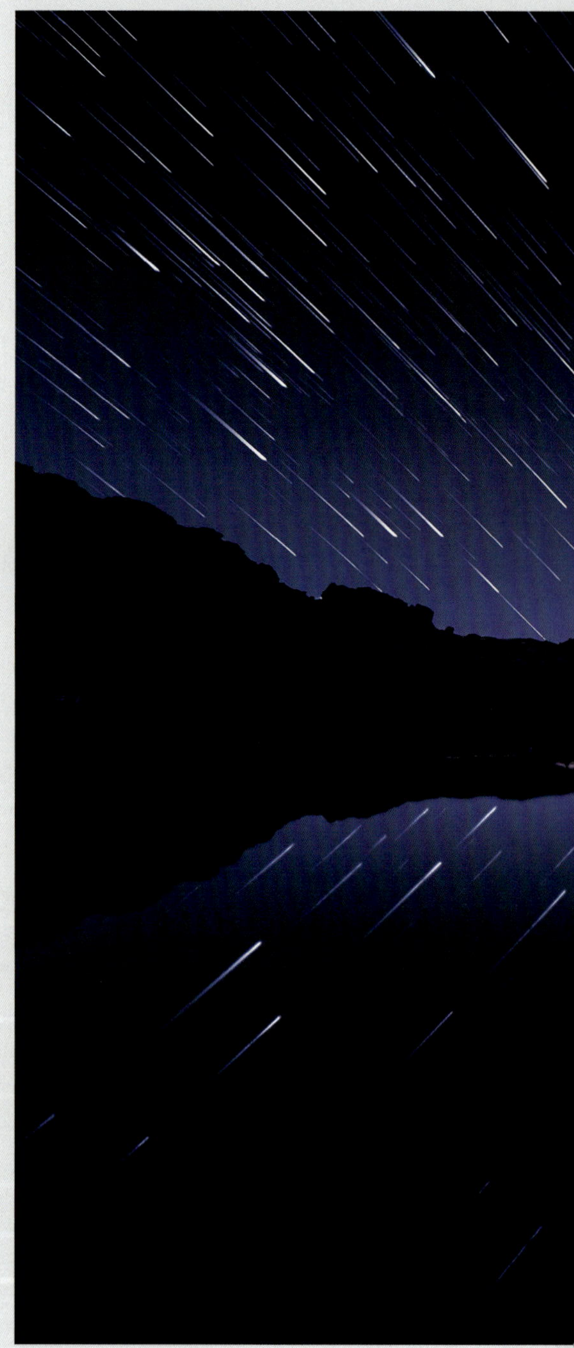

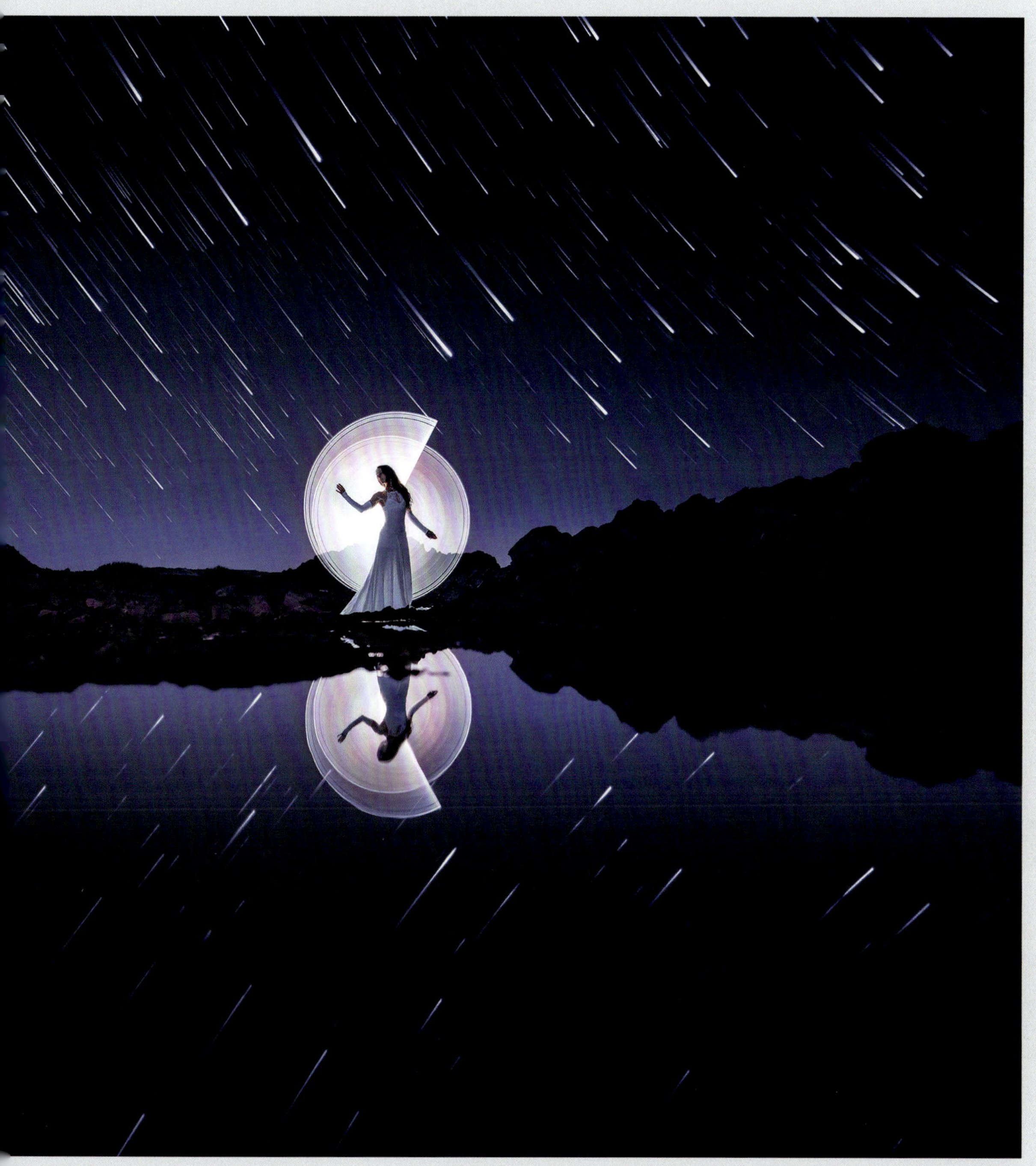

Environment: Rock pool | **Focal length:** 20mm | **Exposure (light painting):** 4 sec. (light painting ~2 sec.), f/1.4, ISO 1600

Exposure (star trails): 30 sec. (40 pictures), f/1.4, ISO 1600

Auroras

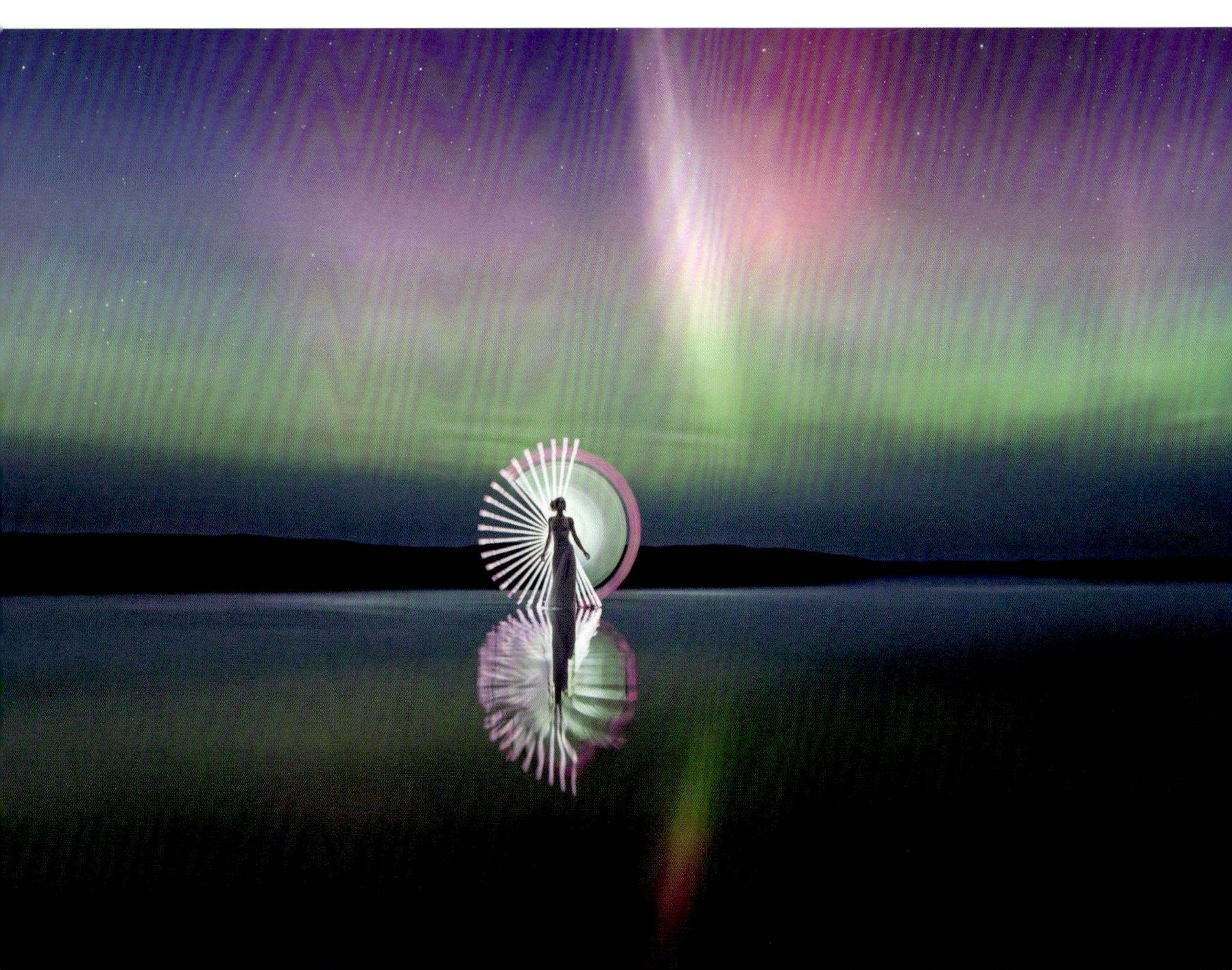

Creating outdoor light-painting images with an aurora as a secondary subject is without doubt one of the most complex and advanced scenarios, but it is also a truly magical phenomenon to include in your photographs. Auroras are visible most nights when the sky gets dark at high latitudes and are more active around the spring and fall equinoxes.

We're not going to go into depth about the science behind them, but auroras occur when charged particles blasted from the Sun interact with Earth's magnetic field (the invisible shield redirecting the solar wind around our planet). As they travel toward the poles, the particles collide with gasses, mainly oxygen and nitrogen, in our upper atmosphere, producing millions of tiny, rapid flashes that we see as colorful dancing lights in the sky.

PLANNING

Although auroras are impossible to predict with complete accuracy, there are a few key points that will help you plan and prepare your light paintings with them. The first of these is to know when they will occur. Looking at the KP index forecast (which measures geomagnetic activity on a scale from 0–9) can give you an idea of the estimated aurora potential up to three days in advance, but it's not good for monitoring aurora activity in real time. Broadly speaking, the higher the KP-index, the further from the poles the auroras become visible.

There are plenty of aurora forecast apps, some of which will send you notifications when the prediction level reaches a threshold of your choice. We currently use Aurora Alerts and SpaceWeatherLive, which provide a pretty accurate forecast indicating the location and intensity of the aurora within a 15–45 minute timeframe. That's not a lot of notice to pack your gear and get on location, but is as close to a "live" update as you can expect.

Keep in mind that this is often referred to as "aurora chasing," and there will be nights when you're out for a long time and nothing happens. This is part of what makes it even more special when you witness a strong aurora.

As well as being there at the right time, you also need to be in the right place, and the closer you are to the magnetic poles, the better your chances of seeing the aurora. During a strong geomagnetic storm you can see the dancing lights over the horizon at mid-latitude locations, quite far from the auroral oval (a ring-shaped zone around each magnetic pole where auroras are most frequently observed).

For that reason, find a location with as little obstruction over the horizon as you can, pointing north (if you are in the northern hemisphere) or south (in the southern hemisphere). If you can find a location that gives you a bit of freedom in terms of your composition, that's a big bonus. Things change very quickly and you might have to adjust your framing to keep up with the show. If you happen to be close within the auroral oval, the aurora will not only dance over the horizon but above your head as well.

Just like shooting the Milky Way, you'll need a location with a cloudless sky, no moon (ideally), and minimal light pollution in order to see the aurora at its best. The darker your location, the better your chances of capturing vivid displays of light.

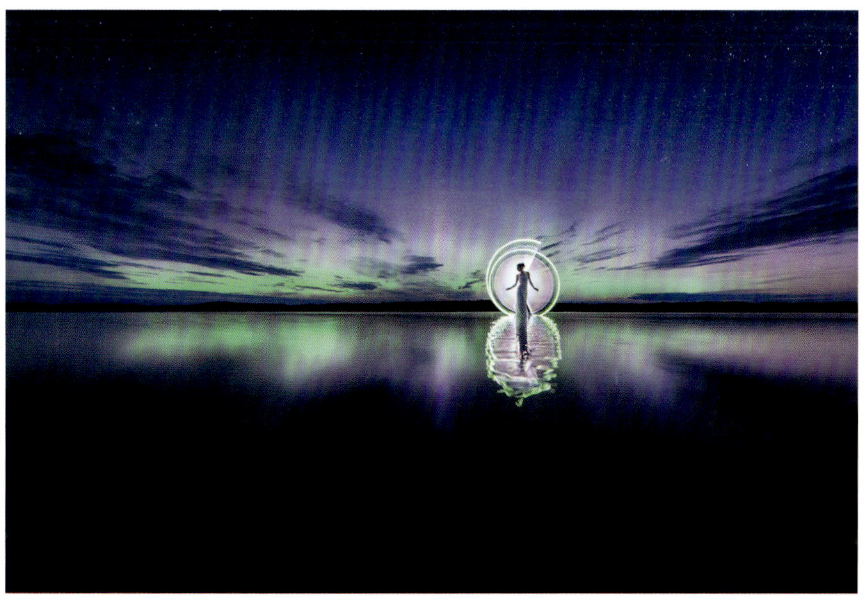

LEFT **Although a clear sky is recommended for auroras, sometimes you can get lucky with clouds and they can enhance your image.**

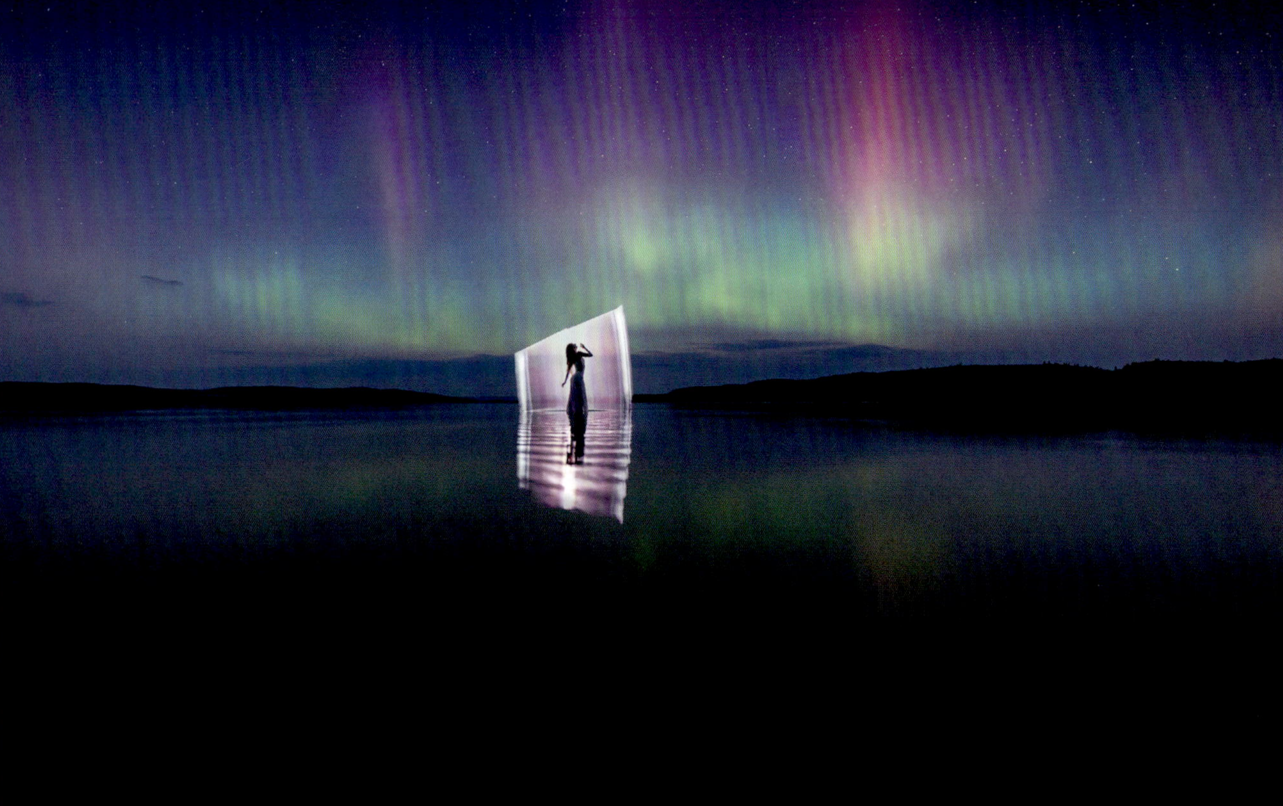

Exposure: 6 sec. (light painting ~2 sec.), f/1.8, ISO 1250 **White balance:** 3200K **Flashlight power:** 50–100 lumens **Tube:** Pinkish tube

CAMERA SETTINGS

The color in the sky will move at various speeds, depending on how active the aurora is. The faster it moves, the more dramatically it can impact your composition, as well as the brightness of the sky.

Auroras are fleeting and unpredictable, which adds to the excitement and challenge of capturing them. Your settings can vary widely, depending on the background, so your exposure will be informed mainly by your location (latitude) and the level of activity of the aurora at a given moment; sometimes it is visible only above the horizon, and at other times it can fill the entire sky.

As the light show evolves, you will need to think fast, adjust your framing rapidly, and/or change your settings every time you go back to the camera, especially if the aurora is very active. Similar to shooting during the blue hour, if you can operate your camera with your eyes closed it will save you some precious time.

Although there's undoubtedly a bit of luck involved in capturing a stunning image of light painting and auroras within a single exposure, we always try because it's unbelievably satisfying when it works. However, it also makes it very difficult to suggest any settings as a starting point: the best advice we can give is to expose for the background, then adjust the power of your light to balance with that.

TOOLS

Choosing a tool that matches or harmonizes with the environment is interesting in this instance, as the colors are pretty unique. Green, purple, pink, and red are not part of our usual spectrum of night sky colors. I find that these four tube/feather colors work best when shooting auroras:

→ Alien tube: Greenish/holographic color
→ CottonCandy tube: Pink/red
→ CottonCandy–Muted tube: Pink/red and desaturated green
→ Pinkish tube: desaturated pink

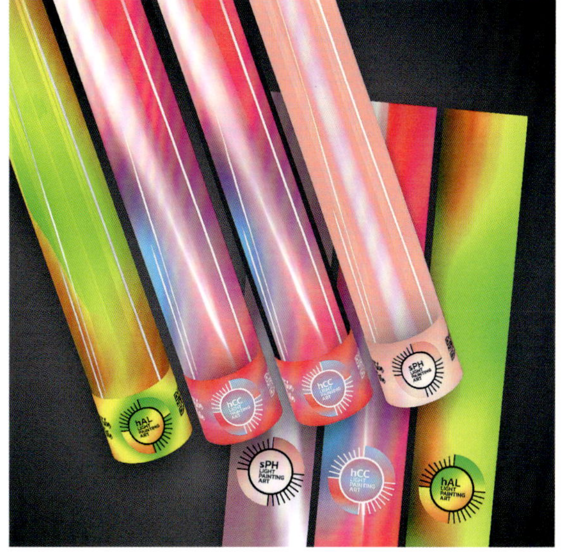

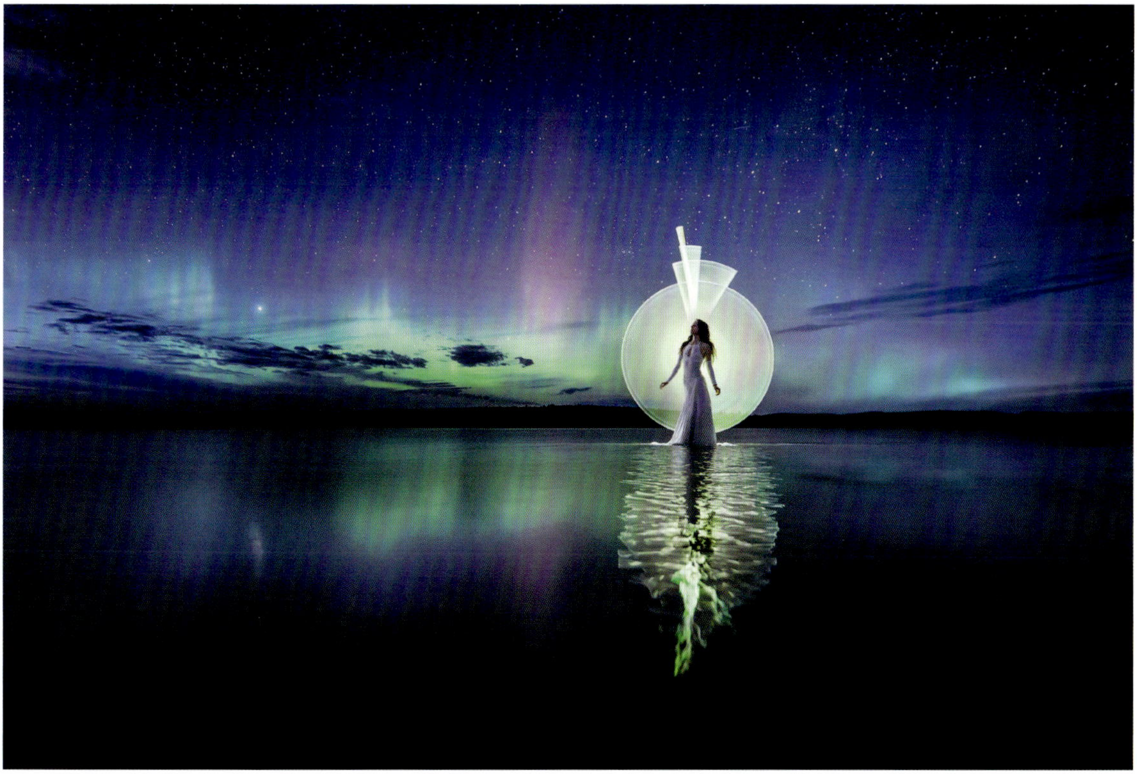

Exposure: 6 sec. (light painting ~2 sec.), f/1.4, ISO 1000 | **White balance:** 3200K | **Flashlight power:** 50–100 lumens | **Tube:** Alien tube

Case Study **Auroras**

Capturing auroras with light painting was something we had been contemplating for a while, slowly brainstorming how we could organize a trip far from home to make it happen. However, 2024 was a year marked by very high solar activity, and on a handful of occasions the conditions made it possible to witness and capture auroras at far more equatorial latitudes than usual. For us, that meant we were only a three-hour drive away from being able to see them over the horizon. Like many people photographing them for the first time, it was an exciting period, as we were quickly trying to learn and adapt to the unique conditions.

In mid-September, the alarm rang at 3am. It felt like we had just gone to bed after our last light-painting session, when we hadn't captured any auroras (the Moon was full in a cloudless sky, throwing an unflattering light on us). This particular morning, though, we were estimating that we might have a 30-minute window during astronomical twilight where the Moon would be close enough to the horizon for us to capture the auroras. The forecast looked favorable, so we kicked ourselves out of bed to drive and then hike to our location.

An hour and a half later we were starting to shoot, waiting for the Moon to get lower and hoping for some magic to happen. Another hour passed and it was getting close to the end of astronomical twilight. A thick cloud of fog was forming behind us, rapidly moving in our direction. But at the same moment, the aurora intensified, with beautiful pink beams of light piercing the sky. There it was. The magic we were waiting for.

We only had time to create this one image. Two minutes later, the fog reached us and the colors of nautical twilight appeared above the horizon. It was over for this aurora shoot, but we were filled with joy, knowing we had captured something truly special during that short-lived moment.

DID YOU NOTICE?

There is a yellow tint in the sky at the left side of the frame. When this image was created, the full moon was very close to the horizon (1.5 degrees elevation) and it set less than 15 minutes after this shot was taken. Yet although the Moon was low enough to be hidden behind the forest trees (which explains why it's not lighting Kim) we can still feel its presence when we look at the sky.

Environment: Lake | **Focal length:** 14mm | **Exposure:** 5 sec. (light painting ~2 sec.), f/1.8, ISO 800

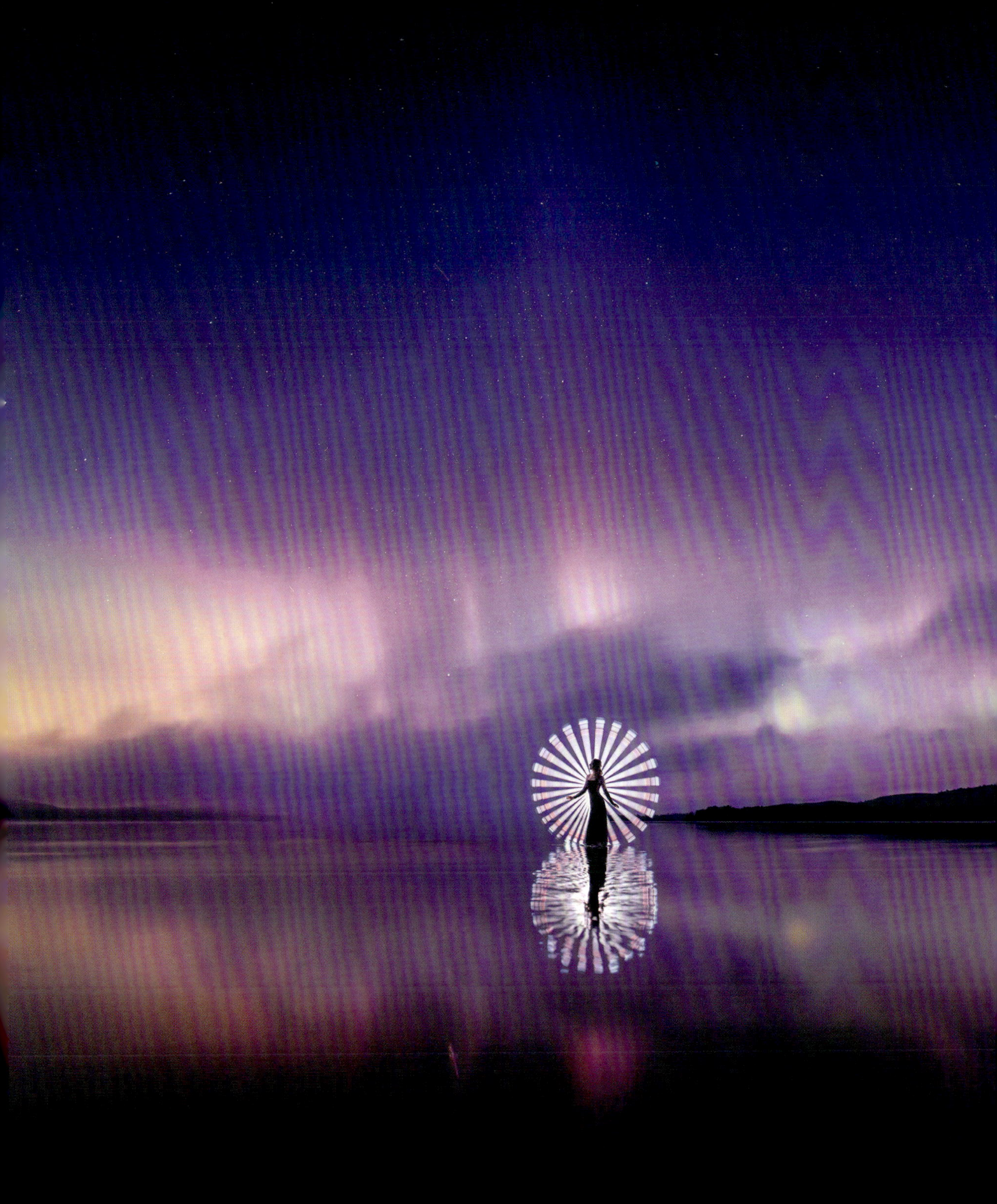

Windy nights

Wind can be encountered in almost any location, but it's up to you to decide if you want to embrace the additional challenge of shooting in windy conditions. When the average wind speed exceeds around 15mph (24km/h), we start to see environmental impacts that we need to consider when we shoot. Dust, sand, and light objects are raised from the ground, and small waves are formed on water. When the wind increases to 30mph (48km/h) the waves grow and it can be harder to walk against the wind, making it more difficult for your model to remain still during a long exposure. The average wind speed is usually accompanied by stronger wind gusts, and these sudden and brief increases can carry away light pieces of equipment without mercy.

The stronger the wind, the more challenging the process becomes. The temperature may be significantly colder, which never makes things easier, and it might become harder to communicate. On a more practical level, light-painting shapes are harder to create, because the long, lightweight tools we use can get pushed around, especially by gusts of wind. Precision of movement is decreased.

For these reasons, the rate of success is much lower than if the conditions are calm; the subject might be blurry due to movement in most of your shots, and many of your light-painting shapes won't look quite how you want them to. All the more reason to celebrate if you get one good image!

But does that mean we should stay comfy at home instead? You know the answer. If you're reading this, then the odds are you're not afraid to embrace a little bit of discomfort for the sake of creation. And as you'll see, the wind can also contribute some magic to your images.

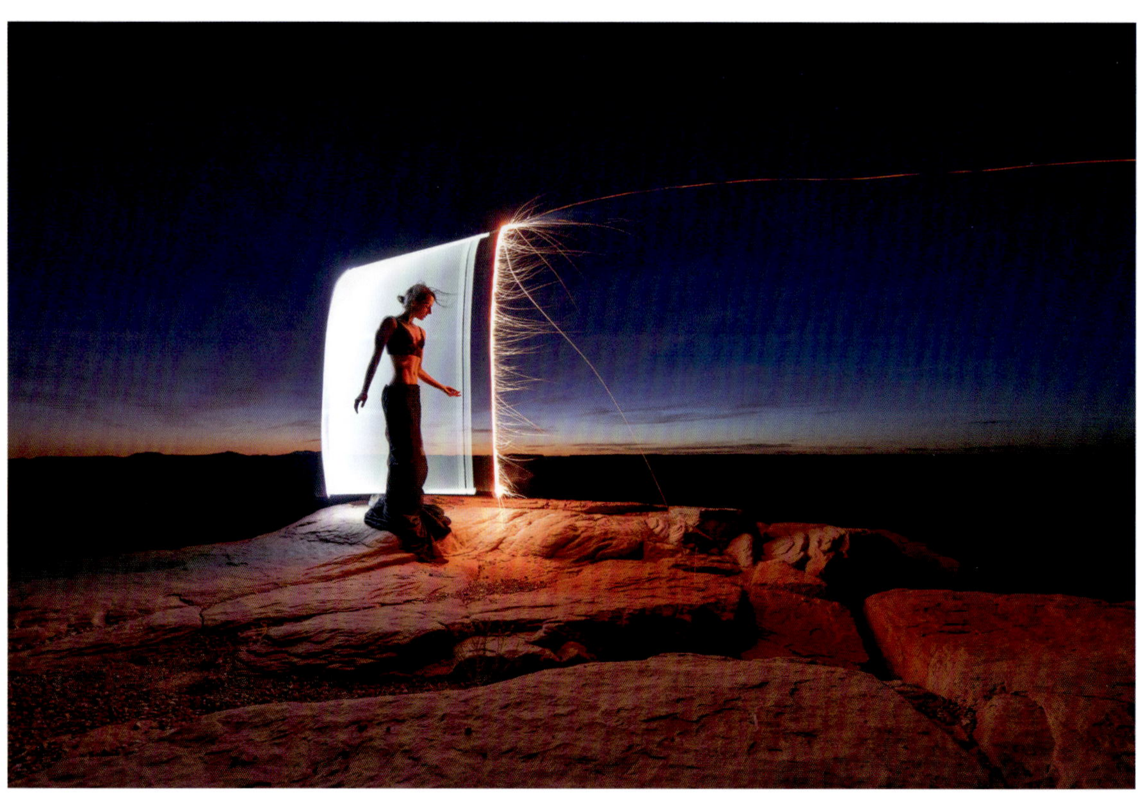

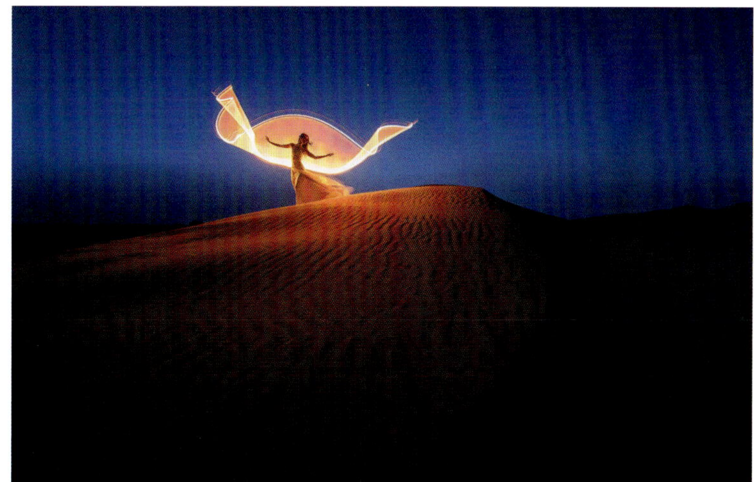

RIGHT **Can you freeze motion during a long exposure? It sounds counterintuitive, but with the right conditions, it's totally achievable. Notice how Kim's hair (and skirt) are captured in motion.**

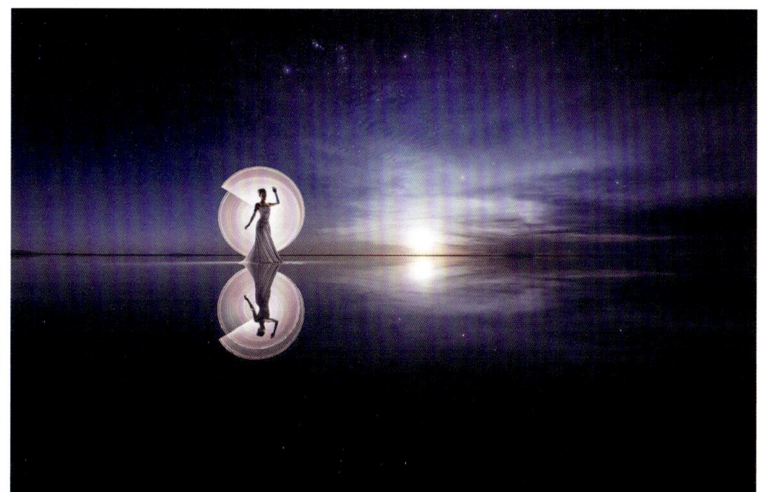

LEFT **Wind will affect reflections on the surface of water, especially if you're shooting in a shallow lake or a puddle. The spectrum can go from a pristine reflection to an absolute abstraction of shapes and colors. These images were taken a few days apart at Salar de Uyuni, Bolivia. The first during a windless night, the second on a windy evening.**

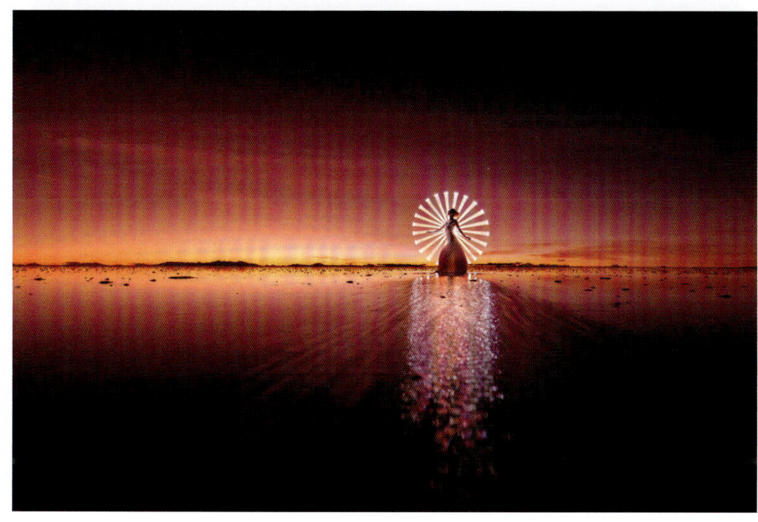

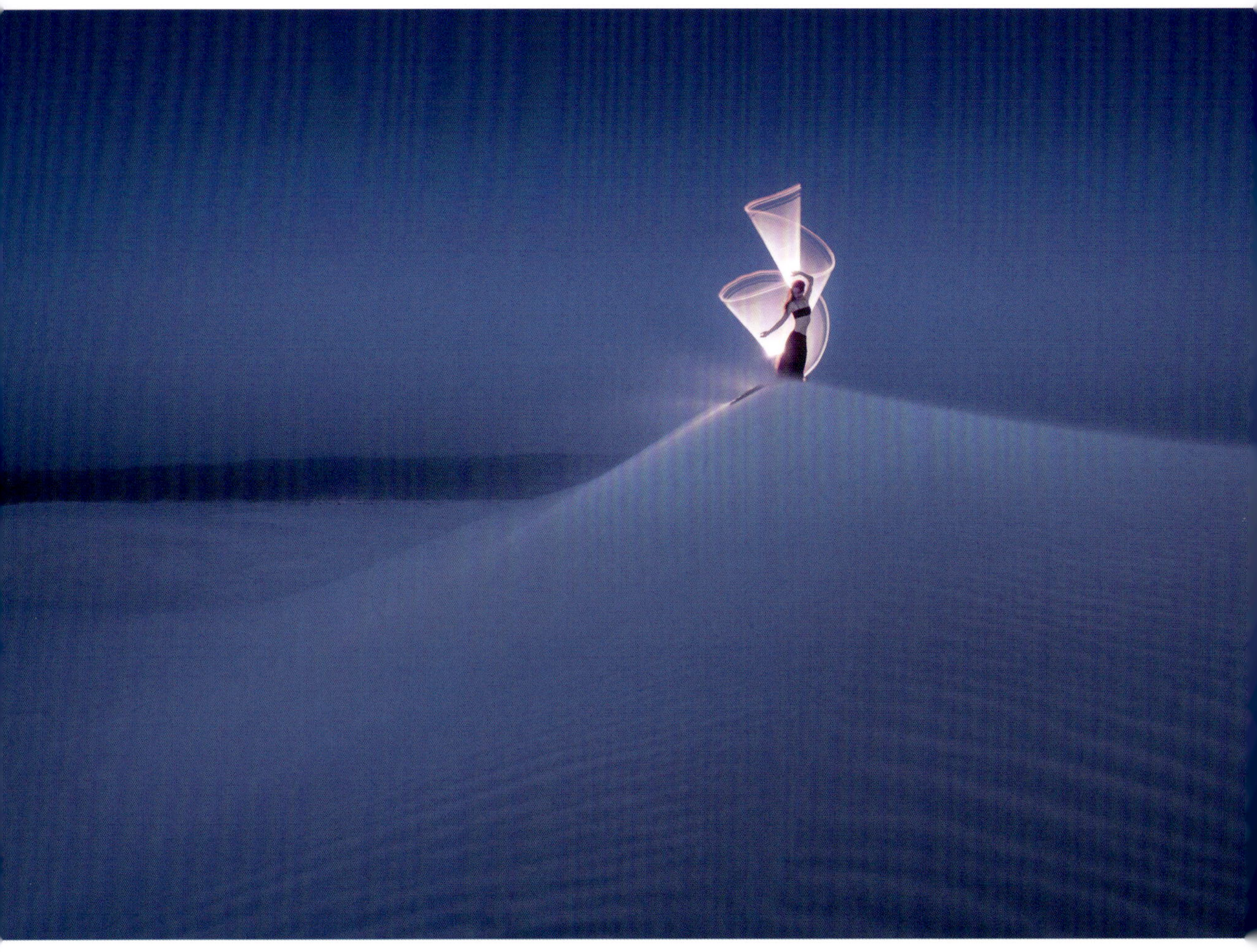

PLANNING

When it's windy, there are several ways that you can adapt the process to maximize your chances of getting an image you'll be satisfied with. To start with, use a sturdy tripod and shoot from a low perspective; add some weight to help stabilize your tripod if you need to. However, be careful around water, because if you shoot too low on a lakeshore there's a chance your camera might get splashed by a wind-driven wave.

Keep your gear organized in your bags while shooting, and keep the bags zipped up. Loose accessories, light-painting tools, and pieces of clothing can easily fly away in the wind. We've lost a few things in the past to learn this lesson!

ABOVE **Strong winds make it possible to capture moving sand if you are in sand dunes. But if you choose to venture there, make sure you keep sand out of your eyes, mouth, and nose!**

When it comes to your light painting, stick to very simple shapes. Doors and lateral shapes are safe options. A single trace at a fast speed will also limit the amount of time your subject is being lit by the tool and therefore improve your chances of a sharp-looking result; even an exposure that's ¼ second shorter can make a difference. But remember that if you move faster, you might have to increase the power of your flashlight to balance the brightness of the light trace with the background.

Finally, ask your model to wear clothing that is less "flowy." Avoid long dresses made of light fabric, and tidy their hair if the wind is strong. If that fails, find a bald bodybuilder in tight apparel to be your model...

CAMERA SETTINGS AND TOOLS

To see our suggested initial camera settings and preferred tools, refer to the section for the type of sky you are shooting (blue hour, stars, and so on).

COMPOSITION

Consider the wind direction in your overall composition. If your model's hair or clothes get lifted, their movement will subtly affect the image. We often try to place the subject so the wind direction draws the eye toward negative space, back to the center.

BELOW **The smoke and light cascading from the sparkler lead toward the negative space.**

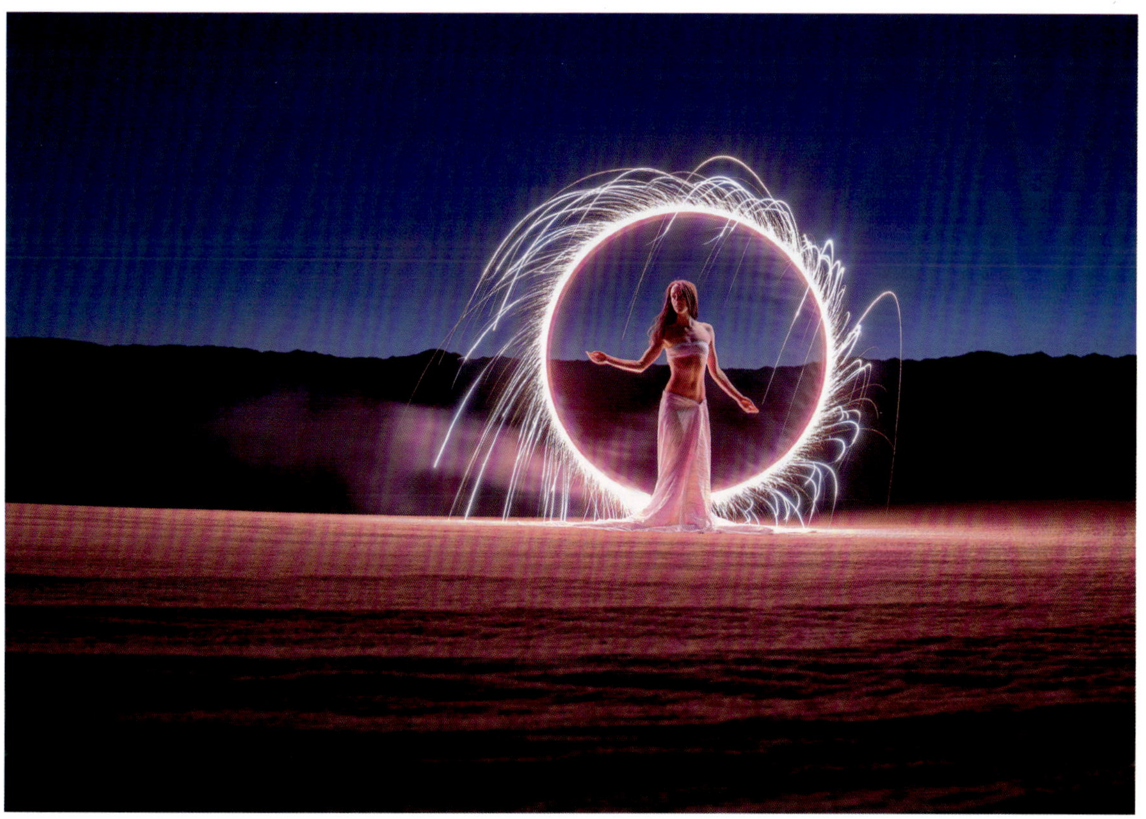

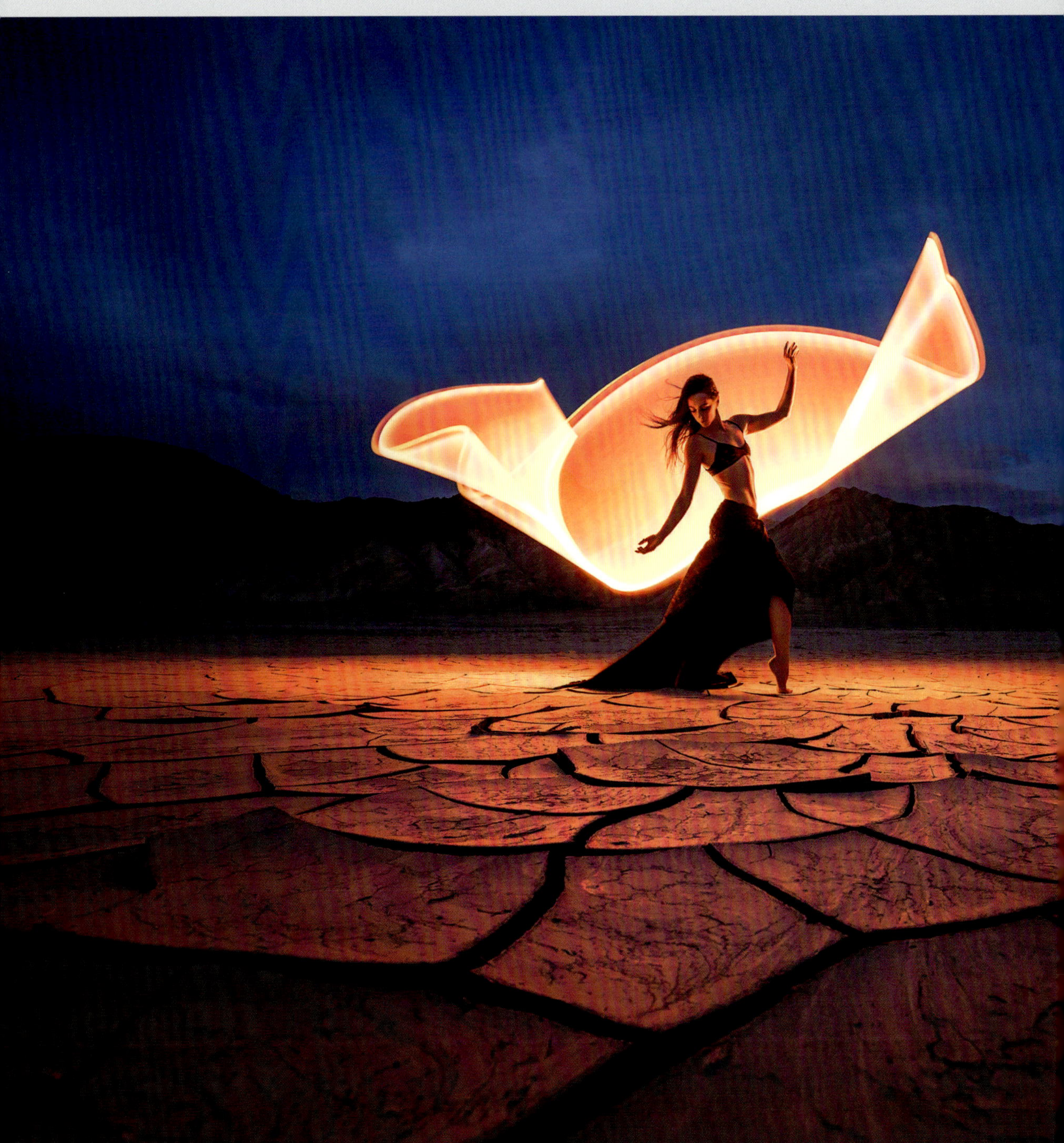

Environment: Desert | **Focal length:** 16mm | **Exposure:** 1.8 sec. (exposure and light painting), f/5, ISO 400

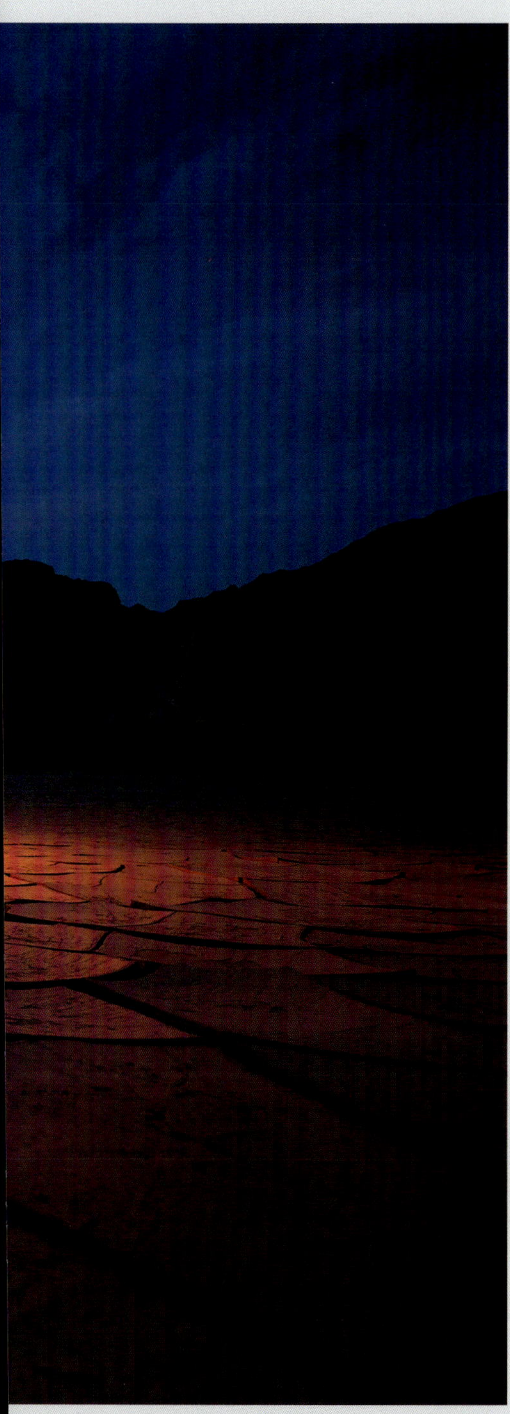

This image is a classic from our body of work. Early in our tube light-painting journey, we had the chance of being guided to a beautiful desert location by a new friend. This was our first time visiting Death Valley National Park, but far from our last.

Since then, we have traveled there many times and created hundreds of images. For a reason we can't totally grasp, this place feels like home to us. And we still haven't explored it all.

ABOUT THE LOCATION

Death Valley National Park is located primarily in California, with part of the park stretching into Nevada. It's the largest National Park in the USA outside of Alaska, and the lowest, hottest, and driest location in North America. A great diversity of amazing landscapes can be seen, including salt flats, canyons, sand dunes, and rugged mountain ranges. For us, the hottest place in North America also means comfortably warm temperatures to shoot in at night.

DID YOU NOTICE?

See the light on Kim's face? This is a good example of how you can adapt your light-painting shape to illuminate your subject. The shape we see at the right side of the picture was the beginning of the light-painting trace, where I started slightly in front of Kim to make sure she would be impacted by the orange light. Like most of our images, this is a single exposure, and in this example every element is well balanced and exposed: the sky, the model, the foreground, and the light painting.

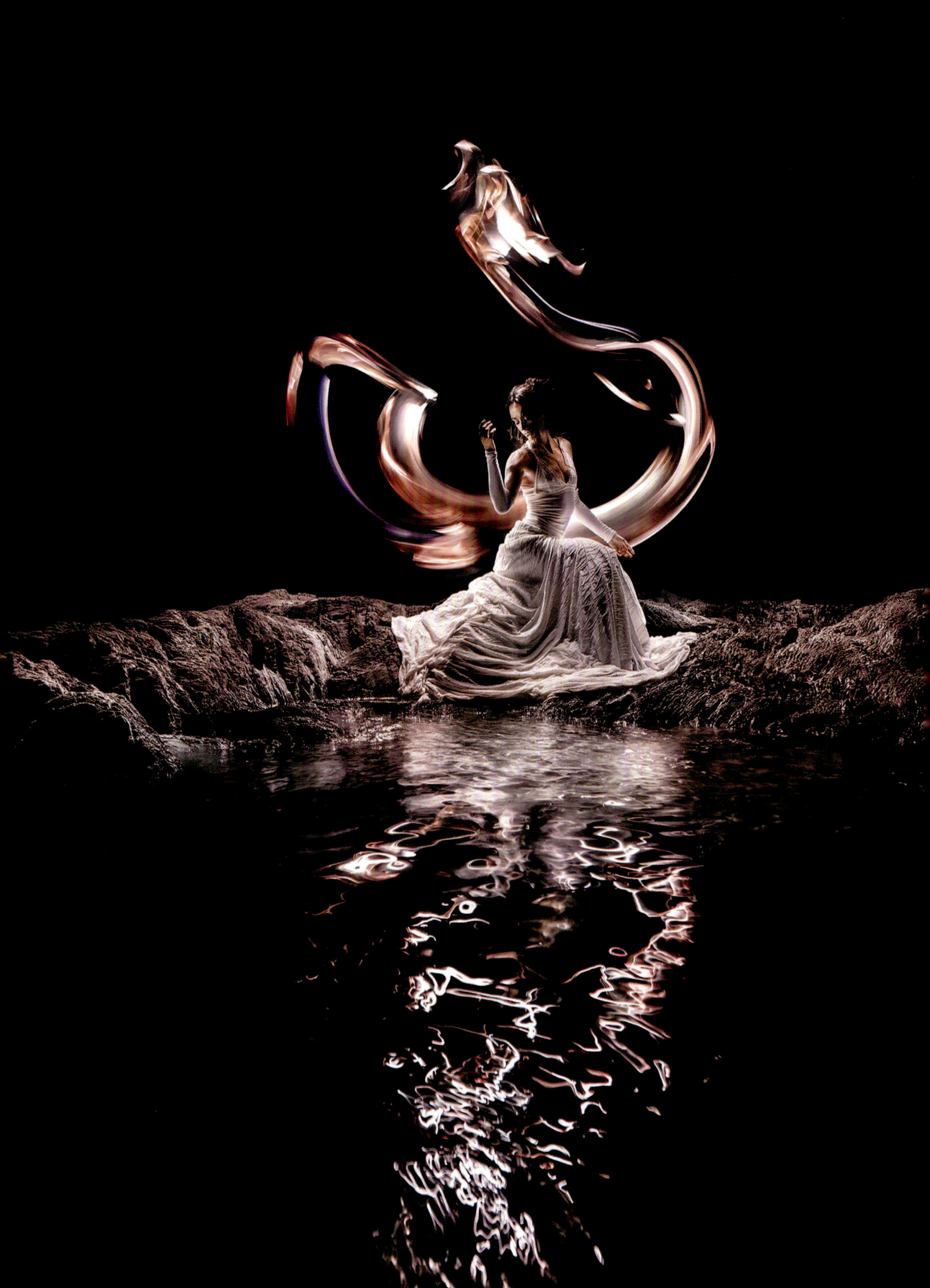

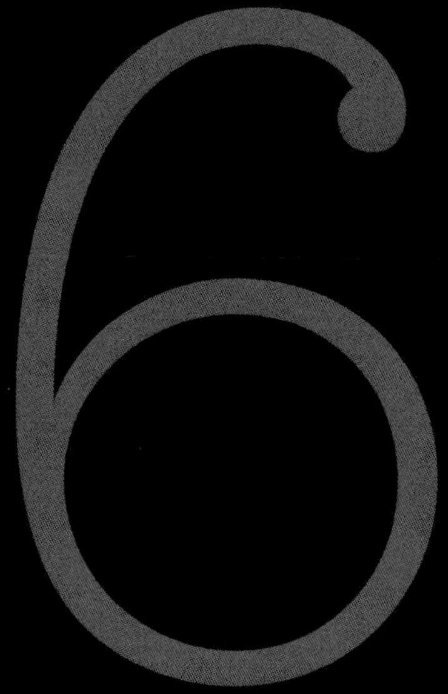

Additional tools & tricks

Once you master the basic principles of light painting, endless possibilities open up to create a wide range of visual effects. This chapter shares a few ideas for you to explore and play with.

Double tubes

Using two long tubes instead of one provides you with a few interesting creative options, such as having an extra-large trace of light, mixing up to four colors, and/or using both strobe and continuous light within a single light-painting shape.

Double tubes allow you to complete some light-painting shapes in half the time; when creating a circle, for example, each tube traces half the shape simultaneously. This results in a faster execution, while maintaining the same exposure time, which can potentially increase the sharpness of the subject in the image.

Using two tubes adds a few constraints, though, especially in the way you hold and manipulate the tool. If you have additional people involved in a shoot (beyond yourself and the model), don't hesitate to give your remote trigger to a friend who can trigger your camera for you, while you manipulate the tubes.

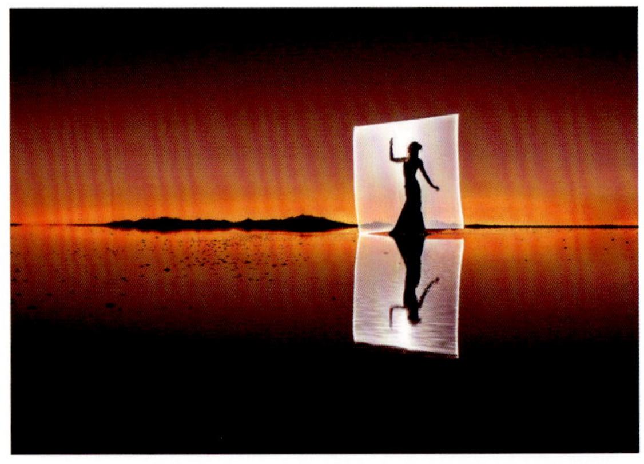

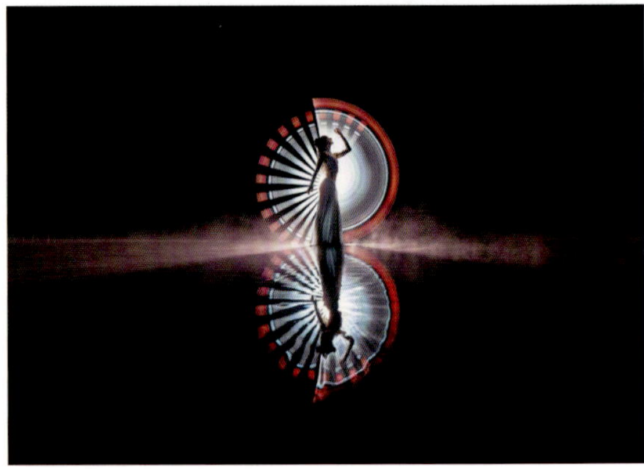

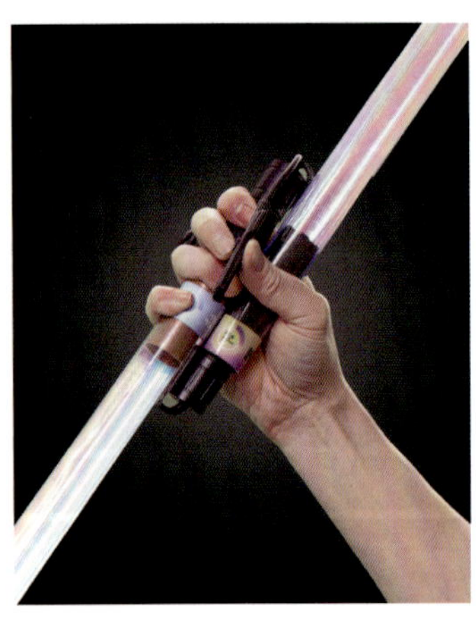

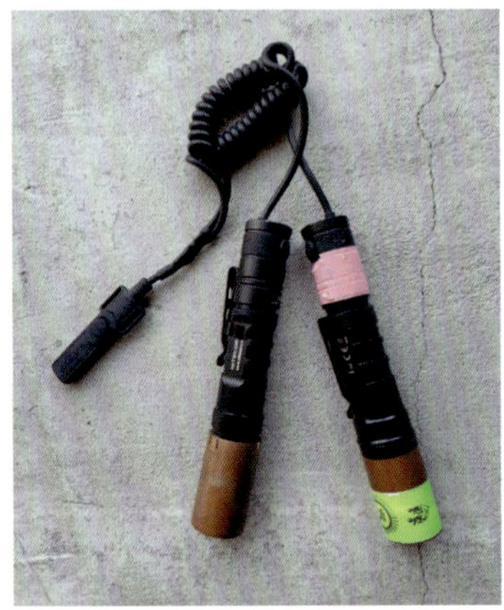

FAR LEFT **This is how I hold two tubes and two flashlights, linked to a single pressure switch to turn on and off the lights. It is a lot to handle with a single hand if you also want to be able to trigger your camera.**

LEFT **Controlling two flashlights with a single switch requires modifying the pressure switch wiring, which is a DIY project. If you're interested in trying it out, you'll find a tutorial at** *lightpainting.art*

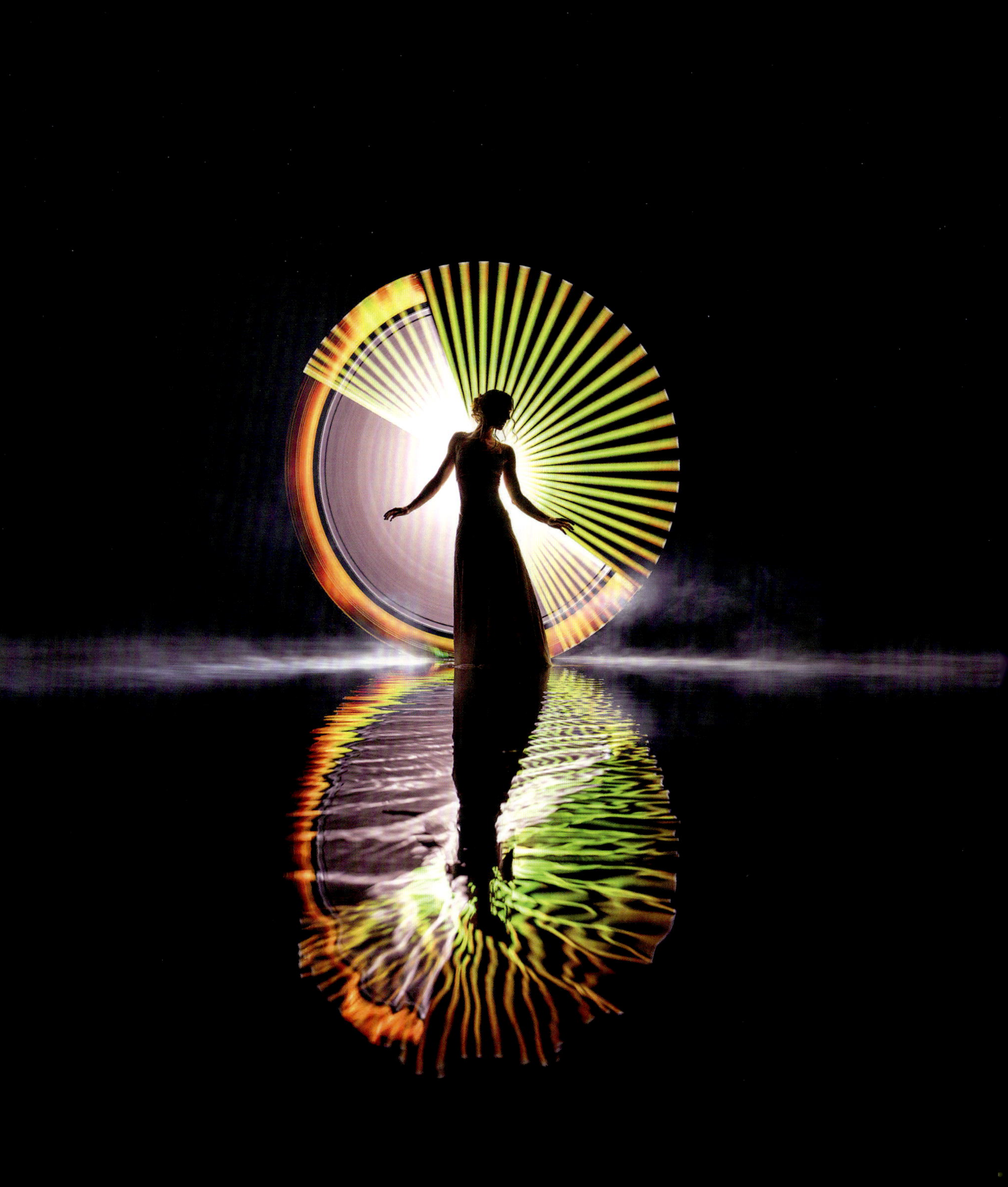

Water, leaves, & sand

Actively incorporating moving natural elements from the environment into your light-painting creations is a great way of playing with the perception of time in your images. The following ideas will help you get started.

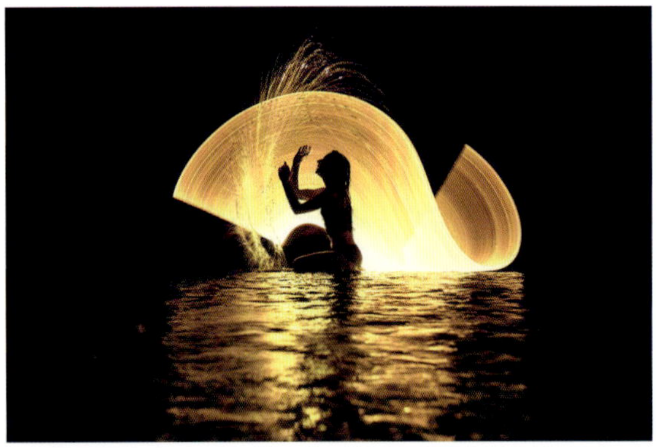

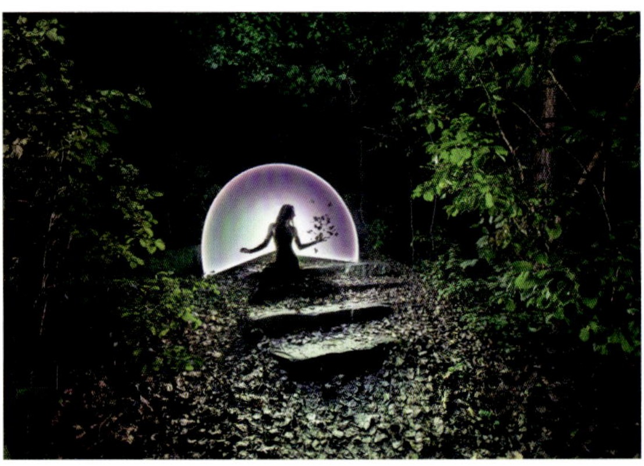

THROWING WATER

This first option is for those who don't mind getting wet. The model throws water in the air and stays still as the light painter paints quickly behind. This is challenging, as the execution speed and timing of both people need to align perfectly in order to capture the water in the air. You might need many, many attempts to achieve a satisfying result!

LEAVES

Throwing leaves can also create an interesting effect. The process is similar to throwing water; the model throws a handful of leaves and then stops moving, while the light painter quickly makes a short light shape behind them. Again, timing and coordination are key, and you may need several attempts to get a good shot. You can also play with other elements. The lighter the element you choose (feathers, for example) the more time you will have to capture it as it falls to the ground.

SPLASHING WATER

A second water-based option is to create a water splash using the light-painting tool. Submerge the feather or outer edge of the tube in the water before making your shape. This creates a subtle but beautiful effect, although be aware that most flashlights are not waterproof, unless you're using a tactical flashlight without a pressure switch.

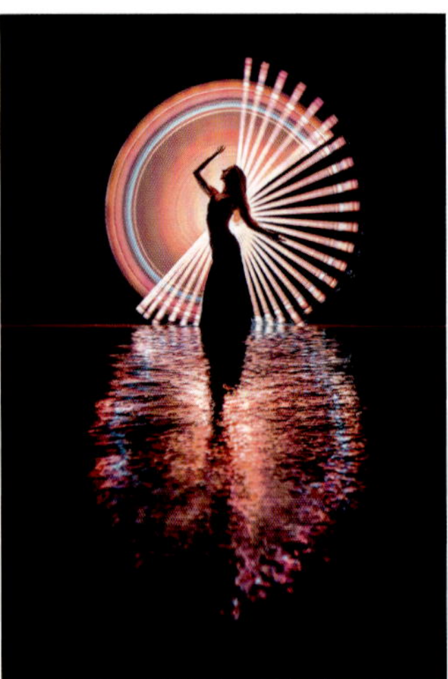

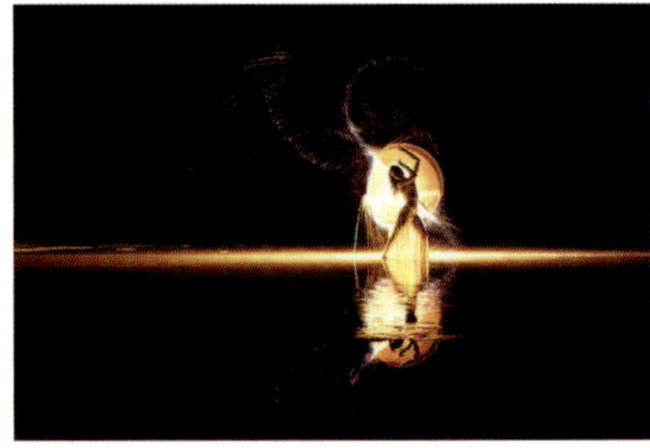

LEFT **You can see the subtle splash of water at the right side of the circle in this photograph.**

BELOW **The splash in this image was not so subtle...**

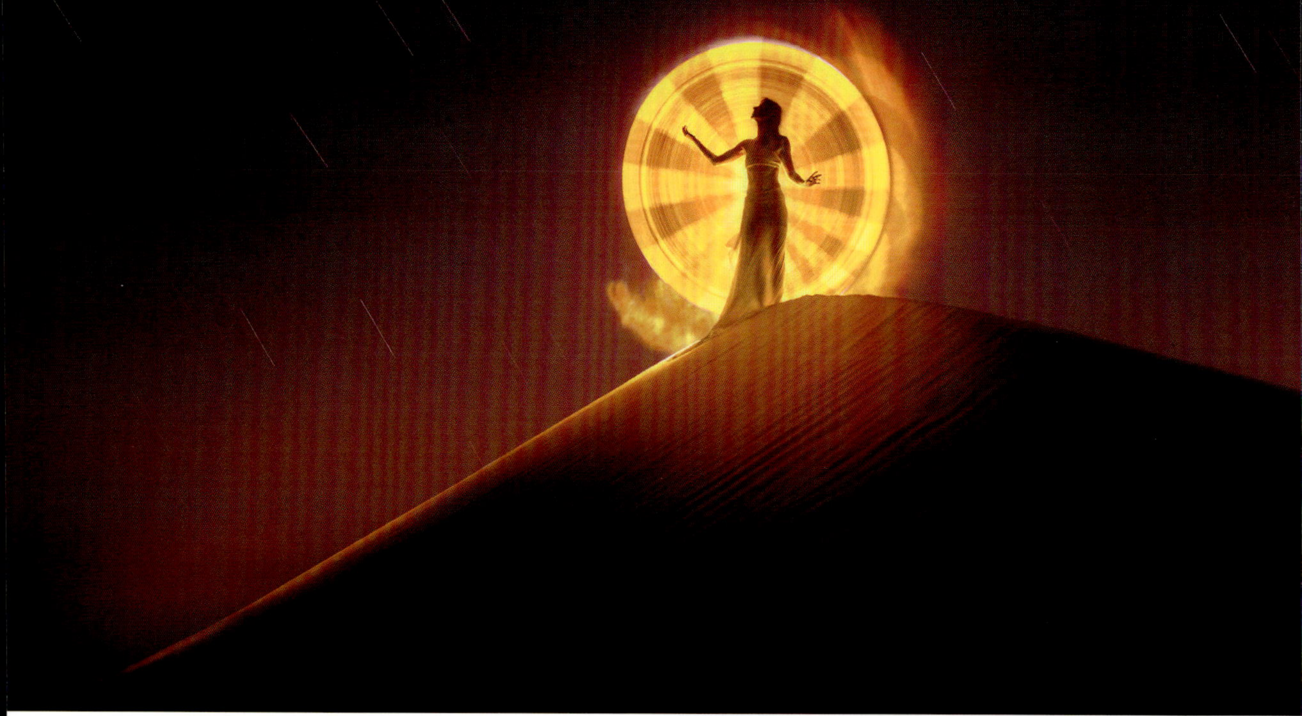

SAND

Unlike water or leaves, sand tends to create a more satisfying effect when it flows steadily down from the hands rather than being tossed in the air. It's very challenging for the model to remain sharp in these types of shots, but it's not impossible. Our favorite tool for this type of sand picture is a black tube with a small RoseBronze tube on top, and a glow cap to bounce the light.

Similar to splashing water, you can also use sand to extend the light trace. Putting the edge of the tube in the sand and scooping some up as you trace a circle, creates a beautiful effect. In order for the sand to be illuminated by the light, the tube needs to allow the light to pass through it (so don't fit a cap to the end of the tube). This is a fairly difficult effect to control, let alone replicate, and the sand needs to be very fine and dry. Again, the success ratio is pretty low, but it's worth trying!

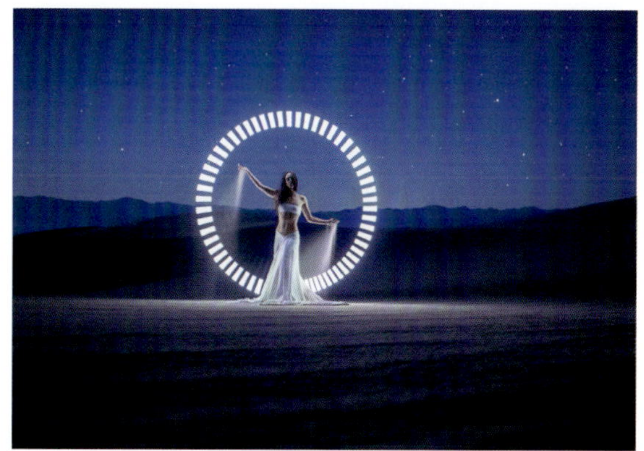

ABOVE **Here, the sand was allowed to flow from one hand at a time, being released right before the light got close to it while tracing the circle.**

Sparklers & fireworks

Sparklers come in various forms and can produce a multitude of visual effects. Depending on where you are located, you will have access to a wide or a very limited range of choices, as legislation varies greatly from one country to another, and even between provinces and states. You may also find there are municipal laws around the use of fireworks, so make sure you check for any restrictions before using them.

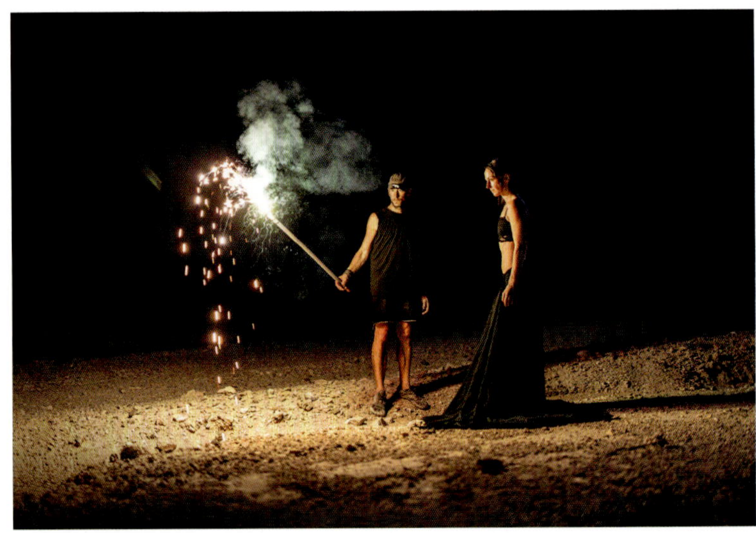

WORKFLOW

1 Attach the sparkler to the end of the tube using hair bands or similar. Use one sparkler at a time and leave a distance between the end of the tube and the burning portion of the sparkler to prevent the heat damaging the plastic tube.

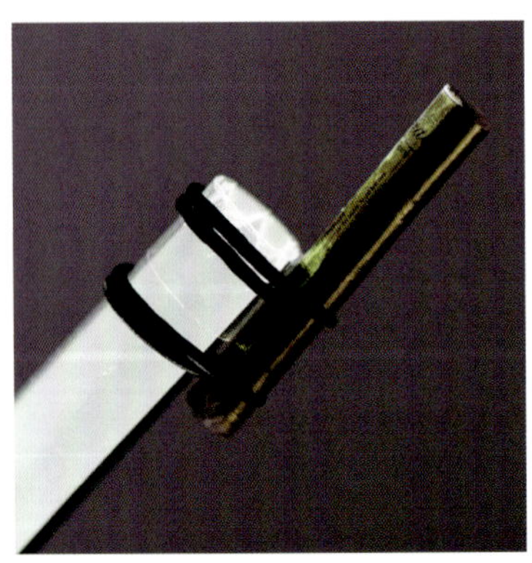

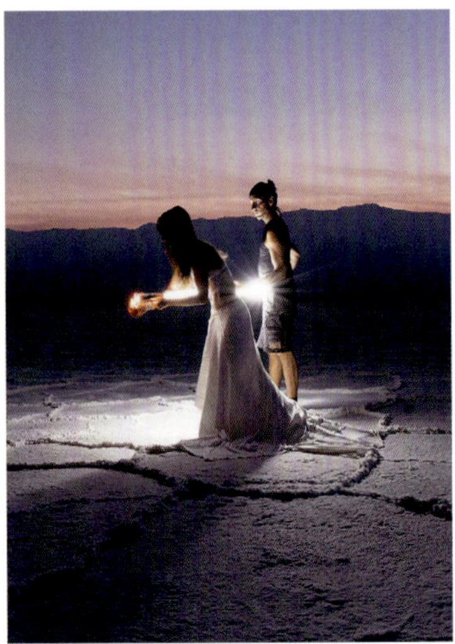

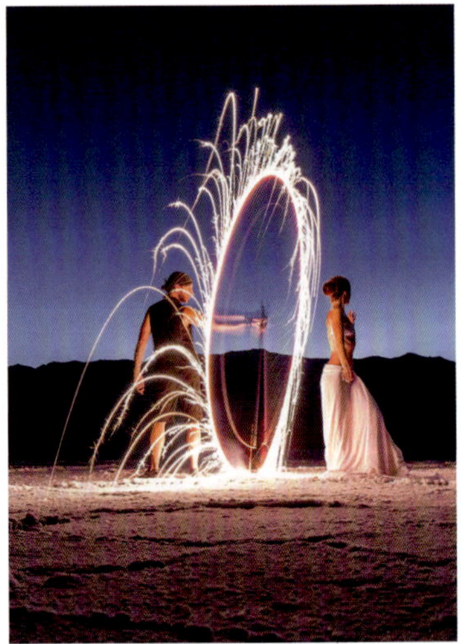

2 Ignite the sparkler. When we are working with sparklers, Kim lights the sparkler while Eric holds the tube, making sure the sparkler (and tube) is horizontal or aimed slightly downward.

3 When the sparkler lights up, create a series of images. We keep going until the sparkler stops burning; they typically last between 30 and 60 seconds.

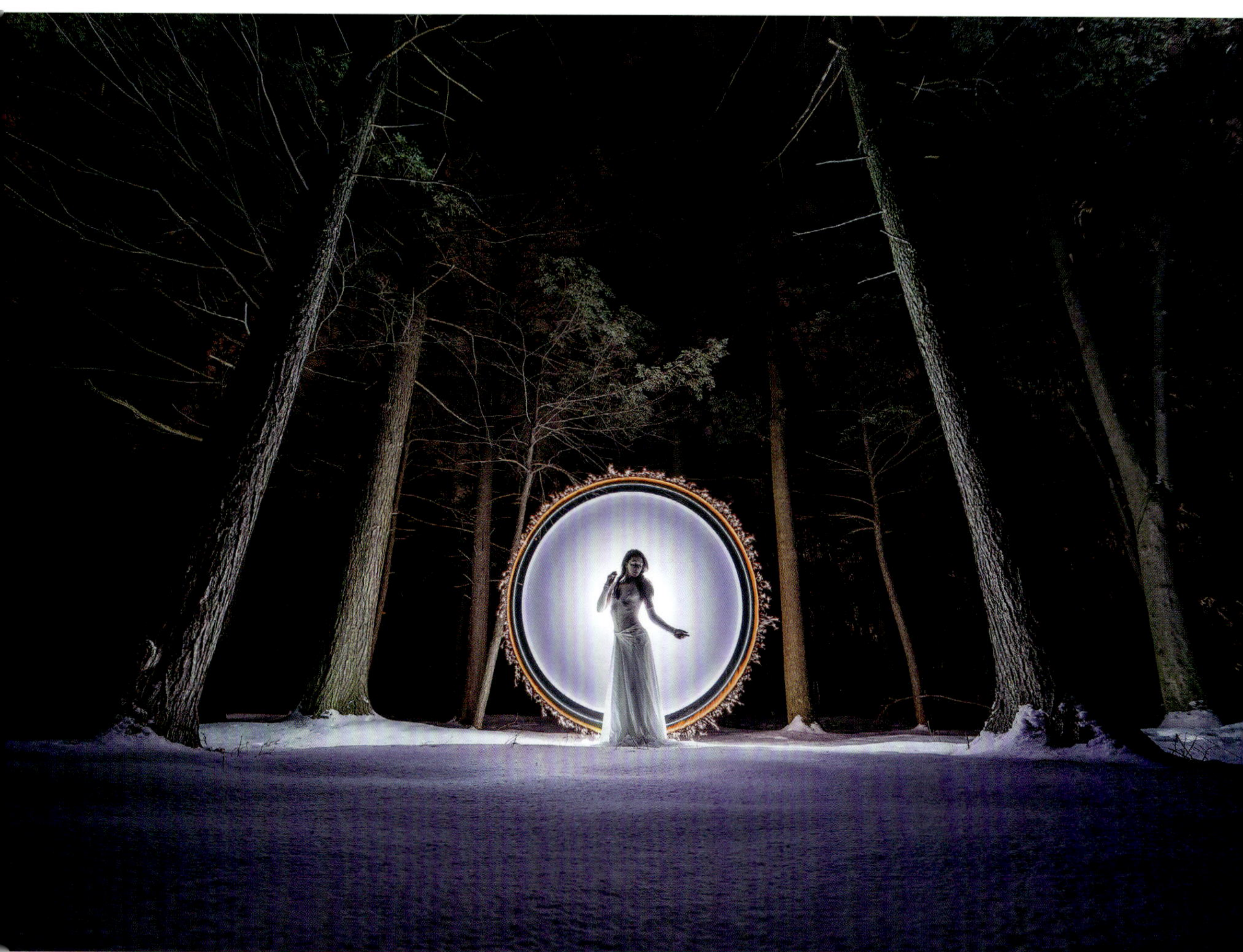

Some sparklers produce long, fountain-like trails, while others create a more subtle sparkly effect. Regardless of the type you chose, sparklers add a dynamic and organic element to the image. For a quick reference on the categories of sparklers and the visuals they produce, see page 169 in the Reference toolkit.

There are a few things you need to be aware of when you are shooting with sparklers, which can affect the general process. For a start, sparklers can't be turned off, so if you are planning on using an inpaint technique, you will need to hide the sparkler somehow for the remaining exposure. Some sparklers can be put in water or sand and won't be extinguished. If not, simply hold the tube pointing down at the end of each shape, at a safe distance from your feet and the model.

Sparklers can be very bright, so most of the time they will illuminate your subject. It also means that most of them can only be used early during the nautical twilight. Beyond that they quickly become too bright to balance with the background. An alternative is to use them when creating black canvas images, without a background (see page 70).

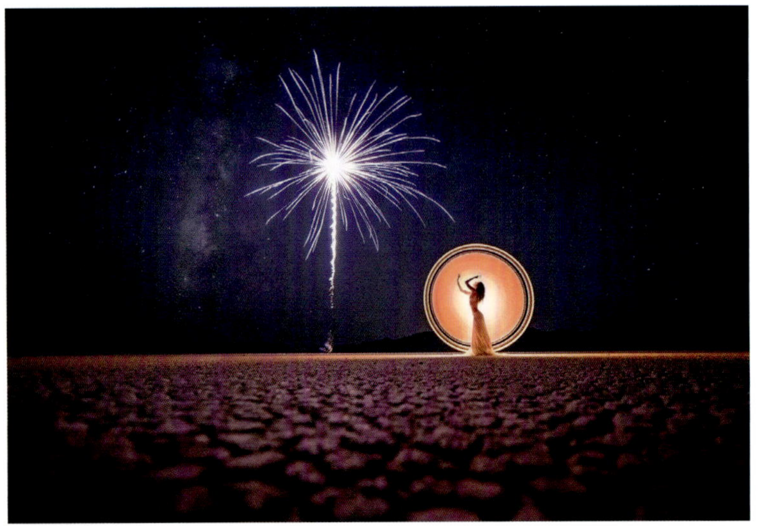

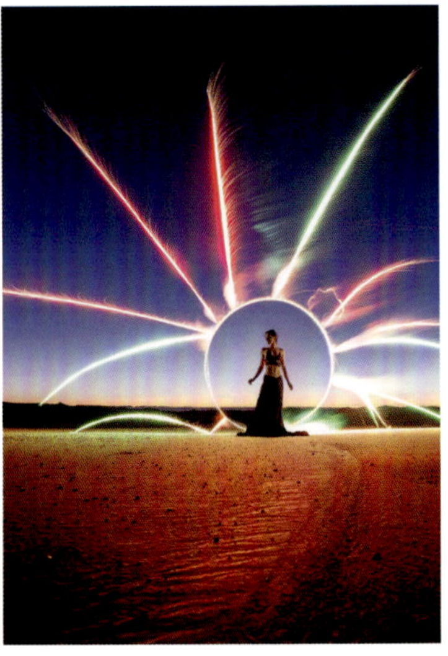

OTHER FIREWORKS

We prefer to work with sparklers, as they are easier to integrate into the light-painting process, but we have occasionally experimented with larger fireworks – the option is there if you want to pursue it.

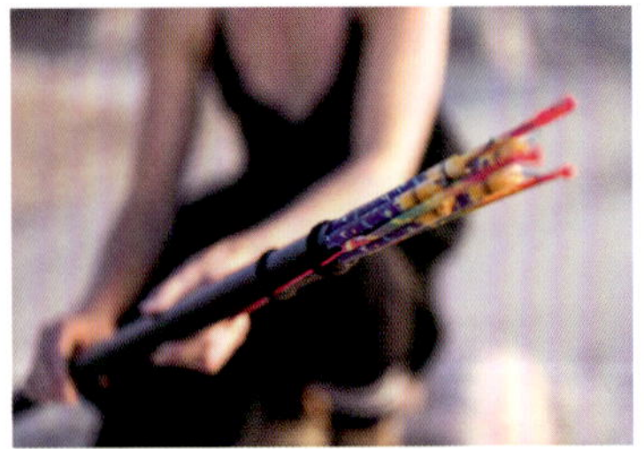

ABOVE **Our once-in-a-lifetime setup: a black tube loaded with roman candles.**

RIGHT **A friend of ours knows how to operate aerial fireworks, so we went to a safe location in the middle of the desert. We communicated using walkie talkies to coordinate the firework launch with the light-painting exposure.**

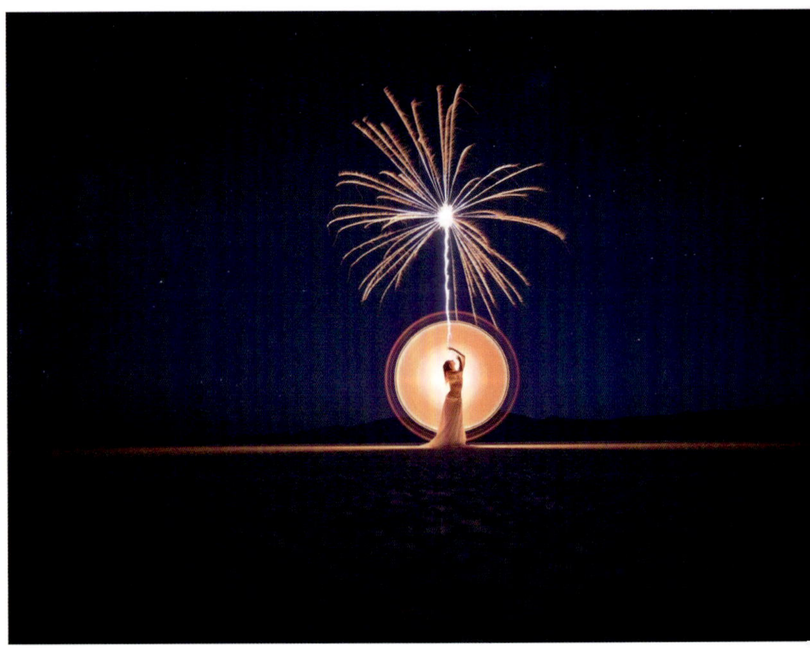

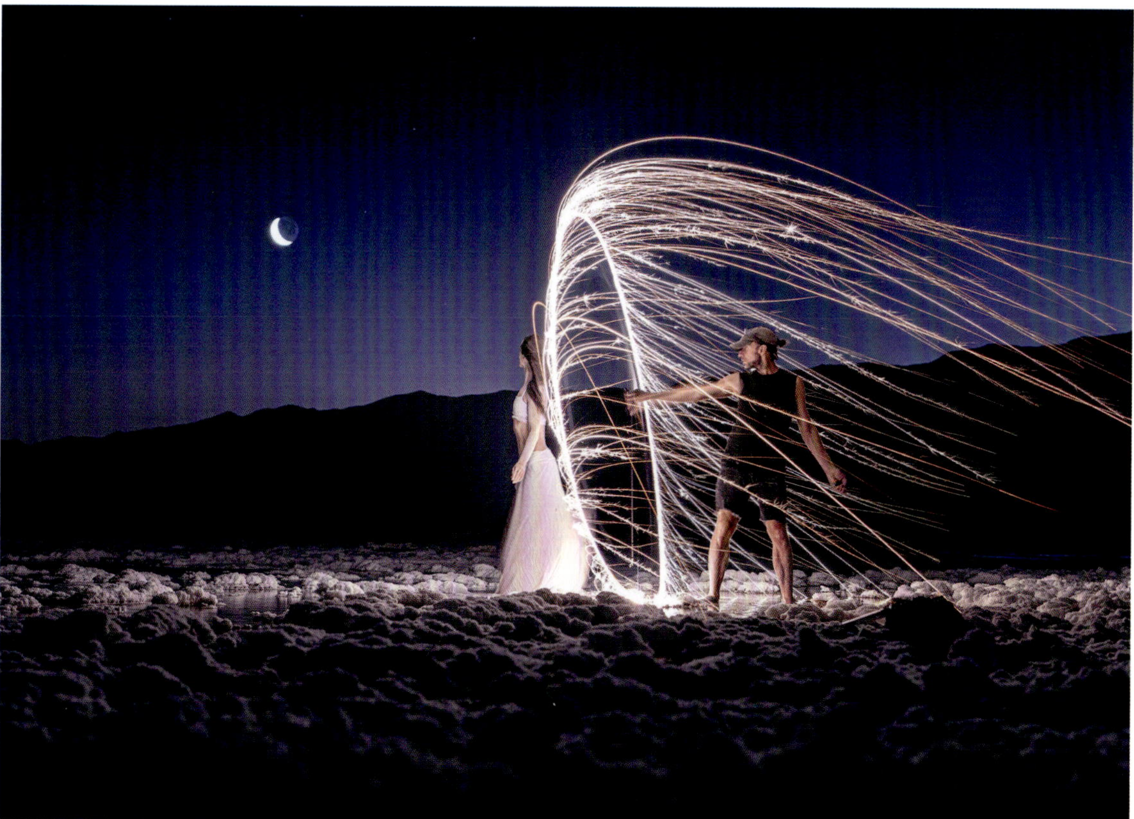

Safety notes

→ Don't use sparklers or fireworks near anything flammable... for obvious reasons.

→ When using sparklers attached to your tube, increase the distance between the tube and the model's body (stand further away).

→ Ask the model to close their eyes or look down, to protect their face.

→ Wear non-flammable clothing (avoid untreated cotton, linen, silk, and cellulose fabric). The thinner the fabric, the more easily it tends to burn. The risk is low, but we have made small holes in a few skirts over the years.

→ Use a windproof butane torch lighter to light the sparkler. Regular lighters are not reliable in windy or humid conditions.

ABOVE **When using sparklers, be mindful of the wind direction. Avoid having the wind blow sparks directly toward you or the model.**

Working solo

All of the images featured so far in this book have included a human subject. While this remains the focus of our approach, the techniques we've shared can be adapted for different subjects, as well as for solo work. Here are a few alternative avenues to explore.

INANIMATE SUBJECT

There's no reason why part of the environment can't become your main subject, or why you can't introduce a new element into the landscape. Whether it is trees, driftwood, sculptures or a bicycle, anything that holds still can serve as a focal point for your light painting. Some members of the community have even used life-size silhouette cutouts and static mannequins to simulate the presence of a human figure without needing a live model.

The big advantage of working with inanimate subjects is that they're incredibly patient. Unlike animals or people, there's almost no risk of motion blur or fatigue. It's also a great opportunity to practice your shapes, refine your technique, and adjust your settings without the potential pressure of collaborating with another person.

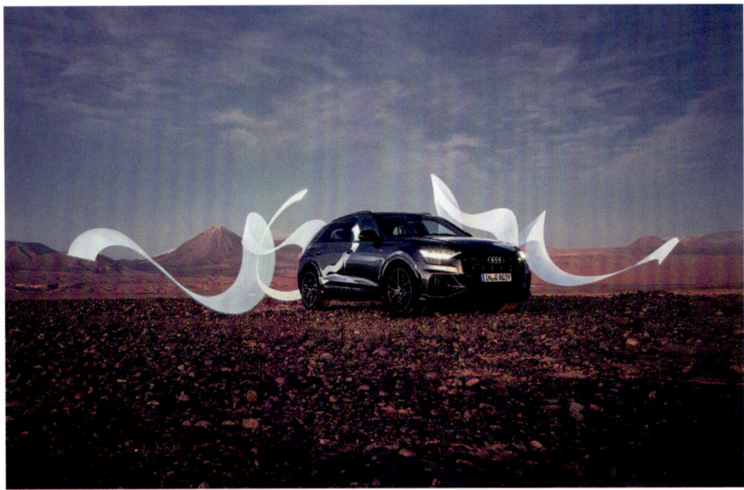

LEFT **This is a rare image we created with a vehicle, captured during the early blue hour. Light painting a large subject like a car often requires a slightly longer exposure than our usual workflow, unless the goal is to create a very minimalistic image.**

ABSTRACT ART

Some artists make abstract light painting their main artistic expression, where the light becomes the subject of the image. In this instance, a smaller tool, such as a light-painting square (see page 140) or an acrylic blade (see page 139), allows more versatility and precision in the painting. This approach can feel harder for some and easier for others, though it usually depends on your interests and skills.

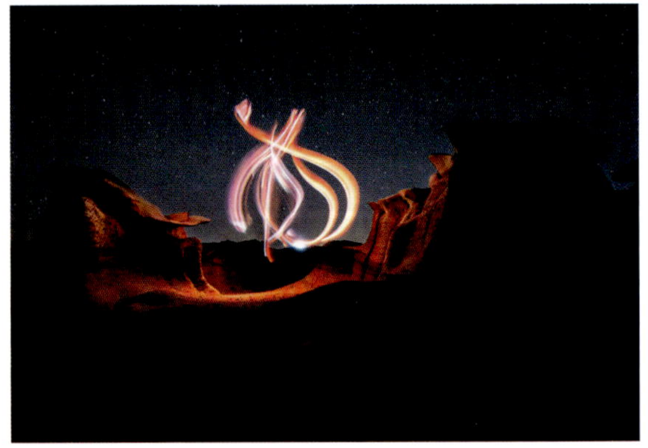

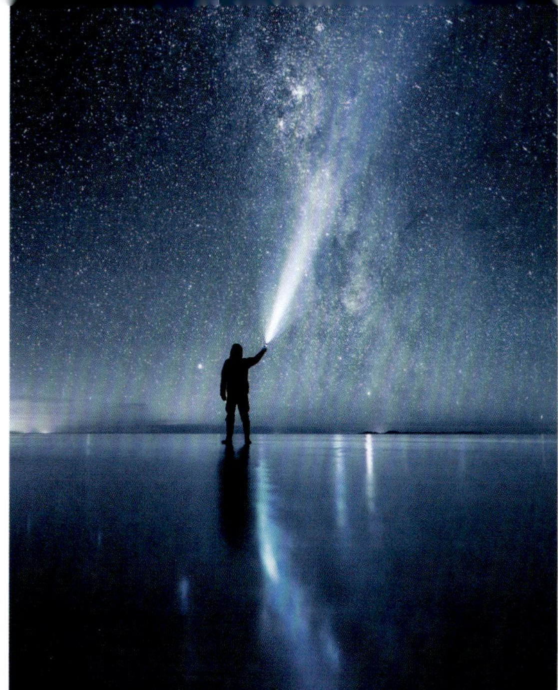

SELF-PORTRAIT

If you like challenges, here's a fun one: be both the light painter and the model! The simplest way of creating a self-portrait is to not move the light. Plant the tube in the ground or hold it straight without moving during the exposure. If you are shooting with a long exposure time (to capture stars, for example) you will need to turn off the flashlight during the shot.

LEFT **Here, Eric used a single flashlight to create a big beam of light in the sky.**

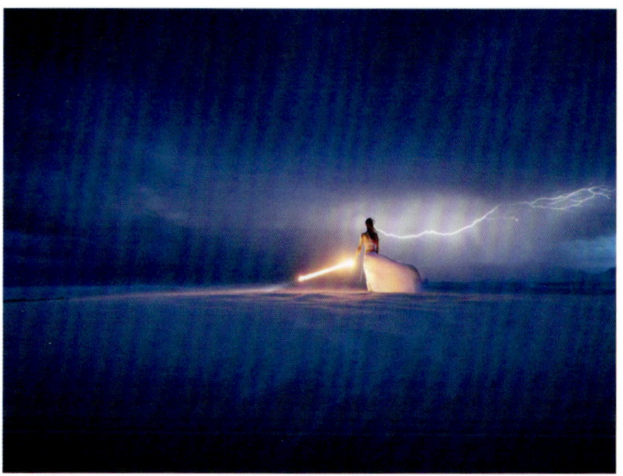

ABOVE **Kim triggered this shot herself, as Eric was running to the cameras to adjust the framing.**

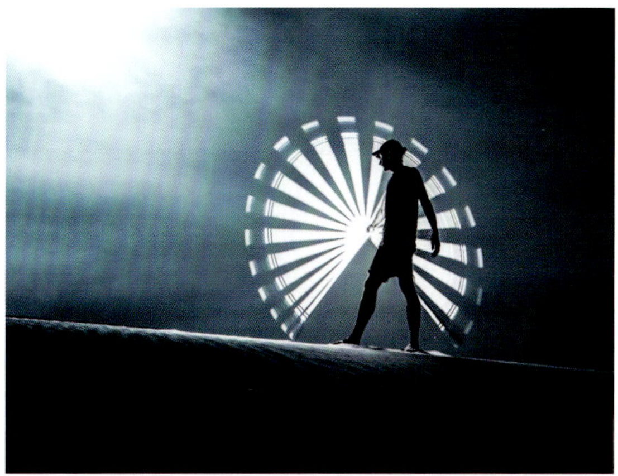

ABOVE **Another self-portrait option is to try to stay motionless while moving the light using one arm.**

FOCUSING

Assessing your composition and focus without someone to help you is definitely a little more challenging, but it's totally achievable. Place an object (such as a backpack or second tripod) exactly where you want the light painting or self-portrait to be. Focus on the object, then go back and mark the object's position before removing it from the frame

– use a small rock or draw an "X" on the ground, depending on the type of surface you're shooting on. Now you can put yourself in the same position, knowing you will be in focus. Just remember to use back button focus or manual focus so the camera doesn't try to adjust the focus when you make your first exposure.

Other tools

We rarely use any tools other than our tubes when we are shooting outdoors, but we have experimented with a number of alternative options over the years to see what visual aesthetic they create.

NEEDLES

The needle is a long acrylic rod that creates a very dim light. We use it by turning the flashlight on and off around the model, slightly changing the angle and height of the tool so it looks unpredictable. The average exposure time needed is 30 seconds or more, making it very hard to get a sharp subject in the final image.

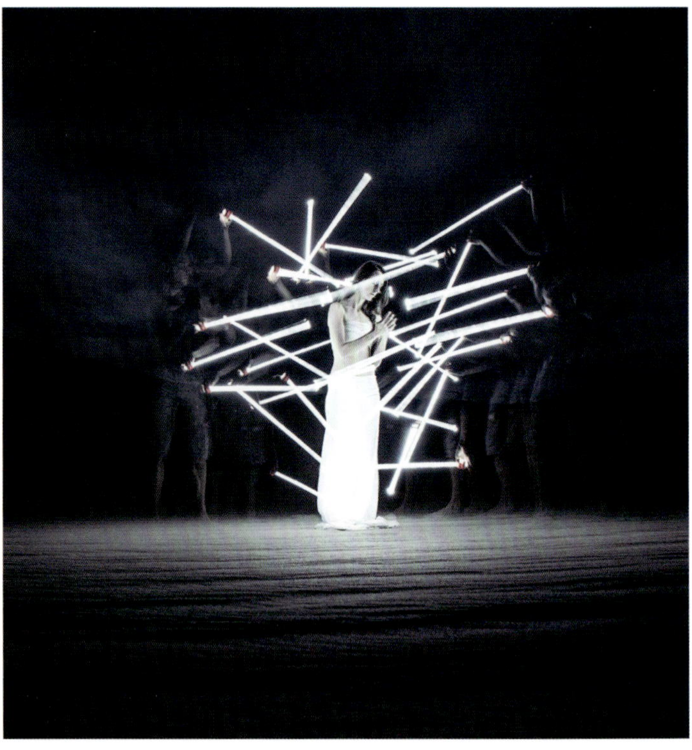

ABOVE **If you look closely, you can see how Eric moves the needle around Kim during the exposure.**

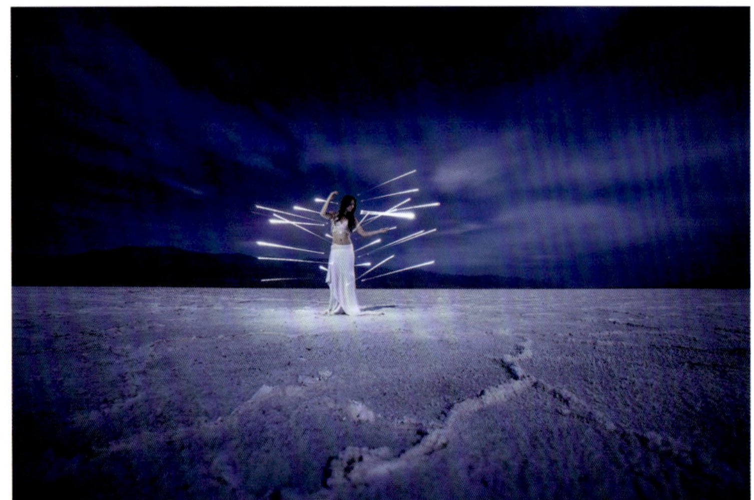

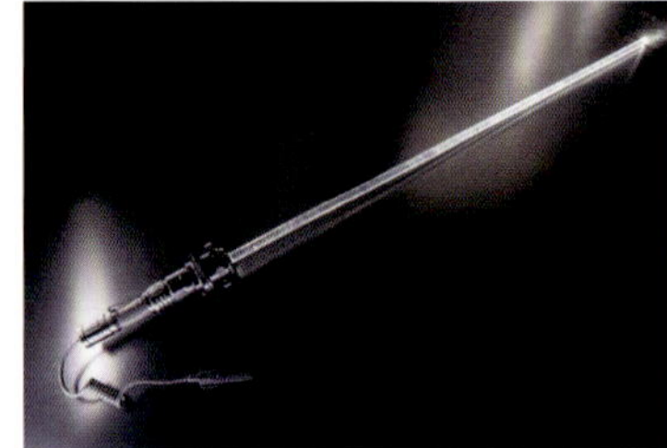

ABOVE **The tool. The Needle doesn't emit light by itself. Like most light-painting tools we use, it needs to be attached to a flashlight.**

ACRYLIC BLADES

Made from clear or frosted acrylic, blades come in a variety of shapes and sizes and offer a high level of control over the shapes and textures you create in the frame. They diffuse light evenly and create some of the sharpest, most defined edges of any tool we use. The acrylic blades can be attached directly to a flashlight or mounted on the end of a light-painting tube.

We love using this tool in the studio, but almost never use it outside. This is simply because it is not a simple tool to create with, so there is still a lot to be explored with it in a landscape setting.

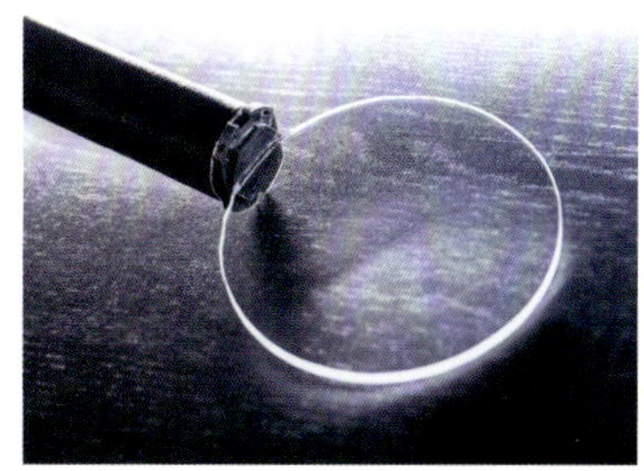

ABOVE **Acrylic blade on top of a tube.**

RIGHT **Images created with this type of tool. The first image is one of our first outdoor light-painting shots, made before we had any tubes. We made it with a DIY acrylic blade attached directly to a flashlight.**

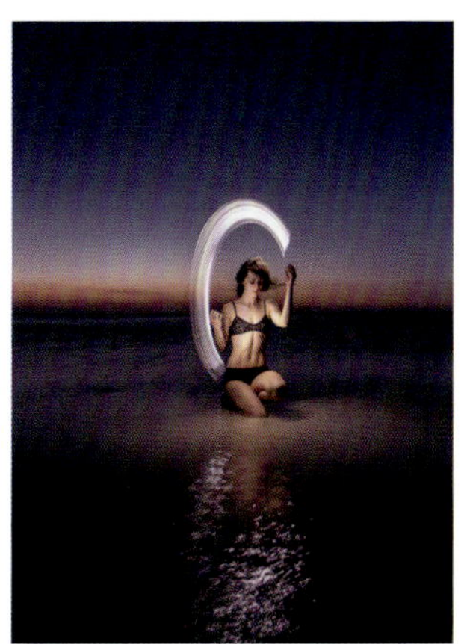

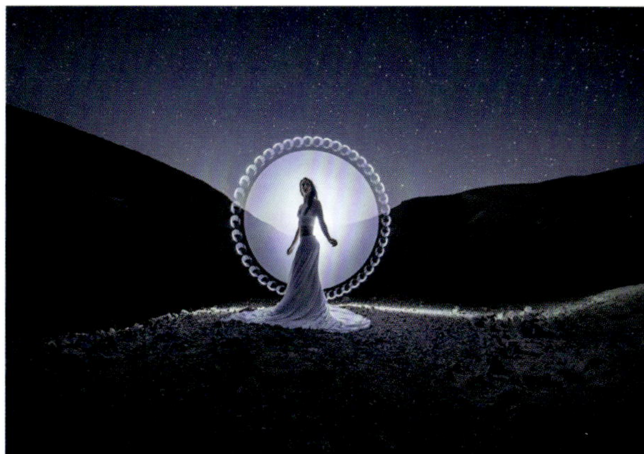

FLASHLIGHT EXPERIMENTS

Experimentation can lead to new possibilities. At one point, we attached small flashlights to the edge of a tube, which eventually led us to mount a small tube on top of a black one. There are many other ways to experiment with flashlights, so let your imagination run wild!

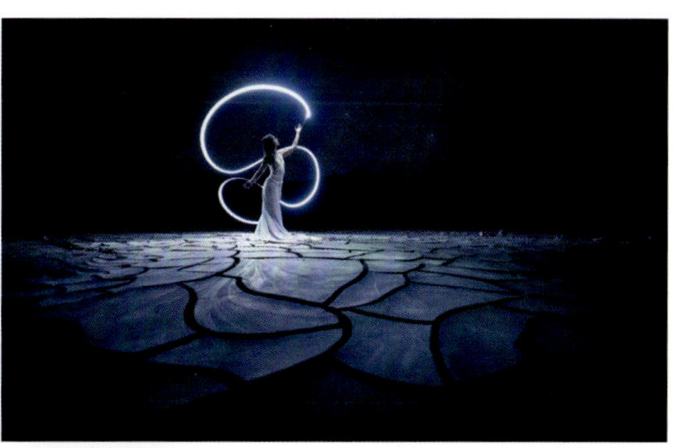

RIGHT **Tactical flashlights are usually waterproof unless they've been modified. For this shot, we attached a flashlight to a small rope and dragged it through the water during the exposure.**

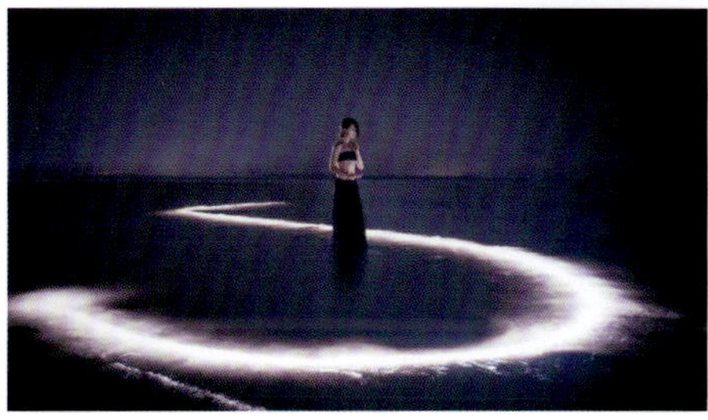

ABOVE **Attaching a small flashlight to the edge of a tube was an early playful experiment that led to a useful discovery we're still using years later. If you try this DIY setup, be careful not to swing it too fast or it might fly into the night!**

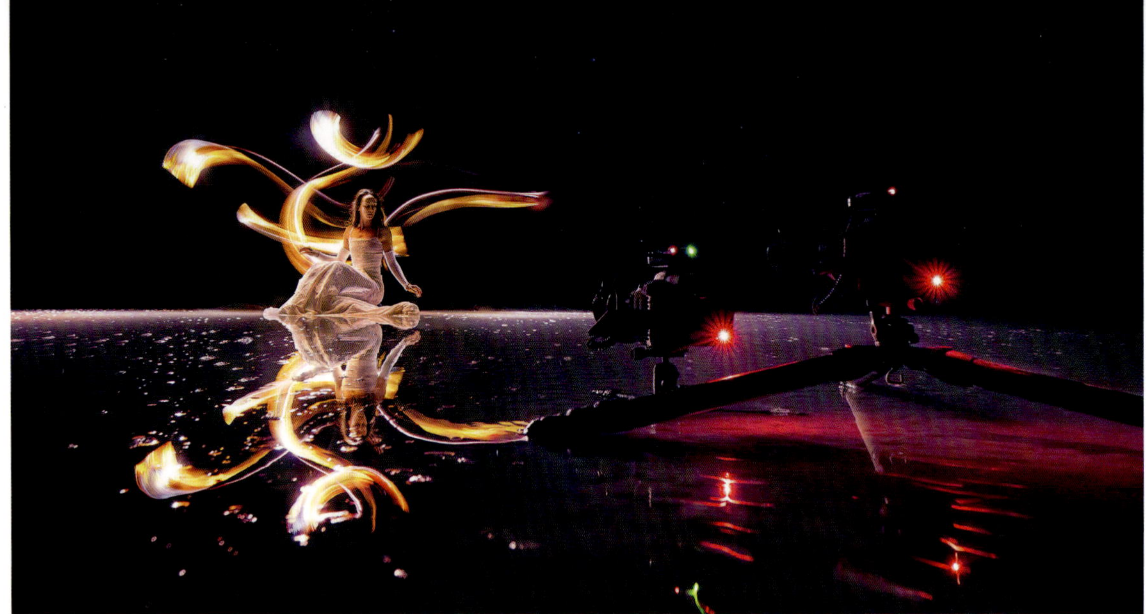

Light-painting square

The light-painting square is not a new tool. In fact, we started using it in the studio in 2013, before experimenting with it outdoors. At the time, the outdoor results were far from satisfying so we put the tool aside and started using tubes instead. However, in 2022 we tried again and this time, with nearly ten years of experience behind us, we achieved something we were proud of.

A light-painting square is a simple square made of holographic material, in which we wrap a flashlight. The tool is incredibly simple, yet much harder to master than tubes, especially when you're working outdoors. This is for a variety of reasons:

→ The tool is much smaller and creates a more concentrated light source. How you hold the flashlight and the square directly impacts the quality of the light.
→ Unlike tubes, it is impossible to "hide" behind this small light source, so you will likely be visible in most of your images.
→ It takes a lot of practice to illuminate the subject properly while also creating beautiful light patterns.
→ Light-painting squares usually require longer exposure times, which increases the risk of a blurry subject, especially when illuminating them multiple times with the tool.

The best way to minimize subject blur is to start with a quick vertical trace of light, close to the subject, with the light aimed toward them to illuminate their face and body. Then, for the rest of the exposure, paint with the tool in the air without pointing the light at the model. This is easier said than done, which is why this tool requires a lot of practice. The success rate is way lower than with the tubes. We probably miss about 90 percent of our shots, and only 2 percent of all our attempts are great results.

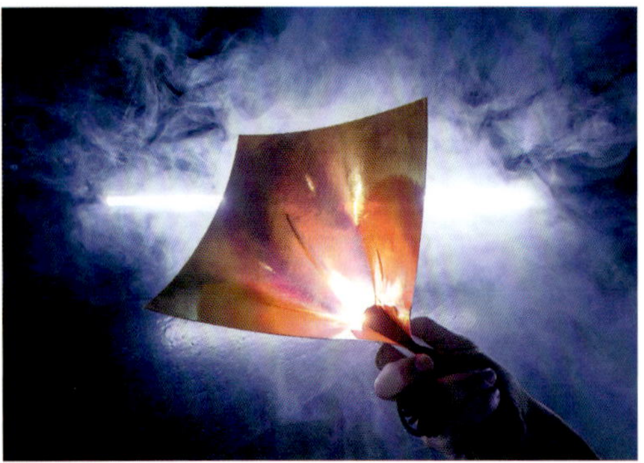

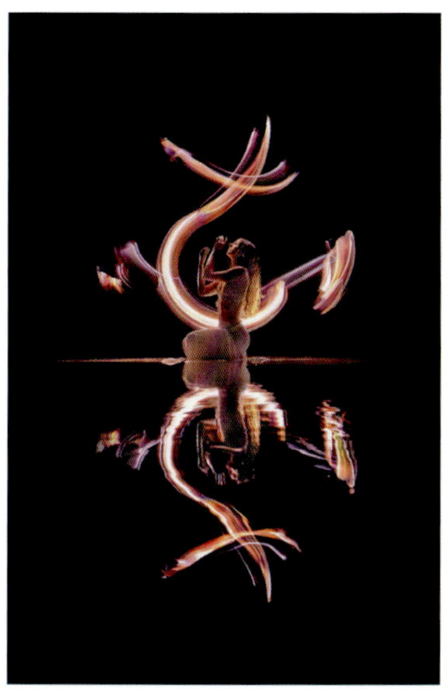
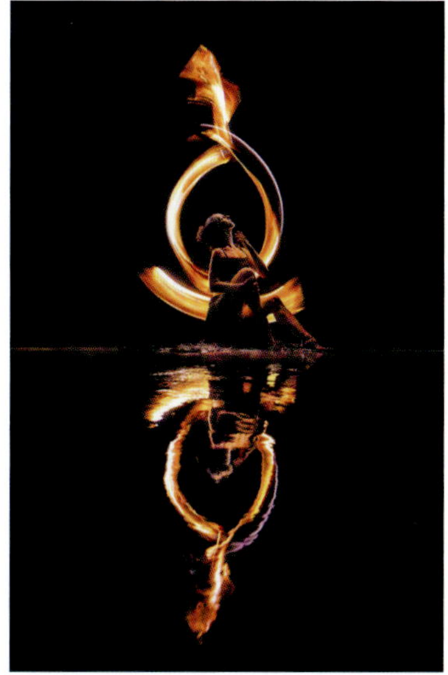
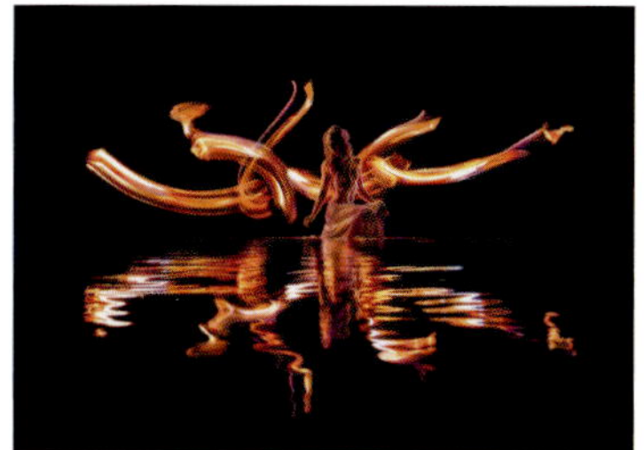
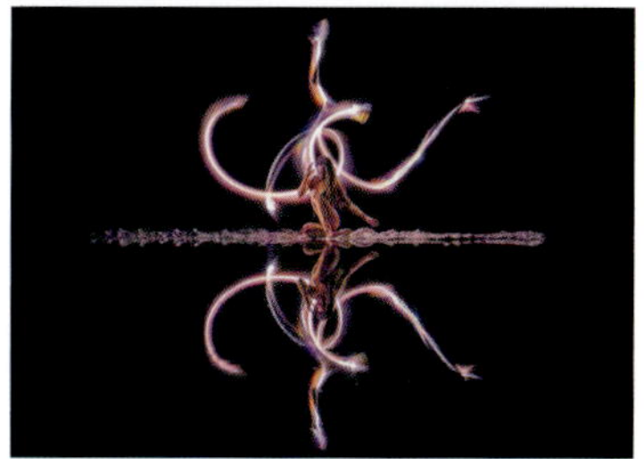

To date, we've mainly used this tool without integrating the landscape in the background. Similar to a black canvas image (see page 70), using a small body of water to reflect the light painting adds an extra layer to the image with the light painting, the model, and their reflection becoming the main subject. For this reason, we usually aim for a central composition when creating with this tool. If the light painter is on dry land (or the water is very shallow) it is easier for them to move freely behind the model, enabling more elaborate shapes to be created.

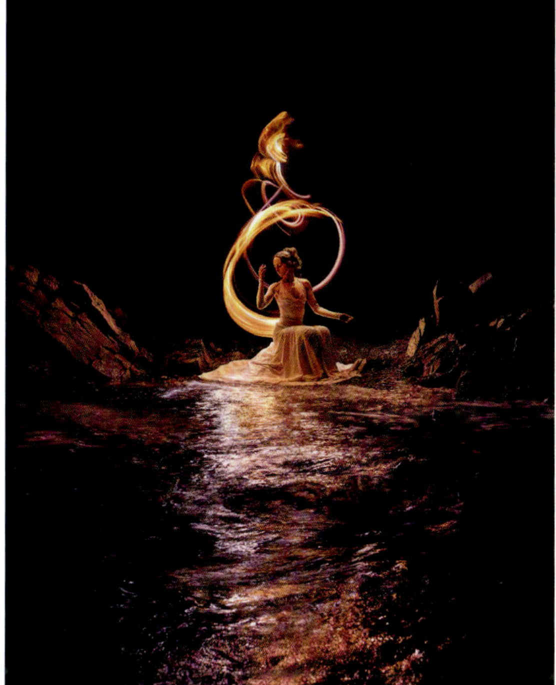

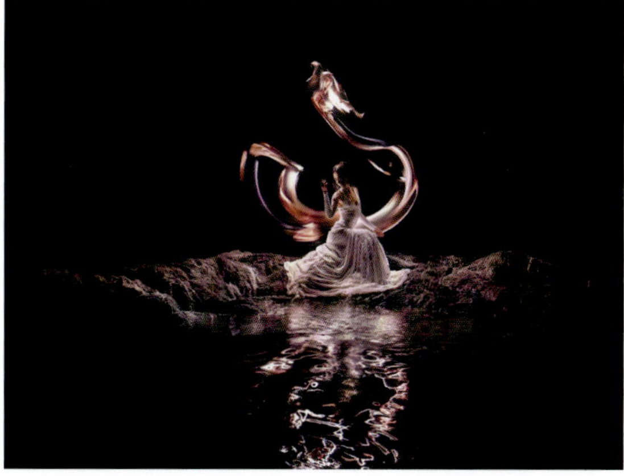

LEFT & ABOVE **Here, we purposefully integrated elements of the landscape, mainly the rock formations around the subject. An additional step of complexity would be to do this during the blue hour or at night with stars.**

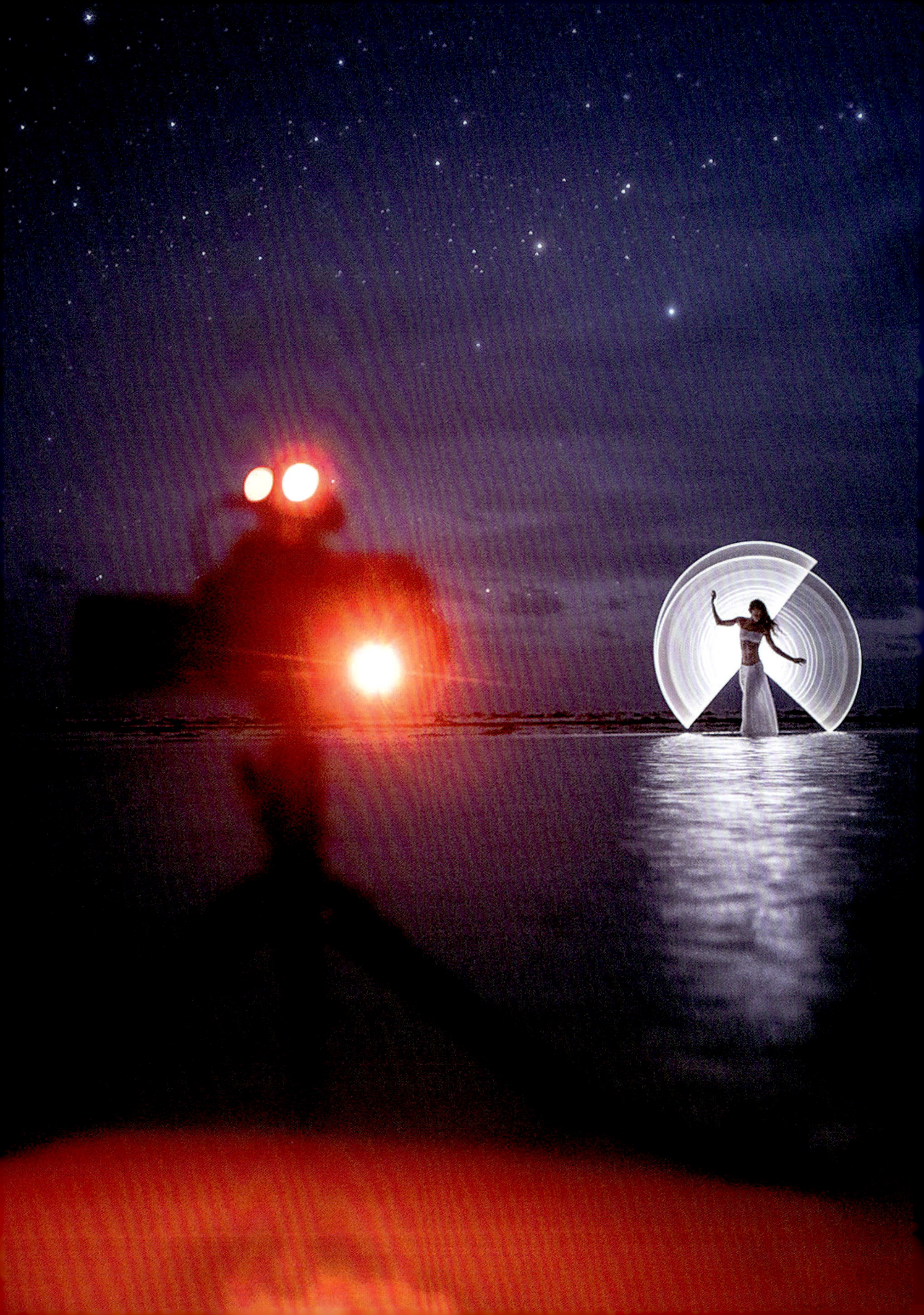

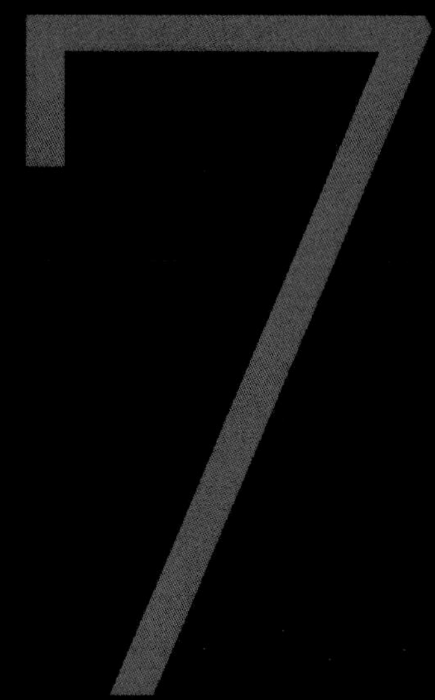

Advanced capture techniques

This section explores advanced capture methods that expand the creative and technical potential of your light painting. Each technique brings challenges, but they offer new ways to document, share, and push your practice further.

Dual cameras

This technique is a creative solution I've developed to increase the level of detail in my final images. Put simply, I use two cameras with different focal lengths to create a high-resolution composite in post-production (see page 156). The main reason I started doing this is so I'd have the option of producing very large, high-quality prints when needed. If you're only planning to share your work on social media, your website, or print small formats, this technique isn't necessary, but for gallery-quality output, it makes a real difference.

Here's how it works: I set up two cameras side by side, positioned as closely together as possible. One camera is fitted with a wide-angle lens (around 14–24mm) to capture the full scene. The other uses a longer focal length (typically 35–50mm) to focus more tightly on the light painting and subject. In post-production, I replace the subject and light-painting areas from the wide shot with those from the close-up, creating a composite that combines the best of both perspectives.

From a technical standpoint, yes, this involves either upscaling the wide-angle shot or downscaling the close-up to match. But both approaches work surprisingly well. The close-up camera captures far more detail in the subject, which is the focal point of the image. Even after being resized, it retains a stunning level of clarity. Meanwhile, the background (usually softer and out of focus) can be upscaled with little to no visible quality loss.

I've been questioned about this technique before, with some arguing that it's unnecessary or overly complicated. But in practice, it's made a dramatic difference in the quality of my prints. This method has become a standard part of my workflow over the past two years, and the results speak for themselves.

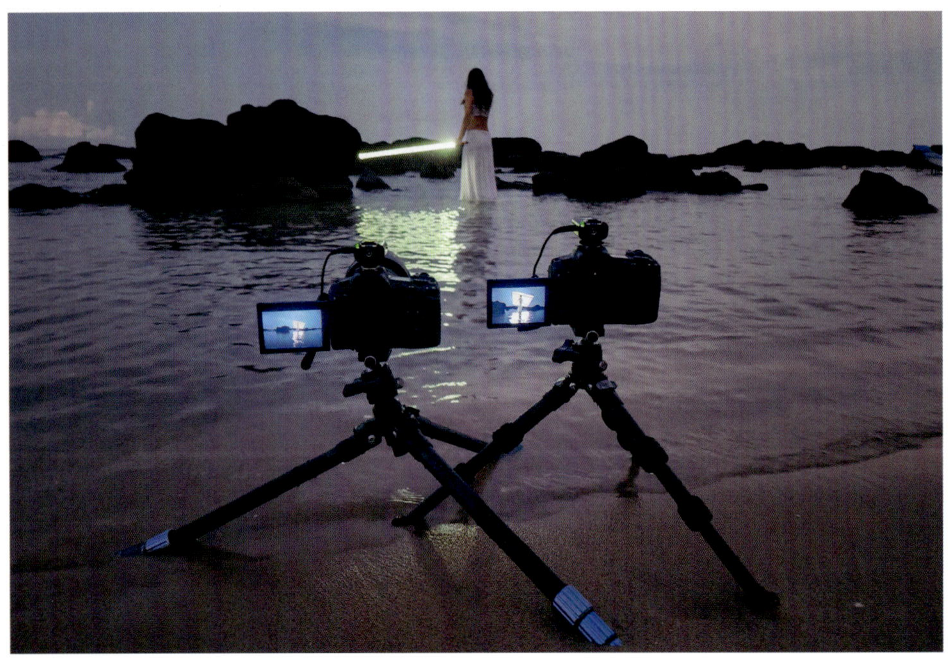

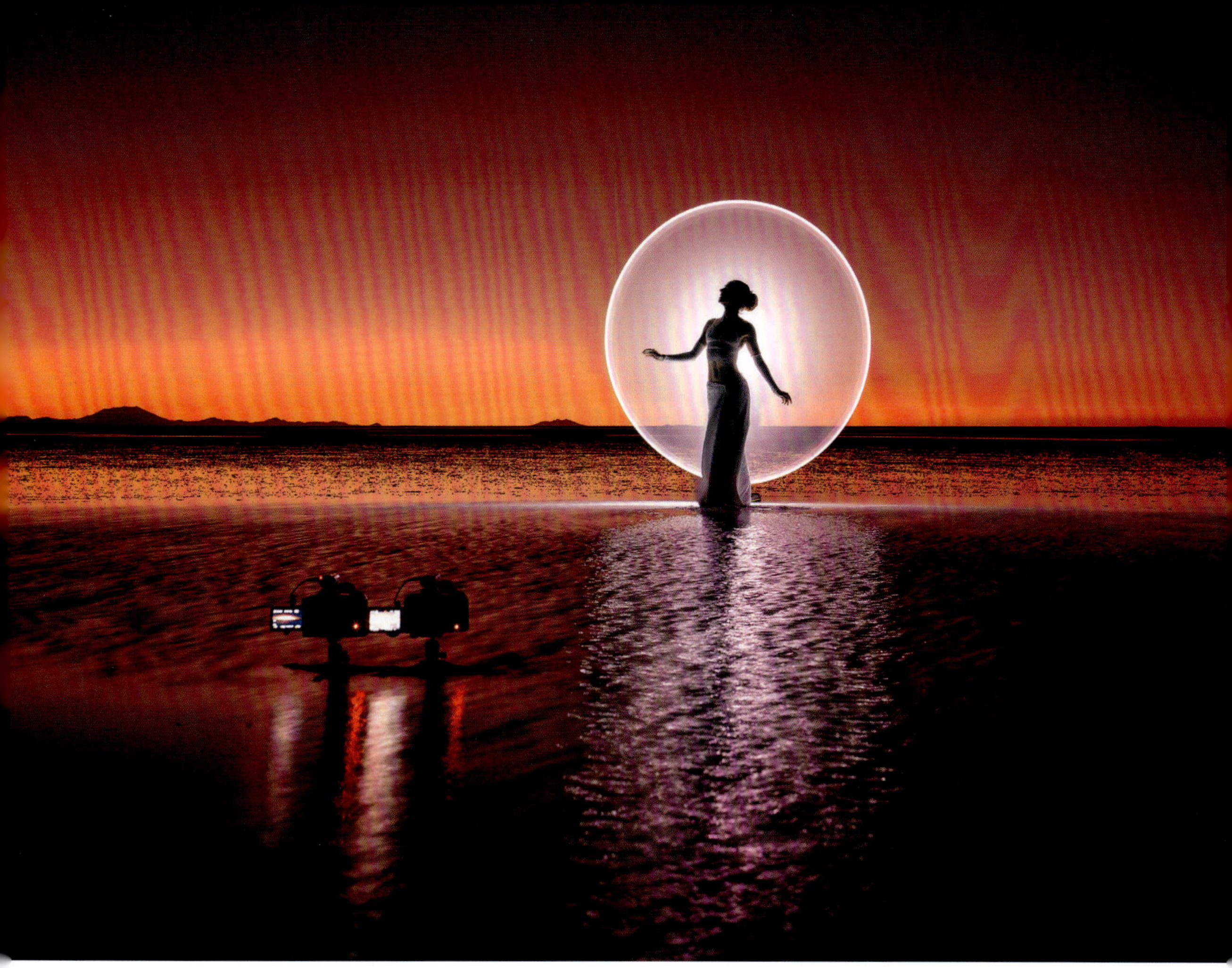

ABOVE **The setup simply involves positioning two cameras side by side.**

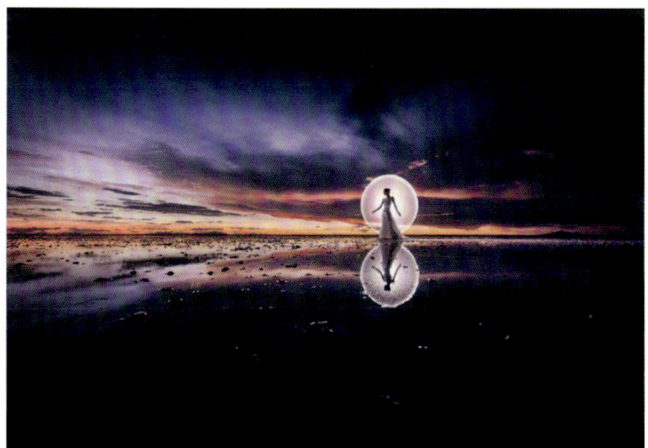

ABOVE **A 14mm focal length was used here for the overall composition.**

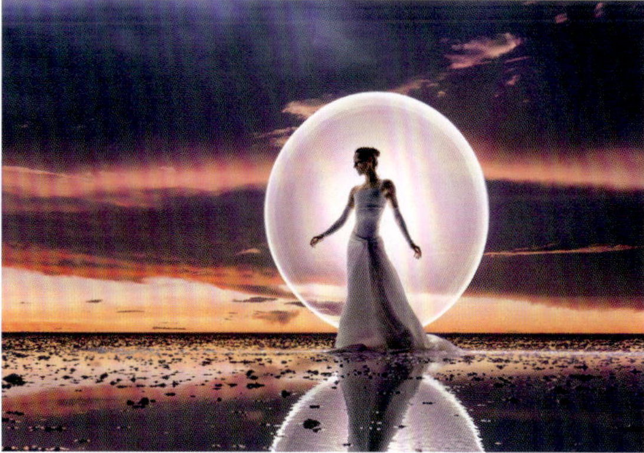

ABOVE **The closer image was taken with a 50mm focal length.**

Timelapse & multiple exposures

Timelapse photography enables you to create a dynamic animation from your light-painting images. By capturing a series of images over time and playing them as a rapid sequence, this technique alters the perception of time, making it appear to move faster. The result is a short video where each image serves as a frame.

To achieve this effect, you need to maintain the same composition throughout the sequence, and your photographs should be taken at regular intervals to capture movement in the scene – typically in the sky, such as stars, the Milky Way, or clouds.

The execution is quite challenging, both for the light painter and the model, as the performance requires sustained focus for a long period of time. The model must remain as motionless as possible for the whole capture, and even if you choose a simple and stable body position, it is a grueling experience. Meanwhile, the light painter must maintain consistency, repeating the same shape over and over while staying hidden behind the model for the duration of the timelapse.

The shorter the distance between the subject and the sky object we want to capture, the faster it will appear to move. This affects how long your timelapse will take to capture: fast-moving subjects, such as clouds, require less total shooting time than slower-moving subjects, such as stars or the Moon. A Milky Way timelapse will take even longer, as each individual exposure needs more time to capture enough light, quickly extending the overall duration of the process.

A simple way to calculate the number of frames you need is to multiply your desired video length (in seconds) by the standard cinematic frame rate of 24fps (frames per second). For example, if you wanted to create a 5-second video, you would need at least 120 frames (5 seconds × 24 fps = 120 frames).

Although some cameras have a built-in timelapse mode, I prefer to capture the images manually. The main reason is because it's easier for me to remain in control of the trigger, and therefore determine precisely when each exposure starts, rather than trying to keep track of where we are by only using the sound from the camera. It's easy to lose the timing when you don't have any visual cues and are relying on the sound of the shutter to guide you.

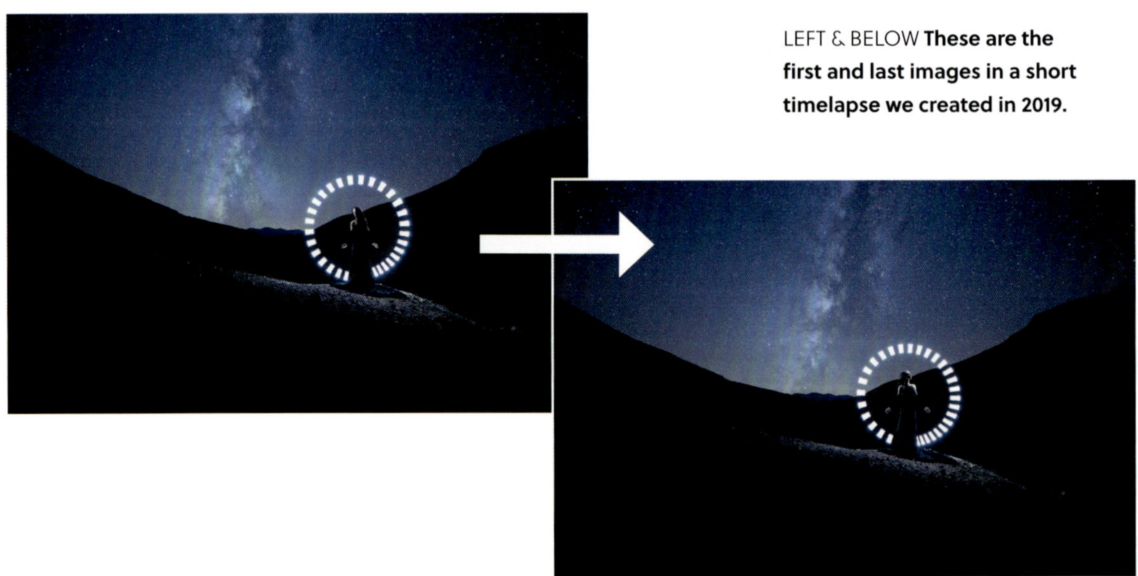

LEFT & BELOW **These are the first and last images in a short timelapse we created in 2019.**

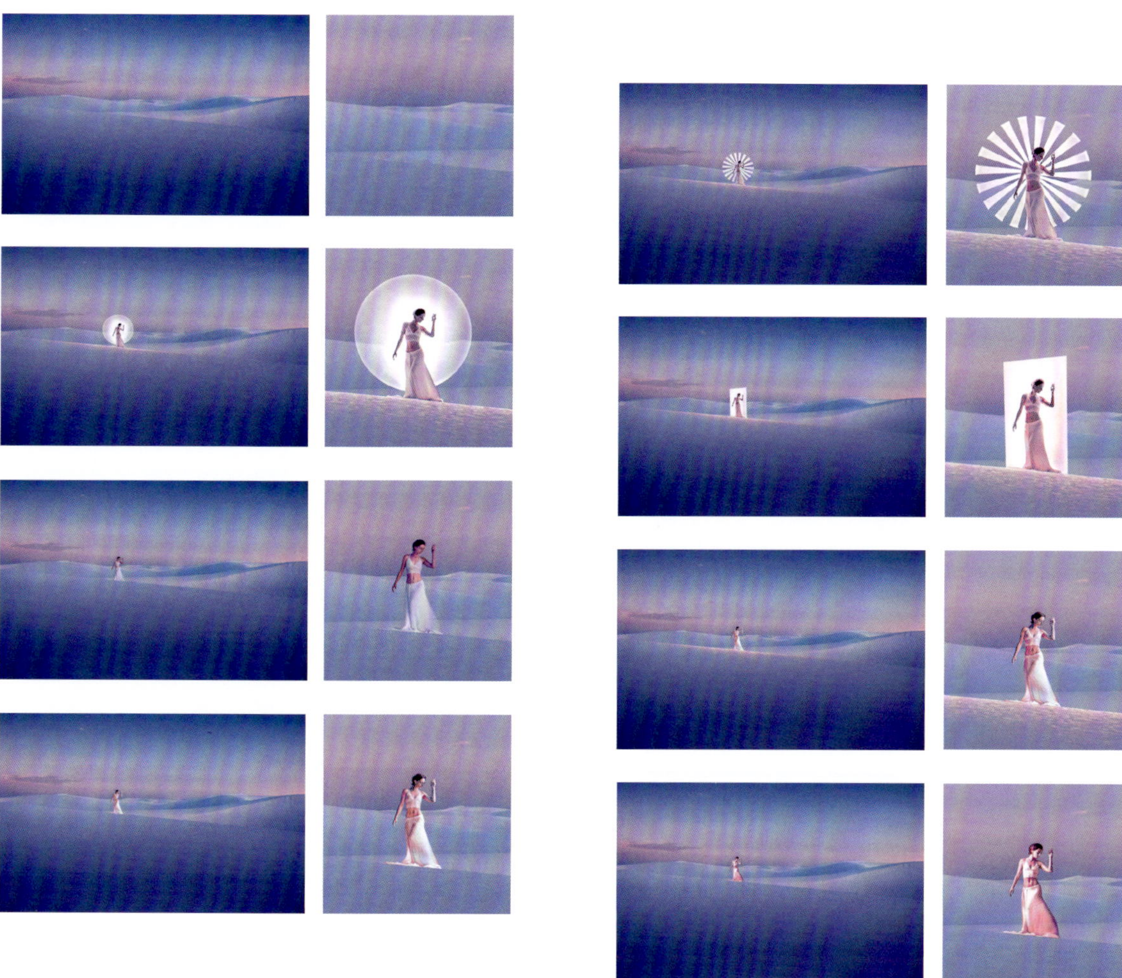

MULTIPLE EXPOSURE ANIMATIONS

Using multiple exposures to animate the light painting is a simpler creative alternative. What is specific to this technique is that what creates the dynamism is mostly the light. Using a series of multiple light-painting shapes with a single pose from the model, we can create short, animated loops. The execution is simpler than a timelapse, and it can be created with a single series of images, using between six and ten pictures.

As the model does their best to stay motionless during the whole time, I will execute a few light-painting shapes (a door, a circle, a circle in strobe, and so on). Then, I'll move to one side of the model and hold the tube to get a side-lit picture of the model's body. Finally, I'll take another shot using just the ambient light (no light painting), with the subject still in position.

From these frames I can play with different combinations, using Photoshop to edit the individual images and Premiere to combine them into a short, animated video.

Filming your sessions

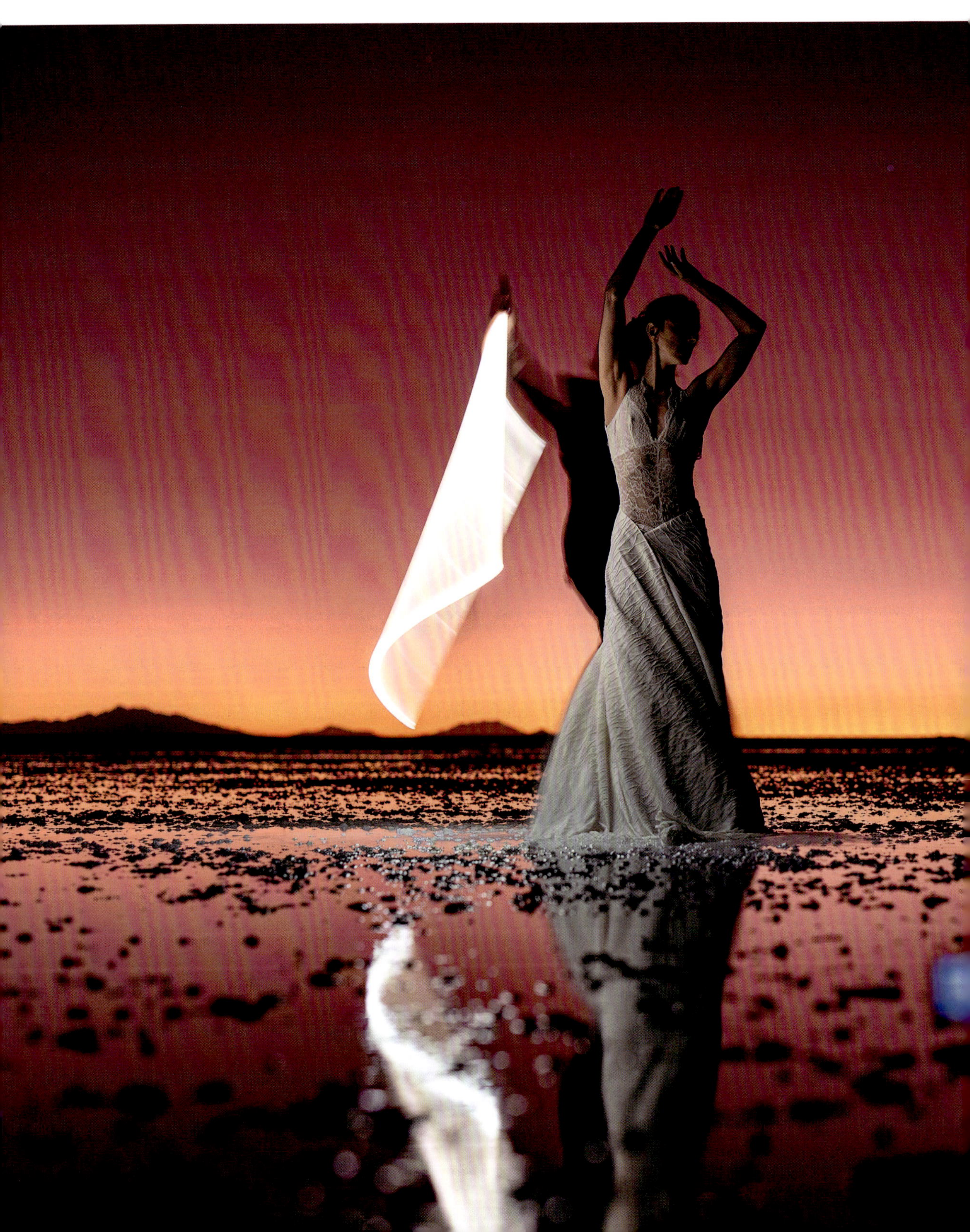

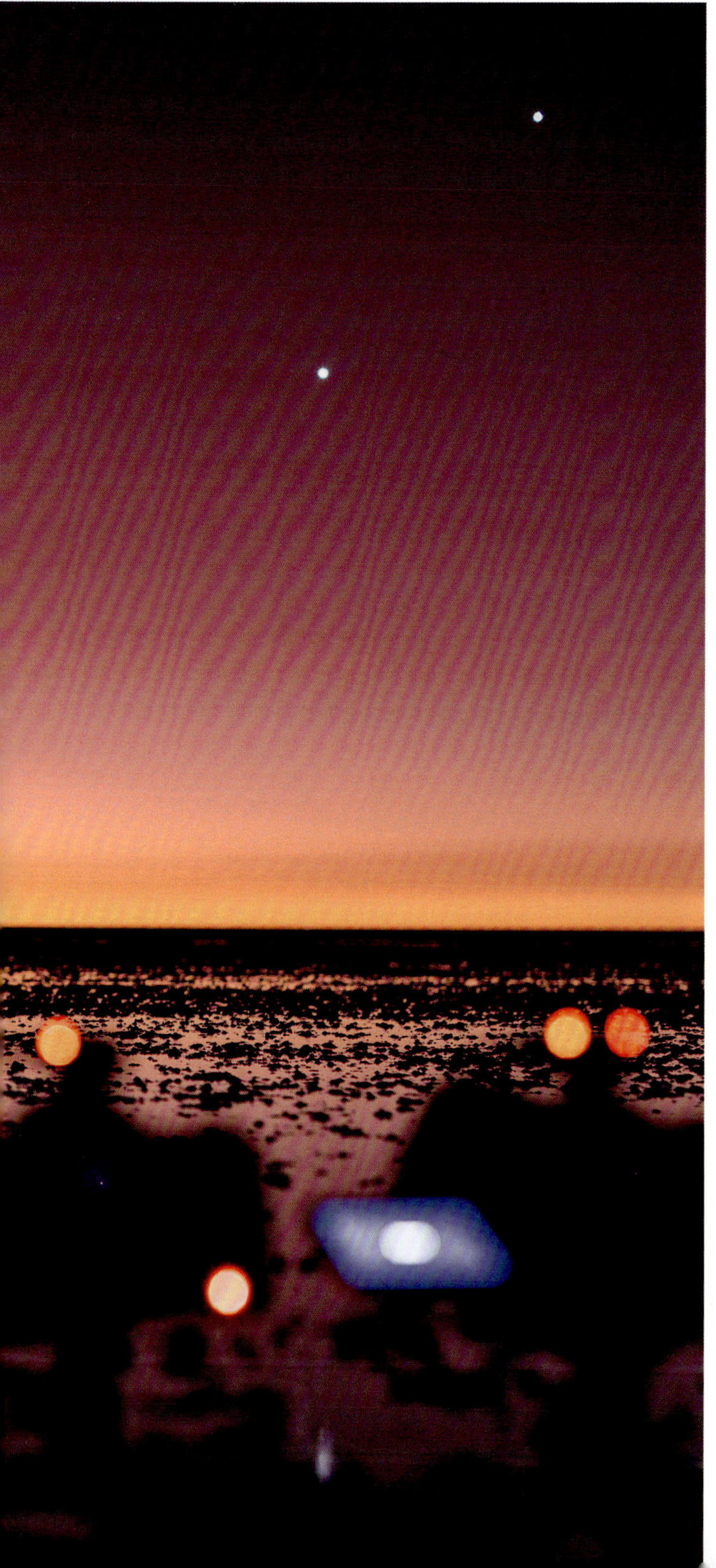

Most of the time we film our sessions, not in their entirety, but at least parts of them. We think it's an interesting thing to add to your process for several reasons:

→ You can learn a lot and improve by watching your own movement.

→ It's a great tool if you ever want to teach what you do to someone else.

→ We find that sharing the process is a beautiful complement to the art itself.

→ In the age of digital manipulation, where it's increasingly hard to differentiate between what is real and what is not, sharing the process of creation demonstrates the technique's authenticity.

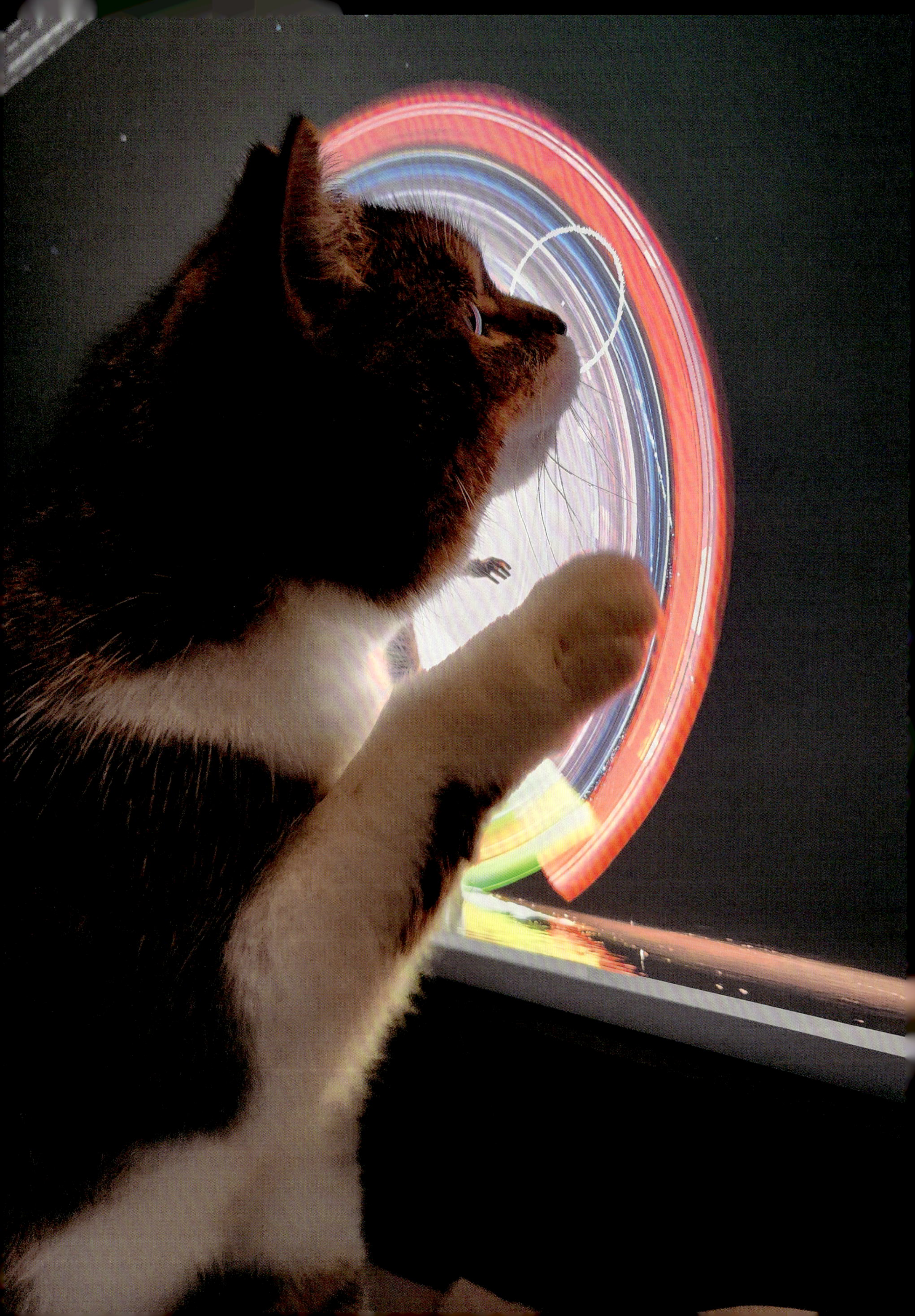

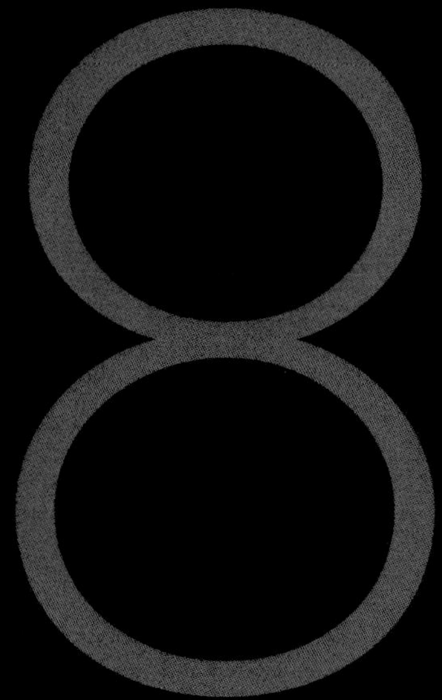

Post-processing

I feel a lot of satisfaction when I capture an image that's well balanced, well composed, and needs minimal adjustments. I prefer spending time outdoors creating images rather than sitting at my computer editing. It's also a sign that the technique has been well executed. However, in some cases, an image can still be improved with a few simple post-processing steps.

Editing essentials

Post-processing techniques continually evolve alongside the tools developed to process our images. We can assume that technologies will keep evolving quite rapidly, so this section may become less accurate as time goes on, but this is how I currently work on my images.

IN CAMERA

It might sound counterintuitive, but your processing decisions start when you are in the field shooting. To avoid the camera making decisions for me, I always shoot Raw, which ensures I have the most information in my files and the widest possible dynamic range. When I open these files on my computer, I work on them as 16-bit images to retain that information, which is especially helpful when it comes to color grading subtle tonal variations in a blue sky.

As mentioned on page 144, I often shoot using two cameras. One records a closer view of my model, and the other gives a wider angle, and I'll merge the two images so I have more details on my model. This is overkill for social media posts but makes a difference if you want to create large prints. We will look at that technique on page 156.

WORKFLOW

I use Adobe Photoshop to process individual images and Adobe Lightroom when I have to batch process images for timelapses or star trails, in addition to Topaz Photo AI and StarStaX when appropriate. Depending on the complexity of the subject and what the end goal is, I can spend anywhere from one minute to two days editing a single picture; if I want to do a large print, I'll go as far as fixing individual stars, combining multiple frames to reveal more detail in the background, and more.

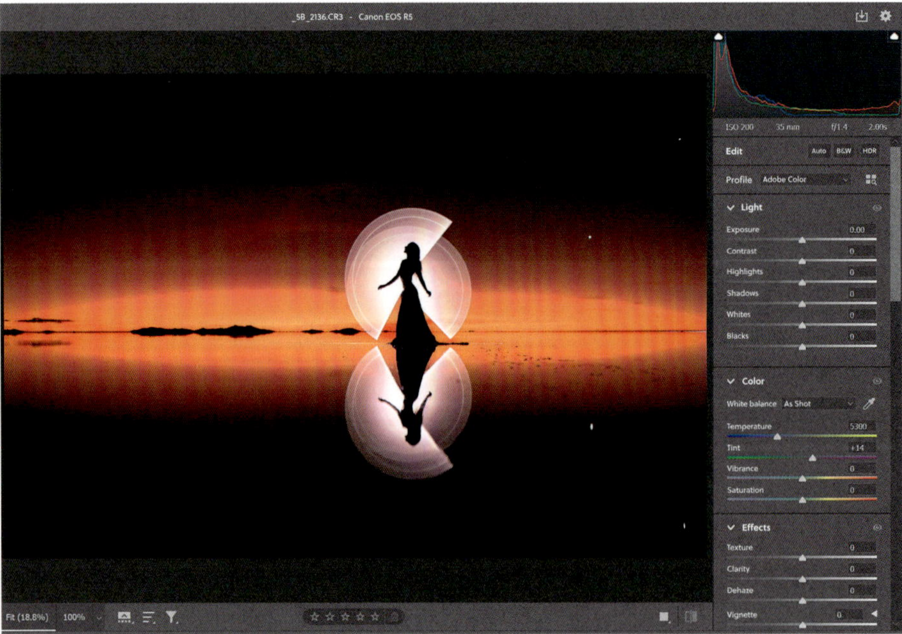

Regardless of the time spent on an image, my workflow generally follows the same pattern. I will start by making minor adjustments and applying noise reduction in Adobe Camera Raw, using AI Denoise and basic slider adjustments. I don't push too far here, as I'm looking to bring a "flat" image into Photoshop. I don't alter the original white balance very much, but will tweak it a bit to the left and to the right to see if I can reveal more colors. I'm not necessarily looking for the final colors here, rather I am trying to extract the most color I can. Sometimes, a minor white balance adjustment on the Raw file can reveal more colors and ease the color grading in Photoshop.

Color grading is the next step, and I do this in Photoshop using Curves, Color Balance, and Hue/Saturation. I'll also make any local adjustments that are needed. I try to do as much of the processing work as I can in a non-destructive way using adjustment layers, smart layers, and linked documents. This even extends to rotating an image, which I do on a smart object that includes all of my layers. To expand an image when the composition is a bit off, I either "stretch" (transform) a selected area, use content-aware fill, or generative fill. It all depends on the type of background I have.

When I'm ready to export an image, I use a ratio template that allows me to export multiple versions of the same file in a non-destructive way. This means I can always go back to the original image and apply changes, and the ratio files will update automatically.

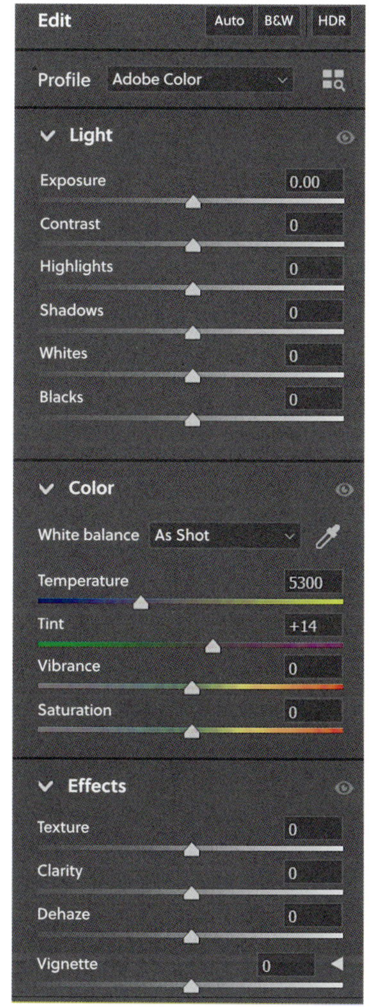

LEFT **This Lightroom screenshot shows all sliders in their original positions, including white balance, showing that no adjustments were made.**

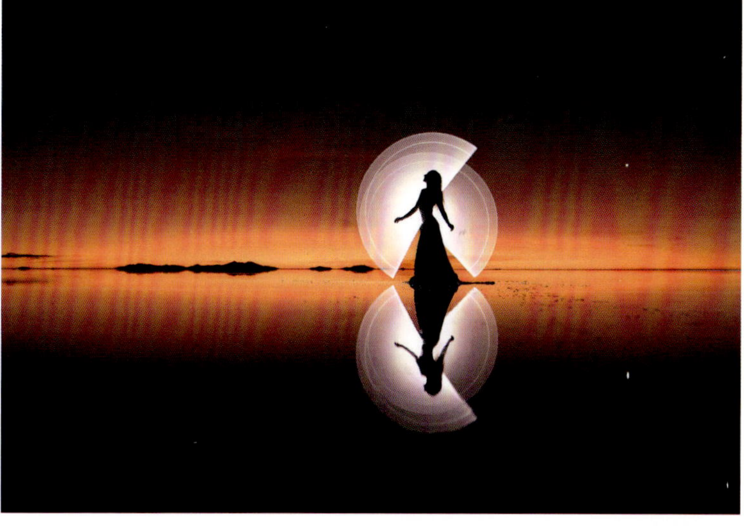

ABOVE **The better your initial capture is, the less editing it will need, which is what I usually aim for. This image required zero editing: it's well balanced, and since I'm not visible, there was nothing to remove.**

Black canvas

With a black canvas image, minimal editing should be required. The main aim is to get pure black around the subject and the light painting, which mostly means crunching the blacks to avoid any hot pixels, stars, or things floating in the water. I typically achieve this by using a black color adjustment layer and a curves adjustment layer, which I mask to ensure a smooth transition leading to the light-painting shape.

With this specific image, I also changed the color of the horizon line from a yellowish-green to desaturated red. This line is actually light that went all the way through the tube, illuminating the water and creating the interesting line. I also brought back stars and bubbles that were darker, using masked adjustment layer curves.

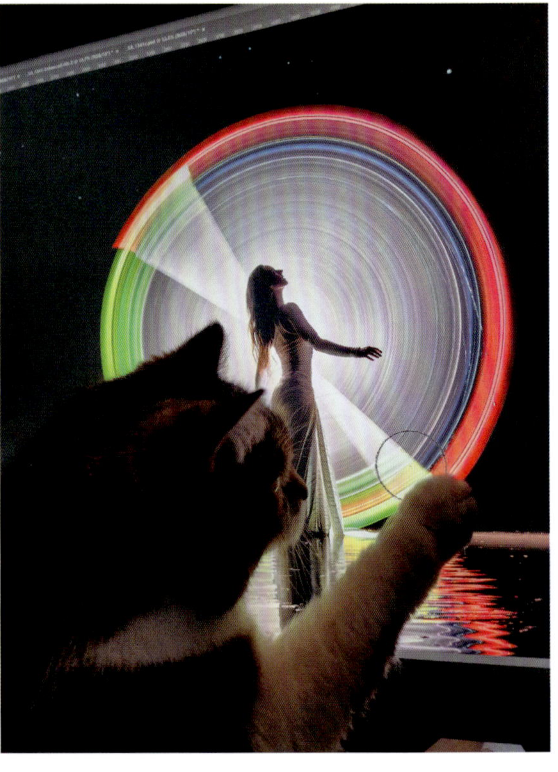

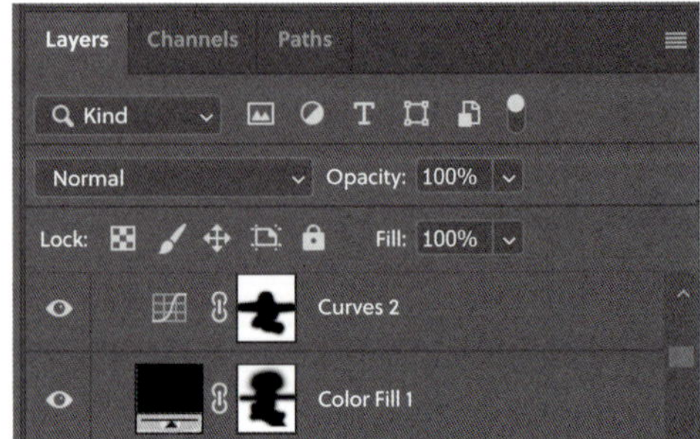

ABOVE **Here's my editing assistant making some subtle last-minute tweaks.**

LEFT **Adjustment sliders. Keeping everything close to original settings**

BELOW **Adjustment layers & layer masks to ensure pure black around the subject.**

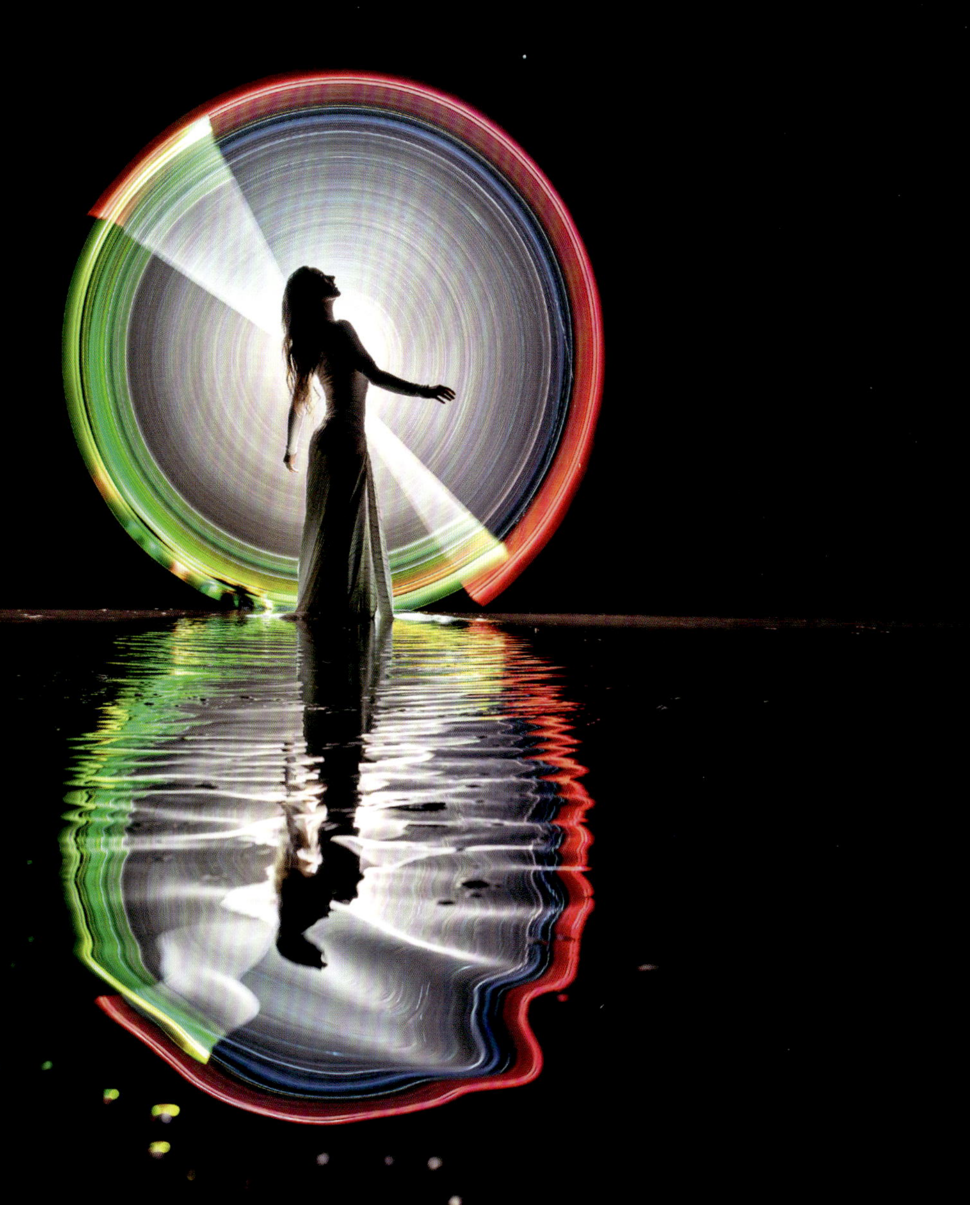

Blue hour

Here's a typical blue hour shot, and in this one, I made a critical mistake due to improper alignment while creating the image. Let's take a look at how to fix it.

As we discussed in chapter 4, alignment behind the subject is crucial during blue hour. A slight misalignment can cause you, or parts of your gear, to become visible in the final image. I chose this specific photo to demonstrate a simple method for correcting that kind of error.

The color grading here is fairly straightforward: a slight increase in Exposure and Contrast, along with a reduction in Highlights and Whites. These adjustments help balance the overall tones and create a more even final result. In this example, I'll also walk you through how I merge a wide-angle shot (14mm) with a portrait shot (35mm) to complete the composition.

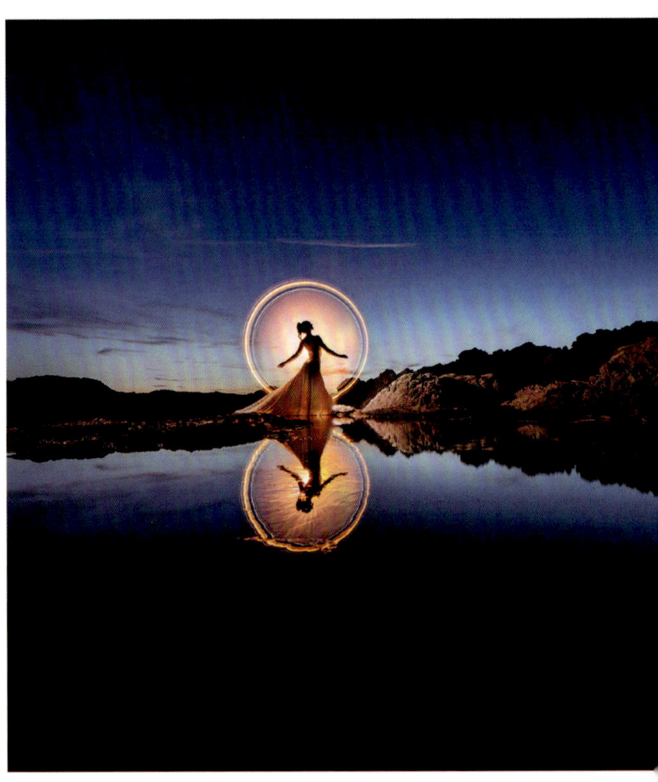

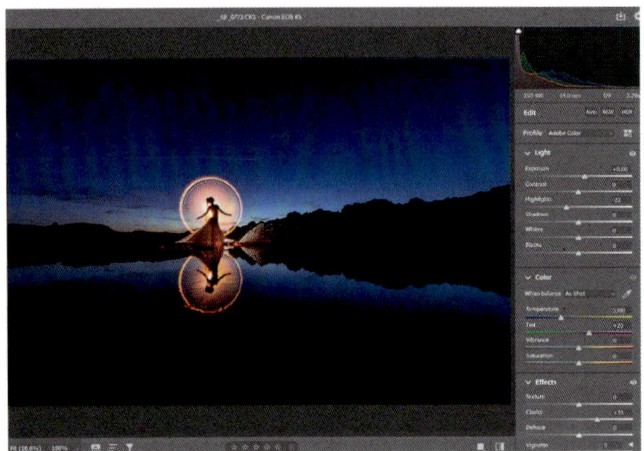

1. Open the wide-angle image and apply your basic editing to your taste.

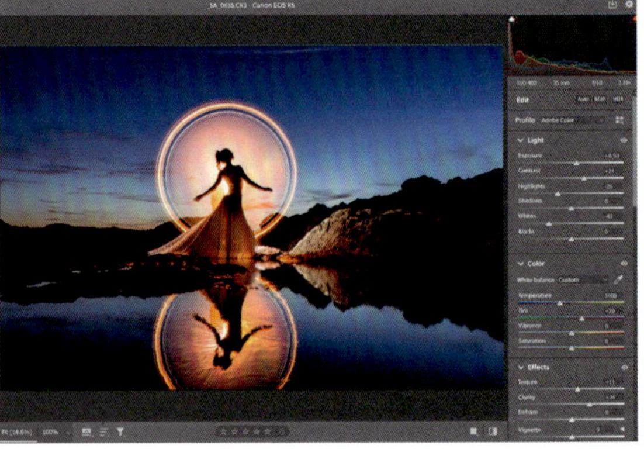

2. Open the close-up image and apply the same settings (More image settings / Apply previous settings), open as an object.

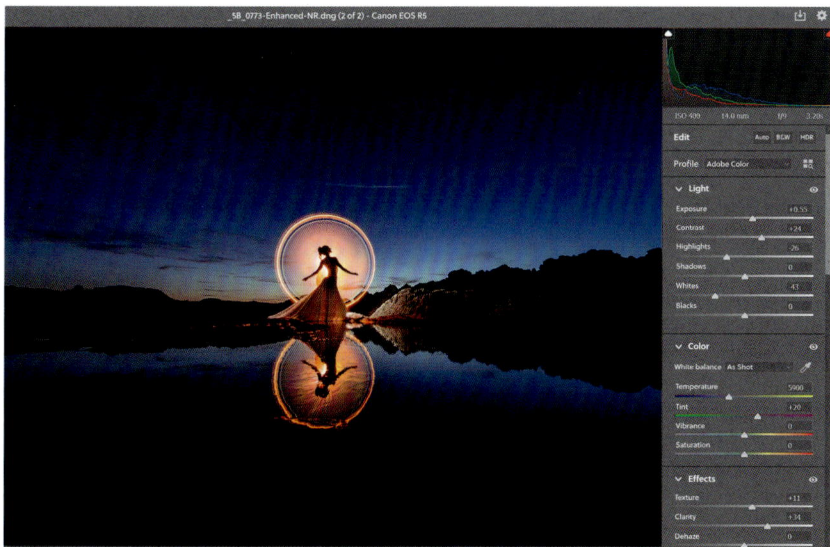

3. Cut the object and paste it on the wide-angle document (the base image).

4. Do a square selection around the subject (including the light painting) and create a mask from this selection. Using a smart object will ensure we can move/resize/edit the close up without losing quality in each step.

5. Change the opacity to 50% and match the subject using the transform tool. That is, try to align as close as you can the subject and the light painting.

6. Go back to opacity 100% and use a black brush and paint over the part you want to remove on your close up. You can keep only the subject, or the subject with its light painting (depending on the situation).

7. Upscale the document. I usually go with twice the resolution of the original image. Once you do this, you'll suddenly get a super-high-quality version of the close up. The background is not going to be on par, but as it is often out of focus (not the main subject), it doesn't matter very much. There's a way to recover some details on the background layer by using Topaz Photo AI or similar.

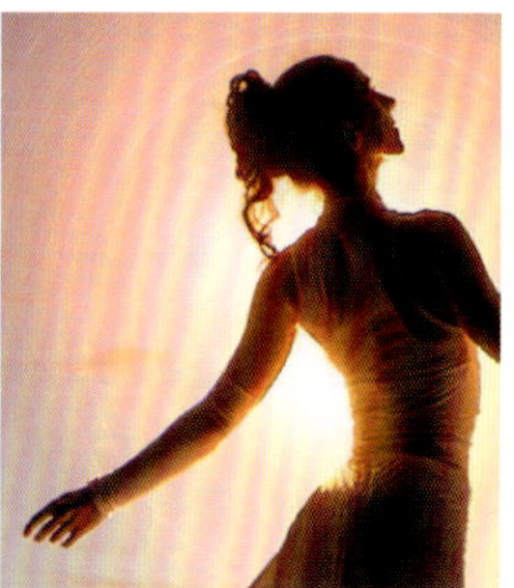 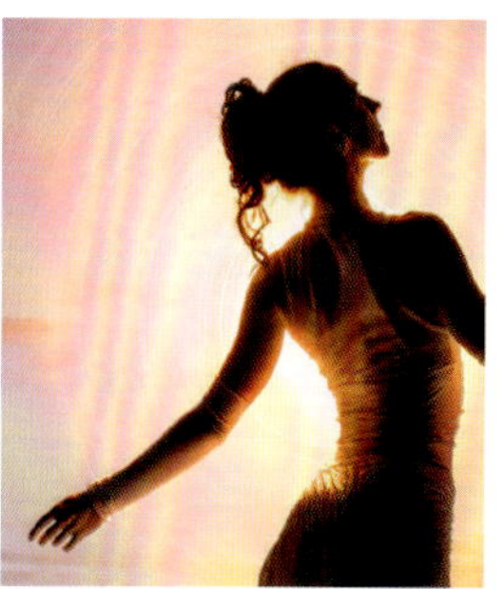

8. Now let's fix the alignment. Simply make a lasso selection in the misaligned area then right click on the area and apply a generative fill.

9. I noticed that the rocks have some weird colors coming from either a lighthouse or a focus light from the participants of this workshop. I evened out these colors by using a Hue/Sat adjustment layer, Colorize, orange color (desaturated). Then I painted over the rocks.

10. Do your final color grading using Hue/Sat and Curve adjustment layers. In this one, I desaturated the blues, saturated the yellows/reds, added some shadows in the top right corner and middle-right.

11. Save your file as TIFF for archiving and JPEG for online publication.

Star trails

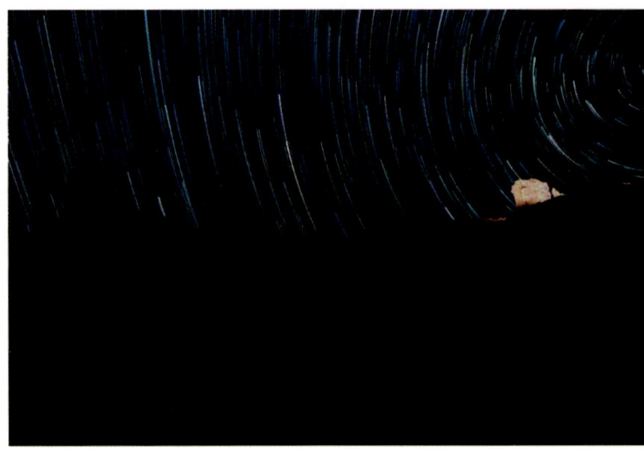

I don't do a lot of star trail photographs, and this is by far the greatest amount of manipulation I will do on any of my images; I find it very tedious and the conditions have to be right in order to come up with something clean. In this example, taken at the Atacama Desert in Chile, I'm doing it the simple way as the rocks are very easy to mask out.

For this shot I took 185 frames, each with an exposure time of 30 seconds, so there was about 90 minutes of shooting in timelapse mode. I shot my 30-second exposures at ISO 200 (to keep noise to a minimum) and set the aperture at f/1.4 to get the giant trails; the white balance was set at 3200K.

MAKING YOUR STAR STACK

Before you can add your subject, you need to create your star trail image, which I do using Lightroom and StarStaX.

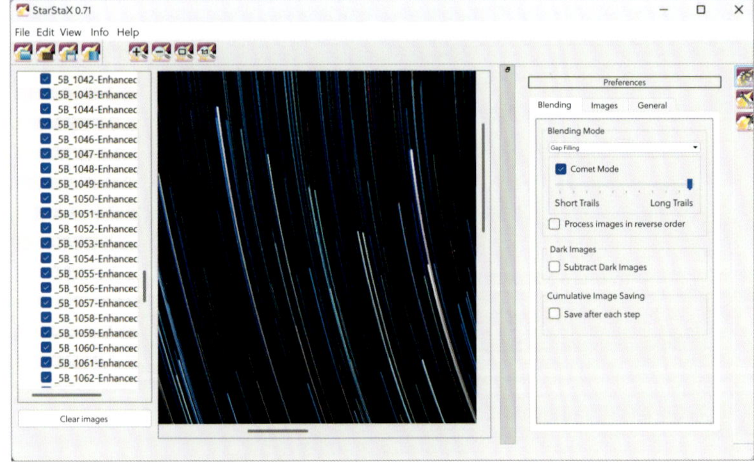

1. When I'm processing a batch of images and the adjustments are going to be the same, I'll use Lightroom to make my basic edits. For this sequence, I increased Contrast, Texture, and Clarity, lowered Shadows, and applied AI Denoise before exporting the images as JPEG files.

2. Once all of the images have been saved, I open them in StarStaX.

3. In StarStaX, I test different combinations of settings to refine the composition, especially when planning to include a subject later on. I experiment with "Comet Mode," adjust the "Trail Length" slider, and sometimes enable "Process images in reverse order" to control the direction and overall feel of the trails. I always use the "Gap Filling" blending mode, as it consistently produces the cleanest and most continuous results. There's no perfect formula here – at some point, the decision to go with longer or shorter trails becomes an artistic one, depending on the mood or story you want the final image to convey.

4. Click on Edit / Start Processing. This process takes a few minutes before you can see the result.

5. Save JPEG and don't worry about the background. We'll use only the star trails from this file.

CREATING YOUR COMPOSITE

Once you've saved your star trail image you can combine it with your light-painting element.

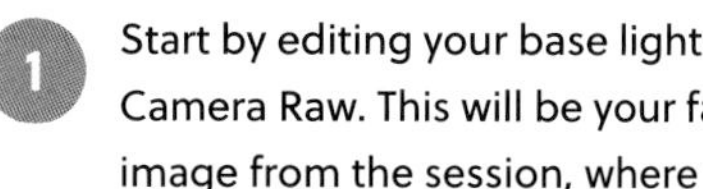

1 Start by editing your base light-painting image in Adobe Camera Raw. This will be your favorite light-painting image from the session, where the camera was in exactly the same place as it was when you shot your star trails.

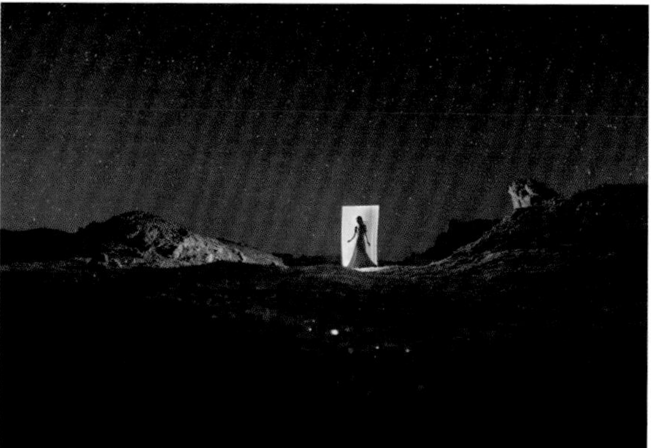

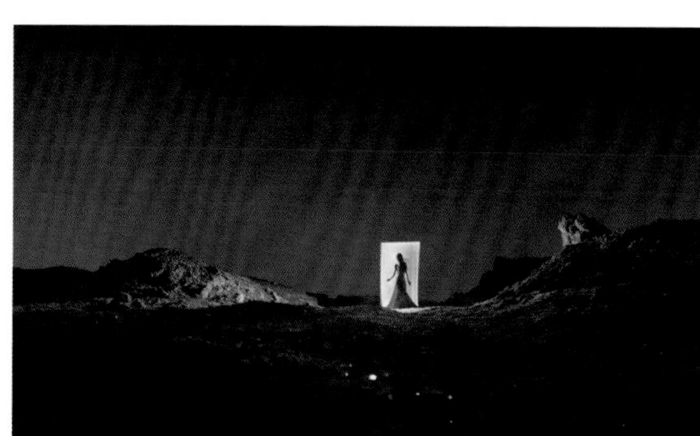

2 Having made your basic edits, open the image in Photoshop. The first step is to clean up the stars, but they are so prominent in this image there's simply no way they can be removed one at a time. Luckily, there's an easy way of doing this.

3 Use the Object Selection Tool to select the foreground (in this example the rocks and subject); invert the selection so the sky is selected; and copy the sky as a new layer. With the new sky layer selected, use the Dust & Scratches filter (found under Denoise) and select a value that makes the stars disappear.

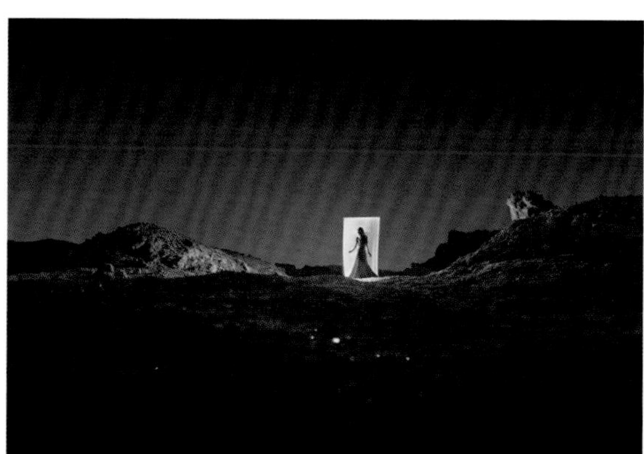

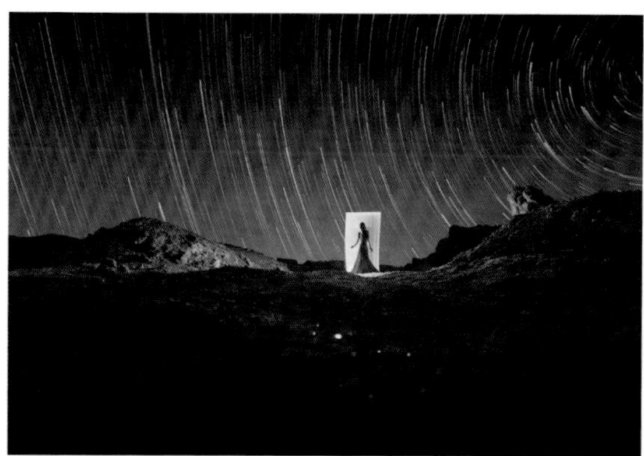

4 In most cases, the previous step is going to be enough to get a clean sky, but in this example some unusual colors were added by some clouds above the rocks, so I added a gradient adjustment mask with the opacity set at 70 percent.

5 Open the star stack image and copy it as a layer on top of your base image. Use the same mask as step 4 (or the sky selection) so that only the trails are visible. Change the star stack layer's blending mode to Lighten or Screen and adjust the brightness to your taste using an adjustment layer above or below the trails layer.

Milky Way

The post-processing of Milky Way images is a perfect blend of technical expertise and artistic expression. In the following instructions, I present two different approaches to editing the Milky Way. The first is a simpler method that uses only Adobe Camera Raw (or Lightroom). The second is more advanced and involves editing in Photoshop using layers and masks.

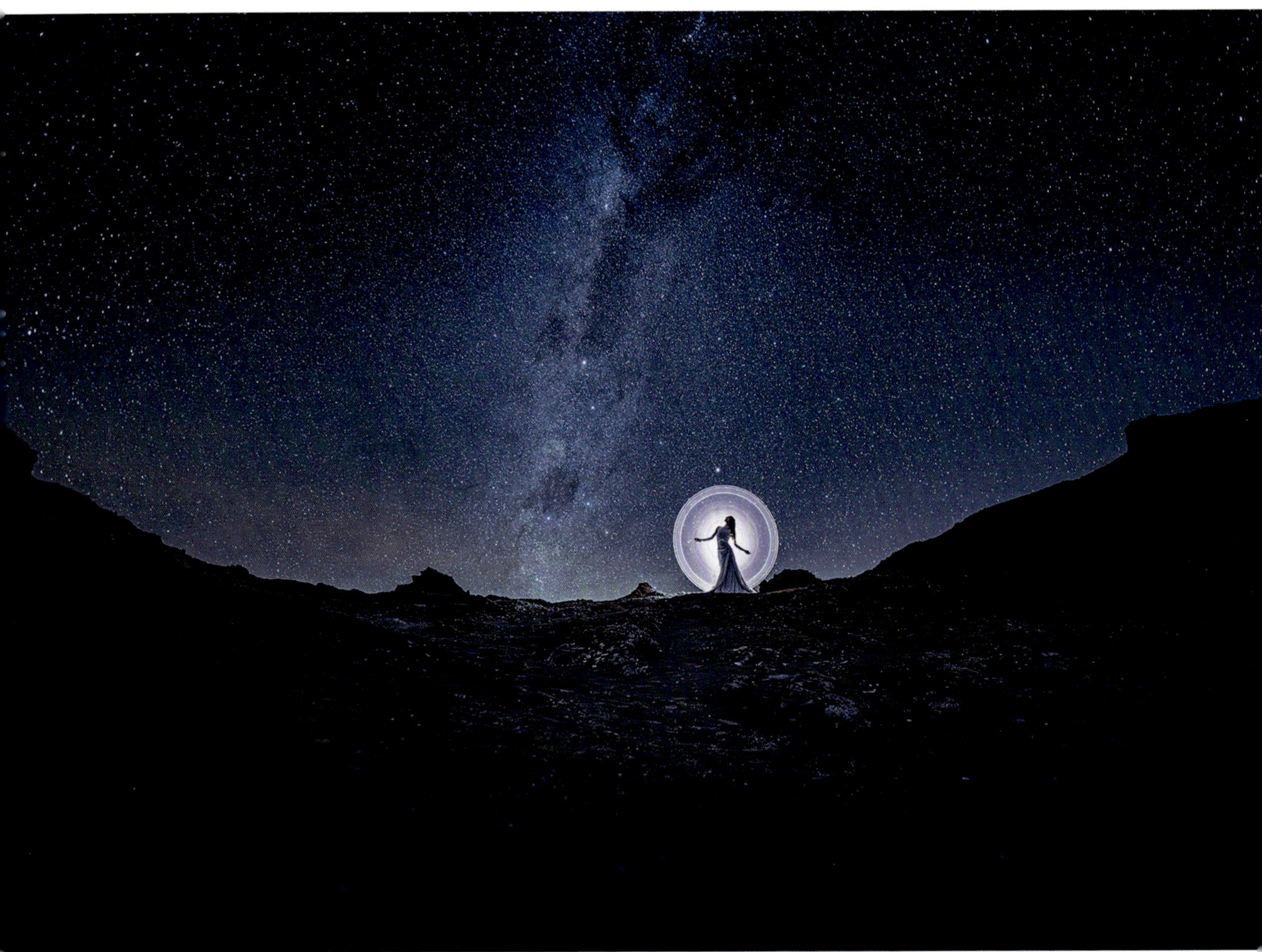

SIMPLE EDIT

1. Open the image in Adobe Camera Raw or Lightroom and begin adjusting the basic sliders to bring out the details in the Milky Way. I typically increase Shadows to reveal more structure in the darker areas and lower Highlights to preserve detail in the brighter parts of the sky. Boosting Clarity and Texture can enhance the overall sharpness and definition of the stars. Be careful not to push these sliders too far, though, as over-editing can introduce noise or create an unnatural look. The goal here is to reveal the richness of the sky while maintaining a natural and balanced feel. You can see the adjustments I made in this example, but keep in mind that the exact settings will vary depending on the image you captured.

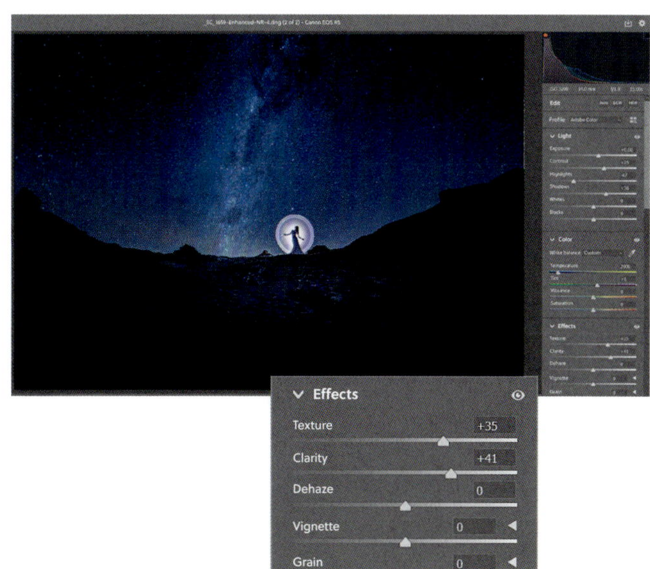

2. Create masks to adjust specific parts of the image without affecting the whole frame. In Adobe Camera Raw, click on the Masking tool (the circular icon in the toolbar) to get started. You can then choose different types of masks, like a Radial Gradient, which lets you apply adjustments in a circular or oval area. For this image, I used three separate radial masks:

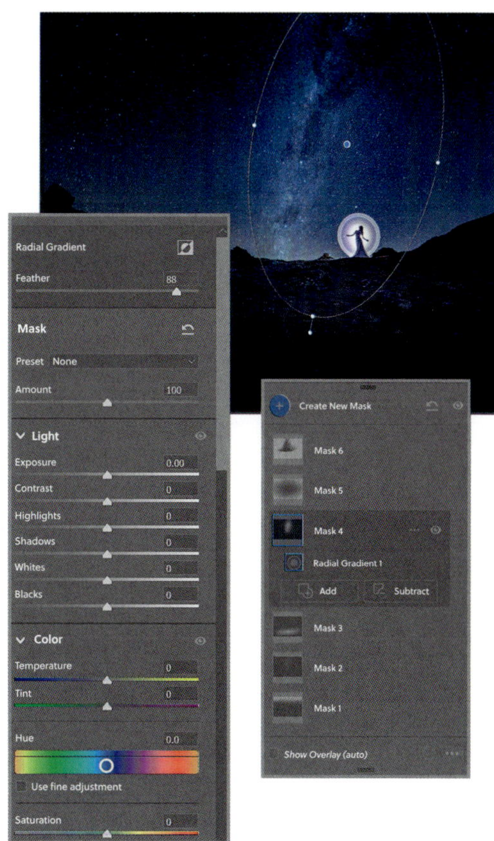

→ One over the Milky Way to slightly boost Exposure (+10) and Clarity (+15), making the core stand out more.

→ A second mask over the top of the foreground to increase Exposure (+20) and bring out more detail.

→ A third, inverted radial mask placed in the center of the image to create a subtle vignette by lowering Exposure (-15) around the edges.

→ These masks help guide the viewer's eye and balance the light across the scene.

→ Don't worry about getting it perfect, just experiment and adjust the size, shape, and feathering of each mask to blend the effect naturally.

3. When you are finished, convert and save your image.

ADVANCED EDIT

1 Open the Raw file in Adobe Camera Raw and start by evaluating the image to see how much detail is available in both the shadows and highlights. This can be hard to judge at first glance, as Raw images often look flat or underexposed. Try increasing the Exposure slightly and lifting the Shadows slider to reveal what's hidden in the darker areas. In this particular shot, the original composition is strong (we won't need to crop or rotate) and there's plenty of detail to work with in the background, foreground, and on our model.

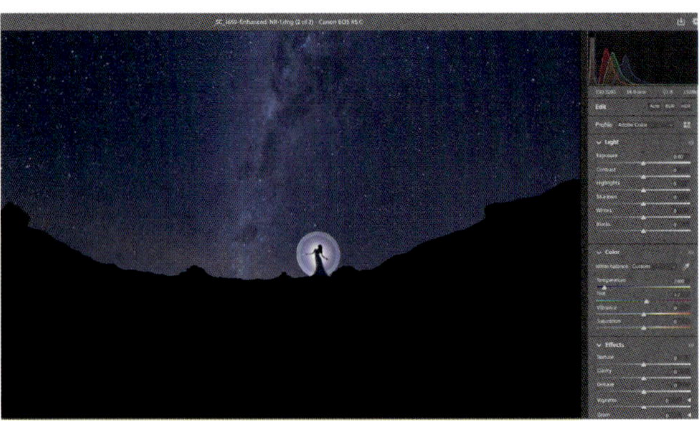

2 My basic settings adjustments were Exposure +0.6, Contrast +17, Highlights -30, Shadows +13, and Clarity +10. Each of these is quite subtle because I want to allow plenty of room for color grading in Photoshop (the more you push the sliders in ACR, the less information you retain for the next steps).

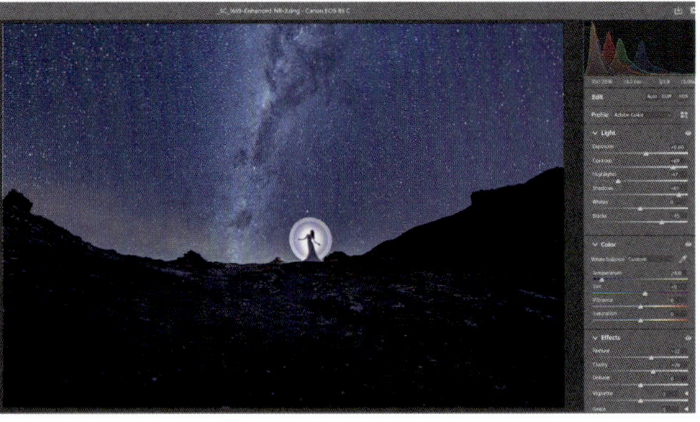

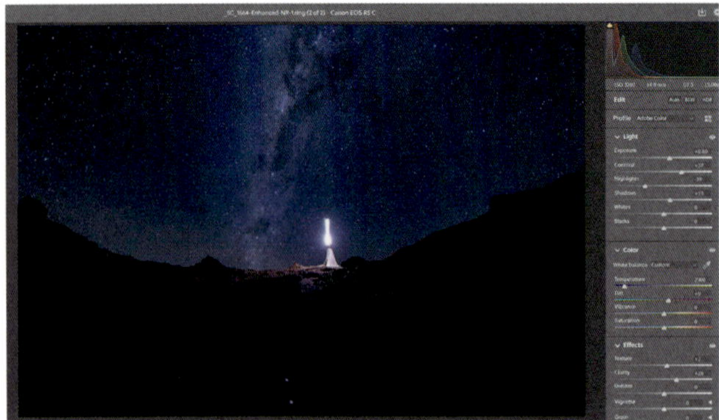

3 The foreground (rocks and dust) look pretty good, and in most cases I would leave it as it is. However, I have the habit of making a deliberate "foreground" shot just in case I want to get more detail without pushing the sliders too far (which would decrease the image quality). The foreground image I'm going to use for this edit has nice contrast and additional illumination on the rocks at the sides of the frame.

4 Bring your base image and your foreground into a single layered file and mask the foreground using the Quick Selection tool.

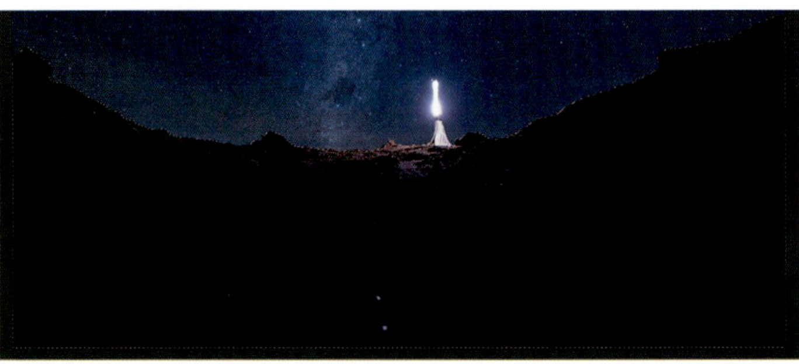

5   Add a Curves adjustment layer with an oval (circular) gradient to darken the outer edges of the sky in the Milky Way area. To avoid affecting the foreground, ensure that the sky and its adjustment layers are placed in a group with a mask that targets only the sky.

6   Add a Hue/Saturation (colorize) adjustment layer for the sky and select a blueish color. This is going to even out the colors in the sky, including the clouds and the Milky Way.

7   Continue with additional color grading (Curves, Color Balance, Hue/Saturation) to accentuate the parts of the image you want to draw attention to.

8   An optional step at this stage is star removal. Sometimes, the number of stars can be overwhelming and add too much visual weight to the upper part of the picture; removing the smaller stars can help restore balance. Start by duplicating your base layer and create a layer mask so you are only working on the sky. Apply the Dust & Scratches filter with a radius of 1px to automatically treat the smallest stars as dust and remove them. Reduce the opacity of your duplicate layer to about 50 percent (this will bring the stars back faintly, which avoids an unnatural-looking night sky).

9   With this image, I removed some footprints and tweaked the light distribution below the subject before exporting the JPEGs in multiple ratios.

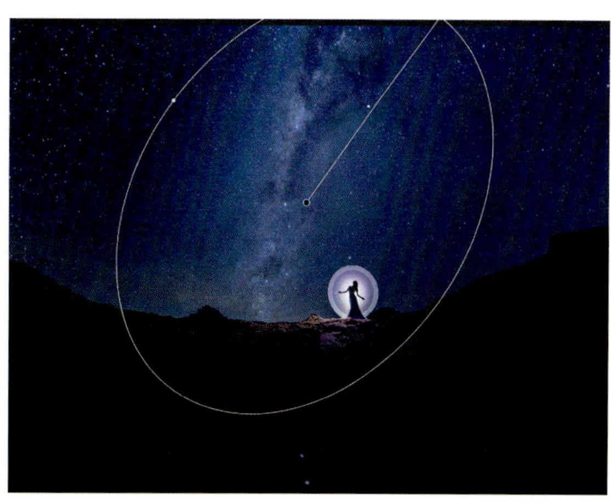

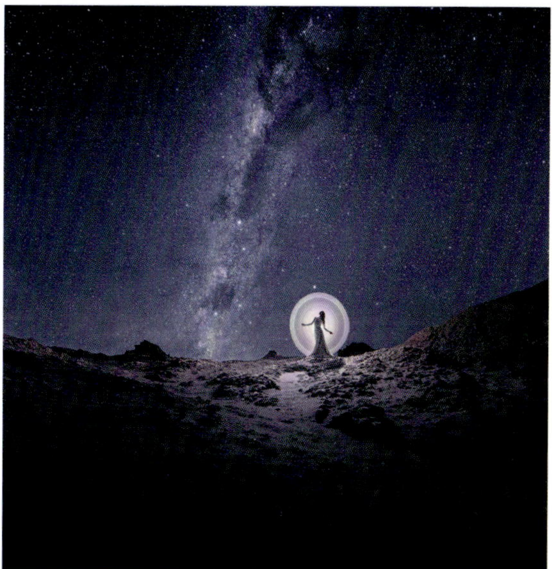

Testing the image

Once I'm happy with an edited image, I generally flip the picture left-to-right and look at it again. This is a simple yet revealing exercise that resets your perception, as if seeing the image for the first time. It lets you take a fresh look at the visual weight distribution within the frame and think about how your attention moves through the image. Do your eyes go where you intended them to, or do you notice something that feels unbalanced? Even if you've worked on an image for several hours, don't be afraid to change the final crop or make further adjustments if it leads to a better balance.

FAQ

This section answers the most common questions we're asked about our light-painting techniques, equipment, and process. Most of them are explained in greater detail within the book.

Are your images composites?
No. Most of the images in this book were created with a single exposure.

Do you use a flash to illuminate your subject?
No. The subject is mainly lit by the light-painting trace, and sometimes by the natural ambient light.

How do you light your subject?
With the light-painting tool and ambient light (see chapter 4).

How do you create a perfect circle?
It's a mix of optimal alignment behind the subject, body positioning, and an extended arm during rotation (see chapter 4).

What tool are you using to create these images?
For outdoor light painting we mostly use tubes. At their simplest, these are plastic tubes with a flashlight inserted at the base, but it can get much more sophisticated than that. I use different colors and accessories depending on the shade and effect I want to create.

Where can I get your tubes?
Our tubes are available at Lightpainting.store

Can I make my own tubes?
Yes! The simplest way to make one from scratch is to roll a piece of plastic (clear polyester or acetate) and secure it with hair elastics or rubber bands. If you live in North America, fluorescent tube guards can usually be found in hardware stores.

Do I need a flashlight adapter for the tubes?
No. Some companies sell adapters that are advertised for use with our tubes, but that's mainly because they also sell flashlights with a diameter that is too large to fit directly. We don't recommend adapters because they make the grip less sturdy and alter the light quality of the tool. The most efficient approach in our experience is to use a flashlight with a diameter of 1 inch (2.5cm) or less, which fits directly into the tube and provides the optimal light distribution.

Do you ever use LED programmable devices instead of tubes? If not, why not?
I don't use or recommend LED programmable devices, because they are usually heavier than tubes. Their weight is also distributed along the entire tool, which makes them harder to manipulate and limits the range of movements that can be done with them. I prefer my tools to be simple and lightweight.

Do you use filters on your lens?
No. ND filters, polarizers, grads, light pollution filters, and so on will all block a certain amount of light, which affects the light painting. It's an unnecessary accessory when you're shooting in low-light conditions, as you'll often already be at the limit of "acceptable" settings to capture a quality image. I don't want to block more light from entering the camera.

Do you need to wear black clothing to do outdoor light painting?
Not necessarily. Although wearing black won't reflect the light, the light painter will still be visible in the shot if their body blocks the light coming from the background (sky). The most important factor is your positioning and alignment, not clothing color.

Why don't you use a smartphone app to trigger and see the image instead of using a remote and going back to your camera between series?
I find that the potential advantages don't outweigh the inconveniences. A smartphone is an extra piece of gear to set up, and in my experience it is less efficient and breaks the creative flow. Even with a smartphone preview, I'd still need to go back to the

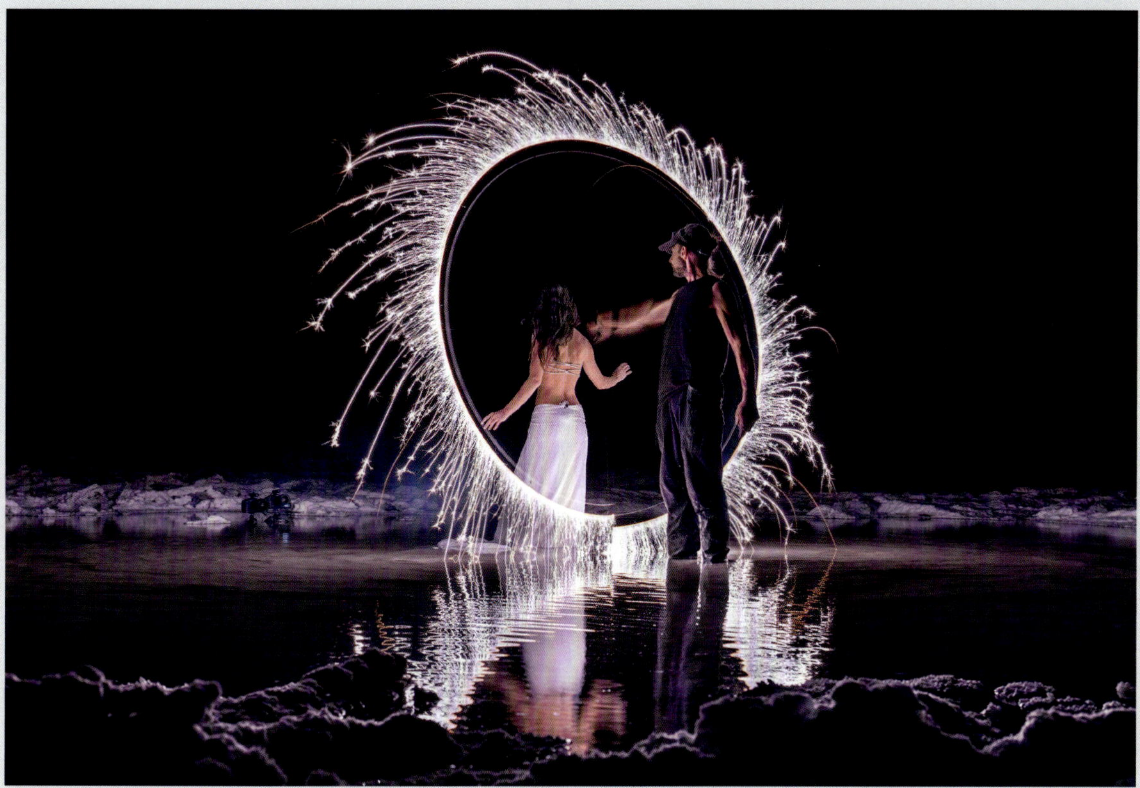

camera to adjust the composition, which is often necessary between series.

How far from the model do you stand when you do the light painting?
It depends on the shape I'm creating. If I want to move the light in front of the subject on one side, I'll start closer, but if I stay behind the model the whole time, I'm usually about an arm's length back from her.

How do you travel with your tubes?
We use a long bag for the tubes, usually adding our tripods and some clothes to get extra weight and padding. If we're flying, the bag needs to be checked-in as oversized luggage.

Do I need expensive photography gear to start creating?
No! Although lenses with a wider aperture will give you a better-quality result when shooting in low light (when you want to include stars or the Milky Way) you can definitely shoot black canvas or forest scenes at night with an older DSLR and an entry level lens, or even with your smartphone.

Where does Kim get her outfits?
I mostly use long pieces of fabric that I attach with safety pins! They're easy to carry and care for. I match the "skirt" with different tops – some are pieces that I buy and modify, others I make myself. It's not sophisticated but totally aligns with our desire to embrace simplicity.

Reference toolkit

EQUIPMENT CHECKLIST

- Camera and lens
- Spare batteries
- Tripod
- Remote triggers
- Spare batteries

- Tubes
- Flashlights
- Spare batteries
- Pressure switch
- Light-painting accessories

- Feathers, sparklers, caps
- Hair elastics
- Windproof lighter

TUBES COLOR REFERENCE

This is a list of tubes we frequently use outdoors, along with their respective reference image. The white balance setting will affect the perceived colors; this is more apparent with some tubes than it is for others, which is why we have included two pictures in some instances.

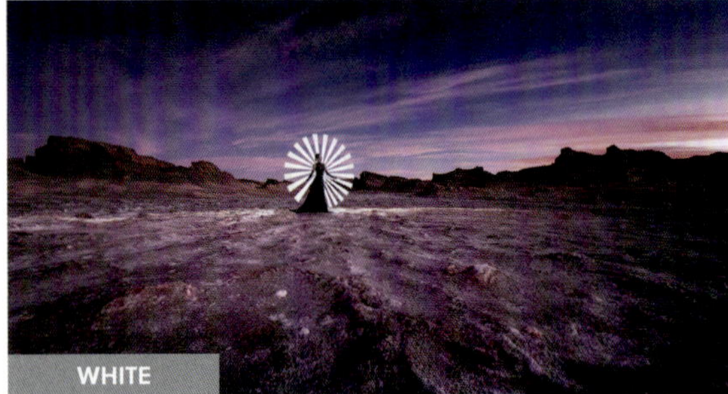

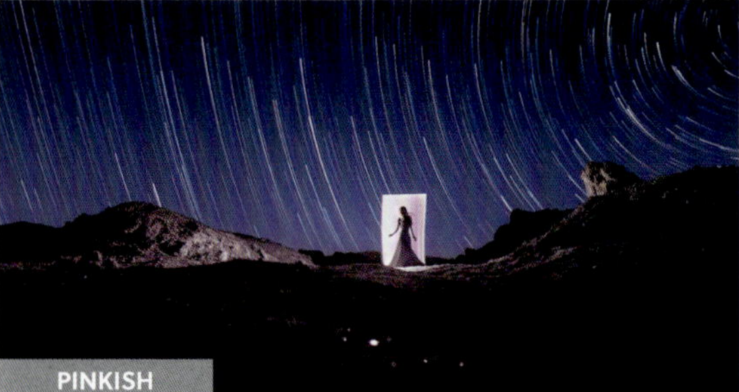

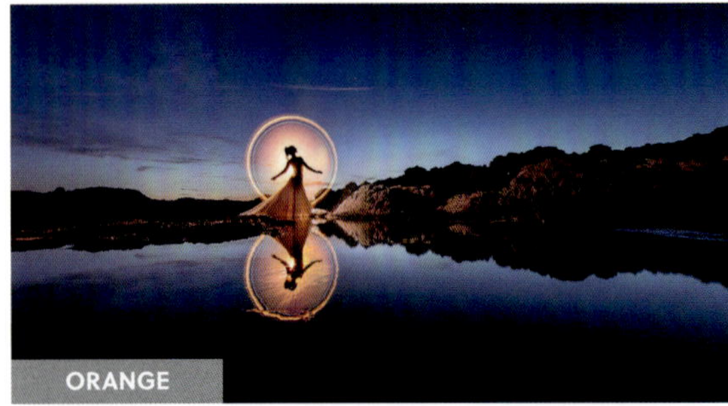

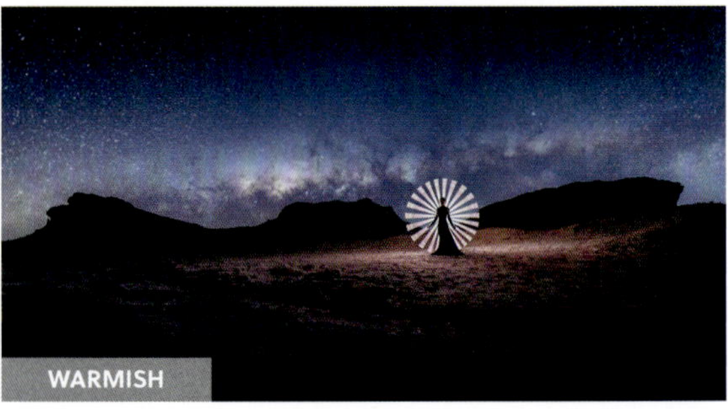

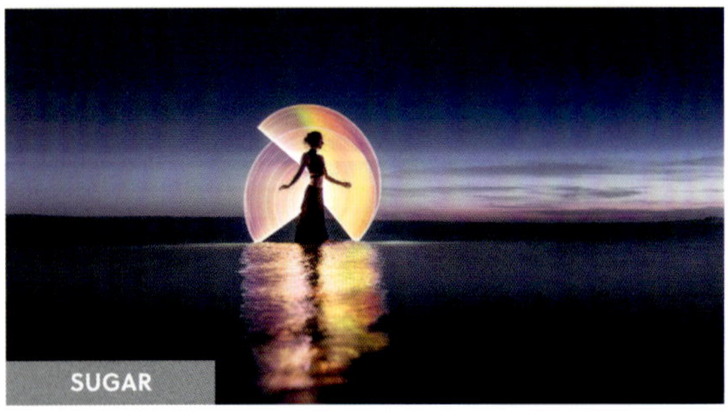

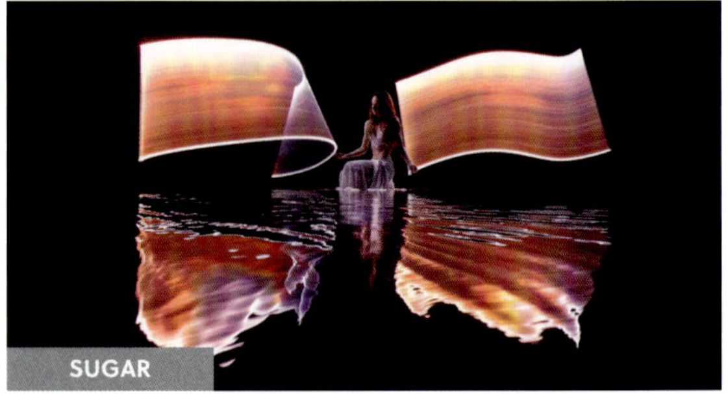

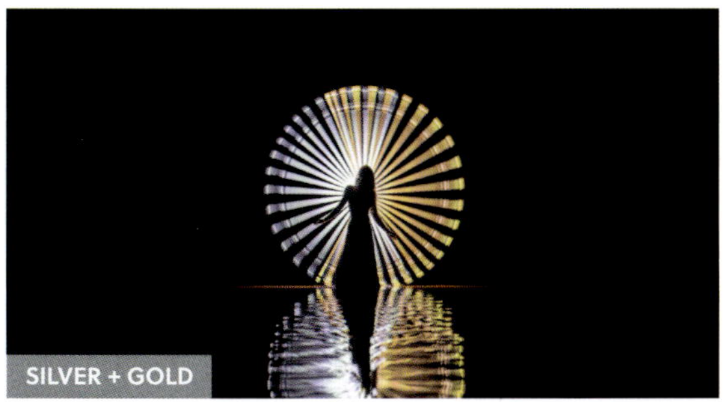

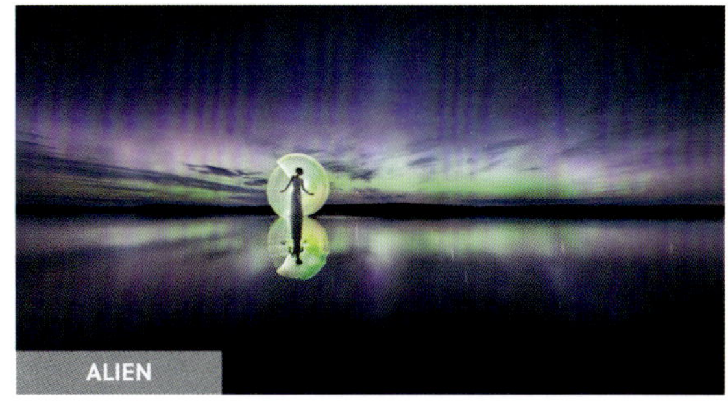

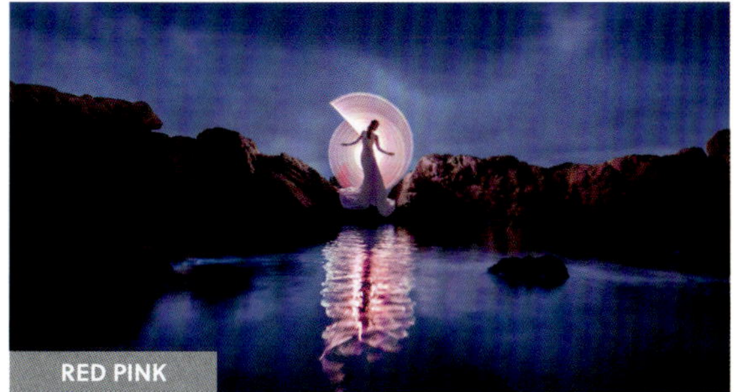

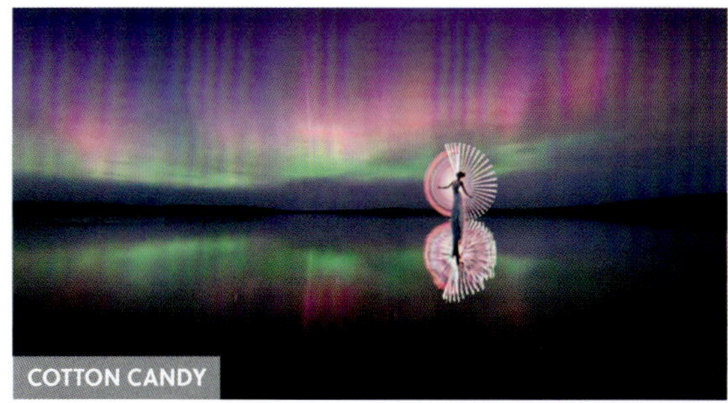

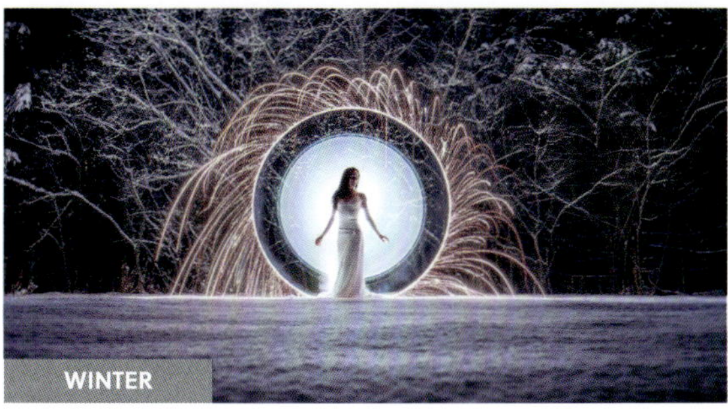

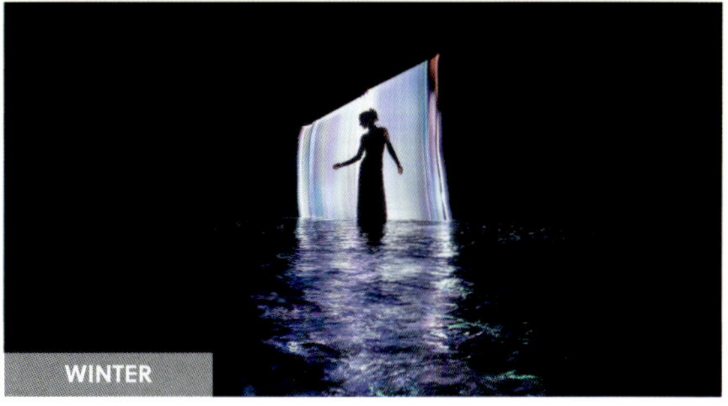

SOLID VS. MILKY COLORS

Some tubes are produced in both Solid and Milky varieties. They both create very similar colors, but different qualities of light. Solid tubes are "directional" and emit light in one direction, making it easier for the light painter to disappear. They generally deliver higher contrast than Milky tubes. By comparison, Milky tubes are diffused, emitting light in all directions. This makes it harder for the light painter to disappear, but the tube throws a softer and more even light on to the ground.

Each tube has a matching feather, but the color choice is up to you. You can use a feather that matches the tube, a complementary one, or a colorful one on top of a neutral-colored tube to add a splash of color. These options can add subtle changes to your images.

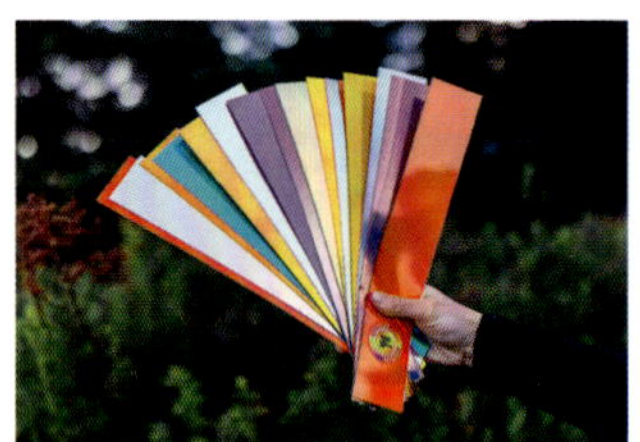

TUBES DATASHEET

Type	LPT name	Code	Colors	Brightness	Temp	Usage
Holographic	Rainbow	hRB	Rainbow	6	3800	Studio
Holographic	Sugar	hSG	Yellow, Purple	5	3800	Studio, blue hour, black canvas
Holographic	Alien	hAL	Green, Yellow, Red	6	3400	Studio, auroras, black canvas
Holographic	RainbowTrout	hRT	Pink, Rainbow	6	4500	Studio, black canvas
Holographic	Sunset	hSN	Orange, Purple	6	4200	Blue hour
Holographic	Winter	hWN	Blue, Cyan	7	4200	Snow, black canvas
Holographic	CottonCandy	hCC	Cyan, Red, Pink	5	3200	Auroras
Holographic	RedPink	hRP	Red, Pink	7	4800	Blue hour
Solid	Solid White	sWT	White	10	5200	Blue hour, black canvas
Solid	Solid Warmish	sWH	Desaturated orange	7	3200	Stars, moon
Solid	Solid Pinkish	sPH	Desaturated pink	8	3600	Stars, moon
Solid	Solid Orange	sOR	Orange	8	4600	Blue hour
Solid	Solid Red	sRD	Red	4	5200	Studio, black canvas
Solid	Solid Amber	sAB	Amber	6	4600	Studio, black canvas
Solid	Solid Yellow	sYL	Yellow	8	5200	Studio, black canvas
Solid	Solid Lime	sLM	Lime	7	5200	Studio, black canvas
Olympic	Olympic Gold	oGD	Gold	6	4600	Studio, black canvas
Olympic	Olympic Silver	oSV	Silver	6	5200	Studio, black canvas
Olympic	Olympic RoseBronze	oRB	Pink	5	3600	Studio, black canvas
Milky	Milky White	mWT	White	8	5200	Blue hour, black canvas
Milky	Milky Warmish	mWH	Desaturated orange	5	3200	Stars, moon
Milky	Milky Pinkish	mPH	Desaturated pink	5	3600	Stars, moon, auroras
Milky	Milky Orange	mOR	Orange	7	4200	Blue hour

OPTIMAL TUBE COLOR SELECTION

Moon	Black canvas	Blue hour	Stars	Milky Way	Winter landscape	Auroras
Warmish, Pinkish	All the colors, especially the Holographic series	Solid White, Solid Orange, Sugar, Sunset, RedPink	Warmish, Pinkish	Warmish, Pinkish, Black	Winter	CottonCandy, CottonCandy Muted, Alien, Pinkish

SPARKLERS

Different types of sparklers produce very distinct visual effects, depending on their composition and burn characteristics. This chart provides an overview of common categories, indicates whether they generate smoke, and shows a reference image created with each one.

Category	Effect	Smoke	Example
Traditional sparklers	Cascade of golden light and sizzling sparks.	No	
Cake or ice fountains	Bright, silver fountains intended to be put on a cake. They produce a thicker effect than a traditional sparkler.	No	
Morning Glory	Multi-colored sparkler. Emits small pyrotechnic stars when it changes colors.	Yes	
Rosy Posy	Multi-colored fountain sparkler. It goes from purple, green, silver, pink, and blue as it burns.	Yes	
Tooth Fairy	Bright silver fountains.	No	
Rainbow fountain	Multi-colored sparkler. Creates a much bigger fountain effect than the previous ones.	No	

SETTINGS

The following settings are suggestions to get you started, but you'll likely need to adjust them based on the conditions at your location. In all cases, the main goal is to expose for the background. As blue hour progresses (from the start of nautical twilight to the end of astronomical twilight), your camera settings must adapt to the fading light. This table helps visualize how each element changes during the transition. The duration of blue hour varies by location and season, but the progression remains consistent. (Times in parentheses indicate the light-painting duration within the overall exposure.)

BLUE HOUR SETTINGS

Blue hour from 18:10 to 19:06 (56 minutes)							
ISO ▲	100	200	400	800	1250	1600	3200
Av ▲	f/13	f/8	f/6.3	f/4	f/2.8	f/2.2	f/1.4
Tv ▲	1.5s	1.9s	2s	2.2s	4s (2s)	6s (2s)	8s (2s)
WB	5200K	4800K	5200K	4200K	3700K	3400K	3200K
🔦 ▼	3000 lm	1000 lm	800 lm	500 lm	200 lm	150 lm	50 lm
🕐	5/56 (18:15)	12/56 (18:22)	19/56 (18:29)	25/56 (18:35)	36/56 (18:46)	45/56 (18:55)	– (19:14)

NIGHT SETTINGS

	Full moon (between 30 degrees and ~10 degrees elevation)	Full moon (close to horizon)	Black canvas	Stars	Milky Way	Star trails	Winter (forest)	Aurora
ISO	400	1600	200	3200	3200	200	200	Variable
Av	f/2.8	f/1.8	f/6.3	f/1.8	f/1.8	f/1.8	f/5.6	–
Tv	4s (2s)	4s (2s)	4s (2-4s)	8s (2s)	8s (2s)	30s	2s	–
WB	~4000K	3200K	See p168	3200K	3200K	3200K	5200K	–
🔦	200–400 lm	50–100 lm	Maximum power ideally 1000+ lumens	50–100 lm	50–100 lm	N/A	Maximum power ideally 1000+ lumens	–

IMAGE REVIEW CHECKLIST

In traditional low-light photography, the histogram is often the go-to tool for assessing exposure. However, in the context of outdoor light painting, especially the way we work, exposure evaluation functions a little differently.

Every time we return to the camera after a series, we rely primarily on the image preview on the monitor. This visual feedback helps us to assess what worked, what needs adjusting and what direction to take creatively. Even though the on-screen preview isn't perfect for judging exposure, especially in low-light environments, it remains our most practical tool for making creative decisions on the spot.

While histograms can offer a more technical view of exposure, we find they fall short in this context. They don't reflect how well the light painting is balanced with the ambient light, nor do they help assess shape brightness, visual composition or subject sharpness.

For a more technical exposure check, the histogram can help if you know how to interpret it. But in our experience, outdoor light painting rarely produces histograms that follow the usual rules. Personally, I almost never use them in the field.

Here is the checklist I run through to efficiently evaluate our results and keep the creative process moving forward:

FRAMING & COMPOSITION

- [ ] Strong composition?
- [ ] Horizon straight?
- [ ] Subject well-placed in frame?

EXPOSURE & BALANCE

- [ ] Background properly exposed?
- [ ] Foreground properly exposed?
- [ ] Light-painting brightness balanced with background?
- [ ] Slight transparency in light shape (when desired)?

SUBJECT & MOTION

- [ ] Subject's pose enhances the image?
- [ ] Pose aligns well with light shape?
- [ ] Subject sharp? If blurry, motion or focus?

DESIGN & COLOR

- [ ] Light shape visually coherent?
- [ ] Color choice works with environment?

This is just the beginning

"Do the best you can until you know better.
Then when you know better, do better."

Maya Angelou

Everything in life is in constant transformation. With that in mind, we aim to evolve, change, and grow for as long as we're able to. And we wish the same for you. We are conscious that as we keep learning, we'll do our best to adjust and improve what and how we teach in years to come. But as of now, this is the best we know and we're confident it is a solid foundation for you to build on.

Our hope is to inspire some of you to be curious and go outside, in nature, with others. To play, create, and connect. Mistakes are part of the process. At least that has been our experience. The more we show up, practice our skills, and release the need to control the outcome, the more space is left for magic to happen. We believe techniques and technologies should be at the service of creativity. The more we master the former, the more freedom we have to create something that is greater than any technical prowess.

Use what you learn in this book as a technique and it might impact your photographic journey. Use it as an artistic outlet and who knows, it might change much more than your photography. Maybe it will have a positive impact on peoples' lives, as it has had and continues to have on ours.

We can't help but to think that by focusing on the outdoor aspect of our practice in this book, we chose to put aside the whole studio part, which is equally dear to us. That might need to become a book of its own in the future... who knows.

As we continue exploring, we'll keep sharing. And maybe some of you will choose to do the same. Because there is still so much more to do and so much space for other artistic voices and perspectives.

We've been saying this for a decade now and it still resonates today as we write these last words:

This is just the beginning.

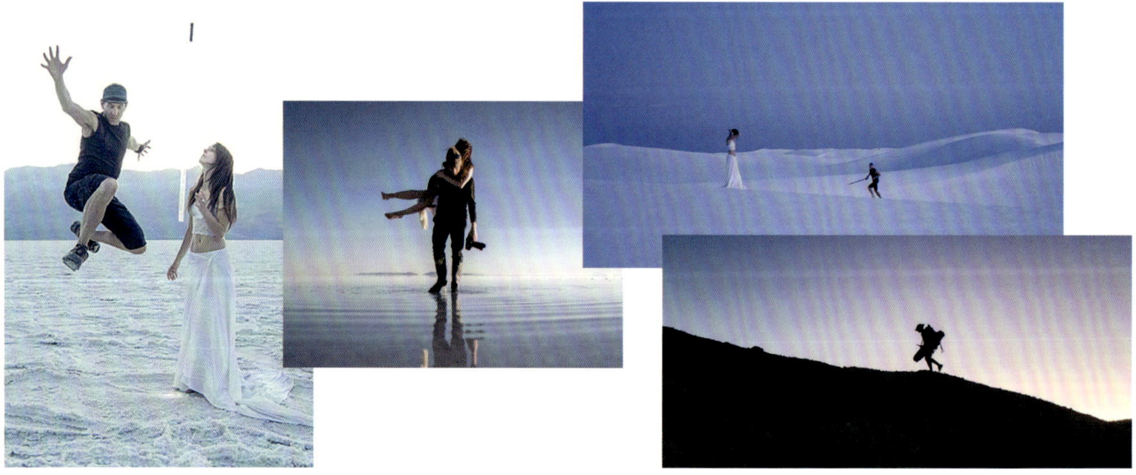

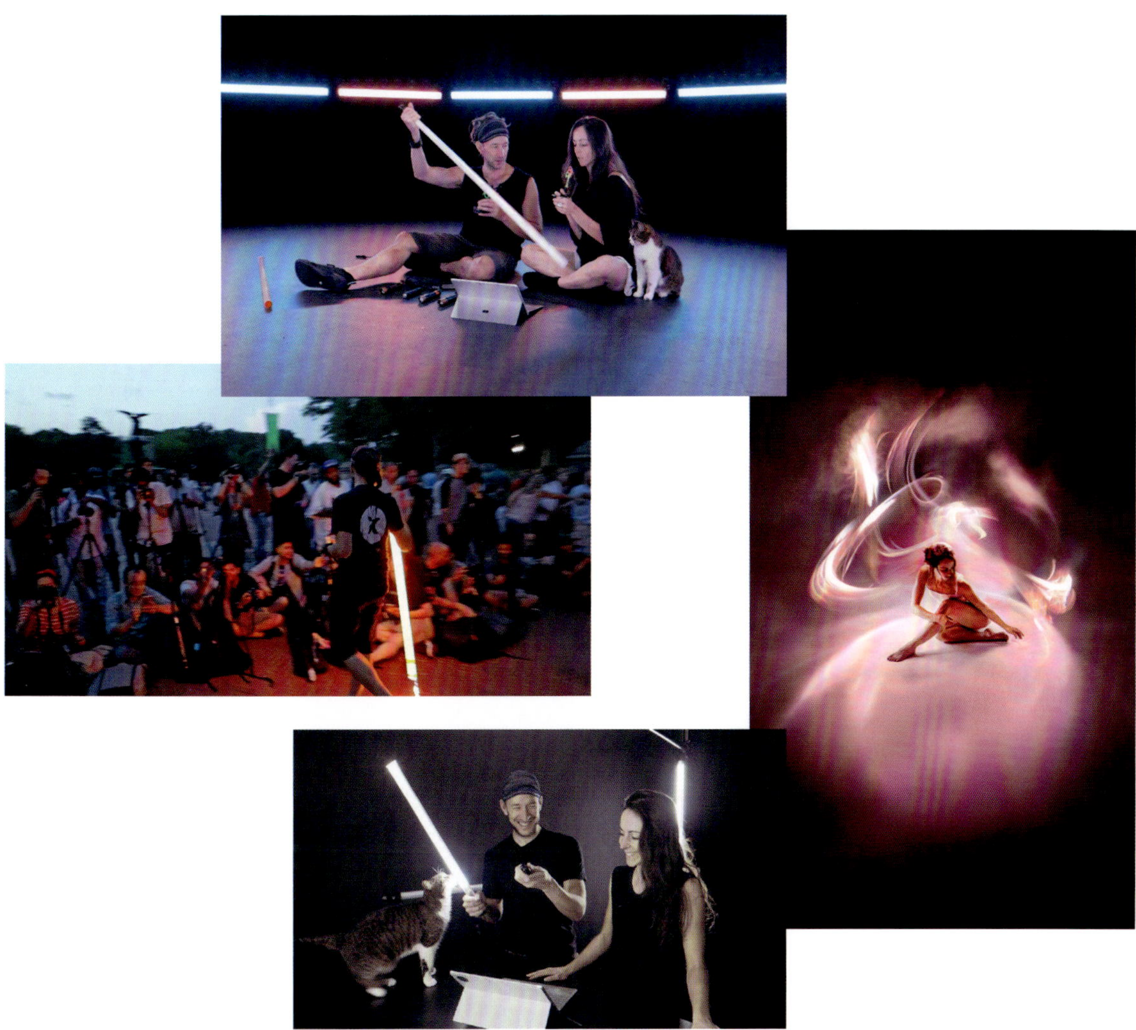

Experiences and life are more enjoyable (and meaningful) when shared.

This book, and more importantly, this technique, wouldn't exist without the community. The many people who joined us on this journey, asking questions, challenging us, and generously sharing their experiments made us strive to improve ourselves and how we explain things. The desire to share makes us understand what we do better, making us better at what we do. We truly enjoy the process of creation, but sharing the journey with you is an essential reason that keeps us going. Watching the artform evolve as others make this technique their own, experiment, and contribute by passing on their knowledge is one of the most exciting things we could have hoped to witness.

From one small iteration to the next, we've learned from others as much as they have from us. You can be part of this cycle if you wish to. If you want to connect with us and other photographers exploring this technique, here's where to start:

lightpainting.art

There, you'll find links to our free resources – including tutorials, blog posts, community groups, and inspiration from the artist's community.

Glossary

Ambient light: Natural light present in a scene (sunlight or moonlight, for example).

Astronomical twilight: Period when the Sun is between 12 and 18 degrees below the horizon. During this time the sky is dark enough for most stars to be visible with the naked eye, but there may still be some faint illumination on the horizon.

Auroral oval: Ring-shaped region around Earth's magnetic poles where auroras are most frequently observed due to the concentration of charged particles along the Earth's magnetic field lines.

Blue hour: Period encompassing the nautical and astronomical twilights. Optimal moment of twilight to capture outdoor light-painting images using the techniques shared in this book.

Celestial poles: The north and south celestial poles are two imaginary extensions of the Earth's poles into space. They are the points in the sky where Earth's axis of rotation intersects the celestial sphere. At night, the stars appear to rotate around them.

Celestial sphere: Imaginary sphere surrounding Earth, onto which all celestial objects (stars, planets, and deep-sky objects) are projected. The concept is used in astronomy as a reference system to map the positions of celestial objects.

Civil twilight: Period when the Sun is between 0 and 6 degrees below the horizon. During this time there is enough natural light for most outdoor activities, but the brightest stars and planets may be visible.

Dimmer: Device that allows the brightness of a light source to be adjusted, providing control over the intensity of light trails during light painting.

Galactic center (or Milky Way core): Brightest and most detailed part of the Milky Way galaxy, where a supermassive black hole called Sagittarius A* is located.

Holographic tubes: Light-painting tools that create rainbow or prismatic effects when light passes through them, producing multi-colored light trails during a long exposure.

Inpaint: Light-painting technique where the light source is turned on and off during a single long exposure, creating one or more distinct light trails within the frame. This technique offers greater creative control but requires a flashlight with an easy-to-access on/off switch.

Milky tubes: Light-painting tools that emit diffuse, omnidirectional light. Milky tubes create soft and even light on their surroundings.

Nautical twilight: Period when the Sun is between 6 and 12 degrees below the horizon. Most stars are visible, and the horizon is still visible with the naked eye.

Outpaint: Light-painting technique where the light is kept on continuously throughout an exposure, creating unbroken trails that match the exposure time. A straightforward, simple, and accessible technique for beginners.

Pressure switch: An attachment for a flashlight that activates the light source when pressed, allowing the light to be controlled precisely during light painting.

Solid tubes: Light-painting tools characterized by their "directional" quality, which emits light in a single direction. Solid tubes generally produce brighter and higher contrast trails than Milky tubes and help the light painter remain invisible in the shot.

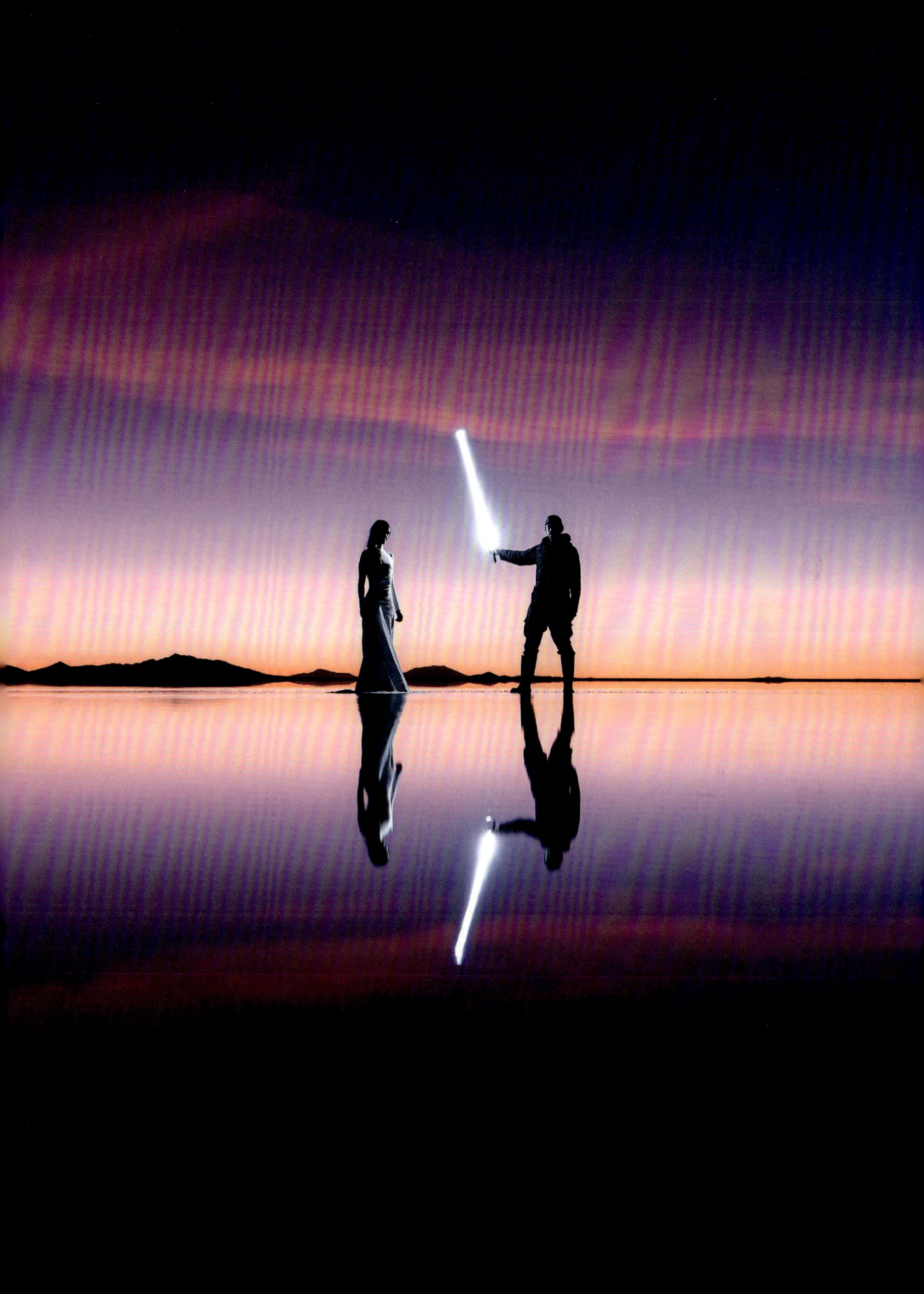

A warm thank you:

To Stephanie, Richard, and the whole team at Octopus for reaching out to us to make this project come to life. Your trust, guidance, and support during this beautiful learning journey has been precious.

To those who've been around since the early days, being patient with us and our French-Canadian accents as we were learning how to teach.

To those who supported us in one way or another over the past 10+ years.

To the beautiful humans we met around the world along the way whom we now call friends and family.

To those who took the time to share with us the impact a simple plastic tube and a flashlight had on their lives.

To those who learned from us and decided to share the technique with others.

To those who dare to see and create magic.

To those who know how to use salami as a tool.

To those who know life is short and choose to play, love, and laugh accordingly.

To those who know that sugar is a color.

To those who don't take themselves seriously but take their craft to heart.

To those who do their best to leave things a little better than they found them.

To those who choose curiosity.

To those who choose kindness.

To those who spread light.

We see you. Please don't stop.

Thank you deeply.

Merci!
Kim & Eric

First published in Great Britain in 2026 by Ilex, an imprint of
Octopus Publishing Group Ltd
Carmelite House
50 Victoria Embankment
London EC4Y 0DZ
www.octopusbooks.co.uk

An Hachette UK Company
www.hachette.co.uk

The authorised representative in the EEA is Hachette Ireland,
8 Castlecourt Centre, Castleknock Road,
Castleknock, Dublin 15, D15 YF6A, Ireland

Text copyright © ERIC PARÉ STUDIO INC 2026

Distributed in the US by Hachette Book Group
1290 Avenue of the Americas, 4th and 5th Floors
New York, NY 10104

Distributed in Canada by Canadian Manda Group
664 Annette St., Toronto, Ontario, Canada M6S 2C8

ISBN 9781840919257

A CIP catalogue record for this book is available from the British Library.

Printed and bound in China

10 9 8 7 6 5 4 3 2 1

Publisher: Alison Starling
Editor: Stephanie Selçuk-Frank
Art Director: Ben Gardiner
Design: Chris Robinson
Assistant Production Manager: Lisa Pinnell

This FSC® label means that materials used for the product have been responsibly sourced.

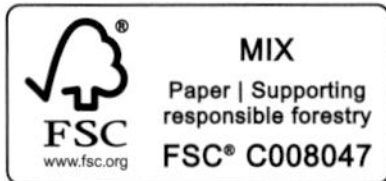